S. Wilkinson

READINGS IN ART HISTORY

VOLUME II

Readings in Art History

VOLUME II • THE RENAISSANCE TO THE PRESENT

Edited by Harold Spencer

CHARLES SCRIBNER'S SONS • NEW YORK

D-8.71[MC]

Printed in the United States of America
SBN 684-41444-9
Library of Congress Catalog Card Number 69-13587

Cover: *Sfera* (*Rotante Primo*), 1966, by Arnaldo Pomodoro.
The Marlborough-Gerson Gallery, New York.

Contents

READINGS IN ART HISTORY

VOLUME II

INTRODUCTION

The aim of this anthology is to assemble a convenient and useful collection of modern writings on the history of Western art. As a supplement to the texts usually assigned in introductory courses in art history, this anthology should prove at least a partial answer to the familiar problem of providing multiple copies of supplementary readings on library reserve shelves. But, apart from its use in surveys of Western art, this anthology will offer a valuable set of readings to any student of Western civilization or of the creativeness of man.

Although each selection stands alone on the merits of its content, the reader will soon discover that patterns tend to develop throughout the anthology and at some level link themes from a number of selections into a logical relationship across time and space. This volume opens, for example, with selections by Erwin Panofsky and John White. Panofsky distinguishes between early fifteenth-century art in the Lowlands and in Italy while at the same time emphasizing the commitment of each of these regional arts to the transcription of the visible world. The selection by John White carries the distinction between the Lowlands and Italy even further by discussing in detail the development of linear perspective in Italy, thus dramatizing the differences between the empirical approach in the north and the theoretical predilections of the Italian artists. Since the representation of space as a three-dimensional continuum, as developed both in Italy and the Lowlands, was to be an underlying assumption for Western art from these Renaissance beginnings to the twentieth century, the theme of these opening selections will be evoked again. To cite but a few of many instances, a variation on the opening themes is developed in Friedlaender's discussion of Caravaggio where the real and spiritual worlds are seen to be dramatically joined in the striking illusionism of that artist's religious paintings; and, much later, in Novotny's paper on the reaction to Impressionism (as well as in Greenberg's article on Cézanne) the dénouement of this centuries-old commitment to illusionistic transcription is finally reached.

Another series of interrelationships can be found in some of the selections that deal with aspects of the Baroque. The brief excerpt from Wölfflin's *Principles of Art History* emphasizes form-concepts in distinguishing between Renaissance and Baroque styles, whereas the article that follows it, John Rupert Martin's essay on the Baroque, stresses the significance of Baroque content and iconography. A few selections later, Rudolf Wittkower treats the sculpture of the great Baroque master, Bernini, primarily in terms of style, calling attention to his pictorial approach. And both Martin and Wittkower call attention to some of Wölfflin's ideas. This kind of cross-reference occurs again and again.

Many of the selections in this volume focus on individual artists. Here there has been an attempt to assemble readings that would demonstrate a variety of critical approaches as well as present a variety of artists. In Yukio Yashiro's sensitive commentary on Botticelli, for example, the sensuous qualities in the artist's work are expressed with a grace appropriate to them. Sydney Freedberg brings an intricate, involuted analysis to the intellectual style of Raphael and the humanist program for his frescoes in the Stanza della Segnatura. The result is harmonic. Anthony Blunt's essay on Michelangelo develops a restricted context in which the artist's weaving of Neoplatonic elements through his ideas about art sets an introspective mood, while Jakob Rosenberg's selection on Rembrandt places that artist in the broad context of his times.

As in the first volume, the editor has chosen readings that range widely in the degree of difficulty they present to the reader, thereby, it is hoped, increasing the flexibility of the anthology.

In some instances it has been necessary to reduce or eliminate footnotes that appeared in the original publications, but this practice has been kept to a minimum. In some cases the requirements of available space were involved, in others it was a matter of special problems—such as footnotes in the selection interlocking too firmly with footnotes and text material elsewhere to permit proper adjustments—that determined the editing. In many instances footnotes leading to specialized study were retained, even though the anthology is aimed primarily at the undergraduate level.

Illustrations, of course, have been limited by necessity, but the editor has included as many as possible in an effort to enhance the usefulness of the anthology. As in the first volume, they have been placed as close as possible to relevant portions of the text, which should prove a welcome convenience. Now and then, illustrations from one selection will be found to relate, directly or indirectly, to another reading, and the choice of illustrations also permits comparisons and suggests problems of art history beyond those examined in the anthology itself.

The headnotes are intended chiefly as bibliographical devices, and, being brief, do not impinge on space better served by the selected readings than by the intrusions of the editor. Except where foreign publications are cited for explanatory purposes relating to particular developments, the bibliographical references are limited to works in English. No anthology can hope to serve perfectly the needs of every situation and the habit of every instructor, but there is enough variety and quality in these selections to meet most situations at least part way.

Although the sequence of the selections approximates customary chronology, thus correlating with traditional periods, some selections will be found to reach beyond the limits of a single period or movement.

This is particularly true of Edgar Wind's discussion of mechanization and art which draws examples from many different eras. As the final selection in the anthology it serves as an evocative colophon, because the questions it raises about the relationship between mechanization and art continue. The implications of this relationship, if they are thoroughly pursued, cannot be confined to the level of techniques and procedures in art for we are impelled to ask the further question whether man, the creature of play and ritual, has been overlooked in our concentration on elaborating man, the tool-maker, as the central motif in the evolution of human society. But lest this seem to lead to a simple rejection of technology, we must remind ourselves that it is altogether possible that all along, man the artificer has been unwittingly the slave of the playing man. This may now be more than an idle question for parlor debate, for the tool-maker has developed poisonous and terrifying toys for the game-playing man. If it is to be argued that these are matters for ecology, economics, and diplomacy, but not for art, one can venture to say that what is at stake is the quality of human life, perhaps its very existence. And that is relevant.

No project of this kind is ever completed without the assistance of many persons and it would be ungracious to conclude this introduction without acknowledging the contributions of at least some of these: my teachers, colleagues, and students from whom I have learned over the years; Miss Sallie Pritchard, for her labors of typing and correspondence; and my wife, whose patience and criticism have aided this project in so many ways.

HAROLD SPENCER

The University of Connecticut

1. PAINTING IN ITALY AND THE LOWLANDS DURING THE FIFTEENTH CENTURY

Erwin Panofsky

INTRODUCTION

A quickening energy infused the art of painting in Western Europe during the early fifteenth century, concentrating about two centers: the Lowlands and Italy. Although painting in both regions was generally committed to a convincing transcription of the visible world, in which space was conceived as a three-dimensional continuum, there was a striking difference between the style of painting that developed in Italy and that of the North.

This selection from Erwin Panofsky's *Early Netherlandish Painting* (1953) defines the characteristic features of these two styles and isolates within each context those conditions and tendencies that contributed to the polarity of the two.

For further reading on the polarization of art in Italy and the Lowlands consult Panofsky's *Renaissance and Renascences in Western Art* (1960), pp. 162–168.

When two men of the sixteenth century as widely disparate as Luther and Michelangelo turned their conversation to painting, they thought only two schools worth mentioning, the Italian and the Flemish. Luther approved of the Flemings, while Michelangelo did not; but neither considered what was produced outside these two great centers. Giorgio Vasari, the sixteenth-century historiographer of art, quite correctly refers to Dürer as a German when deploring his influence upon a great Florentine; but as soon as the discussion takes a more general turn, the same Vasari automatically classifies not only Dürer but also Dürer's forerunner, Martin Schongauer, as "Flemings" operating in Antwerp.

One-sided though it is, such a reduction of the whole diversity of European painting to one antithesis is not without justification when considered in the light of the preceding developments. From about 1430 down to the end of the fifteenth century, Italy and Flanders (or, to be more precise, the Netherlands) had indeed enjoyed a position of undisputed predominance, with all the other schools, their individual differences and merits notwithstanding, depending either on Italy and Flanders in conjunction or on Flanders alone. In England, Germany and Austria, the direct or indirect influence of the "great Netherlandish artists," as Dürer calls them, ruled supreme for two or three successive generations; in France, in the Iberian peninsula, and in such borderline districts as the southern Tyrol, this influence was rivaled but never eclipsed by that of the Italian Quattrocento; and the Italian Quattrocento itself was deeply impressed with the distinctive qualities of Early Flemish painting.

Italian princes, merchants and cardinals commissioned and collected Flemish pictures, invited Flemish painters to Italy, and occasionally sent their Italian protégés to the Netherlands for instruction. Italian writers lavished praise upon the Flemings and some Italian painters were eager to fuse their *buona maniera antica* with what was most admired in the *maniera Fiamminga.* In Colantonio of Naples and Antonello da Messina the Flemish influence is so strong that the latter was long believed to have been a personal pupil of Jan van Eyck. That Ghirlandaio's "St. Jerome" and Botticelli's "St. Augustine," both in the Church of Ognissanti, are patterned after an Eyckian "St. Jerome" then owned by the Medici is common knowledge; and so is the fact that the adoring shepherds in Ghirlandaio's "Nativity" of 1485 were inspired by Hugo van der Goes' Portinari altarpiece, which had reached Florence just three or four years before. When we take into account, in addition to such direct "borrowings," the less palpable but even more important diffusion of a Flemish spirit in psychological approach and pictorial treatment (Piero di Cosimo's landscapes, for example, would be inexplicable without the wings of the Portinari altarpiece just mentioned), the influence of Flanders upon the Italian Quattrocento becomes almost incalculable.

What the Italians of the Renaissance—enthusiasts and skeptics alike—considered as characteristic of this Flemish spirit can be inferred from their own words.

First, there was the splendor of a new technique, the invention of which was ascribed, first by implication and later expressly, to Jan van Eyck himself. Second, and in a measure predicated upon this new technique, there was that adventurous and all-embracing, yet selective, "naturalism" which distilled for the beholder an untold wealth of visual enchantment from everything created by God or contrived by man. "Multicolored soldier's cloaks," writes Cyriacus of Ancona, the greatest antiquarian of his time, in 1449, "garments prodigiously enhanced by purple and gold, blooming meadows, flowers, trees, leafy and shady hills, ornate halls and porticoes, gold really resembling gold, pearls, precious stones, and everything else you would think to have been produced, not by the artifice of human hands but by all-bearing nature herself." Third, there was a peculiar piety which seemed to distinguish the intent of Flemish painting from the more humanistic—and, in a sense, more formalistic—spirit of Italian art. A great lady of fifteenth-century Florence wrote to her son that, whichever picture she might be forced to dispose of, she would not part with a Flemish "Holy Face" because it was "una divota figura e bella"; and Michelangelo is said to have remarked, to the dismay of the saintly Vittoria Colonna, that Flemish paintings would bring tears to the eyes of the devout, though these were mostly "women, young girls, clerics, nuns and gentlefolk without much understanding for the true harmony of art."

The most circumstantial and outstanding tribute is paid to Flemish painting in a collection of biographies, composed in 1455 or 1456 by Bartolommeo Fazio, a humanist from Genoa who lived at the court of Alphonso of Aragon at Naples. Of the four painters included in this *Book of Famous Men* no less than two are Flemings: Jan van Eyck and Roger van der Weyden, the latter still alive at the time of Fazio's writing. Jan van Eyck is referred to as "*the* foremost painter of our age" (*nostri saeculi pictorum princeps*). He is praised for his scholarly and scientific accomplishments and credited with the rediscovery of what Pliny and other classics had known about "the property of pigments"—an obvious allusion to those technical innovations which a good humanist felt bound to derive, by hook or by crook, from classical antiquity. In his descriptions of such individual works as he had seen—unfortunately all of them lost—Fazio, too, untiringly stresses pious sentiment on the one hand, and verisimilitude on the other. He is moved by the grief of Roger van der Weyden's Josephs of Arimathea and Marys, witnessing the Descent from the Cross, and by the Virgin's "dismay, with dignity preserved amidst a flow of tears" when she received the news of Christ's arrest. But no less keen is his enthusiasm for Jan van Eyck's "Map of the World" in which all the places and regions of the earth were represented in recognizable form and at measurable distances; his delight in Jan's "St. Jerome in His Study," where a bookcase, "if you step back a little, seems to recede in space and to display the books in their entirety while he who comes near sees only their upper edges"; and his admiration for a donor's portrait with "a sunbeam stealing through a chink in the wall so that you would think it was the real sun." And Fazio's highest praise is reserved for Jan's picture of a Women's Bath—perhaps a rendering of magic practices—which must have been a *summa* of optical refinements. It included a mirror showing, in addition to the back of a bather represented in front view, whatever else was in the room; an aged woman attendant who "seemed to perspire"; a little dog that lapped up the spilled water; a lamp "looking like one that really burns"; and, furthermore, a landscape—apparently seen through a window—where "horses, people of diminutive size, mountains, woods and castles were elaborated with such artistry that one thing seemed to be separated from the other by fifty miles."

In thus describing the direct juxtaposition of the minutiae of an interior with a vast, almost cosmic panorama, of the microscopic with the telescopic, so to speak, Fazio comes very close to the great secret of Eyckian painting: the simultaneous realization, and, in a sense, reconciliation, of the "two infinites," the infinitesimally small and the infinitely large. It is this secret that intrigued the Italians, and that always eluded them.

II

When we confront Jan van Eyck's famous double portrait of Giovanni Arnolfini and His Bride of 1434 (Fig. 1) with a nearly contemporary and relatively comparable Italian work, such as the "Death of St. Ambrose" in San Clemente at Rome executed about 1430 by Masolino da Panicale (Fig. 2) we observe basic similarities as well as basic differences. In both cases the scene is laid in an interior drawn to scale with the figures and furnished according to upper class standards in fifteenth-century Flanders and Italy, respectively; and in both cases advantage has been taken of that representational method which more than any other single factor distinguishes a "modern" from a medieval work of art (and without which the rendering of such interiors would not have been possible), namely, perspective. The purposes, however, to which this method has been turned are altogether different.

"*Perspectiva*," says Dürer, "is a Latin word and means a '*Durchsehung*'" (a view through something). As coined by Boethius and used by all writers prior to the fifteenth century, the word *perspectiva* refers to *perspicere* in the sense of "seeing clearly," and not in the sense of "seeing through"; a direct translation of the Greek ὀπτική, it designates a mathematical theory of vision and not a mathematical method of graphic representation. Dürer's definition, on the other hand, gives an excellent and brief description of "perspective" as understood in postmedieval usage, including our own. By a "perspective" picture we mean indeed a picture wherein the wall, panel or canvas ceases to be a solid working surface on which images are drawn and painted, and is interpreted—to quote another theorist of the Renaissance, Leone Battista Alberti—as a "kind of window" through which we look out into a section of space. Exact mathematical perspective as developed in the fifteenth century is nothing but a method of making this "view through a window" constructible, and it is well known that the Italians, sig-

1. Jan van Eyck, *Giovanni Arnolfini and His Bride,* 1434, Panel 33″ by $22\frac{1}{2}$″ (National Gallery, London)

2. Masolino da Panicale, Death of St. Ambrose, Fresco, *c.* 1430 (San Clemente, Rome)

nificantly under the guidance of an architect, Filippo Brunelleschi, had achieved this end about 1420 by drawing the mathematical consequences from the window simile. They conceived of the visual rays as of straight lines that form a pyramid or cone having its apex in the eye and its base in the object seen; of the pictorial surface as of a plane intersecting this pyramid or cone; and of the picture itself as of a central projection onto this plane—perfectly analogous to that produced in a photographic camera—which can be constructed by elementary geometrical methods. It should be noted, however, that the Flemings, about thirty years later arrived at a no less "correct" solution on a purely empirical basis, that is to say, not by deriving a workable construction from optical theory, but by subjecting shop traditions and direct visual experience to draftsmanlike schematization until consistency was reached.

However arrived at, the "correct" construction implies the following rules: in the perspective picture all parallel lines, regardless of location and direction, converge in one of an infinite number of "vanishing points"; all parallels intersecting the picture plane at right angles ("orthogonals," often loosely referred to as "vanishing lines" pure and simple) converge in a *central* vanishing point (often loosely called the "point of sight") which can be defined as the foot of the perpendicular dropped from the eye onto the picture plane and which determines the "horizon" of the picture. This horizon is the locus of the vanishing points of all parallels located in horizontal planes, and all equal magnitudes diminish in direct proportion to their distance from the eye. . . .

Modern perspective—whether developed on a theoretical or an empirical basis, whether handled with mathematical precision or intuitive freedom—is a two-edged sword. Since it makes solids and voids equally real and measurable, it can be used for plastic and, if I may say so, topographical purposes on the one hand, and for purely pictorial ones on the other. Perspective permits the artist to clarify the shape and relative location of corporeal things but also to shift the interest to phenomena contingent upon the presence of an extracorporeal medium: the way light behaves when reflected by surfaces of different color and texture or passing through media of different volume and density. Since it makes the appearance of the world dependent upon the freely determined position of the eye, perspective can produce symmetry as well as asymmetry and can keep the beholder at a respectful distance from the scene as well as admit him to the closest intimacy. Since it presupposes the concept of an infinite space, but operates within a limited frame, perspective can emphasize either the one or the other, either the relative completeness of what is actually presented or the absolute transcendence of what is merely implied.

It is these dual possibilities that are exemplified by Jan van Eyck's Arnolfini portrait and the "Death of St. Ambrose" in San Clemente. It matters little—and is in fact hardly perceptible without the application of ruler and compass—that the "Death of St. Ambrose," executed by an artist already familiar with Brunelleschian methods, is fairly "correctly" constructed whereas the Arnolfini portrait is not and has four central vanishing points instead of one. What matters is that the Italian master conceives of light as a quantitative and isolating rather than a qualitative and connective principle, and that he places us before rather than within the picture space. He studies and uses light mainly in terms of rectilinear propagation, employing modeling shadows to characterize the plastic shape of material objects, and castshadows to clarify their relative position. Jan van Eyck, however, studies and uses light, in addition, in terms of diffraction, reflection and diffused reflection. He stresses its action upon surfaces as well as its modification by solids and thereby works that magic so ardently admired throughout the centuries: those reflexes on brass and crystal, that sheen on velvet or fur, that subdued luster of wool or seasoned wood, those flames that look "as though they were really burning," those mirrored images, that colored chiaroscuro pervading the whole room. And where the death chamber of St. Ambrose is a complete and closed unit, entirely contained within the limits of the frame and not communicating with the outside world, the nuptial chamber of the Arnolfinis is, in spite of its cozy narrowness, a slice of infinity. Its walls, floor and ceiling are artfully cut on all sides so as to transcend not only the frame but also the picture plane so that the beholder feels included in the very room; yet the half-open window, disclosing the thin-brick wall of the house and the tiniest strip of garden and sky, creates a kind of osmosis between indoors and outdoors, secluded cell and universal space.

. . . It is a truism that northern Late Gothic tends to individualize where the Italian Renaissance strives for that which is exemplary or, as the phrase goes, for "the ideal," that it accepts the things created by God or produced by man as they present themselves to the eye instead of searching for a universal law or principle to which they more or less successfully endeavor to conform. But it is perhaps more than an accident that the *via moderna* of the North—that nominalistic philosophy which claimed that the quality of reality belongs exclusively to the particular things directly perceived by the senses and to the particular psychological states directly known through inner experience—does not seem to have borne fruit in Italy outside a limited circle of natural scientists; whereas it is in Italy and, more specifically, in Florence that we can witness the resurgence and enthusiastic acceptance of a Neoplatonism according to which, to quote from its greatest spokesman, Marsilio Ficino, "the truth of a created thing consists primarily in the fact that it corresponds entirely to its Idea."

Thus we can understand the peculiarly one-sided relation between Flemish and Italian painting in the fifteenth century. Flanders and Italy shared the basic principles of "modern" art; but they represented the positive and negative poles of one electric circuit and we can easily conceive that during the fifteenth century the current could flow only from north to south. Exploiting the plastic rather than the pictorial possibilities of perspective, the Italians could gracefully accept some of the Flemish achievements and yet go on with the pursuit of that "beauty" which they found embodied in the art of the Greeks and their own ancestors, the Romans: "I solemnly surrender these beautiful statues to the Roman people whence they had once arisen," wrote Sixtus IV when restoring a part of the papal collection to the Capitol. The Flemings, conceiving of perspective as a means of optical enrichment rather than stereographical clarification and unchallenged by the visible remains of classical antiquity, were long unable to understand an idiom so strongly flavored with Hellenism and Latinism. It was, with but a few and well-motivated exceptions, not until the very end of the fifteenth century that Flemish painting came to be drawn into the orbit of the Italian Renaissance, the classicizing influence first sneaking in, as it were, in the shape of such decorative accessories as garlands of fruits and leaves, playful *putti* or ornamental medallions fashioned after classical cameos; and it took the spirit of a new century, the rise of new artistic centers, and even the help of a German, Albrecht Dürer, to open Netherlandish eyes to the more basic values of the Italian *rinascimento.*

2. THE DEVELOPMENT OF THE THEORY OF ARTIFICIAL PERSPECTIVE: BRUNELLESCHI, ALBERTI, AND GHIBERTI

John White

INTRODUCTION

John White's book, *The Birth and Rebirth of Pictorial Space* (1957), focuses on the technical, mathematical, and illusionistic aspects of painting, drawing, and relief. It emphasizes, therefore, the rational and scientific side of the Renaissance which produced the substructure of "pure form" upon which was raised the world of appearances in Italian Renaissance art. But just as there were coexistent in the great works of the Gothic era the complementary factors of mysticism and a "sacred" mathematics, so too, in the Renaissance, the rational and scientific factors accompany symbolism and religious feeling inherited from medieval times. This is clearly revealed in an important study that is, in many ways, complementary to White's book. The work is Rudolf Wittkower's *Architectural Principles in the Age of Humanism* (1952). In demonstrating that Renaissance architecture does indeed contain its measure of symbolical content, Wittkower has contributed significantly to the qualification of the earlier image of the Renaissance as a period in which medieval traditions were quite overthrown, to be replaced by a new, rehumanized worldliness in the spirit of which classical forms were rediscovered as models of an ideal beauty celebrating the capacity of Man rather than the glory of God. Such a view of the Renaissance is not entirely false, but Wittkower's work, in modifying this monolithic concept, brings to our attention the important role played by tradition and religious feeling in the art and architecture of the Renaissance.

It is appropriate here, in relation to this selection by White, to mention a number of works which can be consulted with profit on the subject of visual perception, namely: J. J. Gibson, *The Perception of the Visual World* (1950); Ernst Kris (with E. H. Gombrich), *Psychoanalytical Explorations in Art* (1952); W. H. Ittelson, *The Ames Demonstrations in Perception* (1952); E. H. Gombrich, *Art and Illusion* (1960, 1961); and Rudolf Arnheim, *Art and Visual Perception* (1954), in connection with which one should read Gombrich, *Art and Illusion*, pp. 26–27, and Arnheim's review of this book in *The Art Bulletin*, XLIV, 1 (1962).

The selection that follows is reprinted from John White, *The Birth and Rebirth of Pictorial Space* (1957) by permission of the publishers, Faber and Faber Ltd., London.

FILIPPO BRUNELLESCHI

It is a vivid reminder of the continuity of historical processes that the invention of a mathematically based perspective system during the early years of the fifteenth century was heralded, not by the publication of a treatise, but by the painting of a pair of panels. It is also characteristic of the ever-increasing unity of the arts and sciences in the Renaissance that it was Filippo Brunelleschi, first an architect and second a sculptor, who chose to publicize his new discovery in this way. The importance of the contents of these pictorial manifestos can hardly be overestimated. Although they themselves are lost, it is fortunately possible to reconstruct all their essential compositional features with unusual accuracy.

Antonio Manetti, in his *Life of Brunelleschi,* which was probably written only a few decades after the latter's death, states quite firmly that the new perspective was the master's own creation.[1]

. . . Manetti immediately points out that the new invention contained the rule for the proportional diminution of painted objects which was later codified in treatises such as Alberti's, and which was one of the basic features of artificial perspective. The writer's sense of history is emphasized by his subsequent discussion of the possible existence of a rational perspective system in antiquity, and by his carefully reasoned conclusion that this could not, in any case, affect the stature of Brunelleschi's achievement, as any knowledge of the nature of such a system had undoubtedly since been lost. It is therefore interesting to see, for reasons which will appear later, that before going on to describe the practical applications of the new method, he inserts a long passage insisting how thoroughly modest his hero was, and strongly implying that he was shamefully treated by contemporaries who were not.

Having relieved himself of this outburst of feeling, Manetti describes the painting of "S. Giovanni and the Piazza del Duomo," which was the first of Brunelleschi's demonstration pieces. He records it in these words:[2]

"And this matter of perspective, in the first thing in which he showed it, was in a small panel about half a braccio[3] square, on which he made an exact picture (from outside) of the church of Santo Giovanni di Firenze, and of that church he portrayed, as much as can be seen, at a glance from the outside: and it seems that in order to portray it he placed himself inside the middle door of Santa Maria del Fiore, some three braccia, done with such care and delicacy, and with such accuracy in the colors of the white and black marbles, that there is not a miniaturist who could have done it better; picturing before one's face that part of the piazza which the eye takes in, and so toward the side over against the Misericordia as far as the arch and corner of the Pecori, and so of the side of the column of the miracle of Santo Zenobio as far as the Canto alla Paglia; and as much of that place as is seen in the distance, and for as much of the sky as he had to show, that is where the walls in the picture vanish into the air, he put burnished silver, so that the air and the natural skies might be reflected in it; and thus also the clouds, which are seen in that silver are moved by the wind, when it blows."

The position of all the buildings mentioned, and indeed the whole disposition of the Piazza del Duomo before its westward extension, is well known. The latter enlargement is the only important alteration of shape which has occurred. The key to the accurate reconstruction of Brunelleschi's picture of it lies, however, in Manetti's detailed description of the viewpoint from which it was seen. This is given as some three braccia inside the main, central door of the Duomo. This distance is approximately 1.75 meters. In comparison, the width of the present doorway is about 3.80 meters, a little more than double the previous distance.[4] An actual two to one ratio would mean that anyone standing at the point described by Manetti, and looking out towards the piazza, could swing his eye through an angle of ninety degrees before his view was cut off by the uprights of the door.[5] . . . Since the design of Brunelleschi's panel would only be altered materially by an increase of about thirty degrees in the angle of vision, there is no necessity to modify the original conclusion that he retreated inward about half the width of the doorway in order to design his picture.[6] This distance must be taken from the front of the tunnel-like entrance as a whole, and not from the doorway itself. Otherwise, allowing even the most improbably small depth for Talenti's porch, Brunelleschi's view would have been so restricted that the sides of the Piazza del Duomo would have disappeared completely.[7]

By drawing in Brunelleschi's ninety-degree visual cone on a plan of the piazza as it was in the fifteenth century, it is possible to see how much of it he could have included in his painting. This is done in Fig. 3,[8] which shows that both the Volta de' Pecori and the Canto

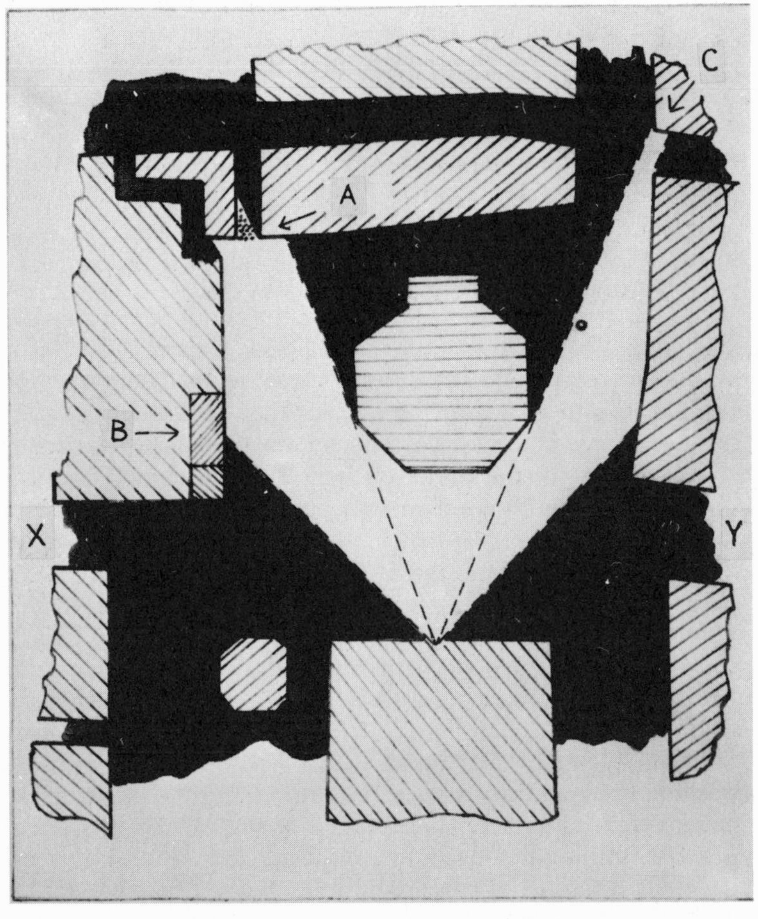

3. A. Volta dei Pecori
B. Misericordia
C. Canto alla Paglia
X. Via de' Calzaioli
Y. Via de' Martelli

alla Paglia, mentioned by Manetti, would indeed have been visible from the main door of the Duomo. Manetti himself does not say that either the Misericordia or the column of S. Zenobius was included in the picture. He merely uses them to identify the left- and right-hand sides of the square. Vasari, however, says that they were actually shown.[9] This fits in with what is revealed by the reconstruction, but throws no light upon Vasari's reliability. His text says nothing that could not have been taken from the passage in Manetti. What is much more interesting is that both to left and right only the receding sides of the piazza are visible. The corners, and forward surfaces of the houses of what are now the Via de' Calzaioli and the Via de' Martelli (Points *X* and *Y* in Fig. 3) cannot have appeared in the picture at all. On either side the picture must have begun immediately with a coulisse running into depth and flanking the graceful octagon of the Baptistery which filled the center of the composition.

The description of the content of the picture being finished, Manetti goes on to say more of its construction.[10]

"In which painting, because the painter needs to presuppose a single place, whence his picture is to be seen, fixed in height and depth and in relation to the sides, as well as in distance, so that it is impossible to get distortions in looking at it, such as appear in the eye at any place which differs from that particular one, he had made a hole in the panel on which there was this painting, which came to be situated in the part of the church of Santo Giovanni, where the eye struck, directly opposite anyone who looked out from the place inside the central door of Santa Maria del Fiore, where he would have been positioned, if he had portrayed it; which hole was as small as a lentil on the side of the painting, and on the back it opened out pyramidally, like a woman's straw hat, to the size of a ducat or a little more. And he wished the eye to be placed at the back, where it was large, by whoever had it to see, with the one hand bringing it close to the eye, and with the other holding a mirror opposite, so that there the painting came to be reflected back; and the distance of the mirror in the other hand, came to about the length of a small braccio; up to that of a true braccio, from the place where he showed that he had been to paint it, as far as the church of Santo Giovanni, which on being seen, with the other circumstances already mentioned of the burnished silver and of the piazza etc. and of the perforation, it seemed as if the real thing was seen: and I have had it in my hand, and I can give testimony."

This passage confirms that, besides showing all of the Piazza del Duomo that was visible from a carefully chosen position, the construction of the picture was dependent upon its being seen from a single viewpoint set at a particular distance from the picture surface. In this case the viewing distance was about twice the width of the painting. There must, therefore, have been a true vanishing point system, with the mathematically controlled rate of diminution which was implied in Manetti's opening remarks on the new discovery.[11]

Manetti's insistence on his familiarity with the work is important from the historian's point of view. His assertion is confirmed by the confidence with which he handles the details of measurement, of construction, and of content, without becoming involved in even venial contradictions. Unfortunately in describing Brunelleschi's second panel, showing the Piazza della Signoria, Manetti says much less about the buildings represented. He makes up for this by being just as definite about the general description of the picture, and about the exact position from which the view was taken. The whole passage runs:[12]

"He made in perspective the piazza of the palace of the Signori of Florence, with everything on it and round about it, as much as can be seen, standing outside the piazza or really on a level with it, along the façade of the church of Santo Romolo, past the corner of the Calimala Francesca, which rises on the aforesaid piazza, a few braccia towards Orto Santo Michele, whence is seen the palace of the Signori, in such a way, that two faces are seen completely, that which is turned toward the West and that which is turned toward the North: so that it is a wonderful thing to see what appears, together with all the things that the view includes in that place. Afterwards Paolo Uccello and other painters did it, who wished to counterfeit and imitate it; of which I have seen more than one, and it was not as well done as that. Here it might be said: why did he not make this picture, being of perspective, with that hole for the eye, like the little panel from the Duomo toward Santo Giovanni? This arose, because the panel of so great a piazza, needed to be so big to put in it so many different things, that it could not, like the Santo Giovanni, be held up to the face with one hand, nor the mirror with the other; for the arm of a man is not of sufficient length that with the mirror in his hand he could hold it at its distance opposite the point, nor so strong, that he could support it. He left it to the discretion of the onlooker as happens in all the other paintings of all the other painters, although the onlooker may not always be discerning. And in the place where he put the burnished silver in that of Santo Giovanni, here he left a void, which he made from the buildings up: and betook himself with it to look at it in a place, where the natural air showed itself from the buildings upward."

Once again the nature of the focused perspective system is underlined. The painting, whilst approaching the normal practice in dispensing with the eyehole and the mirror, still reveals, in its silhouetted upper border, the unusual interest in pure illusionism to be expected in a perspective manifesto demonstrating a new system in the most forceful terms possible.

Manetti makes it clear that, to paint this second panel, Brunelleschi stood in the extreme northwest corner of the Piazza della Signoria (see Fig. 4).[13] Entering the piazza at this point the natural impulse is to look immediately toward the great mass of the Palazzo della Signoria. Flanked, as it is, by lower buildings, it dominates the whole wide expanse of the square, thrusting, corner onward, almost directly at the observer, who sees it with the two visible faces violently foreshortened.[14] The Palazzo is the natural center of the scene, and Manetti's description implies that it was also the center of Brunelleschi's panel. It is the only building which he gives by name. His actual words, "donde si guarda'l palagio de'Signori, in modo, che due faccie si veggono intere," imply that it is the principal focus of interest, and the compositional and perspective center of the picture. They also stress the distinctive characteristic of the extreme oblique setting, its equal emphasis on both the visible, evenly receding surfaces of a building. There seems to be no other reason for his laboring of the point that the two sides shown in their entirety are "quello che'e volta verso ponente e quella ch'e volta verso tramontana." No others can be seen from anywhere inside the piazza.

Taking the Signoria, therefore, to be the center of a balanced composition, it can be seen that the same ninety-degree angle of vision, which Brunelleschi was described as using in the painting of the Baptistery, here takes in the whole of the south and east sides of the piazza. . . .

It is clear that he developed a complete, focused, system of perspective with mathematically regular diminution toward a fixed vanishing point.[15] This directly controlled the onlooker's position in relation to the pictured scene, both in distance and direction. It is the final crystallization of the increasingly close connection between the observer and the pictorial world which had been growing up throughout the previous century. The ever more confident attempts to relate pictorial space to everyday experience of the three-dimensional world—elastic experiments conditioned equally by physical, and psychological factors—are transformed into a logically precise mathematical system. All this is revolutionary in its novelty.

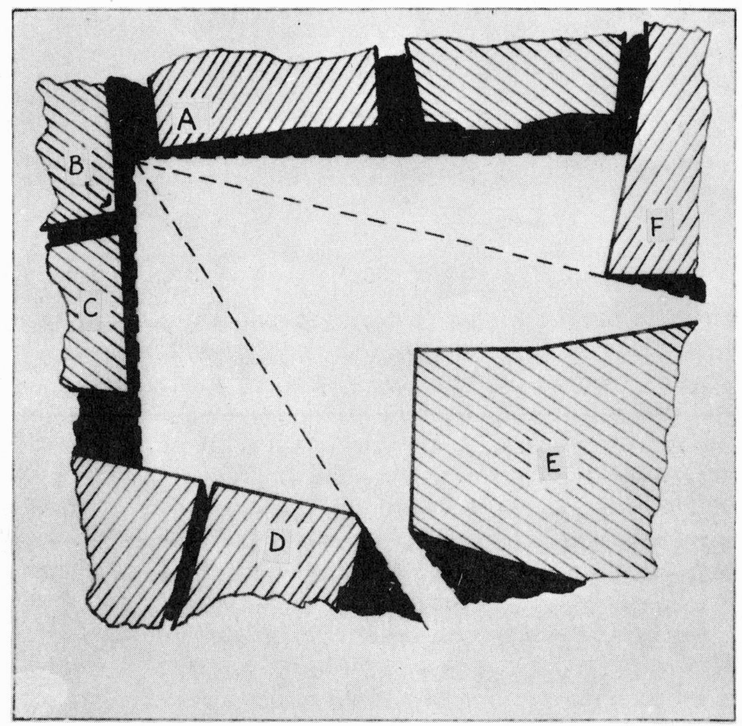

4. A. S. Romolo
B. Canto, Calimala Francesca
C. Tetto dei Pisani
D. Loggia dei Lanzi
E. Signoria
F. Mercanzia

5. Taddeo Gaddi, *Presentation of the Virgin,* 1338, Fresco (Santa Croce, Florence)

At the same time, in the very compositions with which Brunelleschi chose to demonstrate the new invention, he is careful to respect as far as possible the particular, simple, visual truths which underlie the achievements of Giottesque art. In the view of the Piazza del Duomo the whole problem of dealing with the forward surfaces of foreshortened, cubic buildings is, as far as possible, avoided. On either side orthogonal coulisses run inward from the very edge of the painting.[16] In the panel of the Piazza della Signoria, the viewpoint is chosen so as to draw the eye diagonally across the open space. Every building is obliquely set, and the jutting sharpness of the forms must have given dramatic emphasis to the new realism. Nevertheless, in its fundamental structure, the composition is exactly that of Taddeo Gaddi's fresco of "The Presentation of the Virgin" in the Baroncelli Chapel (Fig. 5).

Brunelleschi must have been well aware of the one point of unavoidable conflict between his new mathematical system and the simple observation of reality which underlies the oblique disposition of Giotto's compositions. This conflict he succeeded in reducing to a minimum by the careful selection and manipulation of his viewpoint. The same acute sense of the achievement of the past is revealed in all the forms of Brunelleschi's forward-striding architecture. His perspective manifestos, giving artistic form to a new geometrical construction, can be seen both as a revolution and as a moment of transition.

LEON BATTISTA ALBERTI

It is in Alberti's *Della Pittura*, which he wrote in 1435, that a theory of perspective first attains formal being outside the individual work of art.[17] Theoretical dissertation replaces practical demonstration. The way is open, in art also, for that separation of theory and practice; that particular kind of self-consciousness which, in the wider view, showed itself most significantly in the growing realization of the historical remoteness of antiquity,[18] and which underlies modern scientific achievement.

Alberti starts his treatise by explaining the simple geometric terms which he will have to use. He then begins immediately to describe the pyramid of visual rays which joins the objects that are seen to the beholder's eye.[19] There follows an explanation of the relationship between apparent quantities and the visual angle formed within the eye. In a single sentence Alberti sets forth the fundamental principle of Euclidean optics, and establishes the optical foundation of the pictorial diminution to a point, on which the new perspective system is constructed.[20] The definition of the picture plane as an intersection of the visual pyramid[21] is followed by a demonstration of the fact that all the pictured quantities are proportional to those found in the actual objects which are being reproduced. This also establishes the further fundamental point that there is no distortion of the shape of objects lying parallel to the picture plane. Artificial perspective is therefore, in its treatment of the individual object, essentially a development of the foreshortened frontal system which had reached its highest level of perfection in the Sienese school of the early, and the Paduan and Veronese circles of the late fourteenth century. It is fundamentally opposed in structure to that vision of reality espoused by Giotto and by Ambrogio Lorenzetti.

The new role of the spectator in relation to the picture, which played such an important part in the discussion of Brunelleschi's two panels, is underlined throughout Alberti's treatise, and reflects the growing humanism of the period. This humanist approach is carried into the pictorial world itself when Alberti points out that all the appearances of things are purely relative, and that it is the human figure which alone provides the measure of whatever else the artist cares to represent.[22]

Man's central position as observer of a pictorial world of which he himself is the measure, together with the new reality to which that world aspires, is shown immediately. Alberti describes his actual method of perspective composition, beginning with a suitably large square which he says, "I consider to be an open window through which I view that which will be painted there."[23]

The idea of the imitation of reality as the painter's starting point, which is reiterated in various forms throughout the treatise, reappears in a discussion of the rules of history painting in which he stresses the absurdity of painting large men cooped in tiny houses.[24] He had previously also poured scorn on the old method of foreshortening a squared pavement by successively reducing the distances between transversals by a third.[25] . . .

It is only as a check on accuracy and not as a method of construction that Alberti mentions that "one single straight line will contain the diagonal of many more quadrangles described in the picture."[26] Just as there is no necessity for Brunelleschi to have known the distance point construction in order to paint either of his panels, so there is no evidence in Alberti's writings that he was aware of an alternative and mechanically simpler method of attaining his objective.[27] The apparent failure of the Italian theorists to discover the distance point method, or, if it was known, their definite disinterest in it, seems at first a little curious. It becomes less strange when it is remembered that Alberti's own construction, with its perpendicular intersection of the visual pyramid, diagrammatically illustrates the whole conception of the threefold relationship between the object, the pictorial plane, and the spectator's eye, each time that it is used. The distance point construction—based on the convergence of the diagonals of a square with the horizon line at points of which the distance from the central focus equals that of the observer from the picture plane—this simple construction bypasses the whole conception of the visual pyramid and its pictorial intersection, which finds no clear and diagrammatic reflection in it.

Alberti, in the second book of his *Della Pittura*, goes on to explain how any object, whether angular or circular, can be accurately reproduced on the foreshortened pavement. Its plan is either traced upon the receding plane by direct observation, or else by the transference onto the latter of coordinates obtained upon an unforeshortened square which has been similarly subdivided. The height of its various parts will then be governed by multiples, or fractions, of the vertical distance between the horizon line and the part of the foreshortened plane on which they stand.[28] This distance, if the horizon is at head height, will be equal to the stature of a man.

Even the bare summary of a few aspects of Alberti's new construction reveals the autonomy achieved by the idea of space. During the thirteenth and fourteenth centuries it was possible to see space gradually extending outward from the nucleus of the individual solid object, and moving, stage by stage, toward emancipation from its tyranny. Now the pictorial process is complete. Space is created first, and then the solid objects of the pictured world are arranged within it in accordance with the rules which it dictates. Space now contains the objects by which formerly it was created. The change in pictorial method is a close reflection of the crystallization of ideas which were slowly taking shape in the preceding century, and which were earlier discussed.

The conception of the picture as the plane cross-section of the visual cone, or pyramid, which has its base in the object and its apex in the eye, is similarly the last stage in the slow transformation of the picture plane from the opaque, decorative, surface which was its medieval form.

The artificial perspective, which Alberti codified and himself conceived in part, and which dominated Italian art throughout the fifteenth century, has four principal characteristics. The first two of these are shared by all those centralized, but unfocused, fourteenth-century vanishing axis systems which make use of the foreshortened frontal setting for individual objects. Toward the second two, the leading artists, both of Florence and Siena, had made steady progress by empirical means. The four characteristics are that: (*a*) There is no distortion of straight lines. (*b*) There is no distortion, or foreshortening, of objects or distances parallel to the picture plane, which is therefore given a particular emphasis. (*c*) Orthogonals converge to a single vanishing point dependent on the fixed position of the observer's eye. (*d*) The size of objects diminishes in an exact proportion to their distance from this observer, so that all quantities are measurable. The result is an approximation to an infinite, mathematically homogeneous space, and the creation of a new, and powerful means of giving unity to the pictorial design.

These characteristics are precisely those which stood revealed in the construction which Brunelleschi demonstrated in his paintings of the Florentine piazze. Yet although Alberti places Brunelleschi in the list of six great artists to whom he dedicates his treatise, and although his preface is addressed to him as an architect, there is no reference to him in the text itself. There is therefore nothing to connect his name with the creation of the new perspective which Alberti strongly implies is his own invention.[29] Since the origins of the new idea must have been common knowledge in the circles in which he and Brunelleschi moved, there must clearly be a sense in which his claim is true. He could not otherwise have written in such terms in Florence, and in Brunelleschi's lifetime. There are equally no grounds for a rejection of Manetti's factual account which was also written in the lifetime of many who had known both Brunelleschi and Alberti. The most likely solution seems to be that Brunelleschi was, in fact, the inventor of the basic geometrical constructions which underly the new perspective. He composed his two pictures by the laborious process of first drawing out the plans and elevations of the entire contents, and then combining them upon the panel. Such a procedure arises naturally out of the architect's preoccupation with the plans and elevations of buildings, and also closely follows the pattern established by Vitruvius' few surviving comments on the antique system. This method was afterward abbreviated by Alberti's improved construction which consisted in building a three-dimensional system of coordinates in foreshortening that enabled the artist to determine the relative magnitudes of all the objects which he wished to represent.

. . . It was Alberti, and Alberti alone, who gave expression to the ideas which underlaid and surrounded the bare mathematical skeleton. It was he who related the construction to a complete theory of the status and objectives of pictorial art which was invested with antique authority. It was he who, by reducing the mathematical labor to a minimum, brought the new ideas within the realm of practicality for the ordinary artist. In doing this Alberti gives the method a schematic quality and a rigidity which were not present in Brunelleschi's compositions, for all their trickery of silhouettes and peepholes.

Alberti shows no sign of any awareness of the limitations of his method. It confers upon the artist a hitherto undreamt-of power to intensify and unify the spatial composition, and to harmonize it with the flat pictorial surface which can itself be controlled in a new way. There is no acknowledgement, however, of the points at which these achievements are made possible only by the acceptance of a geometrical convention which runs counter to the artist's visual experience of the details of the world about him. The theoretical perfection of the system, as a system, takes no cognizance of the aesthetic sensibility, and fundamental honesty of eye, which seem to be revealed in Brunelleschi's careful manipulation of his compositions; in his attempt to minimize the conflict between the rigidity of geometrical method and the soft variety of living experience, avoiding, as far as possible, the foreshortened frontal flanking elements which, under the influence of the new perspective, become a standard feature of Renaissance compositions. The contrast between the mathematical and the empirical must not, however, be taken too far. It is not a question of the replacement of a method which is all fidelity to experience by another which is all convention. It is a substitution of one aspect of truth, and one convention, for a different convention and another truth. The softly bowed, centralized oblique composition evolved by Maso actually draws in the apparent dual recession of the individual object, but completely ignores the known and observed rectilinear setting of the series. The new system ignores the first appearance by construction, but acknowledges the known fact, and with it a different appearance. The straight lines of common architectural usage not only can be seen, but are indeed all that is seen by the average modern man.[30] Moreover, when all the conditions postulated by the system are observed, as is hardly ever the case in practice, artificial perspective achieves a scientific accuracy and truth to nature which is quite outside the scope of any other system. Under such conditions, the diminution outward from the visual center of all visible frontal surfaces is taken care of by the natural foreshortenings of the representational surface.

The power generated by Alberti's systematic clarity can be demonstrated by the abrupt change which overtakes the choice of viewpoint in representations of the Piazza della Signoria. In the fourteenth-century fresco of "The Expulsion of the Duke of Athens," and in an early fifteenth-century relief, the Palazzo Vecchio is obliquely set.[31] But this diagonal view of the piazza virtually disappears between the time of Brunelleschi's own design and Stella's etching in the early seventeenth century.[32] In the many well-known views which have survived from the intervening period, the observer is always either situated on the north side of the piazza, looking straight toward the Loggia dei Lanzi, or standing in the middle of the west side and looking straight toward the main façade of the Palazzo. The faces of the buildings are thus made to conform as closely as possible to the axes of an Albertian foreshortened square.[33] No better illustration could be given of the impact of a system of construction upon composition.

The innate pictorial qualities of artificial perspective were not the only sources of its popularity and prestige. Already in the *Della Pittura,* it is used as a lever with which to ease the humble craft of painting into the lordly circle of the liberal arts. With this ascent the formerly humble, but now scientific, painter was to move into the sphere of the princely patrons and attendant men of letters.[34] Social and economic pressures were combined with the aesthetic and the practical. It was Alberti's contribution to the history of spatial realism in painting that, at one blow, made an essential technical improvement and disseminated the new idea in palatable form, whilst harnessing it to the driving force of the whole current of contemporary ideas and aspirations.

LORENZO GHIBERTI

The final document which must take its place beside the work of Brunelleschi and Alberti in the story of the birth of artificial perspective is once more a written text. This is the *Third Commentary,* which Ghiberti wrote in the last years of his life and left unfinished at his death.[35] This *Commentary* does not concern itself with problems of perspective proper, but with what has been called natural perspective or optics. What is more, it does not contain, as far as can be seen, a single item of original material. The text is nothing but a patchwork of quotations from antique and medieval treatises, of which the most important are those of Vitruvius, Alhazen,

Peckham, and Bacon. It is in this very fact that the significance of Ghiberti's work resides. Written after Brunelleschi's painted manifestos, and after Alberti's *Della Pittura* and his own essays in the new perspective for the Porta del Paradiso, it throws some much-needed light upon the relationship between the medieval optics and the new perspective science.

The opening part of the *Commentary* is chiefly concerned with the structure of the eye, and with the theory of vision, which are set forth in a series of excerpts derived from Alhazen, Bacon, and Peckham. Ghiberti was thoroughly up-to-date in his choice of authorities, since the medieval writers were the only available source of knowledge. It was not until later in the century, when artists turned to the serious study of anatomy, giving much-needed impetus to the practice of dissection, that direct observation began to supplement medieval and antique authority. The immediate interest does not, however, lie in these, and in similar passages dealing with proportion, or with reflection and refraction, but in those which treat of the means whereby the size and distance of visible objects are known to the beholder.[36]

In a long series of extracts from Alhazen and Peckham, five main propositions are put forward. These are that: (*a*) Visible things are not comprehended by means of the visual sense alone. (*b*) It is only possible to judge the distance of an object by means of an intervening, continuous, series of regular bodies. (*c*) The visual angle alone is not sufficient for the judgement of size. (*d*) Knowledge of the size of an object depends upon a comparison of the base of the visual pyramid with the angle at its apex, and with the intervening distance. (*e*) Distance is most commonly measured by the surface of the ground and the size of the human body.

The scope of the first proposition is to show, through a complicated argument, that vision is not purely a mechanical function of the eye; that it is meaningless without the operation of the intellect.[37] The understanding of any object in relation to its surroundings is found to depend upon the comprehension of five things. These are its lighting, its color, its remoteness, its parts, and finally, the magnitude of the intervening distance.[38] As a result the nature of the thing seen is not understood "except through discrimination, or recognition, or proof. . . ."[39] This conception of seeing, and of the function of the intellect, is extremely close to that underlying Alberti's *Della Pittura.* It is the particular virtue of the new perspective that it contains within itself the true principles of nature. The processes of measurement and comparison, which alone give meaning to what is seen, attain a mathematical precision beyond the reach of the fallible human eye and mind. If the most recent theories of visual perception seek to supersede this coach and driver view of the relationship of eye and intellect, it is only because the true complexity of the eye and its reflexes are just beginning to be understood. The fact that many of the judgements which Alhazen and Ghiberti, and their successors to the present day, believed, and still believe to take place in the controlling intellect, may actually be automatic responses to stimuli within the eye itself, does not detract from the importance of such ideas for the genesis of the new perspective.[40] Nor does it render them less valuable as a corrective to the crudely mechanical approach which is all too often to be found among writers on the processes of sight and their relation to artistic matters.

The coincidence between the form taken by the new artificial perspective and the analysis of visual experience given by the medieval authorities on optics is carried even further in the second proposition. Here the authority is once more Alhazen, who proves his point by two experiments.[41] In the first he shows how difficult it is to judge the height of clouds above a level plain. Error is almost certain. Yet, if there are mountains which reach into and above these same layers of cloud, the estimation of their height becomes quite easy. Even so, since it is a matter of calculation, it is later shown that only moderate distances can be measured accurately by the eye. Beyond them the visual angle becomes too small, and the spatial divisions are indistinguishable from each other. The second experiment is similar in nature. This time the observer looks through a peephole at the tops of two walls, which lie across the line of vision with their bases out of sight. It is then found to be utterly impossible to tell how far apart the two walls are.[42] It is only by comparison with some known distance that the unknown can be measured. The empirical nature of the judgement of depth is therefore established, and with it the necessity for a continuous, intervening series of regular objects.

"Non igitur comprehenditur quantitas remotionis rei visae a sensu visus, nisi remotio respexerit corpora ordinata continuata."[43] This is matched in Alberti's artificial perspective by the fact that the first operation is the establishment of a regularly subdivided and diminished, rectangular pavement to provide the necessary measuring rod.

The next two propositions are derived from Peckham, who compresses into two short "conclusiones" ideas that Alhazen elaborates in a series of lengthy sections.[44] First Peckham demonstrates that there is no direct connection between the angle at the apex of a triangle and the length of the triangle's base line. The visual angle alone is therefore insufficient as a means of judging size. Then he shows that all apparent sizes depend on a comparison of the visual angle and the base line of the visual pyramid, and that it is only by a further comparison of the latter with the distance intervening between object and observer that its true dimensions can be judged. A hand held in front of the eye will, he observes, blot out a large wall. It is only through a knowledge of their relative distances that their sizes can be compared.

Finally, it is once more in the words of Alhazen that the fifth important conclusion is set forth.[45]

"Bodies, therefore, which are orderly and continuous in relation to the distances of visible objects, are in the majority of cases parts of the ground, and familiar visible things, which are always understood by the visual faculty, and more often they are the surfaces of the ground. . . . The most important of these, the size of which is certified by the visual faculty, is that which is at the feet: since the magnitude of that part, which is at the feet, is understood by the visual sense and by the distinguishing faculty, and the visual sense certifies it by the measurement of the body of man."

This passage is striking in two respects. The first is its similarity to that in which Alberti insists, with added classical allusions, but more restricted purpose, that man is the measuring rod of nature.[46] The second is that it confirms that the ground plane provides the most satisfactory and familiar, ordered, and continuous series of objects which can be used to measure distance. It therefore comes even closer than the second proposition to the formulation of the idea of the foreshortened, rectangular pavement which, in artificial perspective, creates, and measures out, the space that contains all the objects of the pictorial world. The very size of the subdivisions, based upon the stature of a well-built man, stresses the point already made by Alhazen.

These passages, which reveal the medieval view of the visual perception both of size and distance, do not explain the emergence of artificial perspective. They do show, however, a clearly defined conception of visual reality that was potentially fertile ground in a period of rapidly growing interest in the representation of space. It only needed the application of these ideas to representational problems for them to provide the complete basis for a system of perspective. The structure of Alberti's artificial perspective reveals at every stage ideas which are the exact reflection of those found in the medieval texts. It seems most likely that just such an application of optical theory to representational problems lies behind the invention of the new system. Such a process also explains the continued interest in the same texts not only on the part of Ghiberti himself, but also on that of Piero della Francesca and Leonardo da Vinci. The explanation of the necessity for artificial perspective given by Piero in the introduction to the third book of the *De Perspectiva Pingendi* provides, perhaps, the clearest evidence of the close connection of medieval optical and Renaissance perspective thought.[47] He says:

". . . since one part of any quantity is always closer to the eye than another, and the nearer part always appears under a greater angle in relation to the fixed limits, and because it is not possible for the intellect by itself to judge their measurements, that is to say how great the nearer and how great the more distant, therefore I say that perspective is necessary, which discerns all the quantities proportionally like a true science, showing the diminution of any quantity by means of lines."

In this single sentence just those ideas which Ghiberti found in the writings of Alhazen and Peckham are adduced as the justification for artificial perspective. Throughout the medieval texts it is axiomatic that "seeing" involves "knowing," and that the knowledge of distance is one of the elements of this understanding of what is seen. The same conception of sight underlies Alberti's insistence that there must be some rule whereby this knowledge of the painted object can be passed on to the beholder before it can "appear like the real." It is the knowledge of the actual size which gives meaning to the appearance in the eye. It is with the actual size that the scientific painter must concern himself.

This close connection between medieval and Renaissance ideas reveals Ghiberti's intention in writing the *Third Commentary*, which was to deal with natural perspective or optics. He wished to summarize for his contemporaries the conception of visual reality which was the basis and justification of the new system. This had not been done by Alberti, whose treatise, as he himself repeatedly says, is essentially practical rather than theoretical in approach. Whatever doubts may be entertained about the success of Ghiberti's undertaking, mangled as it is in subsequent transcription, the enterprise as such was certainly worthwhile. Ghiberti had himself used Alberti's artificial perspective with great success. It had made an essential contribution to the crowning achievement of his life's work as a sculptor. In the light of his experience, he rightly considered that the new pictorial science did not outmode the medieval writings. On the contrary, it gave them a new immediacy for artists and theorists alike.[48] Ghiberti's very lack of originality, his faithfulness to ancient texts invested with a sudden, new significance, furthers an understanding of the meaning and historical position of the new perspective system.

NOTES

[1] The authorship is not certain, but is usually attributed to Antonio Manetti. All quotations are taken from Antonio Manetti, *Vita di Filippo di Ser Brunellesco*, ed. Elena Toesca (Rome, 1927), in which the attributional arguments are referred to briefly on pp. xi ff. The succeeding passage occurs in op. cit., pp. 9 ff. The nearly literal translation is the present writer's, and is used because in E. G. Holt, *Literary Sources of Art History* (Princeton, 1947), which might otherwise have been quoted, there are, in certain passages, assumptions based upon the knowledge of what follows.

[2] Manetti, op. cit., pp. 10 ff.

[3] The Florentine braccio equalled a distance of .5836 meters at the time of the adoption of the metric system. In the fifteenth century it seems to have been slightly longer, but varied a good deal, often according to the thing being measured. The analyses which follow would only be affected if Manetti had in mind a distance substantially shorter than seems to be the case.

[4] The width of the present door at floor level is slightly less, and above the base molding slightly more than the figure given.

[5] With the actual figures given, the angle of vision would be about ninety-four degrees, but as none of the historical information is exact only the general import of the description can be assessed.

[6] If Talenti's entrance was 3.5 meters deep, the angle of splay would have to be 25 degrees in order to widen the forward opening sufficiently to change the angle of vision by 30 degrees. A greater depth would decrease, and a lesser increase the amount of splay needed, assuming that the width of the door itself was about 6 braccia.

[7] Taking Manetti's measurement from the actual door, the entrance would, assuming that it was rectangular, only have to be about three braccia, or 1.75 meters deep in order to restrict the view in this way.

[8] The diagram was drawn by combining a scale drawing supplied by the Ufficio Technico Erariale di Firenze with the reconstruction of the piazza as it was in 1427 given by G. Carocci in *Studi Storici sul Centro di Firenze* (Florence, 1889), p. 17.

[9] G. Vasari, *Le Vite,* ed. Milanesi (Florence, 1878), Vol. ii, p. 332.

[10] Manetti, op. cit., pp. 11 ff.

[11] In fact Brunelleschi evidently manipulated the viewing distance which, being doubled by the use of a mirror, comes to between $1\frac{1}{2}$ and 2 braccia, or three to four times the width of the panel, giving a visual angle of between 19 and 14 degrees. The reasons for this action are clear. It is impossible to embrace anything like a ninety-degree angle through a hole of the kind described, and the reduced angle actually used is satisfactorily close to the angle of clear vision. It is significant that this manipulation would have greatly accentuated the impact of the forward corners of the piazza had they been included.

[12] Manetti, op. cit., pp. 12 ff.

[13] W. Limburger, *Die Gebäude von Florenz* (Leipzig, 1910), gives the original position of all the buildings mentioned. S. Romolo, p. 149, Calimala Francesca, p. 198.

[14] On entering a rectangle at one of its corners, a diagonal direction of attention is pressed upon the spectator, even where there is no such strong architectural attraction.

[15] No detailed reconstruction of the technical procedure used in drawing these pictures has been attempted, since there is no way of deciding between the various possibilities. It should, however, be noted that the oblique setting could have been accurately achieved without recourse to the distance point construction.

[16] Even so, this would probably allow some at least of the upper parts of the frontal surfaces of various buildings to appear as a result of their uneven heights. This would, however, have far less effect upon the composition than the potentially completely visible frontal surfaces of the buildings in the foreground at the nearer corners of the piazza.

[17] All references are to the critical edition of the Italian text, Leon Battista Alberti, *Della Pittura,* ed. L. Mallè (Florence, 1950). For critical notes on this edition, see C. Grayson, *Studi su Leon Battista Alberti,* Rinascimento, iv (1953), pp. 45–62.

[18] See E. Panofsky, "Renaissance and Renascences," *The Kenyon Review,* Spring, 1944, pp. 201–36.

[19] Alberti, op. cit., fols. 120^{v}–1^{r}, ed. Mallè, pp. 55–8, and fols. 121 ff., ed. Mallè, pp. 58 ff.

[20] Alberti, op. cit., fol. 121^{v}, ed. Mallè, p. 59, para. 3.

[21] Alberti, op. cit., fol. 123^{r}, ed. Mallè, p. 65.

[22] Alberti, op. cit., fol. 124^{r}, ed. Mallè, pp. 68–70.

[23] Alberti, op. cit., fol. 124^{v}, ed. Mallè, p. 70.

[24] Alberti, op. cit., fol. 130^{r}, ed. Mallè, p. 91.

[25] Alberti, op. cit., fol. 124^{v}, ed. Mallè, p. 71.

[26] Alberti, op. cit., fol. 125v, ed. Mallè, p. 73.

[27] The distance point construction, which was popular in the north, is based on the fact that the diagonals of all squares, or, in other words, all lines on any plane which run into the pictorial space at an angle of 45 degrees, meet at a point the distance of which from the vanishing point is equal to that between the picture plane and the eye. (Illus. Panofsky, *Codex Huygens*, p. 96, the observations on diminution being equally false when applied to this method.)

[28] Alberti does not actually use the term "horizon line," but speaks of the "central line." Alberti, op. cit. fol. 128v, ed. Mallè, pp. 86–7.

[29] Alberti, op. cit., fol. 124v, ed. Mallè, pp. 70, 72 in particular.

[30] Panofsky, "Die Perspektive als 'symbolische Form,'" loc. cit., notes 10, 11, pp. 295–6, speaks of the effect of straight line perspective on visual habits. The built-in curves of Greek architecture, and their late rediscovery, are discussed in W. H. Goodyear, *Greek Refinements* (London, 1912).

[31] Illus. A. Lensi, *Palazzo Vecchio* (Milan, 1929), p. 33, p. 30.

[32] A number of modern photographs show the piazza from the same standpoint as that taken by Brunelleschi, but such things are apt to be aesthetically misleading. One of the closest, although from a high viewpoint, is in Lensi, op. cit., p. 45. The nearest artistic approach is probably the Jacques Stella etching of the "Fiesta degli Omaggi," illus. Lensi, op. cit., p. 279, which, however, takes in a wider range of buildings than was possible for the earlier perspective method.

[33] Ghirlandaio's fresco is partially reproduced, and the Vasari and Stradano versions completely shown together with the Savanarola panel, in Lensi, op. cit., pp. 31, 223, 277 and 94. Similar views occur in the background of a portrait attributed to Piero di Cosimo (London, National Gallery No. 895) and in numerous engravings. R. Wittkower, "Brunelleschi and 'Proportion in Perspective,'" *Journal of the Warburg and Courtauld Institutes*, Vol. 16, 1953, pp. 275–91, uses later texts and monuments in order to explain the genesis of Brunelleschi's invention. It is, however, by no means curious that of the small, closely knit circle which included Masaccio and Donatello, it should have been Brunelleschi, the architect and sculptor, who invented the new method, any more than it is curious that Donatello, the sculptor, investigated and exploited its application more thoroughly than any contemporary painter. The separation of the arts was not a feature of the early Renaissance. . . .

[34] For Leonardo's views on the Paragone, which greatly interested him, see I. A. Richter, *Paragone* (London, 1949).

[35] J. von Schlosser, *Ghiberti's Denkwürdigkeiten* (Berlin, 1912), is the definitive modern edition. A very useful concordance and discussion of Ghiberti's relation to his sources is given in G. ten Doesschate, *De Derde Commentaar van Lorenzo Ghiberti in Verband met de Mildeleeuwsche Optiek* (Utrecht, 1940).

[36] Ghiberti, fols. 32v, 37r. Schlosser, op. cit., pp. 126–43.

[37] Alhazen, *Opticae Thesaurus*, ed. Risnerus (Basle, 1572), Bk. ii, sect. 22. Ghiberti, fol. 32v. Schlosser, op. cit., p. 127.

[38] "Remoteness" in this context simply means lack of contact, without any quantitative significance.

[39] Alhazen, op. cit., Bk. ii, sect. 23. Ghiberti, fol. 33r. Schlosser, op. cit., p. 128.

[40] Interesting hypotheses concerning the processes of vision are advanced in J. Gibson, *The Perception of the Visual World* (Cambridge, Mass., 1950).

[41] Alhazen, op. cit., Bk. ü, sect. 25. Ghiberti, fol. 33v. Schlosser, op. cit., p. 131. Similar experiments are still described in modern textbooks of which a particularly interesting example is W. H. Ittelson, *The Ames Demonstrations in Perception* (Princeton, 1952).

[42] There may be some confusion between monocular and binocular vision in this passage, but this is immaterial as the scope of the experiment is only to show the inadequacy of the visual angle for judging distance.

[43] Alhazen, op. cit., Bk. ii, sect. 25.

[44] John Peckham, *Jo. Archiepiscopi Cantuariensis Perspectiva Communis,* ed. Gauricus (1504), Conclusiones 73, 74. Alhazen, op. cit., Bk. ii, sects. 36, 37, 38. Ghiberti, fol. 34v. Schlosser, op. cit., p. 134.

[45] Alhazen, op. cit., Bk. ii, sect. 39. Ghiberti, fol. 35r. Schlosser, op. cit., p. 136.

[46] Alberti, op. cit., fol. 124r, ed. Mallè, pp. 68–70.

[47] Piero della Francesca, *De Prospectiva Pingendi,* ed. N. Fasola (Florence, 1942), p. 129.

[48] The fact that Ghiberti's treatise nowhere overlaps that of Alberti seems, in itself, to show that Ghiberti wrote late in life with full knowledge of Alberti's ideas. It seems likely that Ghiberti's selection from his antique and medieval sources was intended to be a complementary work, filling in the optical and philosophical background, and setting the whole within the historical framework of contemporary artistic developments.

3. THE SENSUOUS BOTTICELLI

Yukio Yashiro

INTRODUCTION

" . . . His delicate creatures were more slender and wavy than the blooms of the wisteria." When he wrote these words, Yukio Yashiro was referring to the Japanese artist, Utamaro. But the image evoked thereby would fit as well the Florentine Botticelli, whom Professor Yashiro does indeed compare to the Japanese master. That Yukio Yashiro's *Sandro Botticelli*, published in 1925 (2nd edition, 1929), is the product of a remarkable sensibility, is repeatedly affirmed by the grace with which the author communicates his perception of Botticelli's sensuous undertones. These emerge as an affective, fragile, and sometimes disturbing presence that haunts the artist's image of the human form, warping it into lovely distortions expressive of spiritual sadness—and desire. To the more familiar analytic and synthetic aspects of Italian Renaissance art, exemplified by empirical observation and anatomical research on the one hand and the interweaving of perspective systems and symbolic geometry on the other, Professor Yashiro here adds a sensuous facet, brilliantly crystallized by Botticelli, but hardly absent from the work of other Renaissance masters. One thinks immediately of Leonardo da Vinci who fully understood, to use Professor Yashiro's phrasing, the "reality of sensuousness."

For other aspects of Botticelli one should consult Ernst Gombrich, "Botticelli's Mythologies: A Study in the Neoplatonic Symbolism of his Circle," *Journal of the Warburg and Courtauld Institutes,* VIII (1945); Arnolfo B. Ferruolo, "Botticelli's Mythologies, Ficino's *De Amore,* Poliziano's *Stanze per la Giostra:* Their Circle of Love," *The Art Bulletin,*

XXXVII (1955); N. A. Pattillo, Jr., "Botticelli as a Colorist," *The Art Bulletin,* XXXVI (1954); and F. Lippman, *Sandro Botticelli's Illustrations for Dante's Divine Comedy* (1896). References are made in this selection to Walter Pater, *The Renaissance* (1873), which contains a frequently-cited essay on Botticelli, and Herbert P. Horne, *Alessandro Botticelli* (1908), which presents most of the documents on the artist. Mention should also be made of Lionello Venturi, *Botticelli* (1937), André Chastel, *Botticelli* (1958), and, of course, Vasari.

The selection that follows is reprinted from Yukio Yashiro, *Sandro Botticelli,* I (1925) by permission of the publishers, The Medici Society, Ltd., London.

This is a book of Art. Its appeal is to the human heart. In the appreciation of Art there is no such thing as authority. Scholarship adorns, even dignifies criticism, but does not authorize it. A critic should not pose as a judge: he is a friend. My wish is to deliver Art from the guidance of specialists and return it to the simple desire of man.

I loved Botticelli and studied him; that is all. I have written down my joy that others may share it, or rather that others may open their eyes and get greater delight from Art in their own way. I long to see my book reach congenial hearts that love beauty, rather than brains of pure scholarship. [From the Preface to *Sandro Botticelli.*]

Let us admit as a healthy and beautiful fact, that the charm of the human body is appreciated, in Art as well as in Nature, chiefly in a sensuous manner. There is no other thing in Nature for the representation of which an artist has so great an employment for his sense-activities. After seeing Botticelli's peculiar sensuousness in the treatment of flowers, we may well expect to find him unparalleled in his treatment of this most precious thing in our sensuous life, the human body.

In an age when anatomy was pursued as the principal study of artists, [he was] moderately well equipped here, and yet how anatomically defective were his figures. He was only a realist in his intention. But there was another Botticelli, the spontaneous one, more essentially himself, who gave the lie to the determined realist. What was this Botticelli? The following pages are intended to serve as an explanation. The core is the Sensuous Botticelli, from which the Sentimental and the Mystic are gradually to develop. For the eludication of Botticelli's genius, his essential indifference to anatomy is, in my view, very important. Paradoxical though it may appear, there is great naturalness in his defective anatomy, so that when looking at it, although you may feel something strange, you will readily acquiesce in the praise usually accorded to Botticelli's realism. This paradox is highly significant. Botticelli could not have made anatomical mistakes through ignorance. He simply deviated from scientific correctness because he had to move with a law more essential. His sensuous inspiration was so strong that it could not bear the restrictions of realism. Sensuousness being itself the most primitive, fundamental faculty of human nature, who can deny that Botticelli, by following it at the expense of the apparent accuracy, did not arrive much nearer to the true Nature? This is what I understand as the key of the complicated relations between his comparative failure as an anatomist and his great success as an artist. Botticelli was a sensuous genius.

Among all the artists of the world, is there any with nerves so delicate in responding to the fine nuances of the human body as Botticelli? Why was he so sensitive? I should like to find some physiological basis for this, but except in his own works, which make me suspect an abnormal keenness for feminine charms on the part of the painter, his biography gives little help. There is a story of his dream about marriage, preserved by "Anonimo Gaddiano," which runs as follows:

"On one occasion, being pressed by Messer Tommaso Soderini to take a wife, he replied to him: I would have you know, that not many nights since, it happened to me, that I dreamed I had taken a wife, and I was so greatly troubled at the thought of it, that I awoke, and in order that I might not fall asleep a second time and dream it over again, I rose and wandered about all night, through Florence, like one distracted: by which Messer Tommaso knew that that was not soil wherein to plant a vineyard." (*Horne*, p. 326.)

How can we interpret this anecdote of his life? It is so vague a story that I wonder if even Dr. Freud, who predicted the whole future career of Leonardo da Vinci from a dream of his infancy, could attempt the same ingènious psychoanalysis of Botticelli's character from this dream. I cannot give any definite interpretation, though I feel an intimate connection between this story and Botticelli's art. The story is usually given as an illustration of the artist's love for jokes, but if joke it was, it came from a serious source.

Another way of approaching Botticelli's real personality is through his portrait, painted by his pupil Filippino Lippi about the year 1482 in the Brancacci Chapel in the Church of the Carmine. This is the only reliable portrait of Botticelli. Filippino was a good-natured and shy soul endowed with considerable descriptive power. Moreover, he was the favorite pupil of the master. As a direct testimony to Botticelli's appearance, one cannot hope for anything better. And what did Botticelli look like? As far as I know, this portrait was generally understood as showing a tired, sensuous type, corresponding well with Vasari's description of Botticelli's boyhood, of his bad health and capricious mood.

Was he not really frail of body, a body in which there were too many nerves, which responded too vividly to all the faint shades of beauty, to the detriment of physical health? His senses were perhaps too acute, while the power to control and unite them to the fixed purposes of life was lacking. He was like a mass of nerves without the sustaining quality of will-power. Thus feminine beauty, the greatest charm for every child of man, he must have felt too keenly. He must have enjoyed and suffered all the conflicting sensations called forth by fair woman. It is only a man of brute nature who can feel only the sensual in regard to sex. Botticelli's super-sensuousness was not of this kind.

Although I am against the prevailing fashion of psychoanalysis, which gives too great an importance to sexual motives, I am more against the puritanical prejudice in understanding great men of the past. Dr. Jens Thiis, in his study of Leonardo's younger days, criticized the vain and frequent attempts of those biographers of Leonardo who described him as a saintly being. In the case of Botticelli, Horne endeavored to endow with a special chastity the personality of his favorite painter, by enumerating details of his life as conducive to the critic's conclusion, such as, that Botticelli's name never was mentioned in conjunction with any woman, and that he lived contentedly all his life as a dependent under the paternal roof. The story of his dream of marriage sounds, in Horne's book, as if Botticelli might have had something of a monk-like feeling towards the fair sex. Dr. Bode, too, after giving the story, refers to Botticelli as the "enemy of marriage," as if Botticelli's pure soul was more inclined to yearn for the fair image than for possession. This is true, as far as it goes, but it is not all. Puritanical interpretation places Botticelli near to the angels. But in him I see the living man.

Besides, it is wrong to consider these painters of the Renaissance in the moralistic light of modern times: their art, which is, after all, the best expression of their life, shows them as extremely human. While Fra Angelico dreamed of female beauty, Botticelli must have been immersed in beautiful sensuousness in order to paint those alluring torsos and limbs. In Fra Angelico you feel the innocent longing for unknown joys; in Botticelli there is rather the sadness of a man who knows all. His story of the dream sounds almost like a disguised confession of a decadent being.

The psychology of the decadent is complex. Overstrung and tired sensuousness is perhaps its basis, which, by its very ardor, leads to embarrassment in the pursuit of desire. Every sensation is so keenly felt that it monopolizes the moment and is soon tired. A decadent man is restless and sad. Usually this type is the product of dissipation, frequent in the over-refined Rococo period and the "fin de siècle," which succeeded it. But it may come spontaneously as in a supersensitive genius like Botticelli's. In normal psychology a sensuous attraction presupposes the desire for physical approach. In supersensitive cases, the physical may repel by its very attraction, as pleasure too acute turns to pain. Botticelli's dream in itself has no interpretation in this way. Putting his alluring female figures together with his strangely serious antipathy against marriage, which can be felt from the story, I cannot help coming to the conclusion that his nature verged on decadent psychology. All through Botticelli's life and art there is always something of duality which was the cause of his unrest and capriciousness.

6. Sandro Botticelli, *Birth of Venus*, c. 1480, Panel 68¼″ by 107¼″ (Uffizi, Florence)

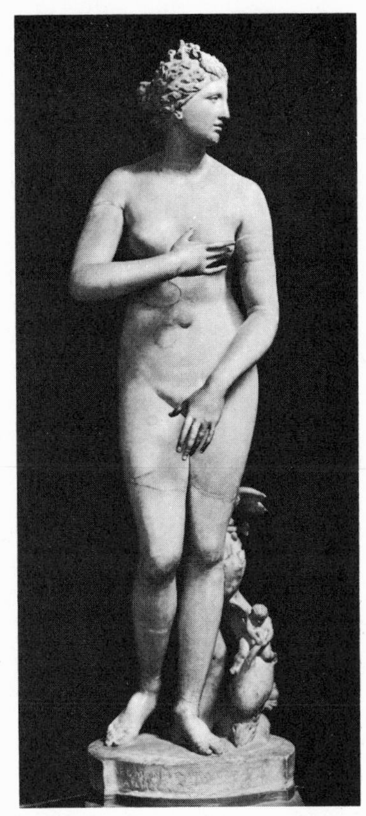

7. *Venus de' Medici,* c. 320–280 B.C. 60¼″ High (Uffizi, Florence)

That the painter of Venus should become converted to the ascetic sect of Savonarola and end his last days in a mystic silence is very symbolic of the whole art and life of Botticelli. He was at bottom a medieval being. But he was born in the age of Hellenic culture. The spirit of the time is so powerful that Botticelli was brought up to play a part which was contrary to his fundamental temperament. In his time he was among the most daring in serving the cult of Venus; he, however, remained essentially the same, a medieval and religious soul, in which a temporary deviation in an opposite direction could not fail to ferment the revolt of his real nature, one day to burst out and upset his whole life. Botticelli was ever a medieval soul, yearning for classic Greece, and as it was beyond his reach, he longed for it all the more. There is no conception of the female figure in Art so remote from Greek ideals as Botticelli's Venuses.

To the medieval mind, contrasted with the classic, a female body was "forbidden fruit." Look at the nervous feeling of shame, shaking every line of Botticelli's Venus, more tremulous than the young hanging willows by the river side. This Venus of the *Birth of Venus* [Fig. 6] must have been modelled from an antique type, of which the *Venus de' Medici* [Fig. 7] in the Uffizi Gallery is the most famous example. There is, however, a whole world of difference. True, the *Venus de' Medici,* being a work of the late period, is apart from the Arcadian innocence of the Golden Age, and the goddess of beauty has become conscious of her nakedness. Compared with Botticelli's, she is still a goddess, a child of the antique world, when everything natural was accepted without shame. Perhaps she is already approaching the time of the birth of Christianity, which, with its contrasted dualism between spiritual salvation and bodily temptation, was to implant a nervous, guilty feeling of shame in the bosom of the descendants of Adam and Eve, and make them cover their nakedness. In the *Venus de' Medici* is just awakened an organic feeling of shyness, a natural instinct for protection. Is she not calm in her beauty thus guarded?

Poor nervous Venus of Botticelli's forbidden vision! She is of the clad race, stripped of her garments. In her bashfulness, she does not know where to look, merely twitching her nervous fingers, anxious to be hidden behind the garment spread by the awaiting Grace. Every line running through the fair pearly body, which Pater called "cadaverous, or at least cold," because, as I think, it is a pale slender body, an aristocratic plant, grown in a secret palace remote from the sun—every line of her body is a silver chord of high-strung nerves conscious of its precious nakedness. Not only her soul is embarrassed, her limbs themselves are suffering from the vulgar gaze.

According to the researches of Horne, Botticelli seems to have followed for the painting the passages from Poliziano's Stanze, where the poet tried among other things to reconstruct, though with inaccuracy, the lost painting of Venus Anodyomene by Apelles. Inaccurate because, although Poliziano expressly says to Antonio Urcèo Codro, in sending him some specimens of his Greek epigrams, "Read first what I have composed in imitation of not a few ancient writers upon the Venus of Apelles, which our Pliny calls Anodyomene and worthily described in certain Greek verses, by which it may still be illustrated," yet Poliziano's description of Venus' hands is different, both from the manner in which Venus Anodyomene, "wringing the ooze out of her hair with her hands," should be represented, and also from the existing statues with the same title. Then why did Poliziano change the position of her hands in this significant way, as is described in the Stanze:

> "La Dea premendo colla destra il crino,
> Collaltra il dolce pomo ricoprissi"

or in the Latin version of Jacques Toussain of Poliziano's Greek epigrams:

The Sensuous Botticelli

> "Et manu quindem gattus mari perfusi capitis
> Dextera stringebat, & resonabat spuma
> —at laeva
> Tegebat pubem adhuc demersam."
> (Cf. *Horne,* p. 150.)

Indeed, there are many Greek statues of Venus beginning with the famous *Venus de' Medici,* with hands in these positions, and it is interesting to notice that this type was preferred by the taste of the time, at variance with Pliny's literary authority. Poliziano, the main supporter of the classic culture of the circle of Lorenzo il Magnifico, tried to regard the naked beauty frankly with the innocent eyes of the Arcadians, but Poliziano, a Quattrocento poet, deceived his intention. His conscience, brought up in Christian morality, could not but feel a strange disturbance at observing the secret beauty, and ended in endowing the nude with his own guilty appreciation. Botticelli had more of a medieval mind, in which the sense of sin was deeply set, so in his vision, religious and sensuous at the same time, Venus must have appeared as an image doubly disturbing. His soul, as it were, in an agony of beautiful sin, seems to be reflected in the trembling but dreamy Venus.

To one who is not sensuous, the question of the flesh is simple. He shuns the danger, or, rather, there is no danger. To Botticelli the spiritual danger, hidden in the flesh, must have been great in proportion with his extreme sensuousness. I imagine that to him the female body was the "white ghost" of medieval fancy. She looms out of the night, menacing him with an awful charm. . . .

I have already referred to Botticelli's Gothic nature. In his conception of the female body he seems more than ever nearer to the Northern than to the Southern temperament. In Greek æsthetic theories, Aristotle very ingeniously distinguished "ethical" art from "pathetic" art, the former indicating the representation of the permanent, steady phase of man, while the latter that of the opposite, the transient. (Cf. P. Gardner, *Principles of Greek Art,* pp. 23 ff.) The Ethos was the essence of Greek Art, with its Olympian serenity, the calm contented philosophy of the intellect, but as civilized luxury gave the Athenians more and more of the refinement of sensibility, and especially after the Peloponnesian Wars shook their sentiment with the cruelty peculiar to civil war, the pathetic side of man and Art was strongly awakened in Greece and became the precursor of Christian Art, the Art of pathos and sentiment. This distinction of Pathos and Ethos in Greek Art applies better between the classic and Christian Arts, between the Southern and Northern. And I suggest that Botticelli's art is an extreme case of the pathetic.

Look at Giorgione's or Titian's or Correggio's nudes, above all Titian's. They are as natural, innocent, and as happy as fine animals basking in the sun. You may feel them dull sometimes: dull, certainly they are, in this sense that their nudity, being natural, fails to excite the pleasure of something uncommon. There is a famous story of Eduard Manet's *Déjeuner sur l'herbe,* now in the Musée des Arts Décoratifs in Paris. It was considered an improper combination of nude women in the society of fully-clad men in the open air. The painter answered this vulgar criticism by pointing out that the same setting, artistically so effective, was painted by Giorgione in the *Concert Champêtre,* and had been under the gaze of the public eyes for years, without causing any scandal. With full sympathy and admiration for Manet, I cannot help noting the great difference between the two pictures, similar in subject but widely apart in conception. The easy calm, not only in facial expression, but in the whole indolent body enjoying the evening air of the Southern summer: where can you find this calm in the work of the most naturalistic of "fin de siècle" painters? In the ancient Venetians, pagan and oriental, there was no question on this happy, caressing evening, of being dressed or undressed. Venus could sleep sweetly by the hillside, nor would she mind the approach of satyrs. But Manet was a modern man, brought up in a modern age, and dressed accordingly in body as well as in mind. Naked flesh produces an unnatural excitation in modern man. If not artistically sophisticated, a blush would be called up by the work of Goya, Manet's real master, the marvellous *Naked Maja* in the Prado Gallery, the most modern, I might say the diabolically modern, conception of the nude.

I hope I have made clear the position occupied by Botticelli among the painters of the nude. It was an extreme case of the "pathetic," Gothic and modern. I think this touches the very core of Botticelli's art, and explains the modern cult of the artist.

Having admitted the pathetic sensuousness as the kernel of Botticelli's genius, we must analyze this sensuousness itself, so that we may arrive at another characteristic, seemingly, but only seemingly, antagonistic to his fundamental sensuousness. This second characteristic distinguishes Botticelli from other sensuous masters.

The psychological processes through which we appreciate plastic art are, besides the visual, the tactile sensation, which plays a part infinitely greater than is generally supposed. That tactile sensation is an important factor in building up our lives has begun to be recognized only recently with the progress of experimental psychology, as it works mostly in a subconscious, uncalculated, reflexive way. But that it does not attract special attention is the sure proof of its frequent use and great importance in life. In the case of appreciating the beauty of the human body, the tactile sensation plays a large part.

The tactile sensation is to be divided into two: the exterior or direct tactile sensation, the enjoyment of the immediate touch, which is closely related with sex sensations, and the interior or indirect tactile sensation, the enjoyment of smooth muscular movements, which make us appreciate in plastic art chiefly the harmony of line. Although these two are derived from the same physiological base, acted on the same nervous system, only dispersed in different places, one on the skin, the other more central in the muscles, and although they seldom act independently, their psychological functions are widely differentiated. The exterior tactile sense may be compared with the tentacles of primitive animals, which are immediately sensitive to outside influences. It is the most practical, most instinctive of senses, which, when too much excited, monopolizes your attention with physical contact, and gives you little opportunity for artistic contemplation. It belongs to the lowest of the senses and is usually, though too hastily, excluded from aesthetic psychology. On the other hand, the inner tactile sense, which feels muscle-movements, is far more abstract, and collectively forms the ideas of Space and Rhythm. This inner tactile sense has its practical side, but, generally speaking, is far apart from animal instincts and greatly contributes to our contemplative life, to which artistic pursuits, however sensuous they may be, belong. I wish to point out that Botticelli's sensuousness, extraordinarily strong in itself, belongs mainly to this inner tactile, and was, of its nature, free from sensuality. I call Botticelli's sensuousness "ethereal sensuousness."

4. RAPHAEL'S FRESCOES IN THE STANZA DELLA SEGNATURA

Sydney J. Freedberg

INTRODUCTION

Sydney Freedberg's *Painting of the High Renaissance in Rome and Florence* is a detailed study of interrelationships in the painting of these two cities from the latter part of the 15th century to 1521. The text weaves back and forth between Florence and Rome and back and forth from artist to artist, developing an intricate evolution of form and style. The selection chosen for this anthology analyzes Raphael's first challenging commission at the papal court of Julius II: a series of frescoes long recognized as both a definitive monument in the classical style of the High Renaissance and the maturation of Raphael's art. The intensity of Freedberg's analysis provokes new insights into the nature of High Renaissance art, particularly with respect to the blend of ingredients that make up what we have called the Classical style.

The prototype for Freedberg's study is a familiar "classic": Heinrich Wölfflin's *Classic Art,* first published in German (1899). It is instructive to read in conjunction with Freedberg's work the reviews of it by Juergen Schulz in *The Art Bulletin,* XLV, 2 (1963), and by Creighton Gilbert, in *The Art Journal,* XXI, 4 (1962). For further reading on Raphael, see Oskar Fischel, *Raphael,* tr. by Bernard Rackham (1948); Edgar Wind, "The Four Elements in Raphael's Stanza della Segnatura," *Journal of the Warburg and Courtauld Institutes,* II (1938–39); Kurt Badt, "Raphael's Incendio del

Borgo," *Journal of the Warburg and Courtauld Institutes,* XXII (1959); J. White and J. Shearman, "Raphael's Tapestries and Their Cartoons," *The Art Bulletin,* XL, 3&4 (1958); H. B. Gutman, "The Medieval Content of Raphael's 'School of Athens,' " *Journal of the History of Ideas,* II (1941); F. Hartt, "Lignum Vitae in Medio Paradisi: The Stanza d'Eliodoro and the Sistine Ceiling," *The Art Bulletin,* XXXII (1950); and John Pope-Hennessy, *The Raphael Cartoons* (1950).

THE STANZA DELLA SEGNATURA. The Sistine Ceiling is perhaps the highest and swiftest flight of spirit ever undertaken by an artist, and in the range of style it explores it may be the longest. In four-odd years of labor Michelangelo accomplished an evolution that embraced, in summary and essential terms, the possibilities of the Classical style from a relatively elementary to an apparently final stage, and also tested its impossibilities. No development in any other artist is comparable to this one in succinctness in time and space. Yet the pattern of development is not unique, and though it was doubtless isolated in its process of generation within Michelangelo's mind, it was not historically isolated in contemporary Rome.

Essentially independently, owing only little to knowledge of Michelangelo's example, Raphael moved in a similar orbit through the development of a mature Classical style: less high and swift, but in compensation investigating the regions through which it moved more broadly and more thoroughly. The distinction between Michelangelo's and Raphael's development depends not only on their different personality, and on their different quality and kind of genius but, as we have observed before, on the habit and aesthetic of their different métier: it is Raphael who explores the Classical style in the more diffuse and more complicated range of the painter's problems. . . .

The given architectural substance of the Stanza was altogether such as to solicit, in the mind of a painter of mature Classical disposition, a whole pictorial decoration that should conform to the internally balancing, centralized unity shaped by the walls themselves. The opportunity implicit in the architectural frame was not merely accepted but decisively exploited by Raphael; like Michelangelo in the Chapel, Raphael created a painted structure far more articulate than the actual Quattrocento space of its Classical aesthetic potential. Each whole wall became, in Raphael's scheme, itself a centralized unit of scanned, controlled expansion into space: a unit that elaborates, extends, and concords with the given architectural form. Almost as much as the sculptural reference is pervasive in the Sistine Ceiling, so is the architectural reference of the pictorial form evident in the Segnatura. In Raphael's enrichment by fictitious architectonic spaces of the simple central structure of the actual room, its effect of form becomes profoundly like that of the contemporary conceptions (as for St. Peter's) of Bramante: the frescoed space becomes a domed quatrefoil, in which responsive curving movements are arranged into a central harmony.

The thematic material that was given Raphael for the decoration of the Segnatura was, even more than the fortunate accident of the given architecture, of a kind to stimulate a Classicizing character of artistic thought. The identity of the author or authors of Raphael's iconography is not known; it is only sure that, unlike Michelangelo, Raphael did not command a culture sufficient to invent his themes or to conceive their symbolic associations. Raphael's problem, vast enough, was to translate a given program (perhaps already earlier invented for Sodoma) into its visible form. What he was called upon to translate was, in the style of its ideas, of one community with the principles of art that he had brought from Florence and which, in part from the stimulus of this program, he was to develop more fully in this place. Unlike the program of the Sistine, in which a Classical cast of form and expression had been given to a profoundly Christian theme, the program of the Segnatura was, inversely, basically Classicizing and only secondarily theological. Its content represents a culminating expression of the humanism of the Renaissance: the program for the Segnatura, produced in Julius' court, is as remarkable a landmark in the history of classicism within Christianity as is the form in which Raphael illustrated it.

The humanist inventors of the program considered, as their starting point, the functions of the room that was to be decorated. These seem, from old tradition, to have been two: this Stanza was apparently the meeting place of the papal tribunal of the *Segnatura*, usually presided over by the Pope in his role as chief officer of the canon and the civil law; and it seems also to have housed the personal library of the Pope, the visible evidence of his character as a Renaissance man of learning, and of his sympathy with humanist letters and Christian humanist philosophy. Both these functions, projections not only of a papal personality in general but of the particular personality of Pope Julius, were to be indicated in the

Stanza, but the key to their union was sought by the humanists in the circumstance that was at once more personal to the Pope and most sympathetic to them: the role of the Stanza as Julius' library. The library was already a concrete expression of these functions, and to the Renaissance observer this was more immediately clear than now, from the habit of arranging libraries of the time according to "faculties," like those of the contemporary university. The Julian reference of the room led to the selection, as the thematic basis of the program, of those "faculties" which were pertinent to him, but these were in any case the ones of widest general significance: theology, law, philosophy (which included natural science), and arts (literary, not visual). These themes once selected, their specific origin, either in Pope Julius or his library, was mostly absorbed—characteristically for the High Renaissance mentality—in their possibilities for making of ideal generalization.

One wall was to be devoted to the description of each of these faculties, illustrated by a rich cast of historical characters brought together on an invented, but noble and meaningful pretext; the historical accent is more literal, but not more deeply felt, than in the Sistine. On the wall devoted to Theology the invention is of an imaginary council of great defenders of the dogmas of the Roman Church, supervised by a heavenly senate of saints and prophets, and presided over by the Trinity. The subject of their disputation is the justification of the doctrine of transubstantiation: a theme at once vastly general in its central importance for Catholic theology, and also topical and personal in its reference to Julius' own veneration and defense of a then disputed article of belief. The wall opposite, which illustrates Philosophy, is an ideal assembly of the great philosophers of the Ancient world, metaphysicians and scientists alike, led jointly by Plato and by Aristotle. In this juxtaposition of Christianity and pre-Christianity, one seeking revelation and the other possessed of it, there is an analogue, but in humanistic terms that are more respectful of the illumination of the Ancients, to the scheme of the whole Sistine Chapel. The wall to the right of the *School of Athens* illustrates the arts, chiefly literary, personified in a gathering of Classical authors and of modern Italian humanists and poets. Certainly, the inventors of this program must have been given the due compliment of a place in this Parnassian court, presided over by Apollo and his Muses. Finally, on the wall across the room the Law is represented. On the lower portion of this wall, to either side of the separating window, are the historical foundations of civil and canon law, in the latter of which Julius acts the part of the giver of the Decretals, Gregory IX; and on the upper portion of the wall is the representation of the three virtues, Prudence, Temperance, and Fortitude, which complement the virtue of Justice.

These are the separate illustrations of the faculties, each one an ideal generalization of actors and of situations, but it is a much higher generalization at which the program aims. It intends to describe not only the dignity of each faculty, but their ideal community: their function in a unity which embraces the highest aspects of man's intellectual, spiritual, and social being. The order in which the scenes are placed upon the walls implies relations. Theology and Philosophy lie across from one another; contrasted, not as irreconcilable opposites but as the classicizing humanists saw them, as complementary avenues to truth: one by faith and spiritual revelation, the other by reason and observation. Poetry and the Arts, which men create by inspiration, contrast with but also complement the Law, which man administers by deliberation and by precedent. The different disciplines, and seemingly opposite ways in which men work within them, are matched and balanced to form together a unity of man's intellectual and spiritual endeavor. Reason and faith, discipline and inspiration, become four walls of one ideal temple of the human mind.

The ideal relation among the faculties on the walls is not only that of their complementary contrast, but of a still more positive association of ideas which is made between each faculty and its adjacent neighbor. Within each wall the actors are arranged in such fashion that those toward one half of the scene have a link in ideal character with those of the adjoining half of the next scene; so in the *School of Athens* it is Plato and his disciples who stand toward the side of Parnassus, and Aristotle toward the Jurisprudence; on the wall of Justice it is the Civil Law that adjoins Philosophy, and the Canon Law that adjoins Theology; in the *Disputà* St. Peter is on the side toward Law and the mystics and visionaries toward the side of Poetry; in the *Parnassus* the Christian poets stand near Theology and the Ancient poets, for the most part, stand toward the *School of Athens.*

This association among the faculties is confirmed on the ceiling in an ideal demonstration which links them still more closely. Between the four enthroned personifications of the faculties, and set at an angle equally between them, the four oblong paintings are so devised in subject as to refer to both faculties that they adjoin: their idea principally illustrates the faculty to the left, but also leads inescapably to that on the right. Between Theology and Justice the oblong painting shows the *Temptation of Adam,* which brought the Fall that made necessary the sacrifice of Christ commemorated in the Eucharist, the subject of the Disputation to the left below. Since this Fall brought a divine judgment upon man, it links the theme of Theology with that of Justice on its right. Between Justice and Philosophy is the *Judgment of Solomon,* the king who here acts in the roles both of philosopher and judge. Between Philosophy and Poetry is an illustration of Astronomy, a branch of "natural" philosophy, in which there is implicit the Platonic doctrine of the harmony of the cosmos that is imitated in the harmonies of art, the "music of the spheres." Finally, completing the interlocking circle of ideas, the *Flaying of Marsyas,* between Poetry and Theology, deals—at the most obvious level only of its meanings—with the double theme of art and the fatal consequence of a challenge of divine authority, implying the results of contest with the sacred dogma of the papal Church. . . .

The painting of the ceiling was a necessary prelude to the major decoration of the Stanza. Beyond the opportunity offered on the ceiling to acquire some mastery of the technique of fresco it was only on the ceiling that Raphael finally attained the capacity, so necessary to the works to come, to make the human form articulate an active human situation. Equally important, the time occupied on the ceiling was a necessary interval in which Rome, Ancient and Julian, aesthetic and literary, could make its decisive impress on the spirit of the artist who, until recently, had been a painter of pictures of Christian devotion for a cultured, but mostly mercantile, Florentine society. By the time Raphael began his paintings of the walls he was possessed by the exalting knowledge of Rome and by the disposition to think and feel—as Michelangelo, by longer Roman experience, as well as private temper, felt already—nobly and universally. What came to happen on the walls of the Stanza della Segnatura is more than a logical development from what we know of Raphael's art before; it is the result of a dramatic magnification, in his new environment, of his personality.

Raphael's first painting on the wall, begun probably fairly early in 1509, was the illustration of Theology [Fig. 8]. This scene is conceived as if it were at once an ideal council of the Church, in

8. Raphael, *Disputà*, 1509, Fresco (Stanza della Segnatura, Vatican)

which its divine and mortal members are gathered to argue and approve the doctrine of transubstantiation, and a symbolic celebration of the Mass; the Eucharist upon the altar is the central object of the energies of the council just as it is the central object of the Mass. It is fixed precisely on the middle axis of the picture and it is upon this object, so small in size but of such vast spiritual meaning, that all the rest of the design focuses. Above and to both sides of the Eucharist the mortal disputants and holy witnesses are disposed in simple, grandly sweeping semicircles which extend, into the depth of the picture, the shape of the arched wall. Higher in the picture is a third and smaller semicircle made of angels and of seraphim, close-packed in upward-rising tiers. The sequence of semicircles, each dense with figures, instantly suggests an effect as of an architecture, like the apsidal half-dome of a church. Exploiting the arched shape of the wall itself, Raphael has conceived an inspired intersection between form and meaning. From the figures who attend the symbolic Mass he has built an apse to house the

Eucharist and the altar on which it stands, making a church more perfect in its substance than any architecture of stone, out of the divine Persons, the Prophets and Apostles, and the wisest of God's theologians.

The development of compositional form and the integration with it of meaning of idea is at a level that makes insignificant the obvious ancestry of the design in such an early monument of Classical style as Bartolommeo's *Judgment,* or in Raphael's own Perugian fresco of S. Severo. The living architecture of this fresco has a clarity, harmony and spaciousness, as well as a sense of scale, like that of an actual architecture; but this painted structure has the flexibility, unarchitectural, of the vital beings out of which it has been made. The great curves echo and reecho in a grandiose accord; but while, in one sense, they repeat each other, in another sense they are at the same time resiliently opposed. Throughout the composition each curve converges meaningfully toward the Eucharist, and every balance swings from it as from a pivot: upon the mute symbol of the Mystery are concentrated not only the spiritual energies of the actors but the formal energies of the design.

As in a real architecture, the solids of the composition here not only shape but give aesthetic personality to the space that they enclose. The unpopulated spaces of the picture have become an aesthetic agent on a scale, and with an emphasis, that, in Fra Bartolommeo's *Judgment,* had been no more than hinted at. The space has not only the accustomed effects of a perspective structure (here still traditional and conservative) but is informed with the animation of the solids that surround and define it. There is no longer, in this space, the quattrocentesque contrast between solids and a measured void but a unity in which space, itself inspired with personality, acts in flexible and complementary concert with the solid forms. This system, expressed for the first time on monumental scale in the *Disputà,* is the normative solution to the problem in Classical pictorial style of relation between substances and spaces; it is a mature midstage in a historical evolution in which Leonardo's *Adoration* and *Last Supper* stand at one end and, as we shall see, Raphael's Tapestry Cartoons at another.

The figures who populate this structure have grown in scale beyond those of Raphael's style in Florence and beyond those, also, of the ceiling; they are as if magnified to accord with the grandeur of the formal and ideal scheme in which they act. Most of the figures tend toward slightly but perceptibly heavier proportion than before, which is supported by a more generous amplitude of drapery. The movement of the body is explicit in articulation in the precise way that Raphael had learned in course of painting of the ceiling, and the draperies are so manipulated as to increase the breadth and clarity of the body's action. The full form and movement of the persons of the *Disputà* conveys, as Raphael's actors rarely had before, a deliberation, a decorum, and even a stateliness that reflects, but even more ennobles, the ideal of behavior of the Classicizing Roman court.

The dignity and Roman sense of decorum in these figure types is new, but the way in which Raphael works with them still depends, even specifically, on lessons learned from Leonardo. The *Disputà* is in a way a fulfillment of ideas first stated in the *Adoration of the Magi,* and several motives indicate that its model was still influential upon Raphael. The left figures of the fresco's lower range particularly recall the by now ancient, but inexhaustible, precedent: there is the same preoccupation as in Leonardo with the differentiation of complementary ideal types, and with the diversifying of expression within a general ideal mood. What Leonardo demonstrates in the *Adoration* in a—by comparison—too tightly interwoven texture is here sorted out into a wonderful lucidity of the component parts.

This process of internal clarifying is in no sense achieved at the expense of the coherence of the whole; it is no more than a function of the whole new power of clarity in Raphael's gestalt. Each individual figure is welded into ineluctable association with its group; and in the group its single parts are bound into a formal and expressive chord of which the resonance is much more than the result of the addition of its parts. As with the figures that compose it each group is distinguished from, yet inescapably associated with the next to make, again, a finally inclusive chorded harmony of whole design.

Within each group Raphael's principle of assembly is, at once, an extension of the principle of counterpoise in harmony, which shapes the posture of the single figure, and a reflection of the synthesis of complementaries which, in ideas of content as well as form, controls the decoration in its entirety. Each posture is related in a rhythmic sequence to the next, and at the same time may be complementary in movement, mass, and place in space. Each group contains, in the meaning of bodily action, in types and in expression of face, a similar interwoven play of complementaries. The relation among groups extends the same conception, of connecting sequences and simultaneous complementary variation of the general idea of form and mood. In the ordering of groups still other considerations are taken into account: of relation not only to the adjacent group but to the countering, other, half of the balancing design and, almost a primary consideration, the expressive function of the group in the development of the picture's whole communicative sense. So in the *Disputà,* in its actively expressive lower range, among those figures who are (unlike the divinely knowledgeable Senate) the "disputants," there is a succession of diverse states of energy and gravity in the groups that move from left to right and inward toward the altar; on the right there is a slower and more even-tempered progress, of figures almost in columnar sequence, which brings the movement of design to rest; here the articulation into groups is not so scanned or so precise.

It is in this manipulation of a multitude into a differentiated harmony of form and expression that Raphael does, in extent and in terms of quality, what neither he nor any of his predecessors in the painting of the Classical style had done before. Conspicuously, the *Disputà* achieves that which Michelangelo, in his contemporary first stories of the Sistine Ceiling, had attempted unsuccessfully to do and then abandoned. Moreover, even in Michelangelo's own special domain of expressive working with the human form, there is no measurable difference at this stage (probably late in 1509) in the evolution of resources of a Classical figure style. In the *Disputà* the compact, spatially developed figure of St. Augustine's scribe is a form at once as unified and as internally complex as is the *Delfica;* the "Bramante" in the foremost group at left is as handsomely counterpoised and as expressive as Michelangelo's *Isaiah,* and perhaps more expressive than the *Joel* whom, in features, he resembles; Raphael's *St. John Baptist* is almost as easy in his pose as the Ignudi of the Sistine's third bay; and the quiet-gesturing, erect figure at the middle left is as Classically recollective in his posture, quite as monumental, and of not less grave a grace, than are the sons of Noah. In all but the magnitude of form and feeling that is Michelangelo's alone, Raphael's contemporary figures are as eloquent as his in the language of the Classical style; and Raphael's development in this respect is as surely independent at this date of Michelangelo as is his remarkable development of composition, in which Michelangelo could offer no aid or example.

The compositional ingenuity that had conceived the idea of exploiting the shape of the wall in the *Disputà* to make of it the basis for a churchly apse is no less demonstrated in the second fresco of the Segnatura, the *Parnassus* [Fig. 9], executed probably in 1510. Here the misfortune of the irregular arched space into which the window juts from below is converted to positive advantage: on and around the intruding window Raphael built the hill of his Parnassus. In this poetic assembly the atmosphere is different from that of the theological gathering in the *Disputà*. Where the *Disputà* evokes a muted and solemn, appropriately celebrant, ardor the *Parnassus* is more lyrically warm, as if in recreation of the atmosphere of a poet's vision of Antiquity. In Raphael's longer residence in Rome, now, he has been exposed successfully to its climate of literary Classicism, but it is more than the subject matter of this fresco that suggests the flavor of an Ancient Classical world. The figures of the *Parnassus* have the accent of an archaeological experience, of Raphael's study in Antiquity of visible analogues of his own Classical style. The Muses of the fresco reflect this experience with something of the excess of enthusiasm of a novelty: they are reconstructions, in Raphael's most sophisticated current vocabulary, of the sensuous beauty of Ancient Classical images, exaggerating (far beyond what is in this case the identifiable and rather insignificant precise Antique source) generic Classicizing characteristics of almost arbitrary perfection of shape and musically cursive sequences of form.

Not only the Muses but all the inhabitants of Parnassus are more Classically conceived than the actors of the *Disputà*, not merely in their imitative Antique cast of drapery and accessories but in the more essential fact of a yet fuller amplitude of form and graver dignity of posture and of movement. The *Sappho*, who introduces us into this intended reconstruction of an Antique world, summarizes the grander Classicism of figure style in the *Parnassus*. Her body is a more plastically ample, richly rounded presence, composed of suave sequences of rhythm. Her movement is a fullest development of contrapposto, slow and easy, yet instinct with latent strength—an impeccable meshing and balancing of muted energy with rich substance. She makes a spatial arabesque of such beauty as before—and only shortly before—only the figures of Leonardo's third *St. Anne* had achieved, and then not with the Classical accent of

9. Raphael, *Parnassus*, 1510, Fresco (Stanza della Segnatura, Vatican)

sensuous splendor and Antique recall of this Raphaelesque form. Measured against the contemporary accomplishment of the Sistine, the Sappho seems a synthesis of Sibyl and Ignudo.

In the position of the Sappho Raphael exploits the awkward given shape of wall with quasi-illusionistic intention, more assertive than in the "Bramante" who plays a comparable role of introduction in the *Disputà*. As with the "Bramante," the movement of the Sappho is directly integrated into a group, here of poets whose measured dignity of stance complements and compensates the variety of her posture. As in the *Disputà*, this leftward and forward group is distinctly articulated from the group that next succeeds. The internal order of this second group is an inversion of the Sapphic group, beginning with the figure of the Ennias—so Ignudo-like—which echoes and varies, in reverse, the figure of the Sappho. The group of Apollo and his Muses is of singular melodiousness, visibly expressing in its form the suave music diffused through it from

Apollo's viol. This melodic line rests in the figure of the last Muse at the right; it then turns gently to descend the slope, moving in accelerating cadence through the figures of this part of the company of poets. Altogether the movement of the composition has a measure of variety—a close-textured alternation of rich arabesque and yielding pause—that is in every way more developed than in the *Disputà*. Again as in the *Disputà*, but with more decisiveness, the figures at the rightward and forward side of the design act to connect their ideal realm and the spectator's space. The principal form here, that of the aged poet, is the complement of the Sappho in sex, age, in compact and forceful shape, and in the direction of his movement; he leads us back to our reality as Sappho led us beyond it.

The *School of Athens* [Fig. 10] (executed probably from late 1510 through mid-1511) also reconstructs an Antique world, but in a mood unlike that of the *Parnassus*, not golden and sensuously warm but crystalline: an atmosphere of high clear thought pervaded by the energies of powerful intelligence. The architecture sets the temper

10. Raphael, *School of Athens*, Fresco, 1510–11 (Stanza della Segnatura, Vatican)

of the scene; Bramantesque, but with a stricter accent than in his actual architecture of recollective Classicism, it creates a stage for the figures that is of lucid order and extraordinary breadth. Its harmony and vastness is not only the frame for its inhabitants but the symbol of the intellectual structure they have built; this man-made architecture contrasts in form and in idea with the fictive heavenly architecture of the *Disputà.* Within this structure, upon the various levels of its deep foreground space, Raphael distributes its population of philosophers in a scheme that absorbs the experience both of the *Parnassus* and the *Disputà:* it has an internal variety still greater than that of one and the final grandiose stability of the other. By comparison with this fresco the design of the *Disputà* seems stilted; the basic harmony of structure, broader and deeper than that of the *Disputà,* has been immeasurably enriched from within.

The ordnance of the actors of the *School of Athens,* like that of the architecture which supports them, is according to a central scheme. Plato and Aristotle, framed by the diminishing sequence of perspective arches, are the focus of this scheme: in them the axes of the composition intersect and on them the orthogonals of the architecture converge. On both sides of their slow-gesturing, majestic forms the other figures expand in counterpoised, but not symmetrical, waves of movement which accelerate in energy as they descend, in a curving and centralizing embrace, toward the front. Unlike the *Disputà,* where the apsidal design frames, but does not enclose space, this figure composition is developed in ground plan so as virtually to surround a central spatial core; this ground plan not only echoes, loosely, the visible system of the Bramantesque architecture to the rear but that of the central ordnance of the entire decoration of the room: it suggests a quatrefoil in shape. The space thus defined by the figures is not only more inclusively and more articulately shaped than in the *Disputà* but there is also here, in comparison with the *Disputà,* a freer and more vigorous intermingling between the figures and the space. Far more than in the *Disputà,* the space of the *School of Athens* is permeated by the higher and more various energies of the figures, and shows the more complex plasticity of their distribution and their individual design. As in the *Disputà,* this space that is shaped by the figures is accompanied by a traditional and conventional space of Quattrocento perspective and both spaces, that formed by the figures and that made by the setting in perspective, are much more effectively combined. The space of the architecture and that of the figures wholly interpenetrate, and reciprocally magnify each other. . . .

In the *School of Athens,* the inheritance of the quattrocentesque concept of perspective space, and Raphael's new concept, of a space made by the figures, work in reinforcing concord and in balance. What Raphael has here first realized so profoundly as a space of figures is, however, distinct in fundamental principle from a perspective system. The space made by perspective may be described as the Early Renaissance's rationalization of an experience of space still based on that of medieval art: perspective serves to rationalize a hitherto unmeasurable, or infinite, continuum. The apprehension of the measurement of space was accompanied by that of the measurement of solids; these were concurrent and consistent, but not synthesized apprehensions. The substances were inserted in the space as loci of the geometrically defined continuum: this projection of consonant but separate experiences, of void and solid, was suspended in an abstract harmony in the reticule of perspective. In this system, as Alberti had defined it, the construction of the stage preceded the setting on it of the players.

As, in the course of the Renaissance, a differently integral, vital sense of human substance was evolved, culminating in the first expressions of High Renaissance Classical figure style, it became increasingly less possible to conceive space only as a preexistent geometric void. Figures of the new kind, as they developed in this mature phase of Classical style, came to move in three dimensions into the air around them, charging it with the emanation of their energies. Space, not only in the intervals between such figures but in the immediate ambience even of a single one of them is no longer precedent to substance or distinct from it: the figure creates space around itself, and in groups and compositions, shapes it. Shaped and charged by the enclosing substances (and in itself observed, in the new style, as mobile textured atmosphere) the space becomes not measured void but a palpable phenomenon: a plastically responsive ether. It is an extension and accessory function of the solid forms, and in this sense, in the *School of Athens,* space and substance have become parts of an experiential unity.

The conception of substance and of its effect on immediately adjacent space is like that in the Ancient Classic style, but no Antique work we know controls so wide and continuous an environment as is in the *School of Athens* with its sense of consistent and connected unity; to achieve this it is precisely the experience of Early Renaissance perspective command over void that must be presupposed. The spatial structure of the *School of Athens* is, like almost every other aspect of High Renaissance Classicism, distinct from Antique analogue and synthesizes Classical rediscovery with the consequence, however transformed, of an ultimately medieval, Christian apprehension of the world.

All this inner unity of space in Raphael's fresco has only limited relation, either by figural devices or perspective, with the space in which the spectator stands. As Leonardo had defined it first, this projection of an ideal world is distinct from ours; it is an accessible but discrete unity. What is in the *School of Athens* as a spatial structure is a synthetic equilibrium, of perspective inheritance and new Classical invention of space shaped by substance; we have observed already that the new Classical component was destined to increase its role. At the climax of Raphael's development of Classicism it would not only eclipse the other; more than this, the sense and the authority of substance, as such, would virtually extinguish even the ancillary function, in design, of space. But now, in this fresco, Raphael has evolved a solution, in terms of purely pictorial aesthetic, of the working of space and substances that is as inaccessible to the sculptural mentality of Michelangelo as it had been to the mind of Classical Antiquity.

The new component in the spatial mechanism of the *School of Athens* is, as we have suggested, a consequence of the matured High Renaissance Classical conception of the human form. In this fresco, this conception has evolved still more; while part of its population is not different from the actors of the *Parnassus* its most prominent figures, those in the foreground, have once more been magnified in their dimension. These figures in particular, but also almost all the others in the painting, are possessed by an energy which now by far exceeds that of the persons of the *Disputà;* they move in, and occupy, space with powerful assertiveness. Because each form is in itself so much developed plastically their gathering together into groups is now more elaborately articulated: to accommodate their spatial movement the enclosing group becomes at once more open within itself and more deep; more than in the *Parnassus* or the *Disputà* we are aware, in the groups of the *School of Athens*, of their expansion as if toward the imaginary fullness of a sphere.

11. Raphael, Cartoon for *School of Athens*, 1509–10, Charcoal and Black Chalk, Heightened with White, 9′2″ by 24′3″ (Galleria Ambrosiana, Milan)

Like the organization of the whole compositional structure, that of its parts is more than before spatially inclusive and expansive.

As is necessary in the Classical proposition, the growth of human form is not a growth of physical dimension only; it is equally a growing of the power of spiritual sensation. The size and breadth of action of the figures answers to their grander and more vital energies of mind. Furthermore, these states of mind, as the faces show them, are not only stronger than in the preceding frescoes but also more explicitly defined; and the body also, in its Classical function of interpenetration with the spirit, is much more explicitly articulate than before of its content. What Raphael achieves in the figures of the *School of Athens* represents a measurably higher development of Classical style. Where, however, in the two earlier frescoes it could be asserted that his development in figure style was, in all but force and magnitude, proceeding *pari passu* with that of Michelangelo, it is now evident that the contemporary accomplishment of Michelangelo in 1511 has explored possibilities of Classical figure style that Raphael has not approached. This is

despite the fact that in the *School of Athens* it becomes for the first time certain that Raphael has studied the Sistine Ceiling, perhaps at first in its half-completed state at the end of 1510.

There is nothing among the figures of the second plan of Raphael's fresco that is not wholly understandable as a consequence of his prior evolution, but the figures of the foreground, exactly those in which he shows himself the most advanced, demand knowledge of Michelangelesque precedent. The *Pythagoras* at the left—still, like the figures just behind him, reminiscent of the models of Leonardo—most strongly shows community with the Sistine Seers; in their developed musculature, complex postures, and extraordinary articulateness of body the youths around Euclid to the right are indebted to the Prophets and Ignudi both. It is the so-called *Heraclitus,* the *Pensieroso* in the center foreground of the fresco (unforeseen in the original cartoon in the Ambrosiana) [Fig. 11], who is most exactly dependent on the Ceiling. This figure, a compound of Michelangelo's *Isaiah* and *Jeremiah,* and so strangely like Michelangelo himself in features and in dress, was added only at the end of painting of the *School of Athens,* after it had been quite finished according to the cartoon. In freedom and immediacy of expressive technique it is advanced much beyond the other figures in this neighborhood. It surely succeeds, in time of conception and in execution, the first official unveiling of the Sistine Ceiling in August 1511.

This addition was provoked by more, however, than a wish to emulate Michelangelo's recent remarkable accomplishment in figure style; it is even more important for its meaning, purely Raphaelesque, within the composition. The *Heraclitus* literally rounds out, to fullness and near-spherical closure, the fresco's spatial scheme and serves in the composition as a final unifying key: it is, almost, a fulcrum for the several parts of the design. Before its meaning of relation to Michelangelo, this figure must be thought of in its significance of a correction to and further fulfillment of the Classical character of Raphael's original design, a correction conceived by Raphael as the fruit of his own development in the interval between invention and completion of the fresco; in this sense it has nothing to do with Michelangelo. It is, however, in this figure that Raphael comes closest to—but yet does not achieve—the sense of scale and of expressive vibrance in the single human figure that is demonstrated by the Michelangelo of this time. The imitation must remain approximate, for it is not motivated, nor inhabited, by the inimitable power of Michelangelo's ideas.

Confined within a less exalted spiritual limit, Raphael's conception of individual humanity does not trespass, even with Michelangelo's guidance, beyond what may be described (in terms of Michelangelo's own development) as a median of idealization. The species of humanity to which Raphael's actors belong, here at his absolute attainment of artistic maturity in the *School of Athens,* is that which Michelangelo had created in the bays of his Ceiling which just precede, but do not quite include, the *Creation of Adam.* However, what may be lacking in concentrated force of each human image is compensated for in Raphael by his quantitative variety of images. Harmonized into a community by their ideal reformation—but a reformation based on their wide, actual, human diversity—the actors of the *School of Athens* represent a concept of mankind much less austere and exclusive than Michelangelo's, but far richer. Like Leonardo before him the mature Raphael continues to believe in the function of art as comment on the multiform experience of the world. Where Michelangelo's art is the expression of an isolated psyche, and his creatures in the Sistine images of man in an essential isolation, the *School of Athens*—and the frescoes of the Segnatura in general—are the expression less of man as an individuality than of the community of men: representations of the greatness that men attain and promote in social concourse.

In the close-woven texture that Raphael makes of this concourse of humanity he exploits a range and kind of orchestration, both of form and of expression, that is closed to Michelangelo. The sum of this pictorial texture is greater than that of its human parts: the single figures may not rise beyond, or even to the standard of Michelangelo's median in the Sistine, but the aesthetic and contentual measure of the whole is not less nobly ideal. More than Michelangelo's pictured world—superb in both senses of the word; too high, too private and too terrible to imply practical example—the world projected here by Raphael conveys an ethic as well as aesthetic sense; here the beautiful is identified with human good.

5. MICHELANGELO'S VIEWS ON ART

Sir Anthony Blunt

INTRODUCTION

In his *Artistic Theory in Italy, 1450–1600* (1940; 2nd edition, 1956), Anthony Blunt traces the artistic theories of the Renaissance from their fully-developed humanist form in the writings of Alberti through the Mannerist doctrines of the sixteenth century.

Of particular interest is the contrast presented by the chapters on Leonardo and Michelangelo. Intensely fascinated by the phenomena of the material world and attuned to "the evidence of the senses," Leonardo emerges representative of the scientific current in Renaissance art. Yet Leonardo's conception of the artist is not that of a mere observer and recorder of phenomena. He is also the imaginative creator, but one whose invention is based nonetheless on the forms of nature. Michelangelo, for all the empirical factors in his conception of the human form, appears initially to comprehend the beauty of the human body as a reflection of the divine in the material world. This notion has its roots in Neoplatonism, which enjoyed an ephemeral popularity in the Italian Renaissance and attracted the artist during his early formative years in Florence. As Michelangelo's religious feeling shifted during the course of his long career towards an increasingly dark and introspective mood, his views on art still retained a measure of Neoplatonic tone. But in these later years, as Blunt demonstrates, he ceased finally to see human beauty as a symbol of the divine. Stylistically as well as chronologically there is a whole lifetime between the physical splendor of his early *David* and the Rondanini *Pietà*, which he left unfinished at his death. What this final work conveys is a spiritual presence, poignant and flawed.

Michelangelo's relationship to the Neoplatonic movement is treated in Erwin Panofsky's *Studies in Iconology* (1939), available in paperback form since 1962. Other readings on Neoplatonism are P. O. Kristeller, *The Philosophy of Marsilio Ficino* (1943); J. C. Nelson, *Renaissance Theory of Love* (1958); E. H. Gombrich, "*Icones Symbolicae:* The Visual Image in Neo-Platonic Thought," *Journal of the Warburg and Courtauld Institutes,* XI (1948); and Erwin Panofsky, *Renaissance and Renascences in Western Art* (1960), especially pp. 182–200. See also the bibliography in the headnotes to the selection on Botticelli by Yukio Yashiro (p. 41).

The selection that follows is reprinted from Anthony Blunt, *Artistic Theory in Italy, 1450–1600,* by permission of the Clarendon Press, Oxford. In this reprint the poetry of Michelangelo, with one exception, is presented in prose translation.

Our sources of knowledge for Michelangelo's views on the Fine Arts are varied. Of his own writings, the letters contain almost nothing of interest from the point of view of theory, since they are nearly all personal or business notes to his family or his patrons. The poems, on the other hand, are of great importance, for though they contain few direct references to the arts, many of them are love poems from which it is possible to deduce in what terms Michelangelo conceived of beauty.

In addition to his own writings we have the evidence of three of his contemporaries. The first of these is the Portuguese painter Francisco de Hollanda, who came to Rome in 1538 and worked his way for a time into Michelangelo's circle. He was probably never very intimate with the latter, and his dialogues[1] were almost certainly written to glorify himself and to show how closely he associated with the master. But however great his conceit may have been, his evidence is of importance, since it deals with a period of Michelangelo's life on which we are not otherwise well informed by his biographers.[2]

The second contemporary source is the biography of Michelangelo in Vasari's *Lives*. It was first published in 1550, but was greatly enlarged and almost entirely rewritten for the second edition of 1568. It contains less material than might be expected, but it gives some account of his methods of working and records some of his opinions.

More important is the third authority, Ascanio Condivi, a pupil of Michelangelo, who published a biography of his master in 1553. The life seems to have been written to correct certain false statements made by Vasari; and, though Condivi was a somewhat naïve character, he is probably more reliable than either Hollanda or Vasari when he reports Michelangelo's own views and statements.

Michelangelo lived to a great age, and his views were constantly developing and changing, so that it is impossible to treat his theories as a single consistent whole. Born in 1475, he was trained under masters who still belonged to the Quattrocento. His earliest works in Rome represent the full blooming of the High Renaissance, but before he died in 1564 Mannerism was firmly established. It is impossible to divide his works or his ideas into sharply separate compartments, but for the present purpose they can be roughly grouped in three periods, if we ignore the very early years from which no documents survive.

In the first period, ending roughly in 1530, Michelangelo's view of the arts is that of High Renaissance humanism. It is most clearly typified in the ceiling of the Sistine Chapel, the *Pietà* in St. Peter's, and the early love-poems. In these works the various elements which made up Michelangelo's early training are clearly visible. Like Leonardo he was heir to the scientific tradition of Florentine painting, but he was also affected by the atmosphere of Neoplatonism in which he grew up. His highest allegiance, however, was to beauty rather than to scientific truth; and although in his early years at least he felt that the attainment of beauty depended in large part on the knowledge of nature, he did not feel the urge to undertake the investigation of natural causes for their own sake. Consequently the observation of nature which he absorbed in the studio of Ghirlandaio could fairly easily be fused with the doctrines of beauty which he learned from the circle of Lorenzo de' Medici. But there was another factor which favored Michelangelo in comparison with Leonardo. Neither Florence nor Milan could provide the latter with the atmosphere of buoyancy which alone can produce a great synthesis such as had been achieved in Florence in the early years of the fifteenth century. In Rome, on the other hand, Michelangelo found a city at the height of its wealth and politically in a leading position for the whole of Italy. In this atmosphere the artist felt at ease with the world, at which he could look out steadily, and which he could reflect directly in his works. A training in Neoplatonism led to a belief in the beauty of the visible universe, above all in human beauty, which was no longer colored by the nostalgic mysticism of Florence. The grandeur of the figures on the Sistine ceiling depends on far more than the simple imitation of natural forms, but its idealization is based on a close knowledge and study of these forms. Whatever heroic quality is added, the foundation is a worship of the beauty of the human body.

In the field of thought the two apparently conflicting systems of Christianity and paganism are still perfectly fused in the Rome of the High Renaissance. The iconographical scheme of the Sistine ceiling frescoes is based on the most erudite theology, but the forms in which it is clothed are those of pagan gods. In Raphael's frescoes in the Stanza della Segnatura the four themes of Theology, Pagan Philosophy, Poetry, and Justice are intricately blended. The catalyst, however, is no longer the hard reason of the Florentines like Alberti, but rather the elaborate Neoplatonism of the later Quattrocento stripped of its more nostalgic elements. In Michelangelo the two faiths were both perfectly sincere. From the days when he was first influenced by the teaching of Savonarola he was a good member of the Catholic Church, though at first without that passionate self-abnegation which came into his faith in the last years of his life.

Michelangelo's belief in the beauty of the material world was very great. His early love-poems reflect this feeling in their expression of strong emotional and often physical passion, directed as much towards visible beauty as toward the spiritual beauty of which the Neoplatonists spoke.[3] Moreover, Michelangelo's contemporaries tell us that he did not merely look at nature, but, throughout his life, studied it scientifically. Condivi speaks of his knowledge of perspective,[4] and both he and Vasari record the care which he devoted to anatomy, not merely learning it at second-hand but dissecting bodies himself.[5]

Michelangelo did not, however, believe in the exact imitation of nature. Vasari says that he made a pencil drawing of Tommaso de' Cavalieri "and neither before nor afterward did he take the portrait of anyone, because he abhorred executing a resemblance to the living subject, unless it were of extraordinary beauty."[6] According to Hollanda his scorn for Flemish painting was based on the same idea: "In Flanders they paint with a view to external exactness . . . without reason or art, without symmetry or proportion, without skillful choice or boldness."[7] This view that the artist must select from nature is in agreement with Alberti, though it is unlikely that the latter would have protested so vigorously against Flemish naturalism. His standards were not the same as those of Michelangelo. Alberti acted according to a strictly rational choice, and sought the typical. Michelangelo pursued the beautiful. Condivi describes his methods as follows, alluding to Zeuxis's painting of the Crotonian Venus:

> He loved not only human beauty but universally every beautiful thing . . . choosing the beauty in nature, as the bees gather honey from the flowers using it afterwards in their works, as all those have done

> who have ever made a noise in painting. That old master who had to paint a Venus was not content to see one virgin only, but studied many, and taking from each her most beautiful and perfect feature gave them to his Venus.[8]

For Michelangelo it is by means of the imagination that the artist attains to a beauty above that of nature, and in this he appears as a Neoplatonist compared with the rational Alberti. To him beauty is the reflection of the divine in the material world.[9] . . . It is clear that the human figure is the particular form in which he finds this divine beauty most clearly manifested: "I can never now perceive Thy eternal light within a mortal being without great longing."[10]

In other cases he talks of the inward image which the beauty of the visible world arouses in his mind. The idea of beauty set up in this way is superior to material beauty, for the mind refines the images which it receives, and makes them approach more nearly the Ideas which exist in it by direct infusion from God . . . .[11]

But at this time Michelangelo still firmly believes that the inward image is dependent on the existence of beauty in the outside world which is transformed by the mind into something nobler. In an early sonnet, written in the form of a dialogue, he asks Love:

> Tell me, Love, I beseech thee, if my eyes truly see the beauty which is the breath of my being, or if it is only an inward image I behold when, wherever I look, I see the carven image of her face.[12]

And Love answers:

> The beauty you behold indeed emanates from her, but it grows greater as it flows through mortal eyes to its nobler abode—the soul. Here it becomes divine, pure, perfect to match the soul's immortality. It is this beauty, not the other, which ever outruns your vision.[13]

These passages may be compared with Raphael's letters to Castiglione, referring to his fresco of Galatea in the Farnesina, in which he says: "To paint a beauty I need to see many beauties, but since there is a dearth of beautiful women, I use a certain idea which comes into my mind."[14]

Michelangelo's views, therefore, in his first period are still related to those of Alberti, but with a strong tinge of Neoplatonic idealism.

For Alberti the artist is entirely dependent on nature in his work, and he can only improve on it by attempting to reach the types at which nature aims. For Michelangelo, on the other hand, the artist, though directly inspired by nature, must make what he sees in nature conform to an ideal standard in his own mind. Compared with Alberti this approach may seem already somewhat unrealistic, but compared with Michelangelo's later views it represents a close and direct connection with nature.

By about 1530 the attempts of the Papacy to form a powerful secular State in Italy had failed. The Reformation had split the Church and incalculably weakened the position of the Pope. Financial disorders of every kind added to the confusion, and the greatest single blow of all had come with the Sack of Rome in 1527, which left Clement VII almost powerless. The whole social structure on which the humanist art of High Renaissance Rome was based was swept away. Instead of a sense of security men felt the general disturbance of events, which seemed to threaten the existence of the Catholic Church and, with it, of the whole of Italian society.

This changed situation affected different generations in different ways. The older humanists, men of Michelangelo's age, had felt that the Roman Church was in need of reform, and had anticipated many of the Pauline features in Luther's theology. The latter forms in some respects a parallel to Italian humanism, for, if the humanists asserted the rights of individual reason, Luther asserted those of individual conscience. The Italian humanists were too closely involved with the Church of Rome as an institution to follow Luther when it became a question of schism in the Church, but, as long as it appeared possible to combine the more moderate doctrines of reform, particularly justification by faith, with fidelity to Rome, many of them were in sympathy with the demands of the German reformers. In this way there was formed a party of humanists who aimed at an internal reform of the Roman Church and a compromise with the Protestants. This party, which later received the official support of Paul III, was led by men like Contarini, Pole, and Sadoleto, with whom were associated as close followers and supporters Vittoria Colonna and Michelangelo. The religion of the latter now became fervent, and took on the form of a serious but not fanatical piety, consonant with his humanistic principles, but gradually modifying them. He belongs, that is to say, to those who wanted to build up a new and spiritualized Catholicism by means of such reforming doctrines as did not destroy the basis of the Roman Church.

This change of outlook naturally affected Michelangelo's art, and the change is most clearly shown in the great work of this period, the fresco of the *Last Judgement* over the altar of the Sistine Chapel, painted for Clement VII and Paul III between 1534 and 1541. This fresco is the work of a man shaken out of his secure position, no longer at ease with the world, and unable to face it directly. Michelangelo does not now deal directly with the visible beauty of the physical world. When he made the *Adam* on the Sistine ceiling he was aiming at a rendering of what would in actual life be a beautiful body, though it was idealized above reality. In the *Last Judgement* his aim was different. Here again nudes appear, but they are heavy and lumpish, with thick limbs, lacking in grace (Fig. 12). The truth is not, as has sometimes been said, that Michelangelo's hand was failing, but that he was no longer interested in physical beauty for its own sake. Instead he used it as a means of conveying an idea, or of revealing a spiritual state. Judged on the humanist standard of 1510 the *Last Judgement* is a failure, and it is not surprising that the admirers of Raphael could not stomach it. But as the most profound expression of the spiritualized Catholicism which Michelangelo practised, it is a masterpiece of equal importance with the ceiling. The ideals of Classic beauty which were relevant in the Sistine ceiling are no longer valid in the *Last Judgement.* Such Classical features as there are, like the Charon and Minos group, are seen through the eyes of Dante and are given a new spiritual significance. The most fundamental principle of the High Renaissance seems here to have been neglected, for there is little reconstruction of the real world, no real space, no perspective, no typical proportions. The artist is intent only on conveying his particular kind of idea, though the means by which he conveys it is still the traditional Renaissance symbol, the human figure.

The new approach to life and to art which is to be found in the *Last Judgement* can also be traced in Michelangelo's writings. In the poems of the thirties and early forties a new attitude toward beauty and toward the problem of love is visible. At this time one of the poet's most frequent themes is that physical beauty passes away, so that love directed toward it cannot give complete satisfaction and is degrading to the mind. . . .[15]

12. Michelangelo, Detail from *Last Judgement,* John the Baptist, 1534–41, Fresco (Sistine Chapel, Vatican)

But this element of bitterness and gloom is balanced by a more optimistic Neoplatonic belief. Love of physical beauty is a cheat, but the true love, that of spiritual beauty, gives perfect satisfaction, does not fade with time, and elevates the mind to the contemplation of the divine. This feeling is expressed most clearly in the poems to Tommaso de' Cavalieri, who dominates Michelangelo's emotional life from 1532 onward. The artist was evidently overwhelmed by the physical beauty of the young man, but he regarded it as an outward sign of spiritual and mental beauty, and the friendship was built upon that basis, though the violence of Michelangelo's passion was no less than in his earlier affections. This is summed up in a sonnet to Cavalieri. . . .[16]

However, not only is love directed toward spiritual qualities, but it has also the effect of raising the lover's mind by means of beauty to a contemplation of the divine beauty and therefore to communion with God. . . .[17]

But it must not be supposed that Michelangelo's view of beauty is wholly incorporeal and spiritualized. Visible beauty is still for him of the greatest significance, since it is the most effective symbol for the true spiritual beauty, and the beauty of man leads more easily than any other means to the contemplation of the divine. Love is stirred up most easily through the eye, which, according to the Neoplatonists, was the noblest of the senses. . . .[18] It is only through the eye that the artist is stimulated to creation and the spectator to contemplation of divine beauty. . . .[19] And it is in the human body that divine beauty is most completely manifested:

> Nowhere does God, in his grace, reveal himself to me more clearly than in some lovely human form, which I love solely because it is a mirrored image of Himself.[20]

The same idea is expressed in the following madrigal by means of the familiar Neoplatonic doctrine that beauty is the light which streams from the face of God:

> Neither my eyes in love with all that is beautiful, nor my soul thirsting for salvation, possess any power that can raise them to Heaven but the contemplation of beautiful things. From the highest Heaven there streams down a splendor which draws desire up toward the stars, and here on earth men call it love. And there is nothing that can captivate, fire and give wisdom to a noble heart as can a face lit with star-like eyes.[21]

At this period of his life, therefore, Michelangelo's poems show strongly the influence of the more mystical elements of Neoplatonism. The strong physical passion of the early love poems has given place to doctrines which make of love the contemplation of an incorporeal beauty. This is only another manifestation of the same tendency which we have traced in the paintings of the second period, such as the *Last Judgement.* It is also the equivalent of the spiritualized form of religion with which Michelangelo was associated in the thirties and forties. In all branches of his art and thought we feel a withdrawal from that direct contact with life which characterized the early period.

It may be suggested that this tendency away from the material and toward the things of the spirit can really be put down to the fact that Michelangelo was growing old. No doubt this provides a part of the explanation, but not the whole of it. Not all old men become spiritually minded. They only become so in certain circumstances, and Michelangelo's mysticism was a mode of escape from finding that his own world had crumbled about him. Age played its part, because had he been younger Michelangelo might have been able to fit himself to the changed circumstances, and have been drawn into the Counter-Reformation movement. But the general situation also played its part in breaking up the foundation on which his life was built.

In those passages of Michelangelo's poems which refer directly to the art of painting and sculpture we find a change corresponding to that in his ideas on beauty in the abstract.

In the first place Michelangelo is much more explicit about the religious function of the arts. Hollanda records a conversation in which Michelangelo explains his idea of the religious painter, who according to him must be skillful in his art and at the same time a man of pious life:

> In order to imitate in some degree the venerable image of Our Lord, it is not enough to be a painter, a great and skillful master; I believe that one must further be of blameless life, even if possible a saint, that the Holy Spirit may inspire one's understanding. . . . Often badly wrought images distract the attention and prevent devotion, at least with persons who have but little; while those which are divinely fashioned excite even those who have little devotion or sensibility to contemplation and tears, and by their austere beauty inspire them with great reverence and fear.[22]

The view which he expresses here is curiously close to that of Savonarola on religious art.[23] We know from Condivi[24] that Savonarola was an important influence in his life, and it is quite likely that his conception of painting as an art devoted to the service of the Church was affected by the teaching of the Dominican.

In the more purely aesthetic part of Michelangelo's writings on the arts the dominant influence in this period is that of Neoplatonism, which affects his view of the relation of painting to the visible world. Painting is no longer talked of as an imitation of nature, and the artist's interest is diverted almost entirely toward the inward mental image, which excels everything that can be found in the visible world:

> Love, thy beauty is not mortal. No face on earth can compare with the image awakened in the heart which you inflame and govern, sustaining it with strange fire, uplifting it on strange wings.[25]

The idea in the mind of the artist is more beautiful than the final work, which is only a feeble reflection of it. According to Condivi Michelangelo "has a most powerful imagination, whence it comes, chiefly, that he is little contented with his works and has always underrated them, his hand not appearing to carry out the ideas he has conceived in his mind."[26]

At this time Michelangelo lays great stress on the divine inspiration of the artist. God is the source of all beauty.[27] . . . And art is a gift received by the artist from heaven.[28] . . . By means of this divine gift the artist can give life to the stone in which he carves his statue.[29] . . . The stone itself, the material part of the work, is useless and dead till the imagination has acted upon it.[30] . . .

Michelangelo's theory of sculpture can be deduced from some of the poems, particularly the sonnet beginning:

> The greatest artist has no conception which a single block of marble does not potentially contain within its mass, but only a hand obedient to the mind can penetrate to this image.[31]

The explanation of this idea is to be found in the fact that when Michelangelo speaks of sculpture he always has in mind sculpture in marble or stone and not modelling in clay. "By sculpture I mean the sort that is executed by cutting away from the block: the sort that is executed by building up resembles painting."[32] For Michel-

13. Michelangelo, *St. Matthew,* 1506, Marble, 8′11″ High (Academy, Florence)

angelo the essential characteristic of sculpture is that the artist starts with a block of stone or marble and cuts away from it till he reveals or discovers the statue in it. This statue is the material equivalent of the idea which the artist had in his own mind; and, since the statue existed potentially in the block before the artist began to work on it, it is in a sense true to say that the idea in the artist's mind also existed potentially in the block, and that all he has done in carving his statue is to discover this idea.

In an early version of . . . [sonnet cxxxiv] Michelangelo gives further indications about his methods:

> After divine and perfect art has conceived the form and attitudes of a human figure, the first-born of this conception is a simple clay model. The second, of rugged live stone, then claims that which the chisel promised, and the conception lives again in such beauty that none may confine its spirit.[33]

This "double birth" corresponds exactly to what we know of Michelangelo's methods as a sculptor. In general he did not make a full-size clay version for a marble statue, but worked instead from a small model, perhaps only a foot high, which kept before him the idea which he had in his mind.[34] Starting from this he attacked the block directly, literally uncovering the statue, so that an unfinished figure like the *St. Matthew* (Fig. 13) gives the impression that it is all in the block and that one could just knock off the superfluous marble and reveal the complete statue.

Certain opinions of Michelangelo's which are recorded by his immediate followers show that he had almost consciously broken with the ideals of the earlier humanists. He was opposed, for instance, to the mathematical methods which formed an important part of Alberti's or Leonardo's theory. Lomazzo records a saying of his that "all the reasonings of geometry and arithmetic, and all the proofs of perspective were of no use to a man without the eye,"[35] and Vasari attributes to him the saying that "it was necessary to have the compasses in the eyes and not in the hand, because the hands work and the eyes judge."[36] He disapproved further of the importance which Alberti and the early Renaissance artists attributed to rules in painting, and he seems not to have sympathized at all with their idea that nature was based on general rules and a general orderliness. He condemns Dürer's treatment of proportion in the human figure as too rigid, saying that this is a matter "for which one cannot make fixed rules, making figures as regular as posts";[37] and, according to Vasari, "he used to make his figures in the proportion of nine, ten, and even twelve faces,[38] seeking nought else but that in putting them all together there should be a certain harmony of grace in the whole, which nature does not present."[39] These opinions all show how far Michelangelo in his later period relied on imagination and individual inspiration rather than on obedience to any fixed standards of beauty. The same is true of his attitude toward architecture, for Vasari writes that

> he departed not a little from the work regulated by measure, order and rule which other men did according to a common use and after Vitruvius and the antiquities, to which he would not conform . . . wherefore the craftsmen owe him an infinite and everlasting obligation, he having broken down the bonds and chains by reason of which they had always followed a beaten path in the execution of their works.[40]

This independence of all rule and the individualism that accompanied it account for the opinion which was generally held in the middle of the sixteenth century that Raphael was the ideal balanced painter, universal in his talent, satisfying all the absolute standards, and obeying all the rules which were supposed to govern the arts, whereas Michelangelo was the eccentric genius, more brilliant than any other artist in his particular field, the drawing of the male nude, but unbalanced and lacking in certain qualities, such as grace and restraint, essential to the great artist. Those, like Dolce and Aretino, who held this view were usually the survivors of Renaissance humanism, unable to follow Michelangelo as he moved on into Mannerism. That this difference of aim was apparent to Michelangelo himself is evident from his remark recorded by Condivi that "Raphael had not his art by nature but acquired it by long study."[41]

In the last fifteen or twenty years of his life we can trace a further change in Michelangelo's art and ideas, though in some ways this change consists in an intensification of the characteristics of the art and ideas of the late thirties and early forties.

After about 1545 the situation of the Papacy changed. The schism with Protestantism had reached a more acute stage, and since the Diet of Ratisbon it had become apparent that any kind of compromise was impossible. Therefore the position of the moderate party to which Michelangelo was attached was steadily weakened. The Church could no longer hope to save itself by their methods and was forced to adopt a much more drastic policy. Even Paul III found himself compelled in his last years to give up his attempts at conciliation and to allow the more fanatical Counter-Reformers to put their ideas into practice. At the Council of Trent the survivors of the Contarini party were defeated, and their rivals, the Jesuits and Caraffa, had their way, gradually establishing their system of blind belief in authority, strict obedience, and absolute rigidity of doctrine.

One result of this change was that the moderates found themselves stranded. They could not sympathize with the new and drastic policy, and yet their own methods seemed useless. Their position was, in fact, hopeless, and for this reason their mysticism gradually takes on a more introspective character.

Michelangelo's most representative work in this period is the last group which he carved, the Rondanini *Pietà* (Fig. 14), left unfinished

14. Michelangelo, Rondanini *Pietà*, *c.* 1555–64, Marble, $77\frac{1}{2}''$ High (Castello Sforzesco, Milan)

at his death, in which he seems to have deprived his human symbols of all corporeal quality and to succeed at last in conveying directly a purely spiritual idea. Like most of the other works of this period, such as the *Pietà* in the Cathedral of Florence, and the group of late drawings, it is concerned with the central features of the Christian faith, the events of the Passion. Michelangelo has given up Classical subjects, but even the religious themes which he treats are no longer those which he preferred in his younger days. Then he chose for his subjects either Old Testament figures, like David, or themes from the New Testament, like the Holy Family, which had a direct and general human appeal. When he carved a *Pietà*, as in St. Peter's, it was conceived as a human tragedy, without much indication of the supernatural implications. The *Pietà* of the last years is an expression of violent, personal, mystical Christian faith, which appears with equal intensity in the drawings for the Crucifixion of the same period.

A corresponding change takes place in Michelangelo's writings. Much of what has been said about his views in the middle period of his life applies even more strongly to his last years. His approach to the world and the arts becomes even more spiritual, but at the same time more specifically Christian. His religious feeling now combines the mystical conception of Neoplatonism with the intense belief in Justification by Faith which he learned from Savonarola and the Contarini group. But he talks less of an abstract divine essence and more of a God whom he addresses personally. We may suppose that his comment on the paintings of Fra Angelico, which shows how much importance he attributed to Christian piety in an artist, was made about this time: "This good man painted with his heart, so that he was able with his pencil to give outward expression to his inner devotion and piety, which I can never achieve, since I do not feel myself to have so well disposed a heart."[42]

He wishes to abandon the whole world and to fix all his thoughts on God, but he feels that he can do nothing without God's grace. . . .[43] All mortal love must be given up. Michelangelo seems no longer to have faith in human beauty as a symbol of the divine. He rather fears it as a distraction from the pure things of the spirit. . . .[44] He hates and fears the things of this world which he regards as temptations, or, at best, as distractions from a higher duty. In passionate repentance he writes:

> I have let the vanities of the world rob me of the time I had for the contemplation of God. Not alone have these vanities caused me to forget His blessings, but God's very blessings have turned me into sinful paths. The things which make others wise make me blind and stupid and slow in recognizing my fault. Hope fails me, yet my desire grows that by Thee I may be freed from the love that possesses me. Dear Lord, halve for me the road that mounts to Heaven, and if I am to climb even this shortened road, my need of Thy help is great. Take from me all liking for what the world holds dear and for such of its fair things as I esteem and prize, so that, before death, I may have some earnest of eternal life.[45]

But most remarkable of all is the sonnet in which he turns not only against the world and mortal beauty but against the imagination itself and against the arts to which it has led him:

> Giunto è già 'l corso della vita mia
> Con tempestoso mar per fragil barca,
> Al comun porto, ov' a render si varca
> Conto e ragion d'ogni opra trista e pia.

Onde l'affettuosa fantasia
  Che l'arte mi fece idol' e monarca
  Conosco or ben, com' era d'error carca
  E quel ch'a mal suo grado ogn' uom desia.
Gli amorosi pensier, già vani e lieti,
  Che fien or s'a duo morte m'avvicino?
  D'una so 'l certo, e l'altra mi minaccia.
Nè pinger nè scolpir fie più che quieti
  L'anima, volta a quell' amor divino,
  Ch'aperse, a prender noi, 'n croce le braccia.[46]

This sonnet is perhaps the supreme proof of the changes that had come over Michelangelo since his youth. It is hard to believe that the humanist creator of the early Bacchus or even the painter of the Sistine ceiling would one day pray to renounce the arts from feelings of Christian piety.

In Michelangelo we have an example of that rare phenomenon, the great artist who is both able and willing to put in writing what he feels about his art. The value of these writings to us depends largely on the light which they throw on the artist's work in painting and sculpture. It is possible to enjoy and even to understand the frescoes on the Sistine roof without reading any of the sonnets, but the appreciation of both the poetry and the paintings can be increased by the comparison of the one with the other; and in the case of Michelangelo's latest works, like the Rondanini *Pietà*, the exposition in words in the late sonnets of the ideas expressed more obscurely, but not less completely, in the carved forms of the statue may provide a clue to the meaning of the latter, for which any one unacquainted with the poems might long search without success. We could deduce the changes traceable in Michelangelo's view of life from his paintings and sculpture, but the evidence of the written word is more compelling, because less liable to misinterpretation; and an hypothesis based on the former is more than doubled in strength when it is confirmed by the latter. The changes that have been traced above, however, are not merely those of a single individual. For Michelangelo was the type of those men who belonged to the Renaissance but lived on into the early stages of the Counter-Reformation. The development in his ideas, therefore, follows the change from one epoch to another, and prepares the way for the art and doctrines of Mannerism.

NOTES

[1] Published in 1548 under the title, *Tractato de Pintura Antigua.*

[2] Hollanda's reliability has often and justifiably been challenged, e.g. by Tietze (cf. "Francisco de Hollanda und Donato Giannottis Dialoge und Michelangelo," *Rep. für Kunstwissenschaft.* [1905], xxviii, p. 295) and, more violently, by C. Aru (cf. "I Dialoghi Romani di Francisco de Hollanda," *L'Arte* [1928], xxxi, p. 117).

[3] Cf. Frey, *Die Dichtungen des Michelagniolo Buonarroti,* Nos. v, vi; and Thode, *Michaelangelo und das Ende der Renaissance* (1903), ii, pp. 138 ff.

[4] M. Holroyd, *Michael Angelo Buonarroti,* 2nd ed., p. 70.

[5] Ibid., p. 64; and Vasari, trans. de Vere (London, 1912–15), ix, p. 103.

[6] Vasari, op. cit., p. 106.

[7] Hollanda, *Four Dialogues of Painting,* trans. A. F. G. Bell, p. 15. It must be remembered, however, that in his youth in Florence, Michelangelo copied the work of a northern artist, Schongauer. He even planned a *Trattato di tutte le maniere de' moti umani, e apparenze, e dell' ossa.*

[8] Condivi, op. cit., p. 74.

[9] Frey, iv, probably 1505–11.

[10] Ibid. xxx, *c.* 1526. For this and the following translations of Michelangelo's poems I am indebted to the late Miss K. T. Butler.

[11] Ibid. xxxiv. 1530: "As my soul, looking through the eyes, draws near to beauty as I first saw it, the inner image grows, while the other recedes, as though shrinkingly and of no account."

[12] Ibid. xxxii. 1529–30.

[13] Ibid.

[14] Passavant, *Rafael* (1839), i. p. 533.

[15] Frey, cix. 34, 1536–46.

[16] Ibid. lxxix, shortly after 1534. The same idea is expressed in xcii, cix. 66 and cix. 101, all probably written in the late thirties or early forties.

[17] Ibid. lxiv. 1533–34; cf. also cix. 99 and xci, both written in the thirties or early forties.

[18] Frey, cix. 104, *c.* 1545: "The heart is slow to love what the eye cannot see."

[19] Ibid. xciv. 1541–44.

[20] Ibid. cix. 105, "To Cavalieri," 1536–42.

[21] Frey, cix. 99, probably 1534–42.

[22] Op. cit., p. 65.

[23] Cf. above, Ch. III.

[24] Op. cit., p. 74.

[25] Frey, lxii, 1533–34.

[26] Condivi, p. 77; cf. Vasari, *Lives,* ix, p. 104.

[27] Frey, ci. 1547.

[28] Ibid. cix. 94, shortly after 1534.

[29] Ibid. cxxxiv, *c.* 1547.

[30] Ibid. lxv, referring to Cavalieri.

[31] Ibid. lxxxiii. 1536–47.

[32] Letter to Varchi, 1549.

[33] Frey, p. 480, sonnet cxxxiv, version I, 1544–46.

[34] Cellini in his *Trattato della Scultura* (ch. iv) records that Michelangelo in general worked without a full-scale model, but that in his later work he sometimes used one. He quotes as examples the statues for the New Sacristy of S. Lorenzo.

[35] Lomazzo, *Trattato,* Bk. v, c. 7.

[36] Vasari, *Lives,* ix, p. 105.

[37] Condivi, p. 69.

[38] Though Vasari writes *teste* here he must mean *faces,* for a figure of twelve *heads* would be too elongated even for a Mannerist.

[39] Vasari, *Lives,* ix, p. 104.

[40] Ibid., p. 44; cf. also Condivi, p. 69. Since Vasari's day the licenses taken by Michelangelo with architecture have often been the subject of less favorable comment, as for instance by Symonds, who accuses him of slipping in his later years into "a Barocco-Mannerism."

[41] Condivi, p. 76.

[42] See Paleotti, *Archiepiscopale Bononiense* (Rome, 1594), p. 81.

[43] Frey, cxlviii, *c.* 1554–55.

[44] Ibid. cxxiii. 1547–50.

[45] Ibid. cl. *c.* 1555.

[46] Frey, cxlvii, *c.* 1554: "In a frail boat, through stormy seas, my life in its course has now reached the harbor, the bar of which all men must cross to render account of good and evil done. Thus I now know how fraught with error was the fond imagination which made Art my idol and my king, and how mistaken that earthly love which all men seek in their own despite. What of those thoughts of love, once light and gay, if now I approach a twofold death. I have certainty of the one and the other menaces me. No brush, no chisel will quieten the soul, once it is turned to the divine love of Him who, upon the Cross, outstretched His arms to take us to Himself."

6. THE ARCHITECTURE OF MICHELANGELO

James S. Ackerman

INTRODUCTION

The creator of such impressive monuments as the *David* and the Medici Tombs in Florence, the Sistine Ceiling and the *Last Judgement* in Rome, is generally granted considerable space as a sculptor and painter in the standard art history survey texts. The attention accorded his architecture is less consistent, varying widely from some three pages of text to two paragraphs or less. Since the sculpture and painting of Michelangelo celebrate in such an awesome way the power of the human form, his images move us. They elevate in our consciousness the tensive ply of our own bodies. The appeal is immediate and strong. This empathic appeal may account to some extent for the relative underexposure of Michelangelo the architect. But it is also worth noting that one of the most important books written during this century on the architecture of the Renaissance—Rudolf Wittkower's *Architectural Principles in the Age of Humanism*—gives relatively little space to the architecture of Michelangelo while dealing extensively with Alberti and Palladio. Here, of course, we must remind ourselves that Alberti and Palladio were theorists, and architectural theory was Professor Wittkower's chief concern in this instance. Furthermore, as Professor Ackerman points out, Michelangelo's own exposition of his architectural "theory" is limited to a fragment of a letter which links architecture to anatomy; and the organic, rather than intellectual, nature of this linkage is apparent both in the sculptural character of Michelangelo's architectural forms and in the creative flux of his building practices.

Serious research on the architecture of Michelangelo could be said to have begun in 1904, with the publication of H. von Geymüller's *Michel-*

angelo Buonarroti als Architekt, and further advanced by Dagobert Frey, *Michelangelo Studien* (1920). Charles de Tolnay's five-volume work on Michelangelo (1943–1960) is the basic study in English on the artist's work in general and James S. Ackerman's two-volume work on the architecture of Michelangelo, from which this selection was taken, is the essential publication on this aspect of the master's career. Other readings are Rudolf Wittkower, "Michelangelo's Biblioteca Laurenziana," *The Art Bulletin,* XVI (1934), an important article on a key monument; and James S. Ackerman "Architectural Practice in the Italian Renaissance," *Journal of the Society of Architectural Historians,* XIII (1954).

The selection that follows is reprinted from James S. Ackerman, *The Architecture of Michelangelo* (A. Zwemmer, Ltd., London, 1961), by permission of the publishers.

In the early years of the sixteenth century the extraordinary power, wealth, and imagination of the Pope, Julius II della Rovere (1503–1513) made Rome the artistic center of Italy and of Europe and attracted there the most distinguished artists of his age. Chiefly for political reasons, the rise of Rome coincided with the decline of great centers of fifteenth-century Italian culture: Florence, Milan, and Urbino. The new "capital" had no eminent painters, sculptors, or architects of its own, so it had to import them; and they hardly could afford to stay at home. This sudden change in the balance of Italian culture had a revolutionary effect on the arts; while the fifteenth-century courts and city-states had produced "schools" of distinct regional characteristics, the new Rome tended to encourage not so much a Roman as an Italian art. No creative Renaissance artist could fail to be inspired and profoundly affected by the experience of encountering simultaneously the works of ancient architects and sculptors—not only in the ever-present ruins but in dozens of newly founded museums and collections—and those of his greatest contemporaries. Like Paris at the beginning of the present century, Rome provided the uniquely favorable conditions for the evolution of new modes of perception and expression.

I described the results as revolutionary. Since Heinrich Wölfflin's great work on this period,[1] the traditional concept of the High Renaissance as the ultimate maturing of the aims of the fifteenth century has been displaced by an awareness that many of the goals of early sixteenth-century artists were formed in vigorous opposition to those of their teachers. What Wölfflin saw in the painting and sculpture was characteristic of architecture, too.

But there is an important difference in the architectural "revolution": it was brought about by one man, Donato Bramante (1444–1514). This reckless but warranted generalization was concocted by a contemporary theorist, twenty-three years after Bramante's death; Sebastian Serlio called him "a man of such gifts in architecture that, with the aid and authority given him by the Pope, one may say that he revived true architecture, which had been buried from the ancients down to that time."[2] Bramante, like Raphael, was born in Urbino; he was trained as a painter and ultimately found a position at the court of Milan under Lodovico Sforza. Already in his first architectural work of the late 1470's his interest in spatial volume, three-dimensional massing, and perspective illusions distinguishes him from his contemporaries, though the effect of his innovations was minimized by a conservative and decorative treatment of the wall surfaces. When Milan fell to the French at the end of the century, Bramante moved on to Rome, where the impact of his first introduction to the grandiose complexes of ancient architecture rapidly matured his style. The ruins served to confirm the validity of his earlier goals; they offered a vocabulary far better suited to his monumental aims than the fussy terra-cotta ornament of Lombardy, and they provided countless models in which his ideal of volumetric space and sculptural mass were impressively realized.

Architecture is a costly form of expression, and the encounter of a uniquely creative imagination with a great tradition could not have been of much consequence without the support of an equally distinguished patron. That Julius II sought to emulate the political grandeur of the Caesars just as Bramante learned to restore the physical grandeur of ancient Rome continually delights historians, because the occasion may be ascribed with equal conviction to political, social, or economic determinants, to the chance convergence of great individuals, or to a crisis of style in the arts.

As soon as Bramante had completed small commissions in his early years in Rome (e.g., the cloister of Santa Maria della Pace, 1500; the *Tempietto* of San Pietro in Montorio, 1502), the Pope saw in his work the echo of his own taste for monumentality and lost interest in Giuliano da Sangallo, the brilliant but more conservative Florentine architect whom he had consistently patronized when a Cardinal. A year after his election to the pontificate, Julius commissioned Bramante to design a new façade for the Vatican Palace and the huge Cortile del Belvedere; in the following year, 1505, he requested plans for the new St. Peter's, to replace the decaying fourth-century Basilica. Another commission of unknown date initiated projects for a "Palace of Justice" that would have rivalled the Vatican if it had been finished.

The new papal buildings confirm the decisive break with early Renaissance architecture already announced in the *Tempietto*. This building, though one of the smallest in Rome, is the key to High Renaissance architecture because it preserves traditional ideals while establishing the forms of a new age. It is traditional in being a perfect central plan, a composition of two abstract geometrical forms: the cylinder and the hemisphere. But fifteenth-century geometry had never (except in the drawings of Leonardo, which surely influenced Bramante) dealt so successfully with solids: buildings before Bramante, even those with some sense of plasticity, seem to be composed of planes, circles and rectangles rather than of cylinders and cubes, and to be articulated by lines rather than by forms. In the *Tempietto* the third dimension is fully realized; its geometric solids are made more convincing by deep niches that reveal the mass and density of the wall. Members are designed to mold light and shade so as to convey an impression of body. We sense that where the earlier architect drew buildings, Bramante modelled them. Because the *Tempietto* recites the vocabulary of ancient architecture more scrupulously than its predecessors, it is often misinterpreted as an imitation of a Roman temple. But just the feature that so profoundly influenced the future—the high drum and hemispherical dome—is without precedent in antiquity, a triumph of the imagination.

In the projects for St. Peter's (Fig. 15) the new style attains maturity. Here for the first time Bramante manages to coordinate his volumetric control of space and his modelling of mass. The key to this achievement is a new concept of the relationship between void and solid. Space ceases to be a mere absence of mass and becomes a dynamic force that pushes against the solids from all directions, squeezing them into forms never dreamed of by geometricians. The wall, now completely malleable, is an expression of an equilibrium between the equally dynamic demands of space and structural necessity. Nothing remains of the fifteenth-century concept of the wall as a plane, because the goal of the architect is no longer to produce an abstract harmony but rather a sequence of purely visual (as opposed to intellectual) experiences of spatial volumes. It is this accent on the eye rather than on the mind that gives precedence to voids over planes.

Bramante's handling of the wall as a malleable body was inspired by Roman architecture, in particular by the great Baths, but this concept of form could not be revived without the technique that made it possible. The structural basis of the Baths was brick-faced

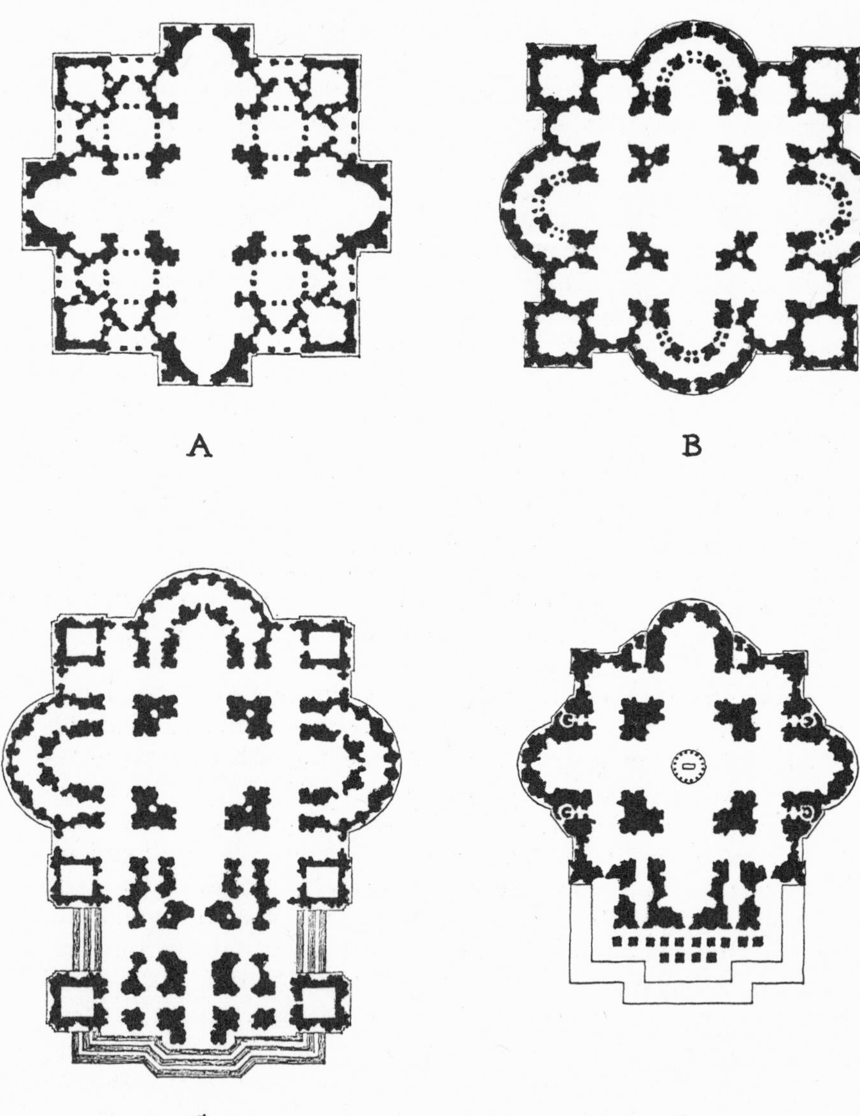

15. Plans for St. Peter's, Rome (After Ackerman, *The Architecture of Michelangelo*, Fig. 11)

A. Bramante, 1506
B. Bramante-Raphael, 1515–1520
C. Sangallo, 1539
D. Michelangelo, 1546–1564

concrete, the most plastic material available to builders. For the Roman architect brick was simply the material that gave rigidity to the concrete, and protected its surface. In the Middle Ages the art of making a strong concrete was virtually forgotten, and bricks, now used as an inexpensive substitute for stone blocks, lost the flexibility afforded by a concrete core. Bramante must have rediscovered the lost art of the Romans. The irrational shapes of the plan of St. Peter's (Fig. 15)—giant slices of toast half eaten by a voracious space—are inconceivable without the cohesiveness of concrete construction, as are the great naves of the Basilica, which could not have been vaulted by early Renaissance structural methods.[3] Bramante willed to Michelangelo and his contemporaries an indispensable technical tool for the development of enriched forms.

In the evolution of the design of St. Peter's, Bramante left for Michelangelo the realization of an important potential in the malleability of concrete-brick construction; for in spite of his flowing forms, the major spatial volumes of his plan are still isolated from one another. The chapels in the angles of the main cross and, more obviously, the four corner towers, are added to the core rather than fused into it, as may be seen more clearly in elevations (Fig. 16).

The dynamic characterization of space and mass which was the essence of Bramante's revolution is equally evident in his secular buildings, even when he was concerned primarily with façades. In the fifteenth century it was the nature of a façade to be planar, but Bramante virtually hid the surface by sculptural projections (half-columns, balconies, window pediments, heavy rustications) and spatial recessions (ground floor arcades, and loggias on the upper story, as in the court of the Belvedere and the façade of the Vatican). These innovations are not motivated by mere distaste for the flat forms of the early Renaissance façade but by a positive awareness of the range of expression available in a varied use of light. His projections capture the sun in brilliant highlights and cast deep shadows; his half-columns softly model the light; his loggias create dark fields that silhouette their columnar supports. In the façades, as in the interior of St. Peter's, the purely sensual delights of vision inspire the design. The philosophical impulse of fifteenth-century architecture had become sensual.

Bramante's style rapidly changed the course of Renaissance architecture. This was due not only to its novelty, but to the unprecedented situation created by the great size of his papal projects: for the first time in the Renaissance it became necessary to organize a modern type of architectural firm with a master in charge of a large number of younger architects who were in one sense junior partners, in another sense pupils. Almost every eminent architect of the first half of the sixteenth century, Michelangelo excepted, worked under Bramante in the Vatican "office": Baldassare Peruzzi, Raphael, Antonio da Sangallo, Giulio Romano, and perhaps Jacopo Sansovino. Of these only Peruzzi actually practiced architecture before Bramante's death (e.g. the Villa Farnesina in Rome, 1509); the others learned their profession at the Vatican and later developed Bramante's innovations into individual styles that dominated the second quarter of the century. The effect was felt all over Italy: Peruzzi built in Siena, Raphael in Florence, Sansovino in Venice, Giulio in Mantua, and Sangallo throughout the Papal States. The death of Julius II in 1513 and of Bramante in 1514 simultaneously removed the coauthors of High Renaissance architecture, leaving the monumental Basilica and palaces in such an inchoate state that the next generation found it hard to determine precisely what the original intentions had been. Paradoxically, this was a favorable misfortune, because it liberated the imagination of the younger architects just as they reached maturity. Raphael, Peruzzi and Sangallo, inheriting the leadership of St. Peter's and the Vatican, were free to compose variations on the theme of their master, and were actually encouraged to do so by successive popes who wanted distinctive evidence of their own patronage.

The fact that Michelangelo's career as an architect began in 1516 is directly related to this historical scene. Michelangelo's animosity toward the powerful Bramante kept him out of architecture during Bramante's lifetime. But the election of a Medici, Leo X (1513–1521), as the successor to Julius II, provided opportunities in Florence. Leo, although he chose Bramante's chief disciple, Raphael, to continue the Vatican projects, needed an architect to complete the construction of San Lorenzo, the major Medici monument in Florence. Michelangelo was the obvious choice for this job because he was not only the leading Florentine artist but also a sculptor-painter, ideally equipped to carry out the half-figurative, half-architectural program envisaged by the Medici family. Besides, the commission served the dual purpose of removing Michelangelo from Rome (Leo said: "he is frightening, one cannot deal with him") and of frustrating the completion of the Tomb of Julius II, which would have competed with Medici splendor.

Although Michelangelo's achievements in Florence proved that he was as eminent in architecture as in the other arts, he was excluded from any important Roman commissions so long as any member of Bramante's circle was alive. When Antonio da Sangallo died in 1546, the only member of the circle who survived was Giulio Romano (Raphael d. 1520, Peruzzi d. 1536), and it is significant that the Fabbrica of St. Peter's called Giulio from Mantua to forestall Michelangelo's appointment as chief architect. But his death, immediately following Sangallo's, finally left the field open to Michelangelo, now 71 years old.

Yet Michelangelo's personal conflict with Bramante cannot by itself explain why the intrigues that it engendered were so successful in excluding him from architectural commissions in Rome. That the popes of this period—Leo X; another Medici, Clement VII (1523–1534); and Paul III, Farnese (1534–1549)—recognized Michelangelo's preeminence is proven by the fact that they tried to monopolize his services as a painter and sculptor. The Medici were even willing to retain him as an architect in Florence after he had fought against them for the independence of the city. The long delay in recognition at Rome must be attributed to the unorthodoxy of his style. It lacked what Vitruvius called *decorum:* a respect for Classical traditions. And in the first half of the century cultivated Roman taste was attuned to a correct antique vocabulary in a classic context. Bramante had formed this taste, and it took a generation to assimilate his innovations.

Raphael was the ideal successor to Bramante. That his concerns as a painter for massive forms and volumetric space in simple compositions of geometric solids were a counterpart of Bramante's architectural goals may be seen in such architectural frescoes as the *School of Athens* and the *Expulsion of Heliodorus.* Consequently, when he succeeded to Bramante's post he could pursue his own interests and at the same time design almost as Bramante would have done if he had lived another six years. If Raphael had been less sympathetic to his master, his architecture would certainly be better known. But in major Vatican works, at the Cortile di San Damaso and Belvedere, the two designers are indistinguishable, and uncertainty about the authorship of projects for St. Peter's has always worried us. In his work outside the papal circle—Palazzo Vidoni-Caffarelli, Palazzo Branconio d'Aquila, Villa Madama in Rome, and Palazzo Pandolfini in Florence—Raphael developed Bramantesque principles and vocabulary into a more individualized expression notable for its greater sophistication, elegance of decoration, and for its success in binding into a unity masses and spaces that Bramante had tended to individualize. The propriety of Raphael's accession to Bramante's throne is further shown by the fact that the very qualities which distinguish him from his predecessor—moderation, respect for continuity, sophistication and elegance, unification of discrete elements—also distinguish his patron, Leo X, from Julius II.

A comparable poetic justice guided the careers of other Bramante followers. Peruzzi, who often worked with the linear and planar means of fifteenth-century architecture while concentrating his great ingenuity on exploring new forms and rhythms in plan and elevation (he was the first to exploit the oval plan and curved façade), was employed more in his native Siena than in Rome. That medieval town must have valued him rather for his superficial conservatism than for the extraordinary inventiveness which had too little opportunity for expression, and which now can only be appreciated properly in hundreds of drawings preserved in the Uffizi Gallery.

Giulio Romano, whose three or four small Roman palaces represent a revolt against Bramante's grandeur in the direction of repression, tightness, and an apparently polemic rejection of plasticity and volume, found himself more at home outside Rome, in the court of Mantua, where the tensions induced by the weakness of humanist duchies in a world of power-states could be given expression in a Mannerist architecture of neurotic fantasy (The Ducal Palace, Palazzo del Tè).

So the Rome which rejected Michelangelo was equally inhospitable to other non-classic architects. Though Peruzzi, as a Bramante follower, was frequently given a chance to aid in the design of St. Peter's and the Vatican and to compete for major commissions (the great hospital of S. Giacomo degli Incurabili, San Giovanni dei Fiorentini), he never was chosen as a chief architect. The victor was always Antonio da Sangallo the Younger, who gave the classic movement its definitive form.

Sangallo's dictatorship in the style of 1520–1545 can be explained more by his propriety than by his eminence; he was probably the least gifted of Bramante's pupils. The first major Renaissance architect to be trained exclusively in the profession, he began as a carpenter at the Vatican in the early years of the century. His practice never had to be set aside for commissions in the other arts and, being a gifted organizer and entrepreneur, he was able not only to undertake all the important civil and military commissions of the papacy but those of private families, among them the Farnese, as well. Nearly a thousand surviving drawings in the Uffizi are evidence of vast building activity throughout central Italy. He is distinguished less for his innovations than for his capacity to apply the experiments and aesthetic of the High Renaissance to the complete repertory of Renaissance building types. The façade of Santo Spirito in Sassia in Rome is the uninspired source of later sixteenth-century façade design; the Banco di Santo Spirito (Rome) has a two story colossal order over a drafted basement in a context that delighted Baroque architects and has never been entirely abandoned; the Farnese palace is the definitive secular structure of the Roman Renaissance, though major components of its design were anticipated by Bramante and Raphael. It is in the plans and models of St. Peter's that the symptomatic weakness of Antonio's architecture may be seen (Fig. 15). The project is unassailable on the grounds of structure or of Vitruvian *decorum*, but it is confusing in its multiplicity: infinite numbers of small members compete for attention and negate the grandeur of scale required by the size of the building; the dome is obese, and the ten-storied campanili are Towers of Babel. Antonio's superior technical and archaeological knowledge proved to be no guarantee of ability to achieve coherence or to control fully such raw materials of architecture as space, proportion, light and scale.

Sangallo, as the first architect of the Renaissance trained in his profession, knew more than his contemporaries about the technical aspects of construction. He was frequently called upon to right major faults in Bramante's structures: to fortify the piers of St. Peter's and the foundations of the Vatican façade, to rebuild the loggie of the Belvedere, which collapsed in 1536, all of necessity to the detriment of the original design. But technical competence was not a preeminent qualification in the eyes of Renaissance critics: Bramante, though called *maestro ruinante* in allusion to his engineering failures, was universally recognized as the superior architect. Of course, this may be attributed simply to a difference in creative ability, or genius, or whatever one may call it, but it raises an important question for Renaissance architecture, and for Michelangelo in particular: was it possible, in the age of Humanism, for an individual to be fully successful as a specialist? Sangallo, in gaining the advantage of a long apprenticeship in architectural construction, lost the benefits of a generalized body of theoretical knowledge and principles traditionally passed on in the studios of painters and sculptors. Problems of proportion, perspective (the control of space), composition, lighting, etc, as encountered in the figurative arts, were more important in the development of Renaissance architecture than structural concerns, partly because, by contrast to the Gothic period or to the nineteenth century, technology was restricted to a minor role.

In our day, when the concern for technique has threatened to overwhelm all other values in architecture, it is difficult to appreciate the Renaissance view that sculptors and painters were uniquely qualified as architects by their understanding of universal formal problems. The view was vindicated by the fact that it was the artist who made major technical advances—the technician merely interpreted traditional practices.

The Renaissance architect was forced into a preoccupation with broad principles in one way or another. First of all, he had to find a way to justify a revival of pagan grandeur in a Christian society; this involved, among other dilemmas, a rationalization of the conflicting architectural principles of antiquity and the Middle Ages. Further, as is demonstrated by Sangallo's failure to construct a theory out of devoted study of Vitruvius and Roman monuments, antiquity itself taught no clear and consistent body of principles. To give order to a chaos of inherited concepts, many Renaissance architects—Alberti, Francesco di Giorgio and others in the fifteenth century, Palladio in the sixteenth—developed and published theories of architecture of a metaphysical-mathematical cast. But formalized philosophies were not the sole solution; it is intriguing that nothing was written about architecture (or any other art) in the High Renaissance. This reveals a desire to solve the same problems in a new way; a reaction in all the arts against the abstract principles of the fifteenth century produced a temporary shift from intellectual-philosophical precepts to visual and psychological ones that could better be expressed in form than in words. This change of emphasis is a key to Michelangelo's achievement, and for this reason I begin the study of his work with some observations on what we know of his architectural ideas.

MICHELANGELO'S "THEORY" OF ARCHITECTURE

Michelangelo, one of the greatest creative geniuses in the history of architecture, frequently claimed that he was not an architect.[4] The claim is more than a sculptor's expression of modesty: it is a key to the understanding of his buildings, which are conceived as if the masses of a structure were organic forms capable of being molded and carved, of expressing movement, of forming symphonies of light, shadow and texture, like a statue. The only surviving evidence of Michelangelo's theory of architecture is the fragment of a letter of unknown date and destination in which this identity of architecture with painting and sculpture is expressed in a manner unique in the Renaissance:

> Reverend Sir (Cardinal Rodolfo Pio?): When a plan has diverse parts, all those (parts) that are of one kind of quality and quantity must be adorned in the same way, and in the same style, and likewise the portions that correspond [e.g. portions in which a feature of the plan is mirrored, as in the four equal arms of St. Peter's]. But where the plan is entirely changed in form, it is not only permissible but necessary in consequence entirely to change the adornments and likewise their corresponding portions; the means are unrestricted (and may be chosen) at will [or: as the adornments require]; similarly the nose, which is in the center of the face, has no commitment either to one or the other eye, but one hand is really obliged to be like the other and one eye like the other in relation to the sides (of the body), and to its correspondences. And surely, the architectural members derive [*dipendono*] from human members. Whoever has not been or is not a good master of the figure and likewise of anatomy cannot understand (anything) of it. . . .[5]

It is not unusual for Renaissance theorists to relate architectural forms to those of the human body; in one way or another this association, which may be traced back to ancient Greece and is echoed in Vitruvius, appears in all theories of the age of humanism. What is unique in Michelangelo is the conception of the simile as a relationship which might be called organic, in distinction to the abstract one proposed by other Renaissance architects and writers. It is anatomy, rather than number and geometry, that becomes the basic discipline for the architect; the parts of a building are compared, not to the ideal overall proportions of the human body but, significantly, to its functions. The reference to eyes, nose, and arms even suggests an implication of mobility; the building lives and breathes.

This scrap of a letter cannot be taken as evidence of a theory of architecture: in fact, it expresses an attitude which in the Renaissance might have been called antitheoretical. But there is more in it than the fantasy of a sculptor, and it may be used as a key to the individuality of Michelangelo's architectural style, primarily because it defines his conscious and thoroughgoing break with the principles of early Renaissance architecture.

When fifteenth-century writers spoke of deriving architectural forms from the human body, they did not think of the body as a living organism, but as a microcosm of the universe, a form created in God's image, and created with the same perfect harmony that determines the movement of the spheres or musical consonances.[6] This harmony could not be discovered empirically, since it was an ideal unattainable in actuality, but it could be symbolized mathematically. Thus the ideal human form was expressed either in numerical or geometrical formulae: numerical proportions were established for the body that determined simple relationships between the parts and the whole (e.g., head : body = 1 : 7) or the body was inscribed within a square or a circle or some combination of the two, sometimes with the navel exactly in the center. Architectural proportions and forms could then be associated with these formulae.

This entirely intellectual attempt to humanize architecture really made it peculiarly abstract, for rather than actually deriving useful mathematical symbols and proportions from a study of the body, it forced the body, like Procrustes, into figures already idealized by a long metaphysical tradition traceable to Plato and Pythagoras. The perfect mathematical figures and ratios and the way in which they were used to establish the form and proportions of buildings remained quite unaffected by this attempt to "humanize" them. But if reference to the human body was superfluous in practice, it gave fifteenth-century architects a timely philosophical justification for their method and helped to transform them from medieval craftsmen to Renaissance humanists.

If the human body was to be adapted by the fifteenth-century theorist to a system of proportions, it had to be treated as a static object to be analyzed into a complex of numerically or geometrically interrelated parts. This method inevitably emphasized units: the whole became a harmony among discrete members. By contrast, Michelangelo's demand for an architecture based on anatomy was motivated by a desire to restore the indivisibility of the human form, a unity to be found in the function of the brain and of the nerve and muscle systems, rather than in external appearances.

Michelangelo was fully aware of the significance of these differences and felt compelled to attack the abstract analytical principles of his predecessors and contemporaries. Condivi noted (ch. LII):

> I know well that when he read Albrecht Dürer,[7] it seemed to him a very weak thing, seeing with his (great) insight how much more beautiful and useful was his own concept of this problem [the human figure]. And to tell the truth, Albrecht deals only with the measurement and variety of bodies, concerning which no sure rule can be given, conceiving his figures upright like posts. But what is more important, he says not a word about human actions and gestures.

At the same time, Condivi speaks of Michelangelo's desire to write a treatise on anatomy with emphasis on human *moti* and *apparenze*. Obviously this treatise would not have made use of abstract ratio and geometry; nor would it have been the more empirical one that Leonardo might have written; for the words *moti* (suggesting "emotions" as well as "motions") and *apparenze* imply that Michelangelo would have emphasized the psychological and visual *effects* of bodily functions.

Michelangelo sensed the necessary relationship between the figurative penetration into human beings that gave his art its unique psychological force, and a literal penetration that would reveal the workings of nerves, muscles and bones. His study of anatomy, in contrast to Leonardo's, was motivated by an incalculably important shift from an objective to a subjective approach to reality.

Early Renaissance theories of proportion, when applied to buildings, produced architecture that was abstract in the sense that its primary aim was to achieve ideal mathematical harmonies out of the interrelationship of the parts of a building. Simple geometrical figures were preferred for the plan; walls and openings were thought of as rectangles that could be given a desired quality through the ratio of height to width. Given the basic concept of well-proportioned planes, the ultimate aim of architectural design was to produce a three-dimensional structure in which the planes would be harmonically interrelated. At its best, this principle of design produced a highly sophisticated and subtle architecture, but it was vulnerable to the same criticism that Michelangelo directed against the contemporary system of figural proportion. It emphasized the unit and failed to take into account the effect on the character of forms brought about by movement—in architecture, the movement of the observer through and around buildings—and by environmental conditions, particularly light. It could easily produce a paper architecture more successful on the drawing board than in three dimensions.

Toward the end of the fifteenth century, architects and painters began to be more concerned with three-dimensional effects, particularly those produced by solid forms emphasized by gradations of light and shadow. Leonardo pioneered in the movement away from the planar concept of architecture in a series of drawings which, while still dependent for their effect on mathematical ratios, employed the forms of solid, rather than of plane geometry: cubes, cylinders, hemispheres. Leonardo's theoretical experiments must have inspired the extraordinary innovations of Bramante discussed in the Introduction. These innovations, which substituted mass and spatial volume for planar design cannot, however, be taken as evidence of a fundamental change in architectural theory. I believe that Bramante still thought in terms of proportion and ratio, as demonstrated by his tendency to emphasize the interplay of distinct parts in a building. In his project for St. Peter's the exterior masses and interior spaces are semi-independent units harmoniously related to the central core (Fig. 16).

Seen in this perspective, Michelangelo's approach to architecture appears as a radical departure from Renaissance tradition. His association of architecture to the human form was no longer a philosophical abstraction, a mathematical metaphor. By thinking of buildings as organisms, he changed the concept of architectural design from the static one produced by a system of predetermined proportions to a dynamic one in which members would be integrated by the suggestion of muscular power. In this way the action and reaction of structural forces in a building—which today we describe as tension, compression, stress, etc,—could be interpreted

16. Caradosso, Medal of Bramante's Project, St. Peter's, 1506 (The British Museum, London)

in humanized terms. But, if structural forces gave Michelangelo a theme, he refused to be confined to expressing the ways in which they actually operated: humanization overcame the laws of statics in his designs to the point at which a mass as weighty as the dome of St. Peter's can appear to rise, or a relatively light attic-facing to oppress.

While fifteenth-century architecture required of the observer a certain degree of intellectual contemplation to appreciate its symbolic relationships, Michelangelo's was to suggest an immediate identification of our own physical functions with those of the building. This organic approach suggests the injection of the principle of empathy into Renaissance aesthetics by its search for a physical and psychological bond between observer and object.

In Michelangelo's drawings we can see how the concept was put into practice.[8] Initial studies for a building are vigorous impressions of a whole which search for a certain quality of sculptural form even before the structural system is determined (Figs. 17, 20). Often they even deny the exigencies of statics, which enter only at a later stage to discipline fantasy. Details remain indeterminate until the overall form is fixed, but at that point they are designed with that sense of coherence with an unseen whole which we find in Michelangelo's sketches of disembodied hands or heads. Drawings of windows, doors, cornices are intended to convey to the mason a

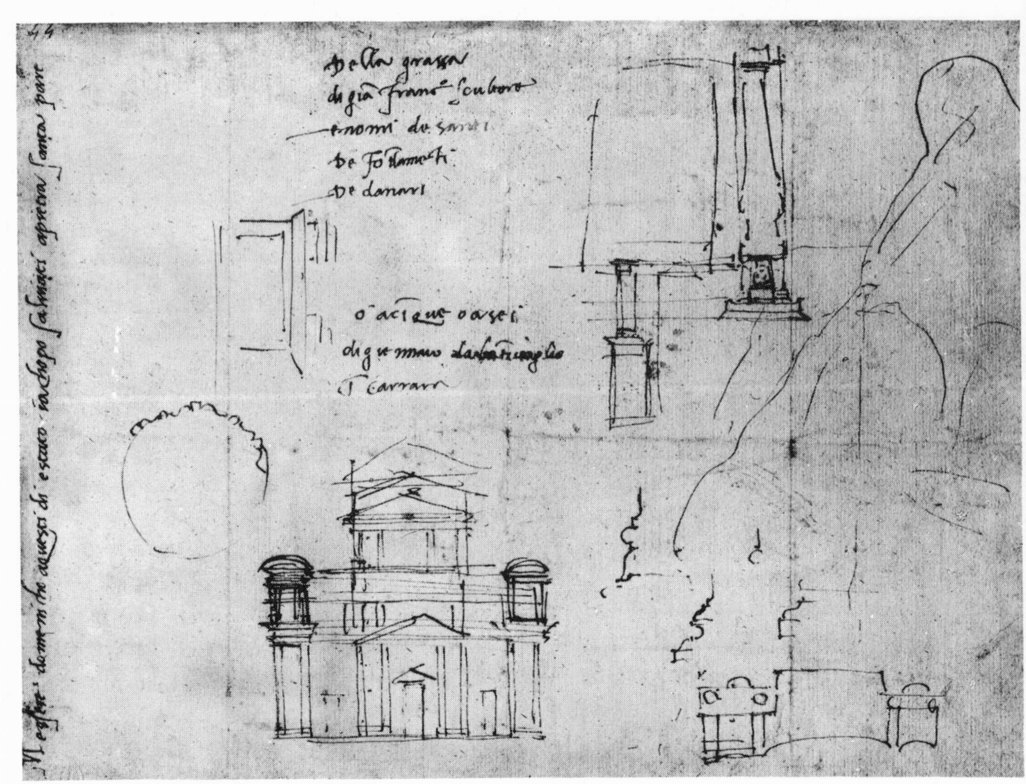

17. Michelangelo, Façade Project, San Lorenzo (Casa Buonarroti, Florence)

vivid experience rather than calculated measured instructions for carvings (Fig. 18). Where his contemporaries would sketch profiles to assure the proper ratio of a channel to a torus, Michelangelo worked for the evocation of physical power; where they copied Roman capitals and entablatures among the ruins to achieve a certain orthodoxy of detail, Michelangelo's occasional copies are highly personalized reinterpretations of just those remains that mirrored his own taste for dynamic form. Rome provided other architects with a corpus of rules but gave Michelangelo a spark for explosions of fancy, a standard that he honored more in the breach than in the observance.

This indifference to antique canons shocked Michelangelo's contemporaries, who felt that it was the unique distinction of their age to have revived Roman architecture. They interpreted a comparable indifference in fifteenth-century architects as evidence of a faltering, quasi-medieval search for the classic perfection of the early 1500's. Implicit in humanist philosophy was the concept that the goal of endeavor, whether in art, government, or science, was to equal—not to surpass—the ancients. Thus, Michelangelo's bizarre variations on Classic orders, coming on the heels of the climactic achievements of Bramante and Raphael, frightened Vasari, who dared not find fault with the Master, but worried that others might emulate him. When Michelangelo claimed for his design of San Giovanni dei Fiorentini in Rome that it surpassed both the Greeks and the Romans, the Renaissance concept was already obsolete; for the moment any improvement on antiquity is conceivable, the door is opened for a modern philosophy of free experiment and limitless progress.

18. Michelangelo (or Assistant), Study for a Window-Frame (Ashmolean Museum, Oxford)

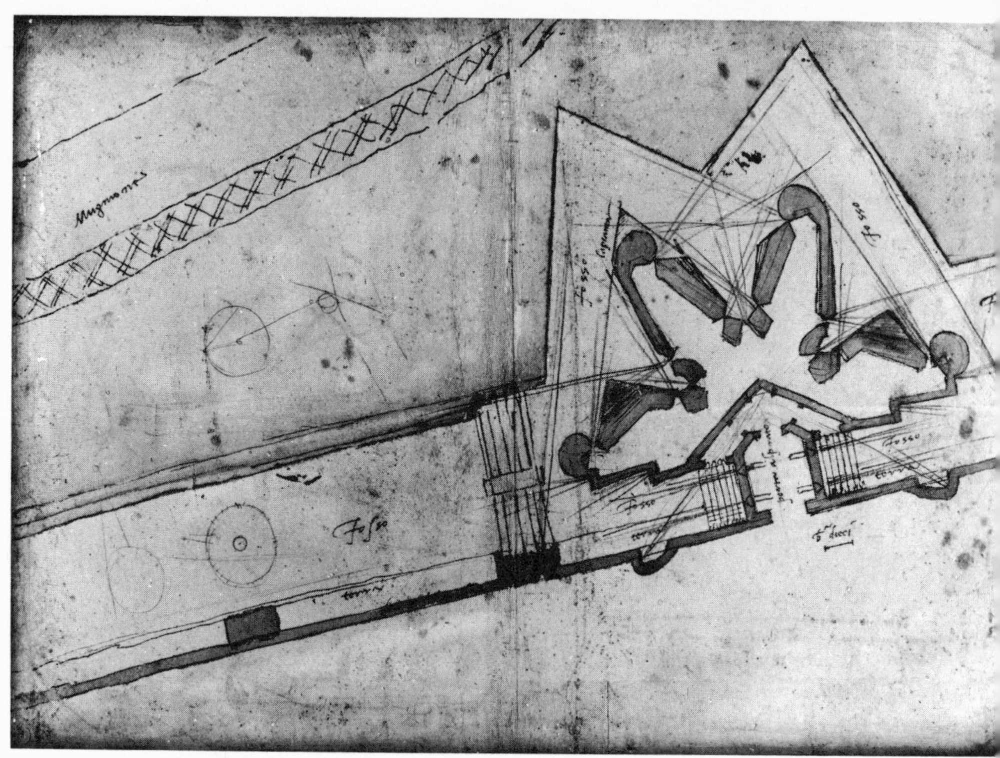

19. Michelangelo, Project for Gate Fortifications, Porta al Prato (Casa Buonarroti, Florence)

Michelangelo's plan studies appear as organisms capable of motion: the fortification drawings obey a biological rather than a structural imperative (Fig. 19). But even in more orthodox plans (Fig. 20) the masses swell and contract as if in response to the effort of support. Elevation sketches minimize the planes of the wall to accent plastic forms—columns, pilasters, entablatures, frames, etc.—which dramatize the interaction of load and support. I say "dramatize" because the sculptural members, seen as bones and muscles, create an imagined epic of conflicting forces, while it is the anonymous wall that does the mundane job of stabilizing the structure. In building, the wall is further distinguished from its expressive articulation by the choice and treatment of materials.

By contrast to contemporaries trained in fifteenth-century proportions, Michelangelo rarely indicated measurements or scale on his drawings, never worked to a module, and avoided the ruler and compass until the design was finally determined. From the start he dealt with qualities rather than quantities. In choosing ink washes and chalk rather than the pen, he evoked the quality of stone, and the most tentative preliminary sketches are likely to contain indica-

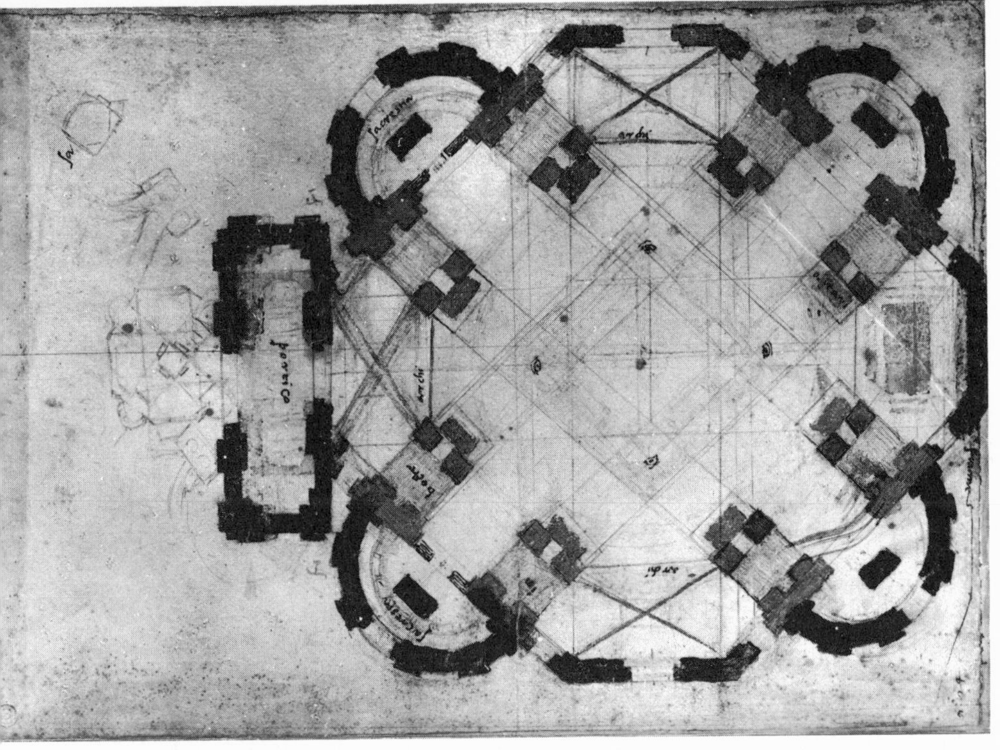

20. Michelangelo, Plan Project, San Giovanni de' Fiorentini, 1559 (Casa Buonarroti, Florence)

tions of light and shadow (Fig. 18); the observer is there before the building is designed.

Michelangelo rarely made perspective sketches, because he thought of the observer as being in motion and hesitated to visualize buildings from a fixed point. To study three-dimensional effects he made clay models. The introduction of modelling into architectural practice again demonstrates the identity of sculpture and architecture in Michelangelo's mind. It is also a further sign of his revolt against early Renaissance principles, since the malleability of the material precludes any suggestion of mathematical relationships or even any independence of parts: only the whole could be studied in terra-cotta. We can infer that when Michelangelo used clay models he sought effects of mass rather than of enclosed space, as in his paintings, where the spatial environment exists only as a receptacle for the bodies. The architectural drawings show the same preference; they communicate mass by contrast to those of Bramante or Sangallo, where lines are drawn around spaces.

This approach to architecture, being sculptural, inevitably was reinforced by a special sensitivity to materials and to effects of light.

Michelangelo capitalized upon the structure of his materials because of his desire to get a maximum contrast between members used to express force or tension and "neutral" wall surfaces. He invariably minimized the peculiarities of surface materials such as stucco and brick, while he carved and finished the plastic members in order to evoke—even to exaggerate—the quality and texture of the stone. No one had a comparable sensitivity to the character of the traditional Roman masonry, Travertine, the pitted striations of which became richly expressive in his design.

In speaking of modern architecture we often associate sensitivity to materials with an exposition of their technical functions, but in Michelangelo's work the latter is characteristically absent. In laying masonry, Michelangelo notably avoided any emphasis on the unit (block or brick). He disguised joints as much as possible in order to avoid conflict between the part and the whole, and to sustain the experience of the building as an organism. He was the only architect of his time who did not use quoins, and he rarely employed rusticated or drafted masonry, the favored Renaissance means of stressing the individuality of the block. If his buildings were to communicate muscular force, the cubic pieces had to be disguised.

Light, for Michelangelo, was not merely a means of illuminating forms; it was an element of form itself. The plastic members of a building were not designed to be seen as stable and defined elements but as changing conformations of highlight and shadow. Much of Michelangelo's unorthodoxy in the use of antique detail can be explained by his desire to increase the versatility of light effects. If more of his interiors had been completed according to his design, I believe we would find an astounding variety of compositions in light, creating moods quite unknown in the Renaissance. It is fascinating to imagine, for example, what the interior of St. Peter's might have been like if the lantern had been screened by an interior canopy as Michelangelo planned. No doubt Michelangelo's sympathetic adjustment to the brilliance of the Mediterranean sun was a factor that inhibited the exportation of his style to hazier northern countries, where the intellectual reserve of Palladio was much preferred.

The common practice in the sixteenth century of building from large wooden scale models, rather than from drawings, explains the absence of any complete plans or elevations among Michelangelo's surviving sketches. But these sketches differ from those of other Renaissance designers in one significant respect: with two or three exceptions none represents even a small detail as it was ultimately built. It was Michelangelo's habit to keep his design in a constant state of flux until every detail was ready for carving, a method entirely consistent with his organic approach. His conception of a building literally grew, and a change in any part involved sympathetic changes in other parts. The final solution was not reached even in the model: the wooden model for St. Peter's was executed without an attic, and probably without a façade or dome, in order to permit Michelangelo to alter those portions in response to his impressions of the body of the building as it was constructed. There and at the Farnese palace, wooden mockups of cornices were made to full scale and hoisted into position to enable the architect to judge, and possibly to redesign, his project at the last moment; had funds been available he doubtless would have destroyed portions already finished in order to improve them, as he did with his later sculptures. In all his work he seems to have carried the generative drive to a point at which it became an obstacle to completion, an obstacle so frustrating that most of his architectural projects were not executed, and no building was completed according to his plans. So contemporary engravers had to record his projects by combining scattered records of different stages in the process of conception with touches of pure fancy. And the problem is the same for the modern historian. We shall never know for certain what Michelangelo's unexecuted projects—whether abandoned or partly completed—were to have been; in fact, the attempt to do so implies at the outset a misunderstanding of his conception of architecture. To visualize any of Michelangelo's designs, we must seek to capture not a determinate solution, but the spirit and the goals of a process.

NOTES

For a general view of Michelangelo's theories of art, see E. Panofsky, *Idea . . .* (Leipzig and Berlin, 1924), (2nd ed., Berlin, 1960), pp. 64 ff.; *Idem,* "The History of Proportions as a Reflection of the History of Styles," *Meaning in the Visual Arts* (New York, 1955), esp. pp. 88–107; C. de Tolnay, *Werk und Weltbild des Michelangelo* (Zürich, 1949), pp. 87–110. Reflections of Michelangelo's theories appear in Vincenzo Danti, *Il primo libro del trattato delle perfette proporzioni* (Florence, 1567).

[1] Heinrich Wölfflin, *Die klassische Kunst* (Munich, 1899).

[2] *Il terzo libro di Sebastiano Serlio bolognese* (Venice, 1540); quoted from the edition of Venice, 1584, fol. 64v.

[3] On Bramante's revival of Roman vaulting technique, see O. Förster, *Bramante* (Munich, 1956), pp. 277 f.

[4] *Lettere,* p. 431; Wilde 1953, pp. 109 f.; Condivi, ch. LIII.

[5] *Lettere,* p. 554; Schiavo 1949, Fig. 96 (facsimile). Interpreted by Tolnay 1949, p. 95.

[6] On fifteenth-century theory, see: R. Wittkower, *Architectural Principles in the Age of Humanism* (London, 1949); H. Saalman, "Early Renaissance Architectural Theory and Practice in Antonio Filarete's *Trattato* . . . ," *Art Bulletin,* XLI, 1959, pp. 89 ff.

[7] *Vier Bücher von menschlicher Proportion* (Nürnberg, 1528). Cf. E. Panofsky, *Dürer* (Princeton, 1943), pp. 260 f.

[8] On the development of architectural drawing in the Renaissance, see W. Lotz, "Das Raumbild in der italienischen Architekturzeichnung der Renaissance," *Mitt. des Kunsthist. Inst. in Florenz,* VII, 1956, pp. 193 ff.; J. Ackerman, "Architectural Practice in the Italian Renaissance," *Journ. Soc. Architectural Historians,* XIII, 1954, pp. 3 ff.

7. THE ARCHITECTURE OF MANNERISM

Nikolaus Pevsner

INTRODUCTION

Nikolaus Pevsner's article "The Architecture of Mannerism" first appeared in *The Mint,* I, in 1946, and is reprinted here with some additions by Dr. Pevsner especially for this anthology. The current interest in the phenomenon of "Mannerism" in Italian art could be said to have begun in 1914, in a lecture at the University of Freiburg by Walter Friedlaender, which was not published until 1925. This became available in English translation as the first of two essays in Friedlaender's *Mannerism and Anti-Mannerism in Italian Painting* (1957) recognized as the classic definition of these two aspects of sixteenth-century Italian art, and now available in a paperback edition with an excellent introduction by Donald Posner. Pevsner, in the selection below, extends the concept of a Mannerist style into the field of architecture. For other readings on Mannerism in architecture consult Pevsner's bibliography at the end of this article.

The literature on Mannerism has grown considerably since Friedlaender's lecture in 1914. Of works in English, there are Max Dvořák, "El Greco and Mannerism," *Magazine of Art,* XLVI (1953); Harold Wethey, *El Greco and His School* (1962), pp. 53–58; Craig Hugh Smyth, *Mannerism and Maniera* (1963); and Arnold Hauser, *Mannerism: The Crisis of the Renaissance and the Origin of Modern Art,* 2 Vols. (1965), a Marxist approach. A session of the 20th International Congress of Art Historians was devoted to Mannerism, and the papers have been published in *Renaissance and Mannerism, Studies in Western Art, Acts of the Twentieth International Congress of the History of Art,* II (1963). To this list should be added Sydney J. Freedberg, "Observations on the Painting of the Maniera," *The Art Bulle-*

tin, XLVII (1965); Rudolf Wittkower, "Michelangelo's Biblioteca Laurenziana," *The Art Bulletin,* XVI (1934); and Wolfgang Lotz "Architecture in the Later 16th Century," *College Art Journal,* XVII (1958).

The selection that follows is reprinted by permission of the author.

England distrusts generalizations. The tendency is to treat each case on its own merit and leave the perfection of codes of law to more logical and less practical nations. The extent to which this attitude influences political, social and legal matters is familiar. Less familiar is the connection of this weakness or strength of character with the proverbial vagueness of English philosophical terminology.

Taking research into art and architecture as an example, there is plenty of antiquarian and archaeological work going on, but little that reaches broader conclusions as to the characteristic style of a man or a nation or an age—to say nothing of those still broader conclusions which allow for the carving out of aesthetic theories with their appropriate terminology.

The word style in fact is hardly yet accepted in the sense in which the French, the Italians, the Germans, the Americans use it. To the man in the street its foreground meaning is still that which comes up from associations with "stylish," doing something "in style," and so on. "He writes a good style" is nearer to the philosophical meaning of the term. For it is certainly at least one of the legitimate uses of "style" to denote the personal mode of expression of an author and an artist, and if you write of Wordsworth's as against Keats's style or Rembrandt's as against Rubens's you are philosophically precise and yet not likely to be misunderstood even in England.

But when it comes to introducing such terms as Baroque, nobody can be sure whether it will be taken by the English reading public as a synonym of fantastic or—in the deeper sense—as the final essence distilled out of all the individual qualities of all the leading personalities of one particular age. Hobbes's and Spinoza's philosophy, Bernini's and Rembrandt's art, Richelieu's and Cromwell's statecraft have certain fundamentals in common, and on these we can establish a Baroque style of exact meaning.

England has been characteristically slow in accepting this working hypothesis. Continental art history began to investigate the opposed principles of Renaissance and Baroque art in the eighties of last century, chiefly in Switzerland (Wölfflin 1888), Germany (Schmarsow 1897) and Austria (Riegl, before 1905). The final summing up was Wölfflin's famous *Grundbegriffe,* which came out in 1915 and was translated into (bad) English in 1932. But you can still find in the subject catalogues of important libraries under *Artists, Renaissance:* Raphael, Rembrandt, Reynolds, Rubens.

Now, if fixed terms for styles of ages are there to keep a host of data in reasonable order, then there is obviously no point in using such words as Renaissance, Baroque and so on, unless their very job is to keep Raphael, Rembrandt, Rubens and Reynolds apart. Surely the first step in tidying up the vast number of works of art and architecture produced in the West between the fifteenth and the eighteenth centuries is to separate what expresses Renaissance spirit from what is Baroque, to separate, that is to say, the static from the dynamic, the compact from the expansive, the finite from the infinite, the ideal from the over-real or over-expressive.

However, this juxtaposition which, thanks to the relative popularity of Wölfflin's book, can be taken as known to readers of these pages, if not to the general public, is historically inadequate. Wölfflin chose his examples to illustrate the Baroque almost exclusively—and very wisely—from the seventeenth century. And, as he says himself that after 1520 hardly any work of pure Renaissance character was produced, what happened between 1520 and the end of the sixteenth century? Where do Parmigiano, Tintoretto, Greco belong? The Renaissance believes in the beauty and vigor of the human body; the Baroque does; but these three painters and their contemporaries don't. The Renaissance believes in the proud independence of the human personality and the solidity of matter. The Baroque does; but Parmigiano, Tintoretto, and Greco evidently work toward a contraction of all that is material, in order to achieve an exquisite and decadent elegance or a supreme spiritualization.

Neither of these goals is Renaissance, neither is Baroque. And as our eyes learned to see these specific qualities of sixteenth-century art and our minds (thanks to contemporary developments) widened to understand them, a new term had to be coined to label them. Mannerism had for a long time been used to designate certain schools of painting and sculpture in Italy, carrying on the manner of late Raphael, Michelangelo, Correggio and other Renaissance artists, and an Italianizing school in the Netherlands; so the word could easily be widened out to be applicable to the whole style of Italian and perhaps European painting and sculpture of the later sixteenth century. In this new sense Mannerism was first used and its extent and character defined between 1920 and 1925. (Dvořák 1920, Pinder *c.* 1924, W. Friedlaender 1925, Pevsner 1925.) Since then it has become accepted on the Continent and in America. Younger scholars use it in as precise and familiar a way as Renaissance and Baroque.

However, analyses and definitions have proved easier concerning pictures and works of sculpture than concerning buildings. Hardly anything to my knowledge has yet been published in this country about Mannerist architecture, although such books as Anthony Blunt's *Mansart* presuppose familiarity with the term and its architectural implications. So what I propose doing here is to look closely at ten or twelve buildings of the sixteenth century, to prove the incompatibility of their formal and emotional character with that of works both of the Renaissance and the Baroque, and then point to certain characteristic events in contemporary thought and feeling to show the same spirit at work in history and architecture.

Bramante, born in 1444, that is eight years before Leonardo da Vinci, stands at the beginning of the High Renaissance. He died

21. Bramante, Casa Caprini, Rome, Engraving by Antonio Lafreri (The Metropolitan Museum of Art, Harris Brisbane Dick Fund, 1941)

in 1514, just before it came to an end. In his old age he designed the Casa Caprini in Rome which Raphael completed for himself in 1517 (Fig. 21). It has since been altered out of recognition. It is a building of five bays and two floors, a comfortable human size, easily manageable by the surveying eye and easily comprehensible to the mind. The ground-floor is rusticated as a base for the main floor, the *piano nobile,* above. This has coupled columns to frame the windows and the generous wall spaces on their sides and above. All the windows have identical balustrades below and pediments above. An entablature and cornice terminate the façade. A minimum of motifs is used, but with a maximum of care for proportion and detail. Ground-floor and upper floor are of exactly the same height. The proportion of the windows between top of balustrade and foot of pediment is repeated by the proportion of the bays between the columns. No ornament appears anywhere. The Doric columns are unfluted, the metopes undecorated. The effect is of a noble perfection and grave harmony.

Bramante's style inspired a whole group of younger architects in Rome. Raphael, born in 1483, is the most notable of them. To his generation belong Serlio, born in 1475, Peruzzi born in 1481, and Sammicheli born in 1484. Others were young enough to start as Raphael's assistants. The most important of these is Giulio Romano (1499–1546).

The group was dispersed by the Sack of Rome in 1527, which took Sammicheli to Verona, while Giulio Romano had gone to Mantua already a few years before. These two were the first to take the innovations of the Roman High Renaissance to the North of Italy. However, in their works the Renaissance seems to have lost its serenity and most of its balance.

About 1530 Sammicheli designed three palaces at Verona, the Palazzi Canossa, Pompei and Bevilacqua. The first two show him a faithful follower of his master, the third (Fig. 22) is surprisingly original. Here is just as in the case of the Casa Caprini a building of two storeys with a rusticated ground-floor and a first floor with columns to separate the window bays. The entrance was intended to be central so that we have to add in our minds four more bays on the left to the ones actually built. The fenestration of the *piano nobile* is a little more complicated than in the Casa Caprini, but the triumphal arch motif of the openings: low—tall—low or *a—b—a,* is in its perfect symmetry and its pyramidal composition

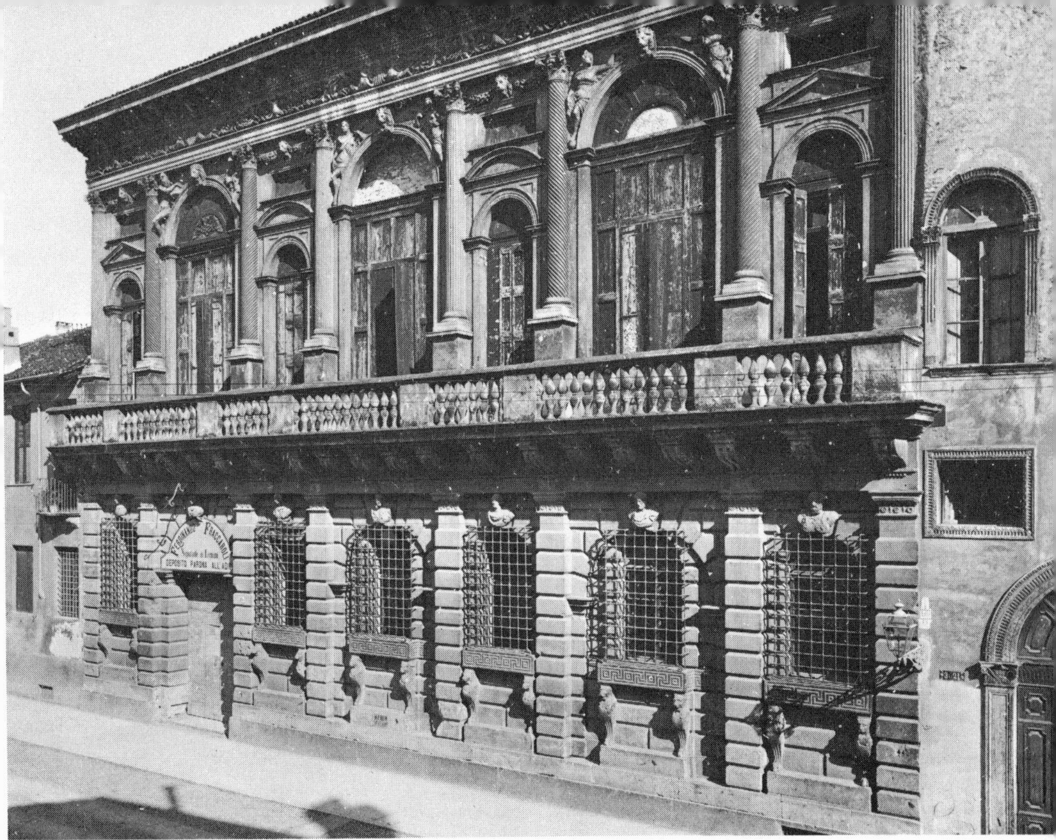

22. Sammicheli, Palazzo Bevilacqua, Verona, *c.* 1529–40

not alien to the Renaissance (Alberti's S. Andrea in Mantua, Bramante's Belvedere Court in the Vatican, etc.). So if the façade of the Palazzo Bevilacqua were simply a five-times-repeated *a—b—a—b—a—b—a—b—a—b—a*, there would be nothing new or embarrassing in it. Nor are a decorated frieze or some figures in the spandrels of the windows ornaments to which the Renaissance, especially in Northern Italy, would necessarily object. It is the details which confuse one as soon as they are studied.

The bays of the ground-floor are not all of the same width. Narrower and broader spaces alternate, but the difference is not marked enough to make one feel certain of its meaning, particularly as all the windows have the same dimensions. The composition of the first floor is even more intricate. The first, the third and the (missing) fifth main windows have columns with spiral fluting, the second and the (missing) fourth straight-fluted columns. That is logical enough, but the pediments above the small windows do not tally with this rhythm at all. If we call the triangular ones α and the segmental ones β we would, over the whole projected extension of the front, get a rhythm looking like this: (from right to missing left) α—β—β—α—α—β. That means that above the central entrance the triumphal arch is rudely thrown out of symmetry. It has two symmetrical spiral columns, but one α and one β pediment. You may say that the little pediments are an afterthought of Sammicheli's to achieve superficial symmetry, when he knew that the palace was not going to be carried on to the left. But even if that is so, no Renaissance architect would have tolerated the presence of two alternatively exclusive rhythms in the finished front. They jar painfully once they have been noticed, and they are not even the only motif of such obstinate illogicality. Another is the uncomfortable balancing of the α and β pediments, especially the segmental β ones, on the round-headed windows.

Victorian ostentatiousness of decoration has made us insensitive to the subtler values of architectural expression. Modern architects suffer from this lack of visual discrimination in the general public. Criticism suffers from it too; this is my excuse for what may be considered unnecessarily close analyses.

How necessary they really are is proved by the fact that Giulio Romano's most famous building at Mantua, the Palazzo del Té, a spacious ducal villa built between 1526 and 1534, appears in textbooks as a characteristic example of the Renaissance style. At a first glance it may well look like that. Yet, is the entrance side really placid and as happily spaced as a Bramante design would be? There are again two storeys, separated by a flat band with a sharply incised key pattern, the ideal Greek solution to the representation of movement in a static ensemble. However, the band is cut up by giant pilasters. Are the two storeys then two, as the band says, or one, as the pilasters say? This lack of clarity would have been intolerable to a pure Renaissance artist. Moreover, pilasters lose their *raison d'être* if they are not spaced regularly, but Giulio breaks that regularity in the very center of his composition to house his three entrances. And he does worse at the corners. To stress these by a coupling of pilasters was in no way against Renaissance feeling. But the two outside pilasters stand closely together, while the two inner ones are separated by niches—a horrid heresy. Then, there is the rustication. The main windows and the doors have imitation-rusticated surrounds of a jagged restless pattern, and those of the doors jut out into and across the horizontal band.

Now all this is not just haphazardly insensitive. It obviously is the expression of a new will, a deliberate attack on the Renaissance ideal of the isolation and balance of all parts, and, what is more, an attack launched surreptitiously by an artist who all the time takes every care to preserve the *dehors* of classical correctness, a care which has indeed deceived observers of several centuries.

Dissonance is even shriller in the façades toward the inner court. Here attached columns (the plain and sober Doric columns of Bramante) replace the pilasters. The rhythm of openings is the simple triumphal arch rhythm (*a—b—a*) of the Renaissance. But why do the pediments lack bases? Why, if rustication is used, should it occur only in odd places? And why, to take the most scandalous breach of etiquette, should every third triglyph be dropped down so as to hang into the zone of the upper windows? It looks as though the building were on the point of collapsing, and that is exactly the impression the architect wished to give: precarious instability instead of the repose of the Golden Age. Evidently, to Giulio and his generation that repose had become unbearable. Restlessness and discomfort appeared as positive values. This is also the reason why the high finish achieved by the Renaissance is placed side by side with rude blocks of unhewn stone, and their incongruous proximity is relished. Nature in the raw becomes for the first time a motif of art. This interpretation of Giulio's rustication is not a modern subtlety. Already in 1537 Serlio wrote about it that it seems "partly a work of nature and partly a work of the artist." The sixth book of his treatise which came out in 1551 is dedicated to nothing but such displays of curious rustication.

Rustication in palace architecture was, it is true, by no means an innovation of the sixteenth century. But when the Early Renaissance uses it, say in Michelozzo's Medici Palace in Florence, it appears as a solid and powerful basis to the noble building of man. Nowhere does it endanger the superiority of the human achievement. In the courtyard of the Palazzo del Té nature breaks into the architect's artificial world, spoiling it and reminding us irritatingly of our own helplessness. How panic-stricken Giulio must sometimes have felt in the presence of nature, is proved by the most famous of his wall-paintings inside the Palazzo del Té, the Hall of the Giants, with walls showing on all sides colossal, brutish giants tumbling down on us amid crashing boulders. Nor can this nightmare of instability, this memento of the untrustworthiness of the

23. Federico Zuccari, Palazzo Zuccari, Rome, 1593 (19th Century Photograph, before Restoration), Now the Biblioteca Hertziana

material world, be set aside as a mere sign of one artist's deranged mind. It adorned one of the main rooms of the Duke's *maison de plaisance* and was apparently widely admired. The distaste of Renaissance perfection must have spread far—that is evident.

At the same time it ought not to be forgotten that in the Hall of Giants the experience may not have been entirely or always nightmarish. There must also have been a *frisson* of pleasant terror, and one should not underestimate this. Preponderance of pleasant over genuine terror can be assumed in the portals of Mannerism shaped as huge open mouths. At Bomarzo in the early sixties—*sacro bosco* or not—the gaping mouth amid giants and monsters in a natural setting may have frightened indeed, but if Alessandro Vittoria in the fifties gave a fireplace in Palladio's Palazzo Thiene this shape, he can only have expected amusement and appreciation of his inventiveness, and one must assume the same in Federico Zuccari's house in the Via Gregoriana [Fig. 23] in Rome in 1590, although there a shock at the uncertainty between almost real monsters, architecturally hewn stone and stone left rude must also have been savored.

Infinitely more seriously Michelangelo had pointed out long before what poignancy there can be between figures seemingly real and the raw block from which they seem to be just emerging. The question has often been asked what made him keep the untreated stone below his reclining figures of *Day* and *Night* and *Morning* and *Evening.* The answer is that he wanted to let them appear in the act of coming to life out of a stony, subhuman preexistence. To shape the image of man entirely liberated from these dark forces must have seemed almost a sacrilege to the young and again the very old Michelangelo. Hence also his many unfinished works.

Again, a different aspect of this new attitude to nature is the Mannerist liking for the grotto. Here such architects as Buontalenti and Palissy employ the highest skill in achieving an elaborate likeness of nature left to herself. There is in this, as well as in Palissy's trick of using casts from lizards, beetles and plants to decorate his bowls and dishes, a good deal of naïve pride, of course, but it should not be forgotten that such verbal imitation of nature, coming as it did, immediately after the great power of idealization which the Renaissance had achieved, is also an admission of defeat and a sign of distrust of human achievement.

To return to Giulio Romano, it must, after the analysis of the Palazzo del Té, be of special interest to see how he expresses himself in a building in which he was entirely free from the wishes of any patron: his own house, built in 1544. Now here he appears at his most formal, evidently determined to prove what was at the time by no means yet accepted: that the artist could be the best mannered of courtiers. We can be sure that he wished to avoid solecisms, yet the design is full of them, according to Renaissance standards. The course between ground-floor and upper floor is pushed up into some sort of fragmentary pediment of the central door; the arch of the door is pressed down into a Tudor shape, and the band which runs along the ground-floor on the level of the imposts of the door arch is broken up into unconnected bits. Or are we to believe that the rusticated frames of the windows conceal the band? This is hardly possible, as any indication of three-dimensionality is absent. All is as flat as paper, and the *piano nobile* windows which one would expect to project with their pediments, are even slightly recessed instead. A most eloquent detail is the decorated bands round the windows. Their ornament seems at first crisp, cool and structurally sound, until it is seen that they run right on into the pediment zone, without any cæsura where structural logic would have placed one. The pediments thus cease to be pediments proper. Their weight is reduced. Nor are the windows shaped strong enough to support weight. This deliberate weakness of the windows makes it impossible for them too to revolt in the sense of the Baroque against the tightness of the arched panels in which they are set.

This denial of expressing strength to carry as well as weight of load is one of the most significant innovations of Mannerist architecture. The Romanesque style had mighty massive walls, the Gothic style shafts soaring-up unimpededly, the Renaissance a balance of upright and horizontal. Now the wall ceases altogether to be mass, just as a figure by Parmigiano, Tintoretto or Greco ceases to be body. Nor is the Mannerist wall a system of active forces, just as there are no convincing active forces in Parmigiano, Tintoretto and Greco. But the result of this is by no means immobility, either in painting or in building, owing to the insistence of the Mannerist on discordant motifs and contradictory directions everywhere.

Peruzzi's Palazzo Massimi alle Colonne in Rome (1535) is also a popular textbook illustration of pure Renaissance. To this the Wölfflin generation has objected that the design of the front is against Renaissance principles, because the excessive weight of the three upper storeys presses down the entrance loggia. Against Renaissance principles the building certainly is, but pressure I fail to see. On the contrary, the curious thing about the façade is its seeming paperiness. It is slightly curved, and that alone gives it something of the appearance of a mere screen. The two rows of top windows have, instead of the substantial pediments of the Renaissance, excessively delicate and flat ornamented surrounds, strap-work of the kind which a little later became so popular in the North. The gradation of parts which the Renaissance had evolved is given up as well. The same smooth pattern of the ashlar stone goes from bottom to top, and the second- and third-floor windows are of identical size. Peruzzi, who had, in the Villa Farnesina twenty-five years before, shown a perfect command of High Renaissance harmonies, has here abandoned them for unstable relations in the flat.

It may need some study to see the Palazzo Massimi in this new light. In Michelangelo's architectural experiments of the twenties no effort is required to see how revolutionary they are. The Laurenziana Library and its anteroom were designed in 1524. The library itself lies fifteen steps above the anteroom, but the anteroom reaches up higher still than the library. This excessive verticalism is yet further emphasized by the many closely set verticals of dark

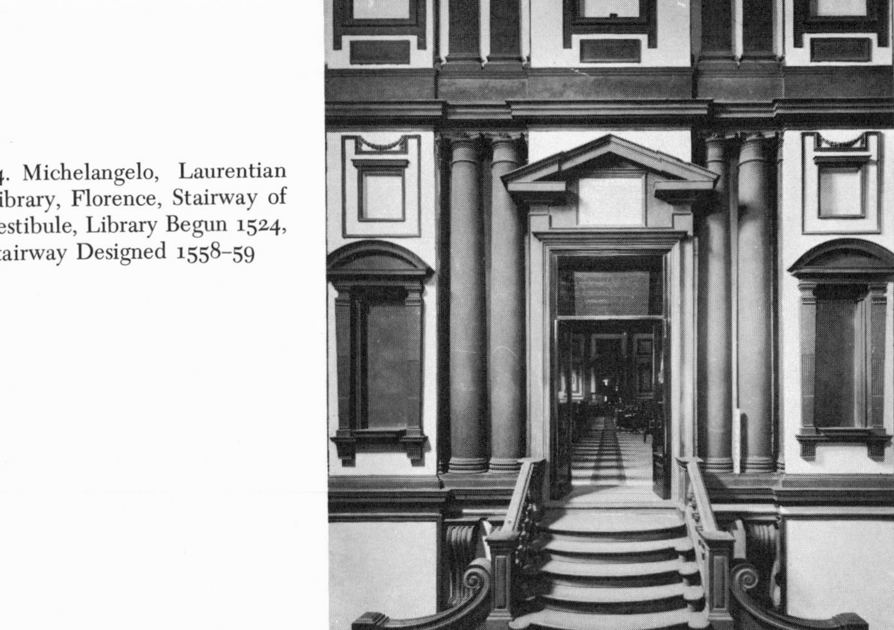

24. Michelangelo, Laurentian Library, Florence, Stairway of Vestibule, Library Begun 1524, Stairway Designed 1558–59

grey marble, streaking the white walls (Fig. 24). The result is a feeling of discomfort which grows worse, when one begins to examine the structural elements in detail. The system is Bramante's approved alternation of window bays (the windows are blind) and coupled Doric columns. But Michelangelo hated Bramante's happy ease; we know that. And so he does all he can to drive out the smooth beauty of his system. His columns, instead of standing out in front of the wall, as all columns have done ever since the first columns were designed, keep farther back than the panels in which the windows are placed. Moreover, they are tightly caged without any of the freedom of development which is their due. They do not support anything either, and they appear to rest precariously on slender brackets. In fact the brackets, themselves encased on left and right, stand farther forward than the columns. So the accepted connection between brackets and columns is broken, just as the accepted connection is broken between columns and bays. No critic has ever, to my knowledge, overlooked these incongruities. But their interpretation has varied a great deal. Burckhardt, the champion of the Renaissance, has called them "evidently a joke of the great master," while Schmarsow, engrossed in his new conception of the Baroque, wrote: "These subdued, encased columns . . . symbolize passionate impetuosity of thought breaking forth and

25. Michelangelo, Detail, Medici Chapel, 1524–34 (San Lorenzo, Florence)

struggling to find an appropriate language." Now this, to my mind, is untrue. I cannot see in the Laurenziana, anything impetuous, any violence, any struggle. Struggle can only arise between forces, and there are no forces in this architecture. Look at the delicate bands of the panels between the brackets, or the lines round the frail-looking niches above the main window zone, or the blind windows themselves, with their square, fluted little brackets below, too weak to carry anything, their tapering and partly fluted pilasters and their capitals retracted where one would expect them to swell out.

Once all this has been observed, it will be patent that, while the columns are indeed painfully incarcerated, they do not revolt. If they did, and if the wall really pressed against them, then one would be justified in speaking of Baroque. Michelangelo's *Slaves* struggle, and they stand indeed at the beginning of a development which the seventeenth-century Baroque was to continue. But Michelangelo's architecture knows no gigantic exertions. It is paralyzed, frozen, as it were, and held by iron discipline in a stiff pose of forced constraint, so accomplished that it even succeeds in appearing elegant: human freedom and human power suppressed, all swelling beauty of the flesh ascetically starved off—a perfect setting for the self-denying etiquette of sixteenth-century society.

The contrast between Michelangelo's architecture and sculpture cannot here be discussed. It is enough to state that Michelangelo (as Raphael, as Correggio) held in his hands the seeds of both Mannerism and Baroque, enough to point to one place where the interaction of the two styles of the future, that of the immediate and that of the later future, becomes most alarmingly evident. The Medici Chapel (Fig. 25) was designed between 1521 and 1534. The tombs of the two Dukes are well enough known. Their composition was to start from violently moving figures of river gods on the floor, lead up to *Day* and *Night*, and *Dawn* and *Evening*, and find its achievement in the somber, brooding figures of the Dukes—expressive, it has been proved, of Plato's Vita Activa and Vita Contemplativa. Now this idea of an "excelsior" through struggle to repose is wholly Baroque; what Mannerism contributes is only the lack of a final triumph. For neither is Giuliano active nor Lorenzo contemplative. Bernini would have given the one Duke wildly reaching-out gestures of triumph, the other an appearance of sensual self-abandon. Such outpourings of feeling Michelangelo never knew. And so he keeps his architecture as frigid, that is as self-consciously precious, as that of the Laurenziana. Detailed analysis of the niches above the low doors is not necessary. The various layers in depth should be observed, the angular excrescences inside pilasters and pediment, the elaborate over-precision of the garlands, and such illogical motifs as the sunk panels of the pilasters and the unmolded block sticking out at the foot of the niche.

But architecture is not all a matter of walls and wall patterns. It is primarily organized space, and of space hardly anything has so far been said. Now it is, of course, much harder to write of space than of walls; for walls can be photographed and space cannot. To experience space it must be wandered through or at least wandered through with one's eyes. It is a process that takes time and could only be re-evoked by film.

Yet it is easy enough to say that no Renaissance architect would have exaggerated height at the expense of width and depth to the extent that Michelangelo does in the Laurenziana. Standing in the anteroom one feels at the bottom of the well or shaft of a mine. There is lack of balance in this from the Renaissance point of view, and from the Baroque point of view lack of the final solution which a wide-windowed dome with paintings of open skies and glories of saints or kings would give. Schmarsow says that this very solution lies in the change-over from the narrow anteroom into the "simple clarity, repose and satisfaction" of the library proper. This again I cannot see. To me the library is excessively long as against its height and certainly as constrained and precious in its details as the anteroom (brackets of the windows, balusters of the blank windows above). So Michelangelo instead of creating a Baroque overflow of dammed forces out into infinite space, keeps his room as rigidly confined as any artist of the Renaissance, but breaks the harmonious proportions and interrelations which dominate Renaissance rooms. In, say, Brunelleschi's Pazzi Chapel a beautifully balanced anteroom is followed by a beautifully balanced main room. In the Laurenziana we are thrown from a room like the shaft of a mine into a room like a tunnel.

This tendency to excess within rigid boundaries is one of the characteristics of Mannerist space. It is well enough known in painting, for instance in Correggio's late Madonnas, or Tintoretto's Last Suppers with the figure of Christ at the far, far end. The most moving of all examples is Tintoretto's painting of the Finding of the Body of St. Mark (Brera, Milan, *c.* 1565). Nowhere else is Mannerist space so irresistible. In architecture this magic suction effect is introduced into Giulio Romano's extremely severe Cathedral at Mantua with its tunnel vault and monotonous columns. This was begun in 1545. But its most familiar and easily acceptable example is no doubt Vasari's Uffizi (Fig. 26). Vasari is the Mannerist *par excellence* of the generation following Giulio's. He lived from 1511 to 1574. He founded the first Academy of Art, a typically Mannerist conception with its connotations of dry rule and social dignity, and wrote the first book on the history of art, his *Vite* of 1555. This again is characteristic of Mannerist mentality: the self-conscious comparison of a late today with a long-past youth and a recent Golden Age. The Uffizi Palace was begun in 1560 to house Grand Ducal offices. It consists of two tall wings along a long and narrow courtyard. The formal elements by now need no special mention: lack of a clear gradation of storeys, uniformity coupled with heretical detail, long, elegant and fragile brackets below double pilasters

26. Vasari, Uffizi, Florence, 1560–74

which are no pilasters at all, and so on. What must be emphasized is the finishing accent of the composition towards the river Arno. Here a loggia open in a spacious Venetian window on the ground floor and originally also in a colonnade on the upper floor replaces the solid wall. This is a favorite Mannerist way of linking room with room, a way in which both a clear Renaissance separation of units and a free Baroque flow through the whole and beyond are avoided. Thus, Palladio's two Venetian churches terminate in the east, not in closed apses, but in arcades—straight in S. Giorgio Maggiore (1565), semi-circular in the Redentore (1577)—behind which back-rooms of indistinguishable dimensions appear. And thus Vasari, and then Vignola (1507–73) and Ammanati (1511–92) designed and built the Villa Giulia, the country *casino* of Pope Julius III (1550–55). It deserves as intensive a description as the Uffizi and the Laurenziana.

The villa is approached from the west, and its buildings and garden stretch to the east (really northwest and southeast). On arriving one sees a façade of seven bays and two storeys with short wings in the same direction but set far back. The archway in leads into a large courtyard with, screening the entrance range and its wings, a semicircular colonnade, rhythmically arranged and containing once more the motif of the Palazzo Massimi, short slim columns with straight lintels and much plain wall, sheer but not heavy-looking, above. These stretches of wall separate three major motifs, in the center of the semicircle a triumphal-arch motif, three arches, low-high-low, but at the ends two fragmentary triumphal arches: low-high only—a painful detail, very Mannerist and of the same nature as that analyzed for the façade of the Palazzo del Té. East of the semicircle is a square part of the courtyard with one-storeyed walls to north and south, that is wholly enclosed—wholly except for one door in the middle of the east wall (the three-bay opening dates from 1900). As one passes through, one enters a loggia open in three arched bays to the east. From here one overlooks a second courtyard, again entirely enclosed, this one three-storeyed. However, the two lower storeys are sunk, i.e. one approaches the courtyard on the second upper floor. Semicircular ramps lead down to the first upper floor, and the ground floor is really at first sight no more than a kind of pit. It is of semicircular shape again but much smaller and surrounded at the top by a balustrade so that from the level of the second courtyard one can look down into it. What is revealed there is a small, cool Nymphaeum with statues of deities in niches and its own miniature east apse where slim caryatids carry the upper balustrade.

If, instead of at once descending by the two ramps, one looks eastward from the loggia between first and second courtyard, one sees another loggia at one's own level and the "Venetian" opening of this allows one to see the grass of a garden lying once more on the level of the first courtyard, i.e. the ground level of the villa. This loggia and the walls to its left and right have more deities in niches, and the east wall of the back garden has as its termination another tripartite piece, with demicolumns and pilasters. So the whole is a sequence of three parts from west to east, all enclosed by solid walls to north and south in such a manner that the progress from the entry to the final set piece of the back garden is rigidly prescribed. The first part is separated from the second by a door,

27. Pirro Ligorio, Casino of Pius IV, Rome, Vatican Gardens, 1558–61

the second from the third by a loggia. Moreover, to add further complexity, the level changes *nel mezzo del cammin* by an unexpected two-storey drop. This sudden change from horizontal to vertical is in the spirit of the Laurenziana, the enclosed progress itself in the spirit of the Uffizi, and also in terms of gardens such as those of the Villa d'Este at Tivoli and the Palazzo Farnese at Caprarola, where there are, it is true, far more varied vistas to be had, but where also no efforts are made to stretch out into infinity as in the Baroque garden at Versailles. Neither do the favorite low loggias on the ground floors of Mannerist buildings indicate infinity—that is, a dark, unsurveyable background of space, as a Rembrandt background. Back walls are too near. The continuity of the façade is broken by such loggias—that is what the Renaissance would have disliked—but the layer of opened-up space is shallow and clearly confined in depth. We have found such loggias at the Palazzo Massimi and the Uffizi. Giulio Romano screens the whole garden front of the Palazzo del Té with them, Palladio all sides of the Basilica at Vicenza. Paladio's Palazzo Chierigati is the most perfect example of this screen technique in palace architecture. It appears again in the addition by Pirro Ligorio (1493–1580) on top of the Belvedere exedra at the Vatican in the early sixties and also in the same architect's Casino of Pius IV, just behind the Vatican (Fig. 27). This was completed in 1561. A main block is separated from a loggia by an oval court with low walls and two side entrances.

The oval, though a favorite spatial element of the Baroque, also owes its introduction into architecture to Mannerism. Oval staircases, elongated in a typically Mannerist way from Bramante's circular staircase in the Vatican, appear in Serlio and Palladio; and Vignola designed an oval dome over the little church of S. Andrea (1554) close to the Villa of Julius and a completely oval church plan for S. Anna dei Palafrenieri shortly before his death. These rooms have nothing yet of the surging and ebbing, ever-varying flow of such oval Baroque buildings as Bernini's S. Andrea al Quirinale and Borromini's S. Agnese. They are not static as centrally planned Renaissance churches might be; but movement is hemmed in, and the preference for oval as against circle may even be due more to the greater elegance of a long-drawn-out curve than to the spatial qualities of the oval.

The loggia behind the oval court of Ligorio's Casino of Pius is open on the ground floor between its four plain Doric columns in order to achieve a contrast of framed vista and wall. However, the wall again seems to have no solidity; it is only a screen just strong enough to act as a background for innumerable ornamental motifs and scenic reliefs displayed in a confusingly intricate manner: overcrowding but no mêlée. The walls of Mannerist rooms are like that too, with crisp stucco work and elegant figures and with inextricably complicated painted actions and allegories. Under their barrel vaults one feels as though inside a jewel chest (*Studiolo* in the Palazzo Vecchio at Florence of 1570, Gallery in the Palazzo Spada in Rome of 1556–60).

But preciosity is only one side of Mannerism. The style in painting would be incomplete without Parmigiano, but also without Tintoretto and Greco and late Michelangelo. For Michelangelo in his last works of sculpture and drawing displays none of the Baroque tendencies of his earlier life. There are no violent actions, no gigantic conflicts in the few Crucifixions and Pietàs of the fifties and sixties, the years in which Michelangelo almost exclusively concentrated on architecture, the work on St. Peter's, the Capitol, the Farnese Palace and so on. Of the candor and depth of his religious feelings we know from his sonnets. What is less known is that, when the Jesuits decided to build a large church in Rome, he offered to design and supervise the work without any fee.

He died before the Gesù was begun. But as the Jesuits were the most powerful religious force of the sixteenth century, it is worth

28. Ammanati, Palazzo del Collegio Romano, Rome, 1570–80's

looking at the emotional qualities of their architecture in Rome. Most people's expectations will probably be disappointed. For somehow the idea has struck root that Jesuit architecture must be in the most flamboyant Baroque fashion, and that this is what one should expect from the Counter-Reformation. Both notions are wrong. Of the real character of the Counter-Reformation more will be said later, of the character of early Jesuit architecture no better examples can be found than the Gesù on the one hand and the Collegio Romano on the other. Both buildings certainly represent Mannerist tendencies and not tendencies of the Baroque. To prove this, the last two of my analyses may be comparisons of the Collegio Romano and the Gesù with a palace and a church of the Baroque in Rome.

The Collegio Romano (Fig. 28) was built by the Jesuits as their University in 1583. The architect was Ammanati (1511–92). The Palazzo di Montecitorio (Fig. 29), the prewar Houses of Parliament of the Kingdom of Italy, was begun by Bernini in 1650 for the Ludovisi family, continued for the Pamfili and then completed as the seat of the Papal Law Courts at the end of the seventeenth century by Gibbs's Roman master, Carlo Fontana. The Collegio

29. Bernini and Fontana, Palazzo di Montecitorio, Rome, Begun 1650, Finished *c.* 1691–1700

Romano is evidently Mannerist in style, and on this uncommonly large scale the style appears particularly uncomfortable. When one stands in front of the building itself and tries to take in its excessive length of twenty bays and excessive height of six storeys and demi-storeys, the total lack of a predominant accent in spite of the stiffest formality otherwise, is most disquieting. The lantern looks as if it were meant as a climax, but it is not, because it is isolated by a balustrade from the rest of the building. Now Bernini—and he was, it should not be forgotten, a restrained architect, as Baroque architects go (though by no means a restrained sculptor and decorator)—leads his composition consistently up to the lantern. The two wings slope back symmetrically in two breaks, pushing forward the seven central bays. These are further distinguished by giant pilasters on the right and left. The treble entrance comes forward beyond the line of the center bays, and the attic above the main cornice, seven times broken, emphasizes the center once more, lifting up the top cornice above the clock and finally surging into the crowning ornament of the lantern. The *piano nobile* is given its due with an almost Renaissance dignity. In fact we know from the history of painting that the founders of the Baroque discovered more to inspire them in the High Renaissance than in Mannerism. Caravaggio's connections with the Raphael of the *Transfiguration* and the Carraccis's with the Raphael of the Farnesina Gallery prove that sufficiently. The art of the first painters of the Baroque is in many ways a grander, less dignified and more melodramatic version of Raphael's last style. Similarly, Bernini's palace is a development of the Palazzo Farnese and of Michelangelo motifs in a more massive, less nobly proportioned and more expansive way.

The Mannerist on the other hand takes care to avoid the impression of weighty masses. He proportions carefully, but with the aim of hurting, rather than pleasing, the eye. And he is certainly far from expansive or melodramatic. The outstanding quality of Ammanati's façade is austerity. Nearly all the windows are to an irritating degree identical. Each storey has the same mezzanine windows above. There is monotony instead of gradation, no crescendo, no climax upward. Nor is there a climax in width. Instead of a central accent, a painfully small, though exquisitely detailed, niche appears in the middle of the middle part. The two symmetrical portals are typically Mannerist in the sense now familiar, with sunk panels in the fragmentary pilasters, square fluted brackets, and everything else to make them look emaciated and of stiff deportment. The large sunk panels of the walls, repeated everywhere, also seem to drain off the substance of the building. They look like plywood with top layers cut back to reveal layers below.

If this frigid, ascetic building is the Jesuit University, what was the Jesuit church in Rome intended to look like when Vignola designed it (Fig. 30)? The foundation stone was laid in 1568. Vignola died before the building was complete. The façade, as well as the upper parts of the interior, are not by him, but by della Porta (who also finished the dome of St. Peter's). According to Vignola's idea the interior was to be dominated by a vast, probably dark, tunnel vault with Mannerist decoration instead of the present painted Baroque glories. The main inner cornice runs through unbroken. It would have driven the visitor eastward into the crossing under the light-shedding dome with a power equal to that of medieval basilicas or of Vasari's Uffizi.

The façade, according to Vignola's intentions, has always been regarded as one of the foundation pieces of the Baroque; and it is indeed more energetically pulled together than contemporary works by other architects. There is consistent development from

30. Vignola, Il Gesù (Façade), Engraving by Antonio Lafreri (The Metropolitan Museum of Art, Harris Brisbane Dick Fund, 1941)

31. Martino Lunghi, S.S. Vincenzo e Anastasio, Rome, 1650

the flat side bays via the slightly projecting middle bays to the center where columns replace the pilasters. This gradation like the crescendo of Vignola's interior from nave to lofty domed crossing (a type incidentally created as early as 1470 by Alberti), has been repeated and intensified by innumerable Baroque architects. But directly one goes for a comparison to a mature Baroque church in Rome, such as the younger Martino Lunghi's SS. Vincenzo e Anastasio of 1650 (Fig. 31), Vignola's Mannerism prevails everywhere. The difference does not only lie in the Baroque's richer orchestration, with all columns and no pilasters. At least as significant is the way in which the columns elbow each other. Vignola has only two breaks in the lower entablature and one in the upper, Lunghi has four and four. He doubles the lower central pediment and trebles the top one. He holds the top storey on the sides by mighty caryatids, where Vignola uses flat, drily profiled side-pieces. But caryatids were popular with Mannerist architects, too. We have seen them in the Casino of Pius. Other famous examples are in Michelangelo's tomb of Julius II and in the sunk fountain of the Villa Giulia in Rome. The Gesù façade has them twice, and again only as an ornament without strength. As this one motif, so the whole façade: in the Baroque a turbulent struggle and a triumphant end, in Mannerism an intricate and conflicting pattern, and no solution anywhere. The final proof of Vignola's Mannerism may easily escape notice unless expressly pointed out. His ground-floor seems to have a logical composition which may be noted thus: *a—b—a, A—B—A, a—b—a.* According to both principles, Renaissance and Baroque, one would expect the top storey to provide a crowning *A—B—A*. In fact, Vignola composes it of *a—A—B—A—a*. How then should '*a*' be understood? as part of *a—b—a* or as part of *a—A—B—A—a*? The resulting disturbance is what the architect wants, just as Sammicheli wanted it in the Bevilacqua Palace and Michelangelo in the Laurenziana.

How can this self-conscious dissenting, frustrated style be accounted for? What made such opposed characters as Michelangelo and Giulio Romano evolve it and the Popes and the Jesuits welcome it?

It is said that in 1513 when Leo X, the first Medici Pope, heard that he had been elected, he exclaimed: "God hath given us the Papacy; now let us enjoy it." Just over fifty years later Pius V was elected. The Vatican under him, we hear from contemporary letters, was like a monastery. Silence was kept at table, and only twice a week was meat served. Leo's interest was hunting and the theater. Pius had been Grand-Inquisitor before he succeeded to the Papacy.

Leo is as characteristic of the High Renaissance as Pius of Mannerism. The end of the Golden Age in art came before or about 1520, with late Raphael and with Pontormo and Rosso. In thought and feeling the break was made in the same years. The Sack of Rome in 1527 is only a convenient reminder of deep inner changes. Groups of men began to assemble, bent on stricter Christian observance. The first of them, the Sodality of Divine Love, was founded in 1518; then new communities and orders quickly followed each other: the Camaldolensians of Monte Corona abandoned their mother house because of its laxity in 1522, the Theatin Order dates from 1524, the Angelican Sisters and the Guastallines date from 1530, the Somasca from 1532, the Barnabites from 1533. The Capuchins separated from the Franciscans in 1535. In the same year the Ursulines were founded; in 1540 came the brothers of the Misericord and, most powerful of all, the Jesuits.

Ignatius of Loyola was born in 1493. His early life was a soldier's. While recovering from wounds received in battle, he conceived the idea of a new militant saintliness. So he retired to Manresa and there prepared himself for his mission with fast and flagellation. Visions haunted him which he tried to overcome. Suppression of human frailty by ever-watchful self-discipline was the hard-gained outcome of his studies—a cold enthusiasm which finds its ultimate form in the *Exercitia Spiritualia* and the system of strict obedience governing early Jesuit organization. Ignatius is only one of many new saints of the sixteenth century. St. Teresa is another (1515–82), and Bernini's Baroque interpretation of her excessively sensitive character should not blind us to her immense organizational talents. Then there are St. Francis Borgia (1510–72), St. Philip Neri (1515–94) a character oddly blended of jollity and mysticism, and St. Charles Borromeo (1538–84) the charitable, miracle-working, ascetic Archbishop of Milan who, we hear, wore chains under his Cardinal's clothing. In a recent article in *La Civiltà Cattolica* twenty-five saints are quoted who died between 1530 and 1600.

Saints and saintliness are exceptional at all ages. But life had changed for everybody in these seventy years. The Inquisition was reintroduced in 1542, censorship of books in 1543. The wars of religion ravaged Germany since the twenties. The struggles of old and new creeds, and then of Anglican and Non-Conformist are one—if not the only—main issue of English sixteenth-century history. In the Netherlands, Protestants fought the Duke of Alba's terror, and in France the conflict led up to the Night of St. Bartholomew.

This period of religious primacy was over in France when Henry IV decided for himself that "Paris was worth a Mass" and returned for purely political reasons into the fold of the Roman Church; it was already over in England during Elizabeth's judicious and magnificently worldly reign, and in Italy when the Jesuits Toledo and Bellarmine agreed to accept cardinalates, when the political ideas of independent Venice (Sarpi) defeated the claims of the Pope, and when Paul V (1605–21) adopted the fashion of the little van Dyck beard which had been created by Henry IV. There is a portrait bust of Paul V by Bernini, and it is enough to compare it with the paintings we have of the Popes of the sixteenth century (for instance, Titian's *Paul III*), to see the difference in character and ambition between the two ages. It is like comparing the Shakespeare of the Sonnets with the Shakespeare of Lear, or Hillyard's with van Dyck's portraits of English noblemen.

Not that "conceitism" ended when the Baroque replaced Mannerism. Many indeed were the innovations of the sixteenth century that lived on through the seventeenth. Such popular Baroque motifs as oval ground plans, broken pediments, twisted columns are of Mannerist origin. Their emotional context, of course, alters their message, just as new dynamic and sensuous qualities distinguish sixteenth- from seventeenth-century mystic poets and courtly poets.

On the other hand, genuine Baroque ideas, first conceived in the world-open days of the Renaissance, kept alive and grew during Mannerism, in spite of its return to medieval mentality. Faith in the autonomy of human thought and the independence of science underlie the precarious and often secret work of such philosophers and scientists as Cardan, Telesio, Sozzini and Bruno. Without them there would be no Galileo, no Spinoza, no Grotius—just as without Vignola's Gesù the favorite scheme of Baroque church architecture would not exist.

After allowance has been made for what connects Mannerism and Baroque—partly by means of a survival of sixteenth-century conceptions into the seventeenth, partly by pioneer work of the sixteenth century towards the seventeenth—it can now safely be said that Mannerism remains a clearly circumscribed style with characteristics as opposed to those of the Baroque as they are to those of the Renaissance. They can be summarized as follows.

Mannerism is a cheerless style, aloof and austere where it wants to show dignity, precious where it wants to be playful. It lacks the robustness of the Baroque as well as the serenity of the Renaissance.

Mannerism has no faith in mankind and no faith in matter. It scorns that bodily beauty in which Renaissance art had excelled and sets against it figures of excessively elongated proportions, sometimes overgraceful, sometimes ascetic. Accordingly it scorns proportions in architecture which are satisfactory to our senses because of their harmony with human proportions. It exaggerates one direction in spatial compositions, as well as in wall compositions, and either breaks symmetry deliberately or over-emphasizes it until it becomes monotony. Moreover, where symmetry is broken, this is not done in the Baroque way to show man conquering matter and subduing it to his will. There is nothing so active in Mannerism. The painter distorts figures to force them into imposed frozen patterns, and the architect designs with seemingly thin materials, which never look strong enough to associate with them the carrying force of the human body, nor ever look massive enough to associate with them the weight of matter pressing down under the force of gravitation. So the Renaissance problem of balance between weighing and carrying and the Baroque problem of a contrast between the two, leading before our eyes to a final victory of one of them, is replaced by an uneasy neutrality rife with potential disturbance everywhere.

Now this is precisely what one must expect from the period which created and developed Mannerism. The great initial impact was the Reformation. It ended the innocence of the Middle Ages in the North and the—very different—innocence of the Renaissance in Italy. It gained for Europe the modern world, a world of science and individualism, but a split world. The Baroque tried valiantly once more to recover singlemindedness—in Italy by means of a self-confident religious enthusiasm, in the North by means of a science with universal claims. Mannerism could not see either of these possible solutions yet. It is a period of tormenting doubt, and rigorous enforcement of no longer self-understood dogma. What individualism had been developed by the Renaissance was to be crushed, and yet could not be crushed. So Mannerist art is full of contradictions: rigid formality and deliberate disturbance, bareness and over-decoration, Greco and Parmigiano, return to medieval mysticism and the appearance of pornography (Giulio Romano, Aretino). For pornography is a sign of sensuousness with a bad conscience, and Mannerism is the first Western style of the troubled conscience.

Remembering once more now the wars of religion, the prosecution of heretics, Spanish etiquette and the Jesuits, the return of the Inquisition and the intricacies of the sonneteers—all this seems consistent. But one warning must be added in conclusion. This essay is a gross over-simplification. Plenty of important men and events have not been mentioned at all or only inadequately. Take, for instance, the most influential of all Italian sixteenth-century architects: Palladio. His case in the history of style, just as that of his Venetian contemporary Veronese, is far too complicated to be as much as outlined here. Renaissance elements are stronger in both of them than in most others of their generation. Of the typically Mannerist disturbances they know little, and their formality avoids the rigid and austere.

But the very fact that Palladio's influence was much more one of the printed page than of the real building is significant. Mannerism is the age of architectural treatises—an innovation, it is true, of the Renaissance (Alberti). Serlio lives almost exclusively in his *Libri d' Architettura,* and Vignola was to the architect and virtuoso of the North the author of the *Regole,* and not of the Gesù. The theory of the Five Orders, revived from antiquity, was now made into a fetish. So Vasari's Academy was bound to appear, and his book on the history of art. Not to do more than enumerate these facts in so casual a way, amounts to a serious omission. Equally serious is the omission of Mannerist work outside Italy, not so much that of Italians abroad as original transalpine work in styles seemingly quite different from Italian Mannerism. That Rosso, Primaticcio and Niccolò dell'Abbate worked at Fontainebleau for Francis I is familiar. Their decoration is among the English perhaps the most widely known example of Mannerism. Goujon also belongs to the Mannerists without doubt, and the style of Lescot, Delorme and the other French-born architects of the mid-sixteenth century can hardly be analyzed under any other term. Again, the Escorial, Philip II's palace-monastery, is evidently a monument of the purest Mannerism, forbidding from outside and frigid and intricate in its interior decoration; but it is essentially Italian in style and, as far as painting goes, the work of Italians: Tibaldi, Cambiaso, Zuccari, Carducci.

So it seems that, concerning the architecture of France and Spain, the application of the term Mannerism affords no problems. But when it comes to the Elizabethan style in England and to its parallels and examples in the Netherlands and Germany, are we still justified in speaking of Mannerism? Wollaton or Hardwick or Hatfield obviously are not Renaissance. Nor are they English Baroque, if St. Paul's and Blenheim are Baroque. Strapwork ornament, in its lifelessness, intricacy and stiff preciosity, is typically Mannerist. But the buoyancy and the sturdy strength of Elizabethan building are wholly absent in Italy, and wholly in harmony with the age of Drake and Raleigh.

However, one should not expect criteria of style always to be applicable to different countries without national modifications. French Romanticism is different from English Romanticism and from German. Yet all three are romantic. Similarly Wren is Baroque, but English Baroque, and the Perpendicular style is Late Gothic, but English Late Gothic. Maybe we shall have to learn the same lesson in the case of Mannerism if we wish for a full understanding of Elizabethan architecture.

FURTHER READING

In English there is still [in 1946] very little: Anthony Blunt's *Artistic Theories in Italy, 1450–1600* (O.U.P., 1940), and some articles in American magazines, especially the *Art Bulletin.* Nothing has as yet appeared on the whole problem of Mannerism or of Mannerist architecture.

MANNERISM IN GENERAL: M. Dvořák: "Greco und der Manierismus" (1920), in *Kunstgeschichte als Geistesgeschichte* (Munich, 1924). W. Friedländer: "Die Entstehung des antiklassischen Stiles . . . um 1520," *Repertorium für Kunstwissenschaft* (1925). N. Pevsner: "Manierismus und Gegenreformation," *Repertorium für Kunstwissenschaft* (1925). E. Panofsky: *Idea* (Leipzig, 1924). W. Pinder: "Zur Physiognomik des Manierismus," in *Die Wissenschaft am Scheidewege* (Leipzig, 1932). N. Pevsner: *Die italienische Malerei vom Ende der Renaissance bis zum ausgehenden Rokoko* (*Handbuch der Kunstwissenschaft*) (Neubabelsberg, 1926–8).

MANNERISM IN ARCHITECTURE: E. Gombrich on Giulio Romano, in *Jahrbuch der kunsthistorischen Sammlungen in Wien* (1935 and 1936). R. Wittkower on Michelangelo's Laurenziana, in *Art Bulletin,* 1934. J. Coolidge on Vignola and the Villa Giulia, in *Marsyas,* 1942, and *Art Bulletin,* 1943. Also E. Panofsky in *Staedel Jahrbuch,* 1930, and E. Michalski in *Zeitschrift für Kunstgeschichte* (1933). A brief summing up is H. Hoffmann: *Hochrenaissance—Manierismus—Frübbarock* (Zürich, 1938).

8. CARAVAGGIO

Walter Friedlaender

INTRODUCTION

Caravaggio died in his thirty-sixth year. His life was bohemian and tempestuous, his temper unruly. Indeed, he has often been pictured as the prototype of the aggressive rebel-artist. Although this image of Caravaggio is not false, it has tended to obscure other equally significant facets of his role in the history of art. Recent scholarship has tended to sight along two general lines: the relationship his work bears both to traditions in Italian painting and the contemporary religious climate in Italy, and to the remarkable influence of his art in Italy and elsewhere.

Friedlaender's *Caravaggio Studies* is not so much a complete monograph on the artist as it is a series of brilliant and provocative essays that reassess the essential character of his art. Of particular interest is Friedlaender's interpretation of the "realism" in Caravaggio's religious paintings in the light of developments within Roman Catholicism brought about by the influence of St. Ignatius Loyola and St. Philip Neri. In such a context, the dramatic intimacy of Caravaggio's religious works develops more profound meanings.

For further reading on Caravaggio, there is Roger Hinks, *Michelangelo Merisi da Caravaggio* (1953); M. A. Graeve, "The Stone of Unction in Caravaggio's Painting for the Chiesa Nuova," *The Art Bulletin*, XL (1958); and an excellent chapter in Rudolf Wittkower, *Art and Architecture in Italy, 1600 to 1750* (1958; rev. ed. 1965). For the influence of Caravaggio's art one should consult Alfred Moir, *The Italian Followers of Caravaggio* (1967); and, by the same author, "Alonzo Rodriguez," *The Art Bulletin*, XLIV, 3 (1962). Benedict Nicholson's *Hendrick Terbrugghen* (1958) is the best study of this leader of the Utrecht Caravaggisti.

No painter ever painted his own mind so forcibly as Michael Angelo Amerigi, surnamed Il Caravaggio. To none nature ever set limits with a more decided hand. Darkness gave him light; into his melancholy cell light stole only with a pale reluctant ray, or broke on it, as flashes on a stormy night. The most vulgar forms he recommended by ideal light and shade, and a tremendous breadth of manner.—HENRY FUSELI, *Lecture II*, 1801, p. 100

In the past few years, Caravaggio's popularity with the public at large has increased astonishingly. Nearly all of his authentic works were brought together in the Milanese exhibition of 1951 and attracted thousands of visitors, some of whom had hardly known his name before. The rediscovery of the artist does not have the same character as the revival of El Greco, the Le Nains, and George de La Tour, because these were essentially provincial painters, and their works had no direct artistic progeny. By contrast, Caravaggio worked in the most important cultural center of his day, Rome, whence his ideas spread to the farthest corners of Europe and were recognized from the beginning by many artists as being something new and revolutionary. His influence, direct or more often indirect, is present in countless seventeenth, eighteenth, and nineteenth century canvases which display realistic or naturalistic features. The enormous impact of his art on later generations, in Spain and in Northern countries even more than Italy, is well known.

Nevertheless most art critics and academicians condemned the "vulgarity" of Caravaggio's paintings, at times even with moral indignation, from Bellori's biography in the seventeenth century, down to Burckhardt's *Cicerone* in the nineteenth. Being themselves committed to a standard of ideal beauty, they found his work no more than a base "imitation of nature" and charged him with having destroyed "good taste." Through two centuries this attitude prevailed, and Caravaggio was classified as a painter of low category. Nor could these opinions have easily been opposed, for the knowledge of his oeuvre was effectively obscured by the innumerable paintings in older collections which were labelled with his name, provided they were dark and realistic. Thus the Caravaggio research, especially the knowledge of his authentic work, was in a state of confusion.

The long and painstaking reconstruction of Caravaggio's oeuvre and the facts and circumstances of his artistic activity has been the work of many excellent scholars for the past forty or fifty years. . . .

It is true that many valuable investigations have been made about Caravaggio's artistic education. His apprenticeship as a very young boy in the shop of a rather mediocre Milanese painter was brought to light long ago by Nikolaus Pevsner. Much has been written about his artistic provenance and of the impressions which he received outside the shop of his provincial master from the surrounding world of North Italian art—from Savoldo, Lotto, Moretto, Antonio Campi and many others—impressions clearly reflected later in the works he executed in Rome. Roberto Longhi, in a famous and spirited article, propounded a theory of almost blood-and-soil character in which he tried to demonstrate Caravaggio's realism as being deeply rooted in the innate realism of Lombard art. Other scholars have vehemently attacked Longhi's Lombard theory as being too one-sided, and have stressed the purely Venetian-Giorgionesque influence on the artist. At present, most critics seem inclined to make a compromise between these two theories. The chapter here on the youth of Caravaggio reviews the many possibilities in Milan as well as in the Veneto which could have influenced Caravaggio's development, although it avoids generalizing conclusions.

Nevertheless, in analyzing Caravaggio's works, little distinction has been made between the impressions which the young artist received (partly subconsciously) from his artistic milieu, and the conscious selection from various paintings which the maturing artist made for the purpose of supplementing his own compositions. Not enough attention has been given to Caravaggio's own special brand of eclecticism, to his avidity in studying the formal details or the themes of many different painters. Observation of this kind is illuminating for the comprehension of Caravaggio's procedures and for the understanding of his personal accomplishment. For this reason it has seemed to me necessary to compare, much more than has been done, Caravaggio's representations (such as the *St. Matthew and the Angel* or the *Deposition*) with those of other painters in Italy and also in the North, not for purely iconographical reasons, but to show how original and even revolutionary his formal and spiritual solutions were.

The intention and meaning of Caravaggio's paintings—their semantics—have been even more neglected. Almost no attempt has been made to understand how his evocative stylistic innovations served as vehicles for the ideas he wanted to express. These devices should not be considered only from an aesthetic point of view but should be comprehended in the deeper sense in which they communicate a meaningful moral idea.

For whatever impressions we may have of Caravaggio's violent and neurotic personality, it is evident from his religious compositions that his artistic expression as a mature artist was dominated by an outspoken ideal. Caravaggio's flower and fruit pieces, half-figures of frivolous boys and musical scenes are extremely charming and amusing, and their loss would certainly be perceptible. However, it should not be forgotten that after the few years in which he produced these youthful, bohemian canvases, he turned his attention almost entirely to the creation of monuments of devotion, all of which are permeated with the same desire to realize the unrealizable, to bring the miracle within the immediate grasp and understanding of everyone.

Caravaggio's treatment of the supernatural as if it were reality, connects him, in my opinion, with the realistic mysticism of past centuries as it was still present in the religious prescriptions of Ignatius of Loyola's *Exercitia Spiritualia.* The essence of Loyola's religious realism was transmitted to Caravaggio through the circle of Rome's most popular and down-to-earth saint, Philip Neri. As far as I know, no one has yet tried to understand the spirit of Caravaggio's religious art in this connection. He is the only painter who expresses, progressively and powerfully, the tendencies of this "low" church in the midst of the high Catholic hierarchy.

A more intense study of the religious movements which permeated the everyday life of the time would clarify to some degree the constantly repeated and often discussed classification of Caravaggio as a mere "naturalist." There is certainly a strong parallel between the direct and sometimes even coarse treatment of religious matters by St. Philip Neri, and the vulgarity in Caravaggio's provoking exhibition of a peasant's dirty feet in the painting of a Madonna, or the swollen body of the Virgin on her death bed. More significantly, Philip Neri was blamed, despised and even persecuted by the regular conservative functionaries and professionals of the clergy just as Caravaggio was blamed by the high lords of the world of art.

To Federico Zuccari, president of the Academy of St. Luke and high priest of the divinely inspired Roman "disegno" (which included not only drawing but the entire learned procedure of art), Caravaggio's method of transferring "natura"—that is to say, the model—directly to the canvas without the medium of preliminary drawings must have seemed a kind of crime against the Holy Spirit. The Roman reactionaries' pretentious conception of art as a kind of transcendental metaphysic, was opposed by Caravaggio's simple, fanatical and almost religious postulate that art speak directly, using the easily understandable terms of the visible world. To the irritation of his rather simple-minded colleague and biographer, Baglione, and to the astonishment of the much more clever and highly educated Bellori, Caravaggio created "arte senza arte," art without understanding what art is. Actually, while Caravaggio as a North Italian tended to think of nature in terms of color and chiaroscuro rather than disegno, as a professional active in Rome he had absorbed much of the structural element in Roman art. One of his most significant functions, in fact, was to bridge the long acknowledged schism between Roman disegno and Venetian colore. With the addition of the moral and social overtones of Caravaggio's painting, there resulted an artistic manifestation which was surprisingly new for Central Italy.

About 1600 one of the Flemish artists who frequented Rome reported to van Mander in Haarlem the emergence in the Roman art world of a curious young painter, who proclaimed loudly the new and rather subversive doctrine, that every work of art not made directly after life is child's play, not even excluding from this preposterous judgment the sacrosanct art of antiquity, or the "Divine Raphael." Such radical statements, though they were doubtlessly made "pour épater le bourgeois," probably gave rise to the assumption that Caravaggio was unable to draw or paint without having a model before him. This accusation, first used by Caravaggio's adversaries to discredit him and his art, later gained currency with such critics as Scanelli and Bellori, who used it to stamp him as a mere naturalist. In reality this derogatory classification, which so prejudiced the judgment of later centuries, was by no means valid, at least in an absolute sense. Caravaggio is quite obviously not a slavish imitator of visible objects, either in his early genre paintings like the *Fortune Teller* (which Bellori cites as an example of his painting directly after life), or in later works such as the *Martyrdom of St. Matthew,* with its stylized figure of the executioner, or the *Flagellation of Christ.* Caravaggio was certainly as well able to alter the appearance of the model or to draw a figure from memory as any of the maniera painters. Even assuming that as a boy he was a recalcitrant student in the shop of Peterzano —and this is not at all improbable—he had surely enough intelligence and ability to master elementary teachings. And to such schooling, "child's play," belongs the knowledge of the graduation of figures according to the distance from the foreground. It was therefore a kind of slander when his critics accused him of using a dark background simply to hide his inability to build up a real pictorial prospettiva. Quite to the contrary, Caravaggio needed this limitation of space to concentrate his composition. He used it to bring the miraculous event directly and persuasively before the eyes and into the heart of the worshiper. The real reason for Caravaggio's censure by the art critics of his day was not a lack of technical ability, but rather his conception of the relationship between the work of art and the worshiper who sees it. Caravaggio's offense was that he had challenged the whole God-given ideology of Roman art, drawing it down to earth from its higher spheres. In spite of these academic criticisms, it was just the directness of Caravaggio's art that brought him notoriety and even popularity. The impression which Caravaggio's paintings made on the populace of his day is difficult to estimate and explain because it is not only an art-historical problem, but a psychological and interpretative one. It involves not only a patient searching and understanding of every individual work but also a comprehension of the significance each work had for the community and for human feelings generally. This knowledge one cannot acquire by reading and interpreting the biographies of art writers of the seventeenth century. Most valuable and interesting though they are for the facts they contain concerning the life and works of Caravaggio, their authors are prejudiced—personally, or by their exclusively artistic or art-theoretical preoccupations. Of all these writers Bellori is the most spirited and erudite. By inserting a vita of Caravaggio in his selection of the most important artists of his period, he showed at least an awareness of the phenomenon "Caravaggio" and its significance from an art historical point of view. But he nevertheless condemns the naturalism of Caravaggio, according to Classicistic-Poussinesque credo, as the "rovina della pittura," the "ruin of the art of painting."

Not for a moment did he try to investigate the deeper roots of this "naturalism," nor did he notice that the "colori poetici," "the colorful poetry," which he observed and admired in his idol, Poussin, are also present—though in a quite different way—in Caravaggio. It was not within the realm of an art writer of the seventeenth century to discover the poetic or dramatic force, and to understand the essence and magnificence of Caravaggio's realism. That would require a writer like Baudelaire. Men like Bellori, Mancini and Scanelli reflect, after all, the opinions of a relatively small circle of artists, literati, and collectors. They were forced to admire the technical novelties of the master, especially in regard to his color, but they did not understand the true intention of his innovations. It is characteristic that Mancini gives the same amount of attention to Giuseppe d'Arpino, the exponent of the late maniera, as to Caravaggio, the leader of the naturalistic school of painting. Similarly, the Marchese Vincenzo Giustiniani praises d'Arpino under the rubric "di maniera" in his somewhat naïve system of categories of painting, while he places Caravaggio (together with Annibale Carracci) in an only slightly higher position. These critics either did not see, or at least did not state, how far superior Caravaggio was as an imaginative artist.

Not one of the biographers explains why Caravaggio, in spite of his strange and individual personality and his violations of decorum, had so many commissions from important churches that he could scarcely carry them out. It is true that such commissions often came from wealthy individuals who wished to dedicate an altarpiece in a church as decoration for their family chapel. Some of these men may have chosen Caravaggio simply because he was in fashion, or because of his artistic skill, but others doubtless appreciated the religious impact of his paintings. Cardinal del Monte, Caravaggio's main protector, may have been one of these, but there is no real evidence to indicate whether this was the reason for his commissions. We have more information in the case of the abbate Giacomo Crescenzi, under whose supervision as trustee for the Contarelli legacy Caravaggio executed his famous paintings in San Luigi. The abbate was one of the closest friends and adherents of St. Philip Neri in his last years. It would not, therefore, be surprising if he had favored Caravaggio because the painter's religious works corresponded in some ways to the sentiments of the Saint.

Thus it was surely not only Caravaggio's technique and method of painting which made so great an impression, but the spiritual content, the new concept of reality, which awoke first curiosity and then admiration. Such feelings may have played a part when the community of painters in Rome urgently requested permission from the agent of the Duke of Mantua to arrange an exhibit of Caravaggio's most moving painting, the *Death of the Virgin,* before it left Rome permanently. The purely painterly beauties of the work, the splendid red curtain and the oblique light traversing the auburn shadows, were of course of the greatest interest and most enjoyable to the professionals and connoisseurs. But more than anything else it must have been the emotional force of the composition which overwhelmed those who saw it. The painting had been opposed by the clergy of S. Maria della Scala allegedly because of the representation of the Mother of Christ in her death as a very poor woman, surrounded by barefooted old men. This social realism, however, tempered and elevated by a consciousness of the mystery of death and resurrection, must have evoked in many of the artists, priests, and laymen privileged to see the painting a feeling that their own emotions were expressed more eloquently by Caravaggio than they could have been by any other artist. . . .

Through the centuries, Caravaggio has been called a mere imitator of nature. His most important and efficient detractor, Bellori, asks the rhetorical question: how a man like Caravaggio could seriously "aspire to art without understanding what art really is," art being understood as the expression of a preconceived idea. Because in the opinion of the Classicistic critics and theorists Caravaggio's art lacked an ideal, there arose a tendency to believe that his religious paintings were nothing but documentary representations of religious events expressed in a commonplace and realistic manner, and without being inspired by any real religious feeling. Nothing could be less true. "Realism" in Caravaggio's works means not so much detailed accuracy in rendering the natural object, as a bringing of the object—the supernatural included—near to the spectator, almost to the degree of physical tangibility. Caravaggio's religious expression has a very special character which, though it does not show the naïveté of a Fra Angelico, the almost

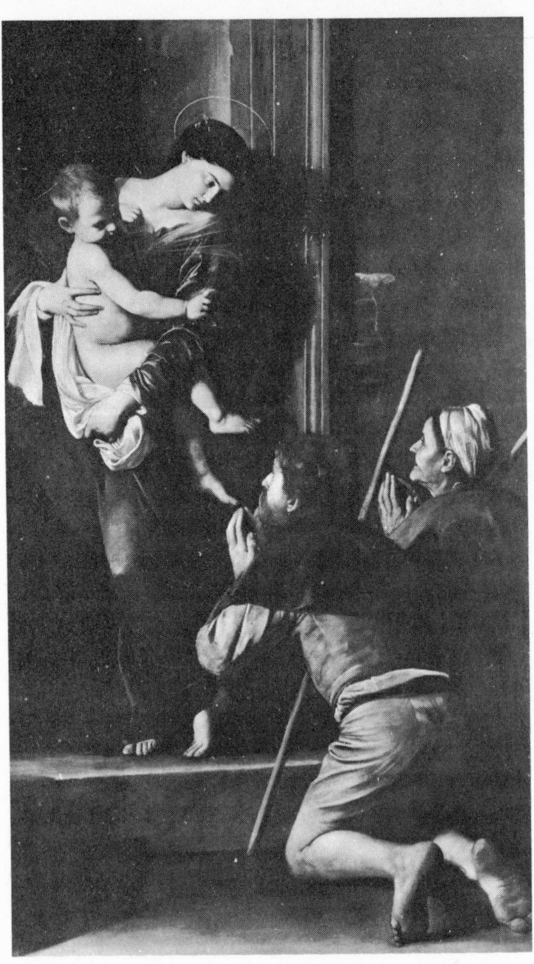

32. Caravaggio, *Madonna di Loreto*, *c.* 1604, Oil on Canvas, $102\frac{3}{8}''$ by 59″ (S. Agustino, Rome)

fanatical spirituality of a Pontormo or Parmigianino, or the sensuous ecstasy of a Bernini, it is surely as sincere and perhaps more revolutionary than the religious expression of these and other artists whose works reflect the religious ideas of their centuries. In the same way, Caravaggio's realistic mysticism is the strongest and most persuasive interpretation of the popular religious movements of the period in which he lived.

Mystery and realism are by no means contradictory. When, in the *Madonna di Loreto* [Fig. 32], Caravaggio places the radiant figure of the Virgin so close to the kneeling peasants that they could easily touch her robe, the perception of the supernatural through the senses is for the spectator perhaps a greater mystery than the abstract vision of a host of angels adoring the name of Christ as painted by Federico Zuccari. This feeling can be traced to the devotional books of the fourteenth and fifteenth centuries, for example Rudolf of Saxony's *Vita Christi* or Thomas à Kempis' *Imitatio Christi*, expressions of the deepest pietistic mysticism which try to direct the human spirit toward perfect harmony with the transcendental order of the universe. In order to achieve this aim, or at least to approach it—because the highest perfection seems unobtainable on this earth—one must be in close contact with the divine by physical means, through the senses. Therefore in these writings the miraculous and transcendental are not emphasized; there is little or no mention of visions or of miracles of the saints, of the Assumption of the Virgin, etc. It is rather the relation of the individual to God that receives stress, and the representations from the life of Christ are intended as models for all mankind. Ignatius of Loyola's *Exercitia Spiritualia* are to a large extent based on these earlier pietistic and mystical doctrines. Here too one finds a great simplification of devotion; there are no visions, no ecstasies, no adoration of the saints or of their relics; the main interest is centered in the individual and his contact with God. St. Ignatius objected strenuously to abstract and scholastic reasoning and to the visionary aspects of medieval theology, which persisted in the more conservative factions of the Counter-Reformation. Instead, he wished Christian mysteries to be contemplated in terms of the actual and tangible. He teaches in the *Exercitia* how to obtain spiritual understanding through the use of the senses, demanding that the exercitant "see with the eyes of the imagination the corporeal place where the object which he wishes to contemplate is found" (Paragraph 47). In another passage, he urges that the exercitant "see the persons with the eyes of the imagination, meditating and contemplating in particular their circumstances," and that he imagine them through the other senses also, to "touch with the interior touch, as, for example, to embrace and kiss the places where such persons trod or sat" (Paragraphs 122 and 125). He asks him to contemplate "the place or cave of the Nativity, how large or how small, how low or how high, and how it was prepared." (*Exercitia*, second week, first day, 2nd Contemplation.) The mysteries of the Passion are to be contemplated in the same concrete and perceptible manner; for example the road along which Christ had to carry the cross to Golgotha, how heavily the cross weighed upon his shoulders, etc. Such an historical or traditional event, known through the gospels, is to be perceived in the imagination

33. Caravaggio, *Conversion of St. Paul,* 1601, Oil on Canvas, $90\frac{1}{2}''$ by $68\frac{7}{8}''$ (Sta. Maria del Populo, Rome)

of the exercising disciple by means of the senses as though it belonged to the actual, tangible world. However, since the event is a part of Christ's Passion, it has a decidedly supernatural connotation and must therefore be contemplated as a mystery; indeed such events are referred to as "mysteries" in the *Exercitia Spiritualia.*

Caravaggio represented the *Conversion of St. Paul* [Fig. 33] with the same kind of sober observation, with the same close sensuous grasp of the factual and tangible, which St. Ignatius would have demanded from the imagination of the exercitant. In composition too the space is strictly limited and precisely measurable. The miraculous light is powerfully visualized without the indication of an ethereal source, and the celestial voice can almost be heard by the spectator, even without the image of Christ who utters it—exactly as it would be heard by the exercitant in his overstimulated imagination. Caravaggio's *Conversion* is a realistic mystery just as are the contemplations of Saint Ignatius, and it is significant that, in the contract of 1600, Tiberio Cerasi specifies this painting, which he ordered, as "the Mystery of the Conversion of St. Paul." Caravaggio's representation of the mystery in completely human terms corresponds closely in spirit to the contemplation of the mysteries in the *Exercitia;* both make the supernatural tangible and understandable to man's spiritual intelligence with the help of the senses. . . .

We have seen that Caravaggio's paintings—particularly the eloquent and monumental works of his mature years—express an astonishingly original and intense religious feeling bearing the imprint of the popular religious movements of his time: the precise spiritual rationalism of St. Ignatius and the informal mysticism and humility of St. Philip. Within this framework, Caravaggio developed his individual religious ideology, dominated by a strong social consciousness. It is probable that the circumstances of his life, the poverty of his early years and other personal difficulties, caused him to rebel against convention and gave him a sharp awareness of the spiritual needs of the individual, whatever his social rank. Again and again in his paintings, Caravaggio shows a deep sympathy for people who are materially poor—for example the poor peasants kneeling before the *Madonna di Loreto* or the simple people at the feet of the *Madonna del Rosario.*

The spiritual language of Caravaggio's paintings did not find an immediate continuation in the works of any other painter. The so-called Caravaggisti were concerned almost exclusively with other aspects of his art, his chiaroscuro effects, his genre subject matter, his color and composition, and they seem to have been unable to comprehend the full meaning of the psychological and social elements of his religious paintings. Such painters as Gentileschi, Saraceni, Manfredi and even Borgianni cannot be called religious painters in the same sense as Caravaggio.

Nor did the religious implications of Caravaggio's works have a very extensive influence outside of Italy. The association of commonplace and familiar figures with sacred events in a few of the early works of Velasquez, such as the *Kitchen Maid* and *Mary and Martha,* remind one of Caravaggio, but they are essentially genre paintings with religious overtones. Much more interesting and significant is the comparison with Rembrandt. Just as Caravaggio was influenced by the ideals of Philip Neri, Rembrandt was, in his later years, inspired by the doctrines of the Mennonites. An interesting parallel can be drawn between the Filippini and the Mennonites, in so far as both were popular religious movements and in a sense spiritually opposed to formalistic and abstract official churches, the one in Holland being the rigid and dogmatic Calvinist Church. In spite of their fundamental differences, both the Filippini and the Mennonites believed in a strict adherence to the Gospels and emphasized the Christian virtues of humility and simplicity, as do all popular pietistic movements. Numerous late religious works of Rembrandt were directly influenced by Mennonite texts and principles in their spiritual content as well as in their subject matter. However, even though both Caravaggio and Rembrandt were men of great spiritual sensitivity and were influenced by similar religious values, their conceptions of religious scenes are fundamentally different. The significant differences between their religious paintings are partly the result of the reasons for which they were painted. Almost all of Caravaggio's religious works, beginning with the San Luigi series, were altarpieces designed for the worship of the Christian community and its members, whereas most of Rembrandt's religious paintings were made not on commission, but as private expressions of his own imaginative impulses, there being no place for paintings in Calvinist churches. Rembrandt could thus treat Old and New Testament subjects in the same impressive manner that he employed for such nonreligious paintings as the *Oath of Julius Civilis* [Fig. 34] or the *Homer*, and he did not have to take into account the spiritual relationship between the worshiper and the sacred scene. Conversely, the principal purpose of Caravaggio's great altarpieces was to depict Christian mysteries so that the worshiper could grasp them in terms of his own life. Rembrandt's aim was not to show miracles in terms of this earth, but to express the radiance of his inner visions. He substantiates these visions in his paintings through his amazing interpretations of human psychology, and, perhaps more, through his spectacular effects of light. In Caravaggio's works the supernatural is always implicit in the actuality of the scene; his light, falling upon the physical objects, evokes from them the supernatural.

It is curious to remark that in France, where there existed a religious atmosphere comparable in many ways to that which St. Philip Neri had created in Rome, almost none of the important artists of the time—Vouet, LeSueur, Philippe de Champaigne—even approached Caravaggio's religious expression. Only in a profane work such as Louis Le Nain's *Repas de Paysans* do we find an expression which is comparable to Caravaggio in its profound piety.

9. DISTINCTIONS BETWEEN RENAISSANCE AND BAROQUE

Heinrich Wölfflin

INTRODUCTION

Heinrich Wölfflin's *Principles of Art History,* which first appeared in German in 1915, and in English translation in 1932, has become a familiar classic in the literature of art. Concentrating on form rather than content, Wölfflin drew up five pairs of concepts with which he distinguished between the formal characteristics of sixteenth- and seventeenth-century art. Although this system was somewhat limiting, failing as it did to recognize the phenomenon of Mannerism in the sixteenth century or to account for the Classicism of a Poussin in the seventeenth, it nevertheless served to emphasize the importance of improving the analytical tools for treating problems of style.

His early *Renaissance und Barock* (1888) is now available in an English translation (1966), as is his late work *The Sense of Form in Art* (1958), first published in German in 1931. His *Classic Art,* translated into English as early as 1903, has seen long service as a college text for Italian Renaissance art.

The brief selection in this anthology is from that portion of the Introduction to *Principles of Art History* in which the paired concepts are initially presented. The selection by John Rupert Martin which follows it explores the character of the Baroque from quite another point of view. Mention should also be made of Rensselaer W. Lee's brilliant article, now available in a paperbound edition, "*Ut Pictura Poesis:* The Humanistic Theory of

Painting," *The Art Bulletin,* XXII (1940), which defines an ideal prevalent in the art of painting from the fifteenth through the eighteenth centuries and, therefore, relevant to the art under discussion in the selections by Wölfflin and Martin. In presenting yet another aspect of art during the Renaissance and Baroque eras, Lee's study, taken together with the selections by Wölfflin and Martin, demonstrates the rich complexity of significant art.

The selection that follows is reprinted from *Principles of Art History* by Heinrich Wölfflin, by permission of the publishers, Dover Publications, Inc., New York, and G. Bell & Sons, Ltd., London.

It is a mistake for art history to work with the clumsy notion of the imitation of nature, as though it were merely a homogeneous process of increasing perfection. All the increase in the "surrender to nature" does not explain how a landscape by Ruysdael differs from one by Patenir, and by the "progressive conquest of reality" we have still not explained the contrast between a head by Frans Hals and one by Dürer. The imitative content, the subject matter, may be as different in itself as possible, the decisive point remains that the conception in each case is based on a different visual schema—a schema which, however, is far more deeply rooted than in mere questions of the progress of imitation. It conditions the architectural work as well as the work of representative art, and a Roman Baroque façade has the same visual denominator as a landscape by Van Goyen.

THE MOST GENERAL REPRESENTATIONAL FORMS

This [chapter] is occupied with the discussion of these universal forms of representation. It does not analyze the beauty of Leonardo but the element in which that beauty became manifest. It does not analyze the representation of nature according to its imitational content, and how, for instance, the naturalism of the sixteenth century may be distinguished from that of the seventeenth, but the mode of perception which lies at the root of the representative arts in the various centuries.

Let us try to sift out these basic forms in the domain of more modern art. We denote the series of periods with the names Early Renaissance, High Renaissance, and Baroque, names which mean little and must lead to misunderstanding in their application to south and north, but are hardly to be ousted now. Unfortunately, the symbolic analogy bud, bloom, decay, plays a secondary and misleading part. If there is in fact a qualitative difference between the fifteenth and sixteenth centuries, in the sense that the fifteenth had gradually to acquire by labor the insight into effects which was at the free disposal of the sixteenth, the (Classic) art of the Cinquecento and the (Baroque) art of the Seicento are equal in point of value. The word Classic here denotes no judgment of value, for Baroque has its classicism too. Baroque (or, let us say, modern art) is neither a rise nor a decline from Classic, but a totally different art. The occidental development of modern times cannot simply be reduced to a curve with rise, height, and decline: it has two culminating points. We can turn our sympathy to one or to the other, but we must realize that that is an arbitrary judgment, just as it is an arbitrary judgment to say that the rose-bush lives its supreme moment in the formation of the flower, the apple tree in that of the fruit.

For the sake of simplicity, we must speak of the sixteenth and seventeenth centuries as units of style, although these periods signify no homogeneous production, and, in particular, the features of the Seicento had begun to take shape long before the year 1600, just as, on the other hand, they long continued to affect the appearance of the eighteenth century. Our object is to compare type with type, the finished with the finished. Of course, in the strictest sense of the word, there is nothing "finished": all historical material is subject to continual transformation; but we must make up our minds to establish the distinctions at a fruitful point, and there to let them speak as contrasts, if we are not to let the whole development slip through our fingers. The preliminary stages of the High Renaissance are not to be ignored, but they represent an archaic form of art, an art of primitives, for whom established pictorial form does not yet exist. But to expose the individual differences which lead from the style of the sixteenth century to that of the seventeenth must be left to a detailed historical survey which will, to tell the truth, only do justice to its task when it has the determining concepts at its disposal.

If we are not mistaken, the development can be reduced, as a provisional formulation, to the following five pairs of concepts:

(1) The development from the linear to the painterly, *i.e.* the development of line as the path of vision and guide of the eye, and the gradual depreciation of line: in more general terms, the perception of the object by its tangible character—in outline and surfaces—on the one hand, and on the other, a perception which is by way of surrendering itself to the mere visual appearance and

can abandon "tangible" design. In the former case the stress is laid on the limits of things; in the other the work tends to look limitless. Seeing by volumes and outlines isolates objects: for the painterly eye, they merge. In the one case interest lies more in the perception of individual material objects as solid, tangible bodies; in the other, in the apprehension of the world as a shifting semblance.

(2) The development from plane to recession. Classic[1] art reduces the parts of a total form to a sequence of planes, the Baroque emphasises depth. Plane is the element of line, extension in one plane the form of the greatest explicitness: with the discounting of the contour comes the discounting of the plane, and the eye relates objects essentially in the direction of forwards and backwards. This is no qualitative difference: with a greater power of representing spatial depths, the innovation has nothing directly to do: it signifies rather a radically different mode of representation, just as "plane style" in our sense is not the style of primitive art, but makes its appearance only at the moment at which foreshortening and spatial illusion are completely mastered.

(3) The development from closed to open form. Every work of art must be a finite whole, and it is a defect if we do not feel that it is self-contained, but the interpretation of this demand in the sixteenth and seventeenth centuries is so different that, in comparison with the loose form of the Baroque, classic design may be taken as *the* form of closed composition. The relaxation of rules, the yielding of tectonic strength, or whatever name we may give to the process, does not merely signify an enhancement of interest, but is a new mode of representation consistently carried out, and hence this factor is to be adopted among the basic forms of representation.

(4) The development from multiplicity to unity. In the system of a classic composition, the single parts, however firmly they may be rooted in the whole, maintain a certain independence. It is not the anarchy of primitive art: the part is conditioned by the whole, and yet does not cease to have its own life. For the spectator, that presupposes an articulation, a progress from part to part, which is a very different operation from perception as a whole, such as the seventeenth century applies and demands. In both styles unity is the chief aim (in contrast to the pre-Classic period which did not yet understand the idea in its true sense), but in the one case unity is achieved by a harmony of free parts, in the other, by a

union of parts in a single theme, or by the subordination, to one unconditioned dominant, of all other elements.

(5) The absolute and the relative clarity of the subject. This is a contrast which at first borders on the contrast between linear and painterly. The representation of things as they are, taken singly and accessible to plastic feeling, and the representation of things as they look, seen as a whole, and rather by their non-plastic qualities. But it is a special feature of the classic age that it developed an ideal of perfect clarity which the fifteenth century only vaguely suspected, and which the seventeenth voluntarily sacrificed. Not that artistic form had become confused, for that always produces an unpleasing effect, but the explicitness of the subject is no longer the sole purpose of the presentment. Composition, light, and color no longer merely serve to define form, but have their own life. There are cases in which absolute clarity has been partly abandoned merely to enhance effect, but "relative" clarity, as a great all-embracing mode of representation, first entered the history of art at the moment at which reality is beheld with an eye to other effects. Even here it is not a difference of quality if the Baroque departed from the ideals of the age of Dürer and Raphael, but, as we have said, a different attitude to the world.

NOTES

[1] "Klassisch." The word "Classic" throughout this book refers to the art of the High Renaissance. It implies, however, not only a historical phase of art, but a special mode of creation of which that art is an instance. (Tr.)

10. THE BAROQUE

John Rupert Martin

INTRODUCTION

In this essay Professor Martin examines the characteristics of Baroque painting and sculpture, ranging beyond a mere consideration of stylistic forms to matters of iconography and content. He identifies a strong current of naturalism which, apart from its embodiment in verisimilitude, contributed to the elevation in the seventeenth century of such genre as landscape and still life. But this naturalism, the author points out, should be distinguished from that of the nineteenth century by its association with a strong allegorical tendency; and he adds the observation that this duality of naturalism and allegory in Baroque art had its counterpart in the duality of naturalism and metaphysics in seventeenth century science and philosophy. Furthermore, in accord with the scientific interests of the age, a preoccupation with psychology was manifest in the frequency of such themes as ecstasy, martyrdom, and humor; and a heightened sense of the infinite was expressed through a preoccupation with space, light, and time. Thus, without homogenizing the variety of styles that coexist within the Baroque era, this selection evokes the presence of an underlying unity of content in the art of the period.

For further reading on interpretations of the Baroque, there is Bernard C. Heyl, "Meanings of Baroque," *Journal of Aesthetics and Art Criticism,* XIX (1961). Baroque problems are extensively treated in volumes V (1946), XII (1954), and XIV (1955) of the above journal. Of special significance is Denis Mahon, *Studies in Seicento Art and Theory* (1947).

On the question of the relation of the Baroque to classical antiquity, one should consult the section of this subject in *Latin American Art and the Baroque Period in Europe, Studies in Western Art, Acts of the Twentieth International Congress of the History of Art,* III (1963). For the various national manifestations of the Baroque there are a number of works: Rudolf Wittkower, *Art and Architecture in Italy, 1600–1750* (1965); *Art in Italy*

1600–1700, Exhibition Catalogue, Detroit Institute of Art (1965); Sir Anthony Blunt, *Art and Architecture in France, 1500–1700* (1953); George Kubler and Martin Soria, *Baroque Art and Architecture in Spain and Latin America* (1959); H. Gerson and E. H. Ter Kuile, *Art and Architecture in Belgium, 1600–1800* (1960); Jakob Rosenberg, Seymour Slive, and E. H. Ter Kuile, *Dutch Art and Architecture, 1600–1800* (1966); Eberhard Hempel, *Baroque Art and Architecture in Central Europe . . .* (1965). Eugène Fromentin, *The Old Masters of Belgium and Holland,* is a perceptive nineteenth-century work by a French artist and writer, available in a paperbound edition (1963) with an introduction by Meyer Schapiro. For the seventeenth-century context, there are D. Ogg, *Europe in the Seventeenth Century,* 5th ed. (1948); G. N. Clark, *The Seventeenth Century* (1947); and such popular well-illustrated surveys of the period as Michael Kitson, *The Age of the Baroque* (1966) and Victor L. Tapie, *The Age of Grandeur* (1966).

The selection that follows is reprinted from John Rupert Martin, "The Baroque from the Point of View of the Art Historian," *Journal of Aesthetics and Art Criticism,* XIV (1955), by permission of the author and the publishers.

THE BAROQUE FROM THE POINT OF VIEW OF THE ART HISTORIAN

Let me say at the outset that by "Baroque" I mean, first, that period which is roughly comprehended by the seventeenth century. I take it, moreover, to designate a set of commonly held attitudes. Thus I regard "Baroque art" as being not only the product of the seventeenth century, but also as being shaped and given its characteristic form by those attitudes. Hence, whatever its original connotation may have been, I do not conceive of the term as applying only to that which is theatrical, sensational or bombastic—as calling up the idea of "a lordly racket," to quote Professor Panofsky.

It is certainly not easy to prove that there is such a thing as "Baroque art," rather than a multitude of heterogeneous works which merely happen to have been executed in the Baroque era—or, if even that term seems tendentious, in the seventeenth century. For we must grant that a single Baroque *style* does not exist: on the contrary, one is almost tempted to speak of the very diversity of styles as one of the distinguishing features of the seventeenth century. Attempts have been made, it is true, to define a coherent stylistic vocabulary for the period. The most brilliant of these was Wölfflin's famous comparison of sixteenth- and seventeenth-century art, from which he drew five pairs of concepts. Thus he was able to point to the contrast between "linear and painterly" modes of vision, between "plane and recession," "closed and open form," "multiplicity and unity," and "clearness and unclearness," as illustrating the artistic qualities of the sixteenth and seventeenth centuries respectively. Penetrating as these observations were (and it would be absurd to disparage Wölfflin's work), it is now evident that his categories have certain limitations. First, as is well known, Wölfflin was interested in form rather than in content; consequently his notion of the Baroque was founded on purely optical (one might almost say "Impressionist") considerations. Second, his conception of a unified Baroque style was only arrived at by neglecting "Classic" artists such as Poussin, although it must be obvious that a comprehensive system which fails to take into account a major artist (no matter how inconvenient) is on that score alone deficient. Third, Wölfflin treated the sixteenth century as an artistic whole, making no distinction between that later phase of it which is now generally termed "Mannerism" and the earlier, classical (or "High Renaissance") phase. Yet it happens that the contrast between Baroque and Mannerism is more striking and illuminating than that between Baroque and High Renaissance. For, as we are now becoming aware, the Baroque came into being not so much through evolution as through revolution; it was deliberately launched, so to speak, in opposition to the principles of Mannerism.

What is required is a definition, not of Baroque stylistic forms, nor yet of Baroque iconography, but of what these reveal to us of Baroque *content.* We shall have to determine the common denominators in all the artistic products of the period—those fundamental attitudes which still persist despite differences of nationality, of individual personality, and even of religious belief, and which are at the same time peculiar to the Baroque era. Needless to say, the few remarks that I shall make here are in no sense intended to answer this requirement. The problem confronting us is much too complicated to be solved in so brief and sketchy a fashion. Furthermore, it is doubtful that it can be satisfactorily solved until we have developed new techniques of scholarship which, by transcending individual areas of specialization (the history of art, of literature, music, philosophy, etc.), will provide us with a more reliable and valid set of criteria than we possess at present. My remarks, then, are of necessity both incomplete and provisional. In order to avoid complications and repetitions, I shall limit myself to the representational arts of painting and sculpture.

Of all the essential characteristics of Baroque art I would place first its naturalism. Verisimilitude, though it takes varying forms, is a principle to which all Baroque artists subscribe. Indeed, it is a factor in the very genesis of the Baroque, conceived as it was in opposition to the stylized conventions and fantasies of Mannerism. It was not merely a careless remark of Caravaggio (who, more than any other, may be credited with inaugurating Baroque naturalism) that the competent painter was one who knew how "to imitate natural things well" (*imitar bene le cose naturali*). Rembrandt too was quoted as saying that "one should be guided only by nature and by no other rules." A similar attitude is encountered in Rubens: in his essay on the imitation of ancient statues (a practice which in general he approved of) he warned against copying their cold and stony luster. These were no idle words, as Rubens' sensuous rendering of the nude makes very clear. Even much later in the century, when academic rules introduced theoretical complications into the creative process, the innately "natural" vision of the Baroque was never supplanted, as witness the portraitists of the age of Louis XIV who, for all their ornateness and rhetoric, are firmly committed to the representation of appearances. It is to this naturalism that we must look to find the most obvious link between Baroque art and thought: the artistic vision of the age that gave birth to the physical sciences was shaped by a respect for visible, material reality.

Naturalism is of course not merely a matter of verisimilitude. Also implicit in the naturalist aesthetic is the widened range of subject-matter, the addition of new categories to the old, accepted themes. Landscape and still life, for example, although they were not "invented" by the Baroque, were during this period elevated to a position of importance such as they had never hitherto enjoyed. The Dutch masters of the seventeenth century perhaps offer the most vivid illustration of the meaning of Baroque naturalism. Owing to their Calvinist background, religious and mythological subjects hold little interest for them, and still less, it would seem, for their patrons. Individually, they are for the most part specialists in limited categories of subject-matter. But collectively they can be said to have dedicated themselves to recording the multifarious aspects of the world and of the life about them: portraiture, both of individuals and of groups, domestic interiors, church interiors, street scenes, scenes of taverns and markets, views of rivers, harbors and ships, rural countrysides at all seasons of the year, still life subjects of every kind, all of these testify to an extraordinary passion for representing everyday facts and occurrences, or, to see it in another light, for crystallizing the shifting patterns of this world into some permanent and enduring form.

In stressing the importance of Baroque naturalism, however, we must guard against oversimplification. We shall gain only a one-sided and distorted view of the Baroque if we confuse the naturalism of the seventeenth century with that of the nineteenth. The gulf between Velazquez and Manet is fully as wide as that which separates Galileo and Darwin; to attempt an equation would be as superficial and erroneous for the first pair as for the second. The student of Baroque art, provided he does not restrict himself to a purely formal analysis, soon comes to realize that its inherent naturalism is inextricably bound up with an equally innate tendency to allegory. It is significant that some of the outstanding "realists" of the Baroque—masters whom the later nineteenth century hailed as "forerunners of Impressionism"—frequently elected to paint allegorical subjects. And characteristically, such allegories were often "concealed" beneath a naturalistic, genre-like exterior: this is especially true of the Spaniard Velazquez and the Hollander Vermeer, two painters whose powers of observation, command of representation and sheer technical mastery might seem to preclude any interest in a non-material reality. In the same way, a surprising number of still life paintings are found, on analysis, to embody a moralizing theme such as *Vanitas,* the abstract idea being made more real by being conveyed in the most immediate and concrete terms possible. These are not isolated examples. The importance of allegory in Rubens, Poussin and Pietro da Cortona is too obvious to require emphasis. The equilibrium of naturalism and allegory, which is one of the distinguishing features of Baroque art, plainly echoes a comparable duality of naturalism and metaphysics in Baroque science and philosophy.

In view of the growing scientific spirit of the time, it is not to be wondered at that Baroque art evinces a deep interest in psychology. We find it exemplified in portraiture, in the power of a Rembrandt, a Velazquez or a Bernini to evoke through a likeness an uncanny sense of presence. But the Baroque concern with the phenomena of personality is not manifested solely in portraits. We can observe it quite as plainly in religious art. Thus there are certain subjects which, though they are in no sense innovations of the seventeenth century, yet recur with such frequency as to show that they have a special psychological appeal. The gospel episode of the Supper at Emmaus, in which the identity of the risen Christ is suddenly and dramatically revealed to two unsuspecting disciples, is such a subject. The Catholic Caravaggio and the Protestant Rembrandt were particularly drawn to it. Or again, in the traditional theme of David with the head of Goliath the Baroque also found new possibilities of interpretation. It is characteristic of the period that the youthful hero is usually presented not as the proud champion elated by his victory, but as a reflective, saddened boy who gazes with something like remorse at his grisly handiwork. In such subjects the Baroque was able to exploit to the full its taste for the portrayal of mixed emotions.

Here we may refer also to another recurrent theme in Baroque religious art: vision and ecstasy. One of the most typical products of seventeenth-century Catholic art is the altarpiece representing, in intensely emotional fashion, a saint in a state of mystical trance, helpless and swooning at the awful realization of divinity. One thinks at once of what is perhaps the greatest work of this kind, Bernini's splendid *Ecstasy of St. Theresa* [Fig. 37]. It is not enough to relate such works merely to the religious sensibilities of the age; for the Mannerist period of the sixteenth century, when religious passions were even more deeply felt, produced nothing comparable to them. Over and above their specifically religious purpose, it appears that artists perceived in these subjects an opportunity to explore the psychology of ecstasy and trance, in which the self seeks to be released from human limitations and absorbed in God.

In the same way the favorite Catholic themes of death and martyrdom, initially brought into existence for reasons of faith, became a vehicle for the portrayal of extreme states of feeling. The unspeakable agony of dismemberment, the intense grief and horror of the onlookers, the feral cruelty of the executioners, these things, we are compelled to admit, are the real subject of many a Baroque martyrdom. The paintings of the Spaniard Ribera are among those that come to mind.

Equally symptomatic of the Baroque awareness of psychological factors is the introduction of humor into the domain of art. Witty and humorous elements can even invade the dignified tradition of monumental fresco painting, as is shown by Annibale Carracci's Gallery in the Farnese palace in Rome, where the decorative figures are not content to play a properly solemn and subordinate rôle, but become positively playful. The sixteenth century, with its ingrained notions of the dignity of art, would have found such levity intolerable. It is significant, too, that this same Annibale Carracci, who may be regarded, with Caravaggio, as one of the founders of the Baroque, was the inventor of caricatures in the modern sense. For caricature, with its comic exaggerations and half-mocking, half-sympathetic intent, in itself reflects an understanding of the complexities of personality. Bernini was fond of drawing caricatures, a number of which have survived. Trivial and hastily executed as they are, they yet derive from the same feeling for humanity that informs his most inspired works of portrait sculpture.

Another of the distinguishing characteristics of Baroque content is what may be called the sense of the infinite. Once again it is hardly necessary to stress the analogy to developments in philosophy, the natural sciences and mathematics. It is not too much to say that the consciousness of infinity pervades the whole epoch and colors all its products. Here it will only be possible to indicate a few of the salient manifestations of that consciousness in works of art.

Some of those subjects which I have just mentioned as illustrating the Baroque interest in psychology may serve also to exemplify the concern with infinity. In Christ's Supper at Emmaus, for example, Baroque artists were able to exploit not only the disciples' sudden realization of their companion's identity, but also the dramatic (because unexpected) intrusion of the infinite and eternal into the everyday world of merely human experience. So also the representation of a saint in mystical ecstasy conjured up the ultimate enlargement of the personality, to the point at which it achieved union with the higher reality. And this desire for expansion of the individual personality (which lies at the very center of the Baroque spirit) is surely to be connected with a new awareness of infinity.

In general, however, the fascination that infinity held for the Baroque artist was expressed in terms of space, light and time. To mention space in Baroque art is to think at once of the widespread interest in landscape, an interest which, incidentally, links together such diverse personalities as Carracci, Rembrandt, Poussin, Rubens, and Vermeer, to name only a few of those who, without being specialists in the subject, turned their attention to landscape at some point in their careers. The typical seventeenth-century landscape painting, with its compelling sweep into depth, and its subordination of humanity to the vaster scale of nature, tells us not only of a fundamentally natural outlook, but something also of the exhilaration which was felt in contemplating the continuum of space.

This is not to say that all Baroque outdoor subjects are monotonously alike. On the contrary, the rich stylistic variety of the period is nowhere more evident than in the widely different approaches to landscape, ranging from the cool serenity of Carracci's idealized nature to the dynamic turbulence of Ruysdael's forest scenes, in which nature seems to be at war with itself; from the generalized, rationally ordered scenery of Poussin, which seems to have been constructed with a kind of Cartesian logic, to the exact and patient portraiture of place which is found in van der Heyden's views of Dutch towns; from the rural countrysides of Rubens, with their emphasis on physical vitality and material abundance, to the classical landscapes of Claude, which breathe an air of poetic evanescence and nostalgia. But varied and multiform as these interpretations may be, they all stem initially from the same sense of wonder at the continuous expanse of the material universe.

We can observe another expression of the Baroque preoccupation with the infinity of space in the great illusionistic ceiling paintings of which the period was so fond. The breath-taking quality and apocalyptic splendor of such ceilings as that of Il Gesù in Rome result largely from the illusion of an unbroken spatial unity, beginning at an infinite celestial distance, penetrating and dissolving the very substance of the roof, and finally seeming to fuse with the actual space of the church interior. And, conversely, the observer experiences something of the thrill of release from the narrow confines of the material world, by subconsciously identifying himself with the figures who are represented as being swept upward into the celestial glory.

But it is not solely through such overtly "spacious" subjects as landscape and heavenly glory that the seventeenth century betrays its feeling for the infinite prolongation of space. One thinks of the various illusionistic devices employed by Baroque artists to dissolve the barrier imposed by the picture plane between the physical space of the observer and the perspective space of the painting: the out-thrust hands which seem to protrude beyond the surface of the canvas (as in Rembrandt's *Night Watch*), the mirrors in which are reflected persons or objects not contained in the picture and therefore to be understood as being in front of it (as in works by Velazquez and Vermeer), these and similar contrivances are aimed not merely at creating a startling, theatrical effect, but at suggesting a continuous, uninterrupted flow of space. Baroque artists were also aware that the limitless can be suggested by the indefinite, as in those Dutch interiors in which an open window or passageway leads provocatively to an undefined space beyond, or as in Caravaggio and Rembrandt, where the very obscurity of the setting seems to hint at deep recessions.

The mention of Caravaggio and Rembrandt, both of whom depend for their expressive power upon effects of luminosity, may also remind us of the extraordinary emphasis that is given to light as a symbol of the infinite in Baroque art. The representation of light may, it is true, take numerous forms. It may be the selective, polarized light of Caravaggio [Fig. 32], descending diagonally from an unspecified external source and throwing certain significant elements into vivid relief, while others are lost to sight in impenetrable shadow. Or it may be Vermeer's sunny daylight, flooding through a casement window and impartially illuminating everything within a perfectly ordered domestic interior. In either case we sense the operation of an external agency which is capable of dissolving the limited confines of the immediate pictorial space, and compels us to feel instead the existence of a boundless, all-pervading spatial expanse. A related phenomenon is the golden luminosity of Rembrandt [Fig. 34] which becomes the symbol of an inner light, seeming to penetrate into the very being of his subjects, and even serving, on occasion, as the vehicle of revelation. Here we may be reminded once more of Bernini's *Ecstasy of St. Theresa,* where the fact of the mystical experience is effectively symbolized by the light which, being admitted through a concealed window above the group, falls upon the saint as the visible sign of the revelation of divinity. Similarly, in those illusionistic ceilings to which we have already referred, the infinity of celestial space is frequently represented in symbolic fashion by a radiant burst of light.

Landscape-painters likewise made use, consciously or unconsciously, of effects of light. It is surely no accident that in many Baroque landscapes the point of maximum depth coincides with the area of greatest brilliance, the glow on the horizon suggesting the endlessness of space. The poignancy of Claude's landscapes owes much to the effect of shimmering sunset which, even while it beckons across the intervening expanse, seems at the same time by its very evanescence to signify transience and eclipse.

Closely allied to the Baroque exploitation of space and light as symbols of infinity is the constant preoccupation with time. This concern, it is hardly necessary to say, is usually expressed in allegorical terms. The theme of Truth revealed by Time, for example, engaged the attentions of Rubens, Poussin and Bernini. Very early in the century we encounter Guido Reni's *Aurora:* the goddess of the dawn heralding the approach of Apollo as he pursues his sunny course through the skies. To penetrate beneath the graceful mythological guise in which the scene is clothed is to feel something of the fascination with the recurring cycle of day and night—the endless revolutions of time. A similar subject by Guercino is made more vivid by its startling illusionism: the figures are seen from below, projected against the vault of heaven, so that to the endlessness of time there is added the infinity of space. In other Baroque artists, notably Salvator Rosa and Jakob van Ruysdael, the obsession with time is reflected in the use of ruins as a symbol of the eternal power of nature and the transience of man and his works. But for the deepest expression of the Baroque concept of time we must look, as Professor Panofsky has observed, to the paintings of Nicolas Poussin. With this master, whom some have sought to characterize as being utterly at odds with the aims and content of the Baroque, time is raised to the stature of a cosmic force, a force that is at once destructive and creative. This conception, which touches upon the very cycle of existence, is expressed not only through iconographical means, but also through the measured, rhythmic movement that animates and gives meaning to his compositions.

These are some of the principal qualities which, as I believe, go to make up the distinctive content of Baroque art. Others might be added; certainly the list is not intended to be final and complete. Moreover, I have necessarily avoided such matters as the lingering vestiges of Mannerism which here and there complicate our understanding of the early Baroque; and I have likewise made no mention of the process of evolution within the Baroque as a whole. But enough has perhaps been said to show why, for most art historians, the word "Baroque" conveys the idea of a unified outlook which is discernible in the artistic products of the seventeenth century.

11. REMBRANDT IN HIS CENTURY

Jakob Rosenberg

INTRODUCTION

Although this selection is primarily concerned with defining Rembrandt's relationship to his times, the spiritual temper and human content of Rembrandt's art are eloquently joined as the writer describes the subjects of Rembrandt's paintings as "humble human beings, bearing the stamp of suffering or old age, but inwardly receptive and therefore open to divine mercy."

Useful beyond its fine assessment of Rembrandt's reputation in his own country, the selection develops a comprehensive view of painting in the Baroque age and evokes, through its references to the relevant literature and to such seventeenth-century figures as Milton and Pascal, the culture in which the art evolved.

The literature on Rembrandt is extensive. For a general view of the period there is Jakob Rosenberg, Seymour Slive, and E. H. Ter Kuile, *Dutch Art and Architecture, 1600 to 1800* (1966). Seymour Slive, *Rembrandt and his Critics: 1630–1730* (1953) is valuable for its treatment of the contemporary and near-contemporary estimate of his work; and C. White, *Rembrandt and his World* (1964) deals with the artist's friends and patrons. Jakob Rosenberg, *Rembrandt,* 2 Vols. (1948), revised in a one-volume edition in 1964, is the standard monograph in English.

For the various aspects of his work, there are a vast number of publications, among which are the following selected titles: Abraham Bredius, *The Paintings of Rembrandt* (1942); Otto Benesch, *The Drawings of Rembrandt,* 6 Vols. (1954–57); Seymour Slive, *Drawings of Rembrandt, With a Selection of Drawings by his Pupils and Followers,* 2 Vols. (1965); Ludwig

Münz, *The Etchings of Rembrandt,* 2 Vols. (1952); G. Biörklund and O. H. Barnard, *Rembrandt's Etchings True and False* (1955); K. G. Boon, *Rembrandt: The Complete Etchings* (1963); Sir Kenneth Clark, *Rembrandt and the Italian Renaissance* (1966); W. R. Valentiner, *Rembrandt and Spinoza* (1957); Wolfgang Stechow, "Rembrandt and Titian," *Art Quarterly,* V (1942); Jakob Rosenberg, "Rembrandt and Mantegna," *Art Quarterly,* XIX (1956); Fritz Saxl, "Rembrandt and Classical Antiquity," *Lectures* (1957); W. S. Heckscher, *Rembrandt's Anatomy of Dr. Nicolaas Tulp: An Iconological Study* (1958); Otto Benesch, "Worldly and Religious Portraits in Rembrandt's Late Work," *Art Quarterly,* XIX (1956); Julius Held, "Rembrandt's Polish Rider," *The Art Bulletin,* XXVI (1944); H. M. Rotermund, "The Motif of Radiance in Rembrandt's Biblical Drawings," *Journal of Warburg and Courtauld Institutes,* XV (1952); and Jakob Rosenberg, "Rembrandt's Technical Means and Their Stylistic Significance," *Technical Studies in the Field of the Fine Arts,* VIII (1940).

The following selection is reprinted from Jakob Rosenberg, *Rembrandt: Life and Work,* Second edition, 1964, published by Phaidon Press Ltd., London, distributed in the U.S.A. by Frederick A. Praeger Inc., New York.

In attempting to understand Rembrandt's significance within his century we must extend our perspective beyond the frontiers of Holland and first find his position within the broad category of Baroque painting.[1] One of the signs of Rembrandt's greatness is the paradoxical fact that his art, while highly individual, repeatedly shows a close affinity to the international trends. It is easy to imagine some of Rembrandt's large-scale creations, such as the *Danaë*, the *Blinding of Samson*, or the *Night Watch*—even such late paintings as the *Conspiracy of Julius Civilis* [Fig. 34]—figuring prominently in a representative exhibition of Baroque art which includes works by Caravaggio and Rubens, Van Dyck and Bernini, Poussin and Velazquez. This would hardly be possible, to the same degree, with any of the other Dutch masters. None of Holland's artists approached so many sides of Baroque art, its imaginative power as well as its strong illusionism, its religious fervor as well as its pictorial breadth and splendor.[2] The majority of the Dutch painters fall into the category of "Little Masters"—a type which grew out of certain national peculiarities and has no close parallel in other countries.

The development of Baroque painting may be traced according to generations, and its leading international representatives during the course of the century were Caravaggio (at the side of the Carracci), Rubens, and Poussin. This means that Italy's initial leadership in painting did not last throughout the century, but was succeeded by that of Flanders and France. However, both Rubens and Poussin still received decisive impulses from Italian sources. We may call the three successive phases which these masters represent the Early Baroque, the High Baroque, and the Classicistic phase of the Baroque. A Late Baroque phase follows, in which the Louis XIV style makes itself felt, with the decorative luster of French courtly taste. We have seen how Rembrandt responded to the main phases of this international development and how he adapted each one to his own ends. As for Caravaggio's influence, Rembrandt's grasp of the chiaroscuro device as a principal means

34. Rembrandt, *Conspiracy of Julius Civilis: The Oath, c.* 1661, Oil on Canvas, $77\frac{3}{16}''$ by $121\frac{5}{8}''$ (Nationalmuseum, Stockholm)

of pictorial expression became a most decisive feature of his art from the very beginning. From Rubens he derived inspiration to treat dramatic themes on a large scale, full of High Baroque vigor and movement—this at least temporarily during the thirties.[3] There followed, in the forties and fifties, Rembrandt's contact with the international trend of Classicism best represented by Poussin, which led the artist to greater simplicity, breadth, and solemnity, and to more tectonic and monumental compositions. Finally, at the end of Rembrandt's career, even a touch of the Louis XIV style may be detected in the coloristic brilliance and the allegorical flavor of such works as the *Jewish Bride* in the Rijksmuseum or the *Family Portrait* in Brunswick.

While Rembrandt thus never lost contact with the broader trends of his period, it is always the powerful individual character of his art that outweighs its international aspects. Therefore, in the previous chapters, the distinctive, personal features have been stressed, rather than those which Rembrandt shared with his contemporaries. And these personal features, as we have observed, underwent certain changes from the first to the second half of Rembrandt's life. It was only later in his development that he departed more radically from the ideals of his time, and then only that his personality manifested its ultimate depth.

If we try to define some of the outstanding characteristics which distinguish Rembrandt from his contemporaries, we think perhaps first of his remarkable independence and his unusual urge to follow his own impulse in the choice of subject matter as well as in interpretation and treatment. Rembrandt was in this respect truly "modern"—perhaps the first modern artist of this kind in history.[4] But Rembrandt's forceful individualism never took a completely arbitrary course; it maintained a firm foundation of universal significance. His spiritual tendency embraced all his subjects—portraiture, landscape, and Biblical painting alike—and since it was linked with an extraordinary human intimacy and empathy, Rembrandt's art comes closer to us than that of the international Baroque, with its more ostentatious character. It is true that the curious blend of the romantic with the realistic which often marks Rembrandt's work is a feature not uncommon in his time. But both these trends, with Rembrandt, were subject to his deep spiritual penetration and thus were relieved of undue theatricality or obviousness. As for his very spontaneous and highly personal technique, this never became an end in itself, but always served the expression of profound human content.

It would be interesting to know how far Rembrandt himself was conscious of his distinctive features, or what theory or opinions he might have formulated to express his own point of view, either in giving instruction to his pupils or in conversations with patrons, fellow artists, and others. Unfortunately we do not have in Rembrandt's case as revealing documents at our disposal as we do for Bernini,[5] Poussin,[6] or Rubens.[7] But there are a few records which, though meager, are not without interest. These records show unmistakably that Rembrandt was opposed to the kind of theory which prevailed in the seventeenth century, particularly the latter half. Joachim von Sandrart complained (as others did also) that Rembrandt "did not hesitate to oppose and contradict our rules of art, such as anatomy and the proportions of the human body, perspective and the usefulness of Classical statues, Raphael's drawings and judicious pictorial disposition, and the academies which are so essential to our professions." And he added, significantly, that Rembrandt, "in doing so, alleged that one should be guided only by nature and by no other rules."[8]

This principle of "nature as the only guide" was obviously a basic point in Rembrandt's aesthetics, and by the term "nature" he must have meant the totality of life as it appeared and appealed to him. (This same point had been the basic principle for Caravaggio, the greatest independent of the beginning of the century, in his defence against academic rules.)

Rembrandt seems to have demanded in addition, from his pupils, a love of nature. We derive this assumption from a conversation among three of Rembrandt's pupils, Carel Fabritius, Abraham Furnerius, and Samuel van Hoogstraten, reported by the last-named in his *Inleyding tot de Hooghe Schoole der Schilder Konst.*[9] Here we are told that the talent of a young artist depends not only upon his love of art but also upon his "being in love with the task of representing the charms of nature."[10] This emphasis upon an emotional approach, rather than a rational and aesthetic one such as contemporary art theories demanded, seems truly Rembrandtesque, if we extend the meaning of the term "nature," as before, to the totality of life.

From the same conversation we learn that "knowledge of the story" is characteristic of good historical painting. This, to be sure, was generally accepted, and no invention of Rembrandt's, but it sounds like a principle that he might have passed on to his pupils. His many religious subjects always show an intimate familiarity with the Biblical text as a basis for his profound interpretation.[11]

A final point in this recorded disputation among Rembrandt's pupils, is the question as to what is the first rule in good composition, and Carel Fabritius answers: "to select and to organize the finest things in nature" (*de edelste natuerlijkheden*). In both respects, selection as well as organization, Rembrandt's work always excelled. We cannot be so sure, however, that the term *edelste* was precisely the word used by Rembrandt. It has a Classicistic connotation which Hoogstraten may have introduced in recording this conversation more than thirty years after his apprenticeship with Rembrandt, when he himself had become thoroughly imbued with the current Classicistic aesthetics. He is probably again thinking of Rembrandt in another passage when he states that a good master ought to "achieve unity in his composition," and subordinate the details to the whole. The passage goes on to mention the *Night Watch*, saying, "Rembrandt, in his painting at the Doelen in Amsterdam, has brought this out very well, but many feel that he has gone too far."[12]

35. Pupil of Rembrandt, Constantyn à Renesse (?), *The Annunciation,* With Alterations by Rembrandt (Kupferstichkabinett, Berlin)

A similar point is stressed by as authentic and direct a source as Sandrart, when he refers to Rembrandt's explicit demand for "universal harmony" in his pictorial organization. Sandrart says that Rembrandt required of the dark accents, which partly obscured his outlines, "nothing but the keeping together of the universal harmony." And he adds, "As regards this latter, he [Rembrandt] was excellent and knew not only how to depict the simplicity of nature accurately but also how to adorn it with natural vigor and powerful emphasis."[13]

As for Rembrandt's method of teaching, we learn, from a number of drawings by his pupils, like the ones by Constantyn à Renesse reproduced here (Fig. 35), that the master often corrected their work by bringing in stronger accents, heightening the articulation as well as the coherence of their compositions—features which are in accord with the statements quoted above.[14]

Finally, there is evidence that Rembrandt demanded absolute independence for his artistic work, presumably for the whole process of creation from the choice of subject matter down to the finishing touches. When he was criticized for the bold and highly personal character of his technique, or his work was mistakenly considered careless or unfinished, he justified himself, according to Houbraken, by saying, "A picture is completed when the master has achieved his intention by it."[15]

These scattered contemporary records about Rembrandt's theoretical remarks do not, by any means, establish a full-fledged theory, but they show that he laid down certain basic points for himself and his pupils. These points reflect primarily the artist's defensive attitude against the current theories of academic Classicism, as well as his strong desire to express himself fully and freely. But there is no insistence, in these records, upon a spiritual approach, so significant in Rembrandt's mature work, nor is there any demand for a spontaneous and personal form of artistic expression. These features were too much a part of his genius, too dependent upon his extraordinary sensibilities and creative powers to be transmitted to others by theories, or compressed into formulas.

In trying to reconstruct the judgement of his contemporaries on Rembrandt's art and personality, we are obliged to rely largely upon late seventeenth-century sources. These records reflect the decline of Rembrandt's reputation after an initial period of extreme popularity which lasted until the forties.[16] After the publication of van Mander's *Schilderboek* in Alkmaar in 1604, art criticism in Holland remained rather inactive until the later years of the century, when the theories of Classicism began to overspread the Continent. By that time the Dutch, German, French, and Italian critics were expressing their opinions on Rembrandt's art in a fairly elaborate and professional form. Their source material was still authentic. Some of the writers, such as Sandrart, Hoogstraten, and de Lairesse, had known Rembrandt personally; others, like Baldinucci and Houbraken, had received direct information from Rembrandt's pupils, or, like Roger de Piles, had lived in Holland at a time when memories of the artist were still fresh. One feels something of a common judgment running through all their accounts, which vary only slightly in appreciation and criticism of Rembrandt's art. His extreme deviations from the standards of Classicism seem to have caused resentment, although his formidable genius commanded considerable respect.[17] Thus a curious mixture of admiration and sharp criticism resulted. We have seen this typical reaction in Sandrart's biography of Rembrandt. It is not very different with the others. The artist's extraordinary native gifts were admitted—his keen observation, his pictorial and coloristic power, the variety and vividness of expression in his figures, and last, but by no means least, his genius in graphic art. But equally strong was the censure for his outright "naturalism," which did not shrink from ugly and vulgar types, from low-life motifs introduced even into the lofty realm of historical painting.[18] The rarity of Classical subjects in Rembrandt's work was also criticized, and his neglect of clear draftsmanship, which was thought to necessitate complete outlining. There was strong objection to the excessive darkness in his pictures. On the whole, the adverse criticism was directed at Rembrandt's violations of the Classic ideals of linear and plastic clarity, of formal perfection and beauty, and nobility of taste. It is particularly interesting and revealing to realize how helpless Rembrandt's contemporaries were before the phenomenon of his introvert tendency—how they blamed him for his slow production and apparent indecision. Equally incomprehensible to them was Rembrandt's highly personal technique in his paintings, misinterpreted as unfinished and resulting from willfulness and carelessness on his part. His drawings and etchings were to a certain degree exempted from this criticism, as we see from the appreciative remarks of Houbraken and others.[19]

What were the reasons that Rembrandt, from his early maturity, was so seriously misunderstood in his own century? Why did his contemporaries deplore his rebellious independence, which some believed was bound to lead to disaster?[20] Was this artist really such a lawbreaker, whose "naturalism" was vulgar and indiscriminate, whose forceful and spontaneous individualism was irreconcilable with a spiritual discipline expressing an ideal of universal significance? Even in raising these questions we feel their absurdity. But seventeenth-century criticism was unable to furnish satisfactory answers, since a proper perspective on Rembrandt's art was barred by the prevailing Classicistic views. The artist himself, with the exception of the few defensive formulas just mentioned, was averse to any more elaborate theorizing, which would have explained the very different spiritual basis of his art and shown the consistency of his attitude. This aversion to theorizing Rembrandt shared with the Dutch painters of his time. To all these artists nature was more important than rules, and none of them—Frans Hals, Vermeer, Ruisdael, Cuyp, nor Pieter de Hooch—have left any trace of a theoretical basis for their art. Neither do we find an adequate critical appreciation of their work in their own day. One may argue that their purely visual approach to nature was a quality peculiar to Dutch painting, and as such appreciated by their countrymen without the need of literary criticism. Huizinga points out in his fine study of Holland's seventeenth-century culture[21] that the Dutch were comparatively inarticulate in their literary expression, while their visual perception and pictorial gift were on an extremely high level. In any case, the situation was such that Holland's writers and critics on art submitted readily to the rules of Classicistic aesthetics as soon as these rules had become firmly established in Italy and France and began to sweep the Continent.

An understanding interpreter of the mature art of Rembrandt in his own day would have faced the difficult task of proving that here also a philosophy was implied—one which could compete with that of Classicism but called for a very different artistic form. This philosophy put truth before beauty. But it was not only the obvious, visual truth of the physical world, but also, penetrating and conditioning it, the spiritual truth which had its roots in the Bible. Rembrandt dealt with man and nature. Both, in his conception, remain dependent upon the Supreme Force that brought them into being. Hence, even his landscapes are not self-sufficient pieces of nature separated from their source and reposing in their own beauty, as, for example, the classic *View of Delft* by Jan Vermeer. They are tied up with the creative process of all earthly life and subject to dynamic changes. There is no such thing, for him, as *nature morte.* Dead peacocks are combined in his still-life paintings with living persons. Rembrandt is unwilling to cut off anything from the continuous stream of creation—even a carcass, as we have seen in his *Slaughtered Ox.* In his figure subjects there is never a staged arrangement, of static finality, such as Poussin offers with great dignity and beauty. Rembrandt's people, wrapped in their own thoughts, are in communication, not with the outside world, like those of Rubens, Van Dyck, or Frans Hals, but with something within themselves that leads, at the same time, beyond themselves. Therefore, an introvert attitude, with Rembrandt, means the search for the spiritual force in man that conditions his life, its origin as well as its course. Man, so to speak, contemplates his state of dependence and accepts it in humility. Nature also is in this same state of dependence, but without knowing it. This puts man in a higher position, and makes him the most worthy subject for the painter. Rembrandt agrees here with Pascal's "toute notre dignité consiste en la pensée."

Since for Rembrandt the essence of truth about man and nature lies in the ultimate relationship of everything created to the Creator, he accepts all things, beautiful or not; their mere existence makes them worthwhile, as issuing from God. Forms, in his compositions, are not allowed to become too definite or to have any finality, since this would break their contact with the life process. If Rembrandt's chiaroscuro has any deeper purpose, it is this: to suggest, to keep alive these mysterious relationships, so true yet so impenetrable for the purely rational approach, so strongly felt by the artist's intuitive and religious mind, yet closed to the view of the aesthete and the Classicist who insist upon beauty and a fully controlled order. While Baroque "naturalism" had nothing to oppose to the Classical ideal save the imitation of nature, Rembrandt's art offered an interpretation of life and nature based upon religious concepts. In his art the Classic and the Biblical worlds, in spite of a certain interpenetration, were no longer indiscriminately mixed, but the former became clearly subordinated to the latter. Thus, one of the oldest problems of Christian civilization was recognized again as a fundamental issue and answered with a new consistency and in a new form.

Small wonder that the consequences for Rembrandt's art were far-reaching. It was not only that he selected subjects of little interest to the Classicists, if not excluded by them: namely, old, sick, or destitute people. In these subjects he discovered the spiritual substance for which the Bible cared most: the human soul in true humility or in sorest need of compassion and salvation. When, on the other hand, Rembrandt did deal with Classical subjects, they were transplanted into a Christian world. His small scene of *Philemon and Baucis* (Br. 481), in the National Gallery in Washington, is bathed in a transcendent atmosphere not unlike that of a *Supper at Emmaus*.[22] His Homer, Aristotle, and Lucretia do not radiate the heroism and self-reliance, the grandeur and beauty, which the Classic concept called for and Baroque naturalism had modified but not really transformed. In Rembrandt's hands the proud figures of the ancient world became humble human beings, bearing the stamp of suffering or old age but inwardly receptive and therefore open to divine mercy.

Just as Rembrandt's contemporaries did not fully comprehend the spiritual attitude implied in his art, they also failed to see the clear interdependence between his ideas and the form he chose for expressing them. Rembrandt was by no means totally opposed to Classic art. We know from his inventory that he owned examples of ancient sculpture and that he admired the art of the great Renaissance masters. He derived motifs from Mantegna, Leonardo, Raphael, Dürer, and Lucas van Leyden. The Venetians exerted a considerable influence upon his style.[23] We have seen that for his own ends Rembrandt employed certain characteristic features of Renaissance art, such as simplicity, breadth, and solemnity, as well as its tectonic and monumental qualities. But other features fundamental to the Classic conception were unacceptable to him.

"Clarity," to the Classicist, meant a complete plastic representation of tangible objects, with no break in their contours, and set within a rationally constructed space. Rembrandt had little use for this kind of clarity, which brought the visible world under a firm control, but excluded any uncertainty and mystery—those intangible elements that were vital to his viewpoint. Rembrandt used both light and shadow in a far more subjective fashion, not primarily to define form, but for their suggestive and evocative qualities. Outlines are broken; they are only partly visible, partly obscured. Space takes on a less geometric character, with less tangible limitations, but suggesting an imperceptible transition from the finite to the infinite. Along with light and dark, color too gains a new symbolical significance, and a vibrating atmosphere pervades the whole picture, heightening the interdependence of all parts and preventing forms and surfaces from becoming isolated or overdistinct.

Rembrandt's concept of "unity" also differed from that of the Classicists. His was a more marked subordination of the individual forms and figures to the comprehensive elements of space, atmosphere, and chiaroscuro, and this symbolized a religious rather than a rational attitude. It replaced the anthropocentric point of view by the concept of man's submission to the spiritual forces of the universe. Compositional "unity," as Rembrandt understood it, was therefore basically different from the concept of unity of a Poussin who demanded for each part its own separate and complete entity. It is true that in these respects (concept of clarity, concept of unity, departure from the anthropocentric viewpoint) Rembrandt was a

Baroque master,[24] but he went beyond the typical Baroque attitude in deepening the function and the significance of these features. His pupils were able to follow him only to a certain degree. Their formal powers were limited and none of them could approach him in the expression of content.

But Rembrandt was not alone in his time in adopting a spiritual attitude that harked back to fundamental Biblical concepts. Two other independents and, like Rembrandt, two of the greatest men of the century, took this course in opposition to the dominating rational and humanistic trend: Milton and Pascal. Science as an unlimited field for man's searching mind is repudiated in *Paradise Lost,* when the Archangel Raphael and Adam discuss astronomical problems. "Adam is exhorted to search rather things more worthy of knowledge," as the argument of Book VIII puts it.

> Whether the Sun predominant in Heav'n
> Rise on the Earth, or Earth rise on the Sun . . .
> Solicit not thy thoughts with matters hid,
> Leave them to God alone.

In *Paradise Regained*[25] the aged and lonely Milton, with all his background of Classical studies, proceeded to characterize Classic thought and culture as the most subtle weapon of Satan, the last resort, as it were, in Satan's attempts to corrupt the purity of Christ's ideas.

And out of his profound faith Blaise Pascal, the great mathematician and thinker, who had absorbed the wisdom of Classic philosophy, reached a similar stand. In resisting the infringement of reason upon faith, Pascal put the realm of the heart into its own place at the side of the realm of the mind. "Le coeur a ses raisons que la raison ne connaît point: on le sait en mille choses." "C'est le coeur qui sent Dieu, et non la raison." These and many more passages in Pascal's *Pensées* strike a note congenial to Rembrandt, although most of official France, and certainly Pascal's compatriot Poussin, took an opposite attitude.

> S'il n'y avait point d'obscurité, l'homme ne sentirait point sa corruption; s'il n'y avait point de lumière, l'homme n'espérerait point de remède. Ainsi, il est non seulement juste, mais utile pour nous, que Dieu soit caché en partie, et découvert en partie, puisqu'il est également dangereux à l'homme de connaître Dieu sans connaître sa misère, et de connaître sa misère sans connaître Dieu.[26]

With this comparison of Rembrandt, Milton, and Pascal we have touched only briefly upon the significant position of three great minds in this controversial century. Each of these men became more or less isolated in his own country, and what they stood for was swept aside by the leading intellectual and artistic trends which lined up with the newly consolidated forces of society, church, and state. Rembrandt's art left hardly a trace in Holland for generations to follow.

In trying to define more closely this much disputed place of Rembrandt in seventeenth-century Holland, it will be of particular interest to listen first to the opinions of two distinguished Dutch scholars: Frederik Schmidt-Degener, the art historian, and Johan Huizinga, the historian of culture. In a brilliant essay on "Rembrandt and Vondel"[27] Schmidt-Degener contrasts the painter and the poet. Vondel is to him the typical representative of the Dutch Baroque which had its roots in Flanders rather than Holland and is characterized by a rhetorical and pictorial splendor. Official Holland, this author holds, always took the side of Flemish pompousness instead of recognizing the true representatives of Dutch character who were modest and reserved and tended to withdraw into themselves.[28] Schmidt-Degener's essay concludes with the statement that the mature Rembrandt not only resisted Baroque tendencies but was on the point of rescuing the great tradition of the Italian Cinquecento from the Baroque trend; that he therefore represents the last of the great Renaissance artists of universal significance, and that it was his official rejection as a monumental painter for the Town Hall of Amsterdam which robbed him of the opportunity to show himself as Raphael's true successor.[29]

Huizinga, in his penetrating study of the Dutch culture of the seventeenth century,[30] sees the best qualities of Dutch art in its unpretentious and sincere rendering of reality, but stresses its limitations both in style and form. According to him Rembrandt was a Romanticist who tried to depict an imaginary world in order to escape the narrowness of his actual surroundings. Thus the artist strove to rival the grandeur of the Baroque but was doomed to fail because of the general weakness of Dutch art on the formal side (*Schwäche des Formgefühls*). Only on a small scale, in graphic art, does he consider that Rembrandt was really successful.

It is clearly evident that these two authors contradict each other. Where, then, lies the truth? Huizinga we believe goes too far in assuming a continuous Baroque tendency as the leading one in Rembrandt's art. We have seen that his work shows a decided change from a Baroque phase in the early part of his career to a style that was closer to classic art yet remained markedly divergent from it. While agreeing with Huizinga that Rembrandt strove to represent an imaginary world since the visual reality around him did not satisfy his creative fancy, we know that he turned from this to a deeper perception of man's inner life, in which the romantic aspect became subordinated to a spiritual tendency.

On the other hand, we feel that Schmidt-Degener, who is well aware of Rembrandt's development in all its phases and has high praise for his artistic achievement, relates the artist's mature style too closely to the Renaissance tradition. He could have reached this conclusion only by overlooking the fundamental difference which exists between Rembrandt's spiritual world and the Classic one. It was this difference, as we have tried to show, which necessitated a very different artistic form, and which conditioned the unclassical features in Rembrandt's late work. Schmidt-Degener may not have admitted this difference as a fundamental one. In fact, he interprets Rembrandt's religious art in the tradition of nineteenth-century humanitarianism,[31] and sees the artist, accordingly, as a forerunner of Jean-Jacques Rousseau and Ernest Renan. One might argue that Rembrandt's art was broad enough to allow this interpretation, and that, by his strong humanization of the Biblical world, the great Dutch master paved the way for the purely humanitarian concept of later centuries. But such an assumption draws Rembrandt too far from the center of his spiritual world and thus means a distortion of historical reality. It is true that Rembrandt was unique in his integration of the actual with the Biblical world, but with him this never deprived the Bible of its transcendental content.

We have seen that Rembrandt shared many features with his own countrymen. The Dutch painters in general showed a considerable independence of Classicism up to the beginning of the Louis XIV period. Like Rembrandt, they accepted nature, rather than academic rules, as their principal guide. Pictorial intimacy and an individual touch characterized their art as well as his. But we know that the typical Dutch painters' notion of nature was limited to the external aspect of life. We have also referred to another limitation which set them apart from Rembrandt: the common Dutch practice of concentrating upon a single category, whether portraiture or genre, landscape, still life, or architectural scenes—not to mention even narrower subdivisions. To Rembrandt this kind of specialization was unthinkable. He brought to each category he dealt with the broader and deeper spirit which characterized his entire outlook, and which raised his art far above a national level.

NOTES

[1] We use the term "Baroque" here in its broadest sense, meaning the whole of seventeenth-century art, not excluding the Classicistic trends within that period. This is possible, since Baroque features are found throughout the century, though in varying degree. In other parts of the book, however, we use "Baroque" in the more specific sense, that is, Baroque as opposed to Classicism. We hope that this rather loose and flexible application of the term (somewhat common in art history) will not confuse the reader. Up to now, better words have not been found to define either the broad meaning of the term, embracing the whole century, or the more specific meaning that signifies only certain characteristic features within this period.

[2] Fromentin called Rembrandt "the least Dutch among the Dutch painters." Alois Riegl expressed the same idea somewhat differently in describing him as "the greatest Romanist among the Dutch of the seventeenth century." See Werner Weisbach, *Rembrandt* (1926), p. 595.

[3] Rembrandt's predilection for excessive Baroque ornamentation (*Ohrmuschelstil*) may also be mentioned in this connection. Carl Neumann, *Rembrandt,* II (4th ed., 1924), pp. 758 ff., devotes to this feature an interesting study.

[4] Frank J. Mather, Jr., *Western European Painting of the Renaissance* (New York, 1939), p. 475, calls Rembrandt "the first rebel genius in painting, the first painter of the modern sort."

[5] Paul Chantelou, *Journal de voyage du Cavalier Bernin en France* (Paris, 1885); Filippo Baldinucci, *Vita des Giovanni Lorenzo Bernini, mit Übersetzung und Kommentar von Alois Riegl* (Vienna, 1912).

[6] G. P. Bellori, *Vite de' pittori, scultori e architetti moderni* (Rome, 1672); André Félibien, *Entretiens sur les vies et les ouvrages des plus excellens peintres anciens et modernes* (1st ed., pt. IV, Paris, 1685); *Correspondance de Nicolas Poussin,* edited by Jouanny (Paris, 1911).

[7] *Correspondance de Rubens.* (*Codex Diplomaticus Rubenianus*), edited by C. Ruelens and Max Rooses, 6 Vols. (Antwerp, 1887–1909).

[8] C. Hofstede de Groot, *Die Urkunden über Rembrandt* (1906), p. 329 [hereinafter "Urk."]; also J. von Sandrart, *Rembrandt, Selected Paintings,* ed. Borenius, p. 21.

[9] Rotterdam, 1678 (Urk., p. 337).

[10] "Dat hy neit alleen schijne de konst te beminnen, maer dat hy in der daet, in de aerdicheden der bevallijke natuur uit te beelden, verlieft is."

[11] In 1641 Philips Angel, in a speech delivered in Leyden on St. Luke's Day (published as *Philips Angels Lof der Schilder Konst* [Leyden, 1642]), praised Rembrandt's *Marriage of Samson* because it showed intimate knowledge of the story as well as the artist's own thoughtfulness (Urk., p. 91).

[12] Urk., p. 338: "De rechte meesters brengen te weeg, dat haer geheele werk eenwezich is . . . Rembrandt heeft dit in zijn stuk op den Doele tot Amsterdam zeer wel, maer na veeler gevoelen al te veel, waergenomen."

[13] J. von Sandrart, *Rembrandt, Selected Paintings,* edited by Borenius, p. 21.

[14] See Hofstede de Groot, "Rembrandt onderwijs aan zijne leerlingen," *Bredius Feest-Bundel,* pp. 74 ff.; also G. Falck, in *Jahrbuch der preussischen Kunstsammlungen,* XLV (1924), pp. 192 ff.

[15] Arnold Houbraken, *De groote Schouburgh der nederlantsche konstschilders en schilderessen,* I (1718), p. 25.

[16] The German painter, Mathias Scheits, who had studied in Holland under Philips Wouwerman, wrote in 1679 some notes about deceased contemporary masters in his copy of van Mander's *Schilderboek.* The remark about Rembrandt contains the following passage which confirms the decline of the artist's reputation toward the end of his life: "Rembrandt . . . wass achtbaer ende groht van aensien door sein konst geworden, het welck doch in 't lest mit hem wat verminderde. . . ." (Urk., p. 348).

[17] The keen French critic, Roger de Piles, went perhaps farthest in the positive appreciation of Rembrandt's art.

[18] The term "historical" painting included Biblical subjects, and, according to the Classicists, ranked highest among the various categories of subject matter. See Félibien, *op. cit.,* and Rensselaer W. Lee, "Ut Pictura Poesis," *Art Bulletin,* XXII (1940), p. 213.

[19] Baldinucci, *op. cit.,* p. 23: "But after it had become commonly known that whoever wanted to be portrayed by him had to sit to him for some two or three months, there were few who came forward. The cause of this slowness was that, immediately after the first work had dried, he took it up again, repainting it with great and small strokes, so that at times the pigment in a given place was raised more than half the thickness of a finger. Hence it may be said of him that he always toiled without rest, painted much and completed very few pictures." Houbraken, *op. cit.,* p. 25: "But it is to be regretted that, with such a bent towards alterations or easily driven towards something else, he should have but half carried out many of his pictures, and even more of his etchings, so that only the completed ones can give us an idea of all the beauty that we would possess from his hand if he had finished everything the way he had begun it."

[20] Andries Pels, in his *Gebruik en misbruik des tooneels* (Amsterdam, 1681), devotes a long passage to Rembrandt, whom he holds up as a warning to those who tend to depart from the traditional paths of art. He ends his criticism with the following lines, lamenting the waste of Rembrandt's genius, his neglect of principles and his excessive independence:

> What a loss it was for art that such a master hand
> Did not use its native strength to better purpose.
> Who surpassed him in the matter of painting?
> But oh! the greater the talent, the more numerous the aberrations
> When it attaches itself to no principles, no rules,
> But imagines it knows everything of itself.

See Urk., p. 352. English translation, *Rembrandt, Selected Paintings,* ed. by Borenius, p. 26.

[21] Johan Huizinga, *Holländische Kultur des siebzehnten Jahrhunderts* (Jena: Diederichs, 1933), pp. 57–58.

[22] See Wolfgang Stechow's article on "The Myth of Philemon and Baucis in Art," *Journal of the Warburg Institute,* IV, 1940–2, pp. 103 ff. Emil Kieser (*op. cit.*, pp. 129 ff.), gives an account of Rembrandt's dealing with Classical motives. He also stresses the fact that Rembrandt endows his Classical subjects with a Biblical flavor.

[23] See J. L. van Rijckevorsel, *Rembrandt en de Traditie.*

[24] See Heinrich Wölfflin's *Principles of Art History* (7th ed., New York, 1932). This author uses the terms "absolute" versus "relative" clarity, and "multiplicity" versus "unity," to distinguish between the Renaissance and Baroque Styles.

[25] Book IV, particularly lines 272–365.

[26] *Oeuvres de Blaise Pascal* (Paris, 1904–14), XIII, *Pensées,* 277, 278, XIV, *Pensées,* 586. Another passage of particular interest is the following (*ibid.*, XIII, 525): "Les philosophes ne prescrivaient point des sentiments proportionnés aux deux états. Ils inspiraient des mouvements de grandeur pure, et ce n'est pas l'état de l'homme. Ils inspiraient des mouvements de bassesse pure, et ce n'est pas l'état de l'homme. Il faut des mouvements de bassesse, non de nature, mais de pénitence; non pour y demeurer, mais pour aller à la grandeur. Il faut des mouvements de grandeur, non de mérite, mais de grâce, et après avoir passé par la bassesse." See also the chapter on the Jews and the Christians beginning with the sentence, "Pour montrer que les vrais Juifs et les vrais Chrétiens n'ont qu'une même religion" (*ibid.*, XIV, 610).

[27] *De Gids,* LXXXIII (1919), pt I, p. 222. German edition: *Rembrandt und der holländische Barock* (Leipzig, 1928). See the review by Hans Jantzen in *Deutsche Literaturzeitung,* Feb. 1, 1930, pp. 226 ff.

[28] "Hollands Wessen spricht aus dem Besten, das Lukas van Leyden schuf und das hat etwas Scheues und Verschlossenes" (*Rembrandt und der holländische Barock,* p. 35).

[29] "Von Rembrandts Hand würde die Folge riesenhafter Kompositionen die Fortsetzung des siebzehnten Jahrhunderts zu Raffaels Stanzen gewesen sein. . . . Mit Rembrandt erscheint der Letzte der Renaissancisten, der Letzte der grossen universalen Meister . . . Rembrandt erweist Europa den Dienst, die Renaissance aus der Barockphase zu retten, in der sie im Begriff war zu versanden" (*ibid.*, pp. 36, 43). For a discussion of Rembrandt's relationship to Classicism see also Ludwig Münz, "Rembrandts Altersstil und die Barockklassik," *Jahrbuch der kunsthistorischen Sammlungen in Wien,* N.F., IX, 1935, pp. 183 ff.

[30] Huizinga, *op. cit.*

[31] "Niemals predigt er Religion. Seine Darstellung der heiligen Geschichten bringt einen gewissen Rationalismus" (*ibid.*, p. 45). Later, in his introduction to the catalogue of the 1935 Rembrandt exhibition (Amsterdam: Rijksmuseum, 1935), Schmidt-Degener slightly modified his point of view without any basic changes.

12. BERNINI

Rudolf Wittkower

INTRODUCTION

One of the outstanding features of Bernini's artistry, whether sculptural or architectural—or that synthesis of these which he mastered to an unusual degree—is its capacity to draw the viewer into physical as well as psychic relationship with its forms. His sculptures, in stressing—even demanding—selected viewing-stations, structure the experience of these works in such a way that even the intervening space is charged with significance. This space, like that in the concert hall or theater, is no mere quantitative element, but the resonant medium through which Bernini's conception is communicated. This orchestration of direct relationships involving the created forms, the beholder, and the ambience that holds them all is environmental in scope and synthetic in method. And nowhere is this better demonstrated than in Bernini's solution to the problem of the Piazza San Pietro and in his design of the Cornaro Chapel, which are the chief foci of the selection by Rudolf Wittkower chosen for this anthology.

In recent years there has been considerable interest in the creation of "environments" where sculptural clusterings and architectural space are joined to empathic images which are sometimes, with almost narcissistic irony, our own reflections. We have also seen how Op Art has absorbed the beholder into its formal configurations by the sheer aggressiveness of its visual magic. One does not easily escape the pull of the Op image except to yank one's eyes from its optical clamps and turn firmly away. It seems reasonable, therefore, to suggest that eyes and sensibilities engaged by these recent developments in art might discover in the grand disposition of space, mass, color, and light in Bernini's art certain affinities that overcome the barriers of time and alien taste.

The chief source for Bernini's life is Filippo Baldinucci's *Vita de Gian Lorenzo Bernini* (1682), now available in an English translation by Catherine

Enggass, with a foreword by Robert Enggass (1966). For Bernini's sculpture the best source in English is Rudolf Wittkower, *Gian Lorenzo Bernini*, 2nd ed. (1966). Among other studies by the same author are his "Works by Bernini at the Royal Academy," *Burlington Magazine*, XCIII (1951); "Bernini Studies—I: The Group of Neptune and Triton," *Burlington Magazine*, XCIV (1952); "Bernini Studies—II: The Bust of Mr. Baker," *ibid.*, XCV (1953), in two parts; "The Role of Classical Models in Bernini's and Poussin's Preparatory Work," *Studies in Western Art, Acts of the Twentieth International Congress of the History of Art*, III (1963). Other works are: A. Underwood, "Notes on Bernini's Towers for St. Peter's in Rome," *The Art Bulletin*, XXI (1939); Pamela Askew, "Relation of Bernini's Architecture to the Architecture of the High Renaissance and of Michelangelo," *Marsyas*, V (1947–49); W. S. Heckscher, "Bernini's Elephant and Obelisk," *The Art Bulletin*, XXIX (1947); Timothy Kitao, "Bernini's Church Facades: Method of Design and the *Contrapposti*," *Journal of the Society of Architectural Historians*, XXIV (1965); and J. S. Pierce, "Visual and Auditory Space in Baroque Rome," *Journal of Aesthetics and Art Criticism*, XVIII (1959).

The following selection is reprinted, by permission, from Rudolf Wittkower, *Art and Architecture in Italy: 1600–1750* (1965), published by Penguin Books Limited.

Few data are needed to outline the life's story of the greatest genius of the Italian Baroque. Bernini was born at Naples on 7 December 1598, the son of a Neapolitan mother and a Florentine father. His father Pietro was a sculptor of more than average talent and moved with his family to Rome in about 1605. Until his death seventy-five years later Gianlorenzo left the city only once for any length of time, when he followed in 1665, at the height of his reputation, Louis XIV's call to Paris. With brief interruptions his career led from success to success, and for more than fifty years, willingly or unwillingly, Roman artists had to bow to his eminence. Only Michelangelo before him was held in similar esteem by the popes, the great, and the artists of his time. Like Michelangelo he regarded sculpture as his calling and was, at the same time, architect, painter, and poet; like Michelangelo he was a born craftsman and marble was his real element; like Michelangelo he was capable of almost superhuman concentration and single-mindedness in pursuing a given task. But unlike the terrible and lonely giant of the sixteenth century, he was a man of infinite charm, a brilliant and witty talker, fond of conviviality, aristocratic in demeanor, a good husband and father, a first-rate organizer, endowed with an unparalleled talent for creating rapidly and with ease.

His father's activity in Paul V's Chapel in S. Maria Maggiore determined the beginning of his career. It was thus that the pope's and Cardinal Scipione Borghese's attention was drawn to the young prodigy and that he, a mere lad of nineteen, entered the orbit of the most lavish patron of the period. Until 1624 he remained in the service of the cardinal, creating, with brief interruptions, the statues and groups which are still in the Villa Borghese. After Urban VIII's accession to the papal throne, his preeminent position in the artistic life of Rome was secured. Soon the most important enterprises were concentrated in his hands, and from 1624 to the end of his days he was almost exclusively engaged on religious works. In February 1629, after Maderno's death, he was appointed "Archi-

36. Bernini, Baldacchino, St. Peter's, Rome, 1624–33

tect to St. Peter's" and, although his activity in that church began as early as 1624 with the commission of the Baldacchino (Fig. 36), the majority of his sculptural, decorative, and architectural contribution lay between 1630 and his death.

In the early 1620s he was one of the most sought-after portrait sculptors, but with the accretion of monumental tasks on an unprecedented scale, less and less time was left him for distractions of this kind. In the later 1620s and in the thirties he had to employ the help of assistants for such minor commissions, and from the last thirty-five years of his life hardly half a dozen portrait busts exist by his hand. The most extensive works—tombs, statues, chapels, churches, fountains, monuments, and the Square of St. Peter's—crowd into the three pontificates of Urban VIII, Innocent X, and Alexander VII. Although he was active to the very end, it was only during the last years that commissions thinned out. From all we can gather, this was due to the general dearth of artistic activity rather than to a decline of his creative capacity in old age. His work as a painter was mainly confined to the 1620s; later he hardly touched a brush and preferred using professional painters to express his ideas. Most of his important architectural designs, on the other hand, belong to the later years of his life, particularly to the period of Alexander VII's reign.

SCULPTURE WITH ONE AND MANY VIEWS

It is one of the strange and ineradicable misapprehensions, due, it seems, to Heinrich Wölfflin's magnetic influence, that Baroque sculpture presents many points of view.[1] The contrary is the case, and nobody has made this clearer than the greatest Baroque artist—Bernini himself. Many readers may, however, immediately recall the Borghese Gallery statues and groups which, standing free in the center of the rooms, invite the beholder to go round them and inspect them from every side. It is usually forgotten that their present position is of fairly recent date and that each of these works was originally placed against a wall. Right from the beginning Bernini "anchored" his statues firmly to their surroundings and with advancing years found new and characteristic devices to assure that they would be viewed from preselected points.

It is, of course, Renaissance statuary that comes to mind when we think of sculpture conceived for one main aspect. Most Renaissance figures leave not a shadow of doubt about the principal view, since by and large they are worked like reliefs with bodies and extremities extending without overlappings in an ideal forward plane. Quite different are Bernini's figures: they extend in depth and often display complex arrangements of contrasting spatial planes and movements. . . . It appears then that Bernini's statues are conceived in depth and that the sensation of their spatial organization should and will always be realized, but that they are nevertheless composed as images for a single principal viewpoint. One must even go a step further in order to get this problem into proper focus. Bernini's figures not only move freely in depth but seem to belong to the same space in which the beholder lives. Differing from Renaissance statuary, his figures need the continuum of space surrounding them and without it they would lose their *raison d'être*. Thus the *David* aims his stone at an imaginary Goliath who must be assumed to be somewhere in space near the beholder; the *Bibiana* is shown in mute communication with God the Father, who, painted on the vault above her, spreads his arms as if to receive her into the empyrean of saints; *Longinus* looks up to the heavenly light falling in from the dome of St. Peter's; *Habakkuk* points to the imaginary laborers in the field while the angel of God is about to remove him to Daniel's den across the space in which the spectator stands. The new conceptual position may now be stated more pointedly: Bernini's statues breathe, as it were, the same air as the beholder, are so "real" that they even share the space continuum with him, and yet remain picture-like works of art in a specific and limited sense; for although they stimulate the beholder to circulate, they require the correct viewpoint not only to reveal their space-absorbing and space-penetrating qualities, but also to grasp fully the meaning of the action or theme represented. To be sure, it is Bernini's persistent rendering of a transitory moment that makes the one-view aspect unavoidable: the climax of an action can be wholly revealed from one viewpoint alone.

While Bernini accepts on a new sophisticated level the Renaissance principle of sculpture with one view, he also incorporates in his work essential features of Mannerist statuary, namely complex axial relationships, broken contours, and protruding extremities. He takes advantage, in other words, of the Mannerist freedom from the limitations imposed by the stone. Many of his figures and groups consist of more than one block, his *Longinus* for instance of no less than five. Mannerist practitioners and theorists, in the first place Benvenuto Cellini, discussed whether a piece of sculpture should have one or many views. Their verdict was a foregone conclusion. Giovanni Bologna in his *Rape of the Sabines* (1579–83) showed how to translate theory into practice and gave a group of several figures an infinite number of equally valid viewpoints. The propagation of multiple viewpoints in sculpture came in the wake of a deep spiritual change, for the socially elevated sculptor of the sixteenth century, refusing to be a mere craftsman, thought in terms of small models of wax or clay. Thus he created, unimpeded by the material restrictions of the block. The Renaissance conception of sculpture as the art of working in stone ("the art of subtracting") began to be turned into the art of working in clay and wax ("modelling," which is done by adding—for Michelangelo a painterly occupation), and this sixteenth-century revolution ultimately led to the decay of sculpture in the nineteenth century. Although Bernini could not accept the many views of Mannerist statuary because they would

37. The Cornaro Chapel, Sta. Maria della Vittoria, Rome, Eighteenth Century Painting (Staatliches Museum, Schwerin)

interfere with his carefully planned subject–object (beholder–work) relationship and, moreover, would prevent the perception at a glance of one center of energy and one climax of action, he did not return to the Renaissance limitations dictated by the block-form, since he wanted to wed his statues to the surrounding space. By combining the single viewpoint of Renaissance statues with the freedom achieved by the Mannerists, Bernini laid the foundation for his new, Baroque, conception of sculpture.

Only on rare occasions did he conceive works for multiple viewpoints. This happened when the conditions under which his works were to be seen were beyond his control. Such is the case of the angels for the Ponte S. Angelo, which had to have a variety of viewpoints for the people crossing the bridge. These angels clearly present three equally favorable views—from the left, the right, and the center; but they do not offer coherent views either in pure profile or from the back, for these aspects are invisible to the passers-by.

During his middle period Bernini brought new and most important ideas to bear upon the problem of defined viewpoints. He placed the group of *St. Teresa and the Angel* in a deep niche under a protective architectural canopy (Fig. 37), and this makes it virtually impossible to see the work unless the beholder stands in the nave of the church exactly on the central axis of the Cornaro Chapel. Enshrined by the framing lines of the architecture, the group has an essentially pictorial character; one may liken it to a *tableau vivant.* The same is true of later designs whenever circumstances permitted. The Cathedra was conceived like an enormous colorful picture framed by the columns of the Baldacchino (Fig. 36). Similarly, the pictorial concepts of the *Constantine* and the *Blessed Lodovica Albertoni* are revealed only when they are looked at from inside the portico of St. Peter's and from the nave of S. Francesco a Ripa respectively. Indeed, the carefully contrived framing devices almost force upon the spectator the correct viewing position.

In spite of their *tableau vivant* character, all these works are still vigorously three-dimensional and vigorously "alive"; they are neither reliefs nor relegated to a limited space. They act on a stage of potentially unlimited extension. They still share, therefore, our space continuum, but at the same time they are far removed from us: they are strange, visionary, unapproachable—like apparitions from another world.

Bernini

COLOR AND LIGHT

It is evident that Bernini's pictorial approach to sculpture cannot be dissociated from two other aspects, color and light, which require special attention.

Polychrome marble sculpture is rather exceptional in the history of European art. The link with the uncolored marbles of ancient Rome was never entirely broken, and it is characteristic that in Florence, for instance, polychromy was almost exclusively reserved for popular works made of cheap materials. But during the late sixteenth century it became fashionable in Rome and elsewhere to combine white marble heads with colored busts, in imitation of a trend in late antique sculpture. The naturalistic element implicit in such works never had any attraction for Bernini. The use of composite or polychrome materials would have interfered with his unified conception of bust or figure. In his Diary the Sieur de Chantelou informs us that Bernini regarded it as the sculptor's most difficult task to produce the impression and effect of color by means of the white marble alone. But in a different sense polychromy was extremely important to him. He needed polychrome settings and the alliance of bronze and marble figures as much for the articulation, emphasis, and differentiation of meaning as for the unrealistic pictorial impression of his large compositions. It may be argued that he followed an established vogue.[2] To a certain extent this is true. Yet in his hands polychromy became a device of subtlety hitherto unknown.

Bernini's tomb of Urban VIII certainly follows the polychrome pattern of the older counterpart, Guglielmo della Porta's tomb of Paul III. But in Bernini's work the white and dark areas are much more carefully balanced and communicate a distinct meaning. The whole central portion is of dark, partly gilded bronze: the sarcophagus, the life-like figure of Death, and the papal statue, i.e. all the parts directly concerned with the deceased. Unlike these with their magic color and light effects, the white marble allegories of Charity and Justice have manifestly a this-worldly quality. It is these figures with their human reactions and their sensual and appealing surface texture that form a transition between the beholder and the papal statue, which by virtue of its somber color alone seems far removed from our sphere of life.

More complex are the color relationships in Bernini's later work. The Cornaro Chapel is, of course, the most perfect example. In the lowest, the human zone, the beholder is faced with a color harmony of warm and glowing tones in red, green, and yellow. St Teresa's vision, the focal point of the whole composition, is dramatically accentuated by the contrast between the dark framing columns and the highly polished whiteness of the group. Other stimuli are brought into play to emphasize the unusual character of the event which shows a seraph piercing her heart with the fiery arrow of divine love, symbol of the saint's mystical union with Christ. The vision takes place in an imaginary realm on a large cloud, magically suspended in mid-air before an iridescent alabaster background. Moreover, concealed and directed light is used in support of the dramatic climax to which the beholder becomes a witness. The light falls through a window of yellow glass hidden behind the pediment and is materialized, as it were, in the golden rays encompassing the group.[3]

It is often observed that Bernini drew here on his experience as stage designer. Although this is probably correct, it distracts from the real problem. For this art is no less and no more "theatrical" than a Late Gothic altarpiece repeating a scene from a mystery play, frozen into permanence. Bernini's approach to the problem of light is in a clearly defined pictorial tradition of which the examples in Baroque painting are legion. The directed heavenly light, as used by Bernini, sanctifies the objects and persons struck by it and singles them out as recipients of divine Grace. The golden rays along which the light seems to travel have yet another meaning. By contrast to the calm, diffused light of the Renaissance, this directed light seems fleeting, transient, impermanent. Impermanence is its very essence. Directed light, therefore, supports the beholder's sensation of the transience of the scene represented: we realize that the moment of divine "illumination" passes as it comes. With his directed light Bernini had found a way of bringing home to the faithful an intensified experience of the supranatural.

No sculptor before Bernini had attempted to use real light in this way. Here in the ambient air of a chapel he did what painters tried to do in their pictures. If it is accepted that he translated back into the three dimensions of real life the illusion of reality rendered by painters in two dimensions, an important insight into the specific character of his pictorial approach to sculpture has been won. His love for chromatic settings now becomes fully intelligible. A work like the Cornaro Chapel was conceived in terms of an enormous picture.

This is true of the chapel as a whole. Higher up the color scheme lightens and on the vaulting the painted sky opens. Angels have pushed aside the clouds so that the heavenly light issuing from the Holy Dove can reach the zone in which the mortals live. The figure of the seraph, brother of the angels painted in the clouds, has descended on the beams of light.

Along the side walls of the chapel, above the doors, appear the members of the Cornaro family kneeling behind prie-dieus and discussing the miracle that takes place on the altar. They live in an illusionist architecture which looks like an extension of the space in which the beholder moves.

In spite of the pictorial character of the design as a whole, Bernini differentiated here as in other cases between various degrees of reality. The members of the Cornaro family seem to be alive like ourselves. They belong to our space and our world. The supranatural event of Teresa's vision is raised to a sphere of its own, removed from that of the beholder mainly by virtue of the isolating canopy and the heavenly light.[4] Finally, much less tangible is the unfathomable infinity of the luminous empyrean. The beholder is drawn into this web of relationships and becomes a witness to the mysterious hierarchy ascending from man to saint and Godhead. . . .

With his revolutionary approach to color and light, Bernini opened a development of immeasurable consequences. It is not sufficiently realized that the pictorial concepts of the mature Bernini furnish the basis not only for many later Roman and North Italian works, but above all for the Austrian and German Baroque. Even the color and light orgies of the Asam brothers add nothing essentially new to the repertory created by Bernini.

THE PIAZZA OF ST. PETER'S

While he was in Paris, Bernini's greatest work, the Square of St. Peter's, was still rising. But by that time all the hurdles had been taken and, moreover, Bernini had a reliable studio with a long and firmly established tradition to look after his interests. His "office" supplied, of course, no more than physical help towards the accom-

38. Aerial View, St. Peter's, Rome

plishment of one of the most complex enterprises in the history of Italian architecture.[5] Bernini alone was responsible for this work which has always been universally admired, he alone had the genius and resourcefulness to find a way through a tangle of topographical and liturgical problems, and only his supreme authority in artistic matters backed by the unfailing support of Pope Alexander VII could overcome intrigues and envious opposition[6] and bring this task to a successful conclusion (Fig. 38). Among a vast number of issues to be considered, particular importance was attached to two ritual ones right from the start. At Easter and on a few other occasions the pope blesses the people of Rome from the Benediction Loggia above the central entrance to the church. It is a blessing symbolically extended to the whole world: it is given *urbi et orbi*. The piazza, therefore, had not only to hold the maximum number of people, while the Loggia had to be visible to as many as possible, but the form of the square itself had to suggest the all-embracing character of the function. Another ceremony to be taken into account was the papal blessing given to pilgrims from a window of the private papal apartment situated in Domenico Fontana's palace on the north side of the piazza. Other hardly less vital considerations pertained to the papal palace. Its old entrance in the northwest corner of the piazza could not be shifted and yet it had to be integrated into the architecture of the whole.[7] The basilica itself required an approach on the grandest scale in keeping with its prominence among the churches of the Catholic world. In addition, covered passageways of some kind were needed for processions and in particular for the solemn ceremonies on the day of Corpus Domini; they were also necessary as protection against sun and rain, for pedestrians as well as for coaches.

Bernini began in the summer of 1656 with the design of a trapezoid piazza enclosed by the traditional type of palace fronts over round-headed arcades. This scheme was soon abandoned for a variety of reasons, not the least because it was of paramount importance to achieve greatest monumentality with as little height as possible. A palazzo front with arcades would have been higher than the present colonnades without attaining equal grandeur. So by March 1657 the first project was superseded by one with arcades of free-standing columns forming a large oval piazza; soon after, in the summer of the same year, Bernini replaced the arcades by colonnades of free-standing columns with a straight entablature above the columns. Only such a colonnade was devoid of any associations with palace fronts and therefore complied with the ceremonial character of the square more fully than an arcaded scheme with its reminiscences of domestic architecture. On ritualistic as well as artistic grounds the enclosure of the piazza had to be kept as low as possible. A high enclosure would have interfered with the visibility of the papal blessing given from the palace window. Moreover, a comparatively low one was also needed in order to "correct" the unsatisfactory impression made by the proportions of the façade of St. Peter's.

This requires a word of explanation. The substructures of Maderno's towers, standing without the intended superstructures, look now as if they were parts of the façade, and this accounts for its excessive length. A number of attempts were made in the post-Maderno period to remedy this fault,[8] before Urban VIII took the fateful decision in 1636 of accepting Bernini's grand design of high towers of three tiers.[9] Of these only the southern one was built, but owing to technical difficulties and personal intrigues construction was interrupted in 1641, and finally in 1646 the tower was altogether dismantled. Since the idea of erecting towers ever again over the present substructures had to be abandoned, Bernini submitted during Innocent X's pontificate new schemes for a radical solution of the old problem.[10] By entirely separating the towers from the façade, he made them structurally safe, at the same time created a rich and varied grouping, and gave the façade itself carefully balanced proportions. His proposals would have involved considerable structural changes and had therefore little chance of success. When engaged on the designs for the piazza, Bernini was once again faced with the intractable problem of the façade. Although he also made an unsuccessful attempt at reviving Michelangelo's tetrastyle portico,[11] which would have broken up the uniform "wall" of the façade, he now had to use optical devices rather than structural changes as a means to rectify the appearance of the building. He evoked the impression of greater height in the façade by joining to it his long and relatively low corridors which continue the order and skyline of the colonnades.[12] The heavy and massive Doric columns of the colonnades and the high and by comparison slender Corinthian columns of the façade form a deliberate contrast. And Bernini chose the unorthodox combination of Doric columns with Ionic entablature[13] not only in order to unify the piazza horizontally but also to accentuate the vertical tendencies in the façade.

For topographical and other reasons Bernini was forced to design the so-called *piazza retta* in front of the church. The length and slant of the northern corridor, and implicitly the form of the *piazza retta,* were determined by the position of the old and venerable entrance to the palace. Continuing the corridor, the new ceremonial staircase, the Scala Regia, begins at the level of the portico of the church. Here the problems seemed overwhelming. For his new staircase he had to make use of the existing north wall and the old upper landing and return flight.[14] By placing a columnar order within the "tunnel" of the main flight and by ingeniously manipulating it, he counteracted the convergence of the walls towards the upper landing and created the impression of an ample and festive staircase.

There was no alternative to the *piazza retta,* and only beyond it was it possible to widen the square. The choice of the oval for the main piazza suggested itself by a variety of considerations. Above all the majestic repose of the widely embracing arms of the colonnades were for Bernini expressive of the dignity and grandeur here required. Moreover, this form contained a specific *concetto.* Bernini himself compared the colonnades to the motherly arms of the Church "which embrace Catholics to reinforce their belief, heretics to reunite them with the Church, and agnostics to enlighten them with the true faith."

Until the beginning of 1667 Bernini intended to close the piazza at the far end opposite the basilica by a short arm continuing exactly the architecture of the long arms. This proves conclusively that for him the square was a kind of forecourt to the church, comparable to an immensely extended atrium. The "third arm" which was never built would have stressed a problem that cannot escape visitors to the piazza. From a near viewpoint the drum of Michelangelo's dome, designed for a centralized building, disappears behind Maderno's long nave and even the visibility of the dome is affected. Like Maderno before him,[15] Bernini was well aware of the fact that no remedy to this problem could possibly be found. In developing his scheme for the piazza, he therefore chose to disregard this matter altogether rather than to attempt an unsatisfactory compromise solution. Early in 1667 construction of the piazza was far enough advanced to begin the "third arm." It was then that Bernini decided to move the "third arm" from the perimeter of the oval back into the Piazza Rusticucci,[16] the square at one time existing at the west end of the Borghi (that is, the two streets leading from the Tiber towards the church). He was led to this last-minute change of plan certainly less by any consideration for the visibility of the dome than by the idea of creating a modest ante-piazza to the oval. By thus forming a kind of counterpart to the *piazza retta,* the whole design would have approached symmetry. In addition, the visitor who entered the piazza under the "third arm" would have been able to embrace the entire perimeter of the oval. It may be recalled that in centralized buildings Bernini demanded a deep entrance because experience shows—so he told the Sieur de Chantelou—that people, on entering a room, take a few steps forward and unless he made allowance for this they would not be able to embrace the shape in its entirety. In S. Andrea al Quirinale he had given a practical exposition of this idea and he now intended to apply it once again to the design of the Piazza of St. Peter's. In both cases the beholder was to be enabled to let his glance sweep round the full oval of the enclosure, in the church to come to rest at the aedicule before the altar and in the piazza at the façade of St. Peter's. Small or large, interior or exterior, a comprehensive and unimpaired view of the whole structure belongs to Bernini's dynamic conception of architecture, which is equally far removed from the static approach of the Renaissance as from the scenic pursuits of northern Italy and the Late Baroque.

The "third arm," this important link between the two long colonnades, remained on paper forever, owing to the death of Alexander VII in 1667. The recent pulling down of the *spina* (the houses between the Borgo Nuovo and Borgo Vecchio), already contemplated by Bernini's pupil Carlo Fontana and, in his wake, by other eighteenth- and nineteenth-century architects,[17] has created a wide roadway from the river to the piazza. This has solved one problem, and only one, namely that of a full view of the drum and dome from the distance; may it be recalled that they were always visible in all their glory from the Ponte S. Angelo, in olden days the only access to the precincts of St. Peter's. To this fictitious gain has been sacrificed Bernini's idea of the enclosed piazza and, with no hope of redress, the scale between the access to the square and the square itself has been reversed. Formerly the narrow Borgo streets opened into the wide expanse of the piazza, a dramatic contrast which intensified the beholder's surprise and feeling of elation.

The most ingenious, most revolutionary, and at the same time most influential feature of Bernini's piazza is the self-contained, free-standing colonnade.[18] Arcades with orders of the type familiar from the Colosseum, used on innumerable occasions from the fifteenth century onwards, always contain a suggestion of a pierced wall and consequently of flatness. Bernini's isolated columns with straight entablature, by contrast, are immensely sculptural elements. When crossing the piazza, our ever-changing view of the columns standing four deep[19] seems to reveal a forest of individual units; and the unison of all these clearly defined statuesque shapes produces a sensation of irresistible mass and power. One experiences almost physically that each column displaces or absorbs some of the infinitude of space, and this impression is strengthened by the glimpses of sky between the columns. No other Italian structure of the post-Renaissance period shows an equally deep affinity with Greece. It is our preconceived ideas about Bernini that dim our vision and prevent us from seeing that this Hellenic quality of the piazza could only be produced by the greatest Baroque artist, who was a sculptor at heart.

As happens with most new and vital ideas, after initial sharp attacks the colonnades became of immense consequence for the further history of architecture. Examples of their influence from Naples to Greenwich and Leningrad need not be enumerated. The aftermath can be followed up for more than two and a half centuries.

NOTES

[1] However, a passage in *Kunstgeschichtliche Grundbegriffe,* first published in 1918, shows that Wölfflin was very well aware that Baroque sculpture has a "picture-like" character and is therefore composed for one viewpoint.

[2] Polychrome settings became common after Sixtus V's chapel in S. Maria Maggiore.

[3] This device is fully effective only in the afternoon, when the sun is in the west.

[4] In the Teresa group, as in the allegories of the tomb of Pope Urban, marble seems to turn into flesh. But the psychological effect is different; for while here the group has its own mysterious setting, there the allegories stand before the niche, in the spectator's space.

[5] The only detailed discussion of the history of the Piazza is in H. Brauer and R. Wittkower, *Die Zeichnungen des Gianlorenzo Bernini* (Berlin, 1931), pp. 64–102. See also V. Mariani, *Significato del portico berniniano di S. Pietro* (Rome, 1935), and the recent interesting contribution by C. Thoenes, *Zeitschrift für Kunstgeschichte,* XXVI (1963), pp. 97–145. Bernini's principal assistants were his brother Luigi, Mattia de' Rossi, Lazzaro Morelli, and the young Carlo Fontana.

[6] Opposition was centered in reactionary ecclesiastical circles. They supported an elaborate counter-project of which twenty-five drawings survive which time and again are attributed to Bernini himself. For the whole problem see Wittkower in *Journal of the Warburg and Courtauld Institutes,* III (1939–40). Also Brauer-Wittkower, pp. 96 ff.

[7] This made it necessary to pull down Ferrabosco's tower [built 1616–17].

[8] Mainly by Ferrabosco; see D. Frey, "Berninis Entwürfe für die Glockentürme von St. Peter in Rom," *Jahrbuch der kunsthistorischen Sammlungen, Wien,* XII (1938), pp. 220 f., figures 243–5.

[9] The complex history of these towers is discussed in Brauer-Wittkower, pp. 37–43; see also Frey, *op. cit.,* and Underwood in *Art Bulletin,* XXI (1939), p. 283; H. Millon in *Art Quarterly,* XXV (1962), p. 229, summarized the whole question.

[10] Brauer-Wittkower, pp. 41 ff., plates 156–7; D. Frey, *op. cit.,* pp. 224 f.

[11] Brauer-Wittkower, plate 164B, and Wittkower in *Bollettino d' Arte,* XXXIV (1949), pp. 129 ff.

[12] Bernini himself talked about this in Paris (Chantelou, *Journal du Voyage du Cav. Bernin en France,* ed. Lalanne [Paris, 1885], pp. 42). Similar arguments also in Bernini's report of 1659–60 (fol. 107v, see Brauer-Wittkower, p. 70).

[13] First used by Pietro da Cortona in S. Maria della Pace.

[14] Brauer-Wittkower, pp. 88 ff. Previous discussion of the Scala Regia with partly different results, Panofsky, *Jahrbuch der Preussischen Kunstsammlungen,* XL (1919) and Voss, *ibid.,* XLIII (1922).

[15] D. Frey, *op. cit.,* 217.

[16] The whole material for this question in Wittkower, *Boll. d' Arte, loc. cit.*

[17] For Carlo Fontana's projects see Coudenhove-Erthal, *op. cit.,* pp. 91 ff. and plate 39. For later and similar projects see T. A. Polazzo, *Da Castel S. Angelo alla basilica di S. Pietro* (Rome, 1948).

[18] This statement is true in spite of the fact that this type of colonnade was first devised by Pietro da Cortona.

[19] There are two passages for pedestrians and between them a wider one for coaches.

13. THE TRANSFORMATION OF CLASSICISM IN THE ART OF INGRES

Walter Friedlaender

INTRODUCTION

Walter Friedlaender's *David to Delacroix,* from which this selection is taken, examines the traditional confrontation of Classicism and Romanticism in French art. The pattern that emerges from this study is not a simple polarity of styles or purposes, but a montage in which the older French rationalist (Poussiniste) and irrationalist (Rubeniste) juxtaposition is complicated by an evolution that parallels the succession of Classical, Mannerist, Early and High Baroque phases of European painting during the 16th and 17th centuries. This scheme of interpenetrating patterns is especially felicitous in Friedlaender's discussion of Ingres, in whose work elements of Classicism and Romanticism mingle with Archaic and Mannerist features. Friedlaender's multifaceted image of Ingres places the artist in a vital relationship both to the artistic context of his era and to such later artists as Manet, Seurat, and Degas.

One should read in conjunction with the following selection the article by Agnes Mongan, "Ingres and the Antique" in *Journal of the Warburg and Courtauld Institutes,* X (1947). There is also the catalogue by Agnes Mongan and Hans Naef, *Ingres: Centennial Exhibition; 1867–1967* (Fogg

Art Museum, Harvard). A recent well-illustrated publication is Robert Rosenblum, *Ingres* (1967). For Homeric themes in Neoclassical art, see Dora Wiebenson, "Subjects from Homer's Iliad in Neoclassical art," *The Art Bulletin,* XLVI (1964).

Of the two main tendencies in French art—the rational or Poussinist and the irrational or Rubenist—the first, the so-called Classicistic current, certainly had the preponderance at the beginning of the nineteenth century. However, in spite of the jealously guarded dominance of the academic school, the opposing Baroque and coloristic tendencies were by no means dead. [There were] . . . elements of this in David himself, and still more clearly in his disciple Gros, whose works seemed to prepare the way for a Neo-Rubenism or a Neobaroque, and independent of the school of David a sort of protobaroque developed by Prudhon. Moreover, there were still irrational elements of a quite different nature, which stemmed from Rousseau and the eighteenth century but which must be called romantic because they were related to the ideas and whims of the romantic writers. Of these elements the most important were the following: an emphasis on sentiment and emotion; a newly awakened interest in nature and landscape; a historicizing tendency, especially evident in the revived interest in the Gothic, which until then had been considered barbarous; a taste for the ghastly, even for the cruel; a new wave of spiritual interest in Catholicism, and finally the inclination toward the primitive and the archaic which resulted in the abstraction and reduction of art forms. By the penetration of these foreign elements into the fabric of its ideals, rational Classicism in the old sense was strongly shaken. David himself and much more so his school were affected by the new ideas and feelings though these did not yet lead to an immediate and decisive change in their general style.

Gradually the reappearance of the two old currents, the linear and the coloristic, became clearly discernible again although they now took on an entirely new meaning as a result of the penetration of both currents with romantic and sentimental elements. At the same time these two currents became more sharply opposed to each other than ever because of the accentuation in each of its specific formal character. Both currents emerged positively only toward the end of the second decade of the century; only in the third decade were they fully developed. The strongly coloristic and High Baroque development, first represented incompletely in Géricault, was then gloriously embodied by Delacroix. This movement is generally called the French romantic school in the proper sense, partly because of its connections with the late romanticism of Victor Hugo, Berlioz, and others.

The contrasting development was the Neoclassicistic current, with its strong concentration on line and structure. This new Classicism was quite different from that of David because of its absorption of new romantic elements, especially that of archaizing abstraction. There was further, a shifting of the classical ideal from Roman antiquity toward the High Renaissance of Raphael. The leader of this movement was Ingres. The fundamental contrast between the two new directions in style is vast, and far more embittered than the battle of the Rubenists and Poussinists in the seventeenth century. To the historical spectator these two implacable antagonisms seem to dominate French painting of the maturing nineteenth century.

Jean Auguste Dominique Ingres (1780–1867) came from the town of Montauban in Gascony. His father, a versatile artisan and entrepreneur in the arts, had moved there from Toulouse. Entering the academy of cultured and conservative Toulouse when he was only twelve, Ingres received a solid training which, though it included drawing from medieval monuments and Gothic choir stalls, naturally had the Latin ideal of form as its constant focus. For the young Ingres the *divino Raffaello,* chief sun of the academic heaven, shone even brighter than the antique; a copy of the "Madonna della Sedia" was his great revelation and the *réligion de Raphael* stayed with him throughout his life, as did his early discovered passion for music and the violin. He said once of himself that he had remained essentially *ce que le petit Ingres était à douze ans.*

When he was seventeen or eighteen he had the great good fortune—as he said himself—to enter David's Paris atelier, escaping thereby from the provinces and coming into the main artistic current of his time. For David's art, as well as his atelier, had become a European phenomenon. Yet David's teaching represented no break for Ingres, because its main tendency moved within that Latin tradition upon which Ingres had been brought up at home. David quickly recognized the extraordinary formal talent of his young pupil, and gave him the opportunity to aid in the execution of his pictures, as, for example, with his "Mme. Récamier." But Ingres was too independent to become a regular "Davidian" and soon, toward 1800, a certain estrangement seems to have come between the master and his twenty-year-old pupil. To be sure, David was broad-minded enough to permit his pupils to pursue aims at variance with his own, but only within certain definite limits, and Ingres seems to have been sympathetic with the Primitifs who, as we have seen, struck David at his weakest point by their pitiless criticism of his "Sabines"—at this time his latest and, he hoped, his most advanced work. To be sure Ingres did not belong to the inner circle of Maurice Quaï—he was not the man for that sort of idealistic eccentricity, not even when he was young. But for a while the strong demands of this sect for primitivism and archaism became so far his own that they resulted in a split between his point of view and that of David and the "School."

Ingres' close connection with this archaistic movement comes out most clearly in a very early work: "Venus Wounded by Diomedes." Venus, wounded in the hand by Diomedes, mounts Mars' chariot, in which, led by Iris, she is to hurry back to Olympus. The choice of a subject out of Homer, the favorite author of the Primitifs, immediately characterizes the work. Even more indicative is its formal relationship to "Etruscan" vase painting, attributable to examples in the Louvre which Ingres must have known. But there was another and more direct influence, that of the famous English sculptor John Flaxman, who was known on the continent less for his sculpture than for his illustrations of Homer, Hesiod, Aeschylus, and Dante. In the form of outline engravings, these attained an extraordinary diffusion. Flaxman was in Paris in 1802 and there saw Ingres' Prix de Rome picture, "Achilles Receives the Ambassadors of Agamemnon" [Fig. 39], which much to David's irritation he held to be the finest picture in Paris. Flaxman looked upon David not only as an "atheist and regicide" but also, after the manner of the Barbus, as a *retardataire* artist. A small drawing by Flaxman for the *Iliad*, showing the scene in which Iris brings Venus to Mars, and illustrating the passage immediately preceding that chosen by Ingres, certainly gave the latter his inspiration for the "Wounded Venus." In Flaxman, Ingres found and realized that for which, in essence, the Barbus were striving: linear abstraction on a primitive foundation, that is, based upon vase painting and

39. Ingres, *Achilles Receives the Ambassadors of Agamemnon,* 1801, Oil on Canvas, 43½″ by 61″ (École des Beaux-Arts, Paris, Photo: Giraudon)

quattrocento drawings. In his picture, likewise, Ingres sought an abstraction which departed from that convention of plastic bodily mass which had until then been the Classical ideal. In Archaic painting with its lack of space alleviated by linear overlappings, with its head turned in profile and so bound into the same plane as the bodies, with its somewhat wooden proportions and stiffly articulated movements (particularly evident in the horses), Ingres and his like-minded contemporaries found an unsurpassed prototype. In this Flaxman had definitely preceded them; and we must recognize that there was an international movement which emphasized "linear abstraction" and "freedom from the Classical."

Ingres' picture, however, is at once richer and more subtle than anything Flaxman had done. What set Ingres apart was his strong feeling for the finest nuances of movement, for the most delicate and lifelike rise and fall of bodily outline, a feeling which breaks through all his archaism to produce living form. . . .

But side by side with this penchant for the Archaic and abstract linear design, Ingres from the very beginning had (though it was overlooked at first) a much stronger passion which inevitably went far to paralyze the first: his lasting love, rooted in him from childhood, for the ripe and self-contained art of Raphael. The imitation of the Archaic Greek style, of the primitive in general, could easily have turned into a merely playful and decorative manner. Among the Barbus the exaggerated desire for abstraction and primitiveness turned into a kind of meaningless game, as to a certain extent it did among the German school of Nazarenes. Ingres escaped falling into this sort of loose and playful formal Mannerism because of his innate desire for living form, for the kind of idealized realism that was embodied in Raphael and those who shared his approach. For Ingres the work of Raphael was not a ghostlike academic dogma, but the individual, the natural, and the living lifted into the realm of ideas. He had such unbounded admiration for Raphael's art that he made it his declared ideal. On the other hand, his youthful "revolution" into linear abstraction and the primitive kept him from becoming a mere follower of the Raphaelite tradition.

In the light of all this, it may be asked whether Ingres can properly be called a Classicist. (Terms such as Gothic, Baroque, Classicistic, etc., are in themselves somewhat ambiguous and unprecise, but for the purposes of demarcation and summary they cannot be lightly abolished.) Nevertheless this question must be answered in the affirmative. To be sure the Classical ideal had now changed; it was no longer the Roman antique as it had been for the second half of the eighteenth century and for David; it was Raphael, but surely Raphael's is the most preeminent position in the Classical canon. And to the degree that this is true every retrospective follower of Raphael is a Classicist. But there we must not overlook the fact that every clearly distinguishable main current is influenced and colored by differing countercurrents and tributary streams. The Archaic, the primitive, the linear-abstract, these are all attributes of a romantic tendency. Ingres' work fell within a period in which romantic sentiment and romantic art were preponderant and basic throughout Europe—in Germany and England as well as in France. And so Ingres' Classicism was necessarily influenced in an essential way by the romantic point of view of his time. The result was a romantic Classicism—in which romantic, irrational, and anticlassical elements (revealed in his subjects as well as his form) penetrate and modify in a particular way the general tone of rational Classicism. As a linear Classicist Ingres was a deadly enemy of the coloristic, Baroque romanticism of Delacroix; as an archaistic romantic he was opposed to the Classicism of David and his adherents. . . .

An artist is attracted to the "primitives" and to "Etruscan" vase paintings because they present the possibility of producing a direct impression by line alone. The "pure contour," because it omits unimportant interior forms, allows a clarification of the essentials. This holds good, above all, for the rendering of character; it is in his outstanding achievement in portraiture that Ingres is closest to us today. Here, too, are fused those two characteristics which are proper to his art: his feeling for linear abstraction and his strongly "classical" feeling for bodily form. By the union of these two he attains both an extreme refinement of contour and a surprisingly precise characterization of the living individual. Perhaps only Bronzino can compete with Ingres in the apparently simple and primitive and yet unsurpassedly refined grasp of the portrait form. It is historically noteworthy that the middle of the sixteenth century, when Bronzino worked in Florence, was a period in which a primitive, archaizing, and what may be called a "Gothic" style superseded the Classicism of the High Renaissance, though still thoroughly impregnated with Classicism's formal language. Thus Bronzino and Ingres worked under artistically similar conditions. . . .

One must not evaluate Ingres exclusively as a draftsman. . . . He built his art upon his drawing as upon a solid rock. He drew continually, everything, everywhere. He said to one of his pupils: "*Voyez-vous, mon enfant,* drawing is the first of the virtues for a painter, it is the foundation, it is everything; a thing well drawn is always well enough painted. So, we shall start drawing, we shall go on drawing, and then we shall draw some more." But in addition to his altogether unusual feeling for the most delicate modulation of line, still further sharpened by incessant practice, he had a clear sense for sensitive gradations of color value, which in the Rivière portrait he pushed to the utmost refinement. Ingres never became a Rubenist, that is, a colorist who paints color as the fusion and dissolution of tones in light. Though David, in spite of his Classicism, could make certain concessions in this direction, such a practice would have been contrary to Ingres' whole nature. For this reason alone Delacroix, whose whole art was built on this (in the narrow sense) coloristic foundation, necessarily became Ingres' hated antipode.

On the other hand, the constructive method of Poussinism, the building up of strongly emphasized surfaces of local color against and behind one another, did not entirely satisfy Ingres' color feeling either. Refinement of line and surface demanded refinement of color values in order to bind the surfaces more closely together. Here, too, one is reminded most of the way in which Parmigianino and Bronzino, the so-called Mannerists of the sixteenth century, employed their colors. Ingres' sensitive feeling for tonalities helped correct any excessive effect of linear abstraction and helped him to give convincing existence to the material and sensuous charm of things. . . .

In 1806 Ingres finally received the Prix de Rome stipend for which, because of international conditions, he had had to wait for years, and so at the age of twenty-six arrived in the promised land of Italy. He belonged there—he was a "southerner," like Poussin or Claude. He could hardly live outside this atmosphere; he was much more Roman (even if completely French in nationality) than his teacher David. "How they deceived me," Ingres is supposed to have said, as he finally stood before the originals—perhaps in the Brancacci chapel, perhaps in front of Raphael. He must have meant that the Classic ideal as expressed by Raphael and also by Masaccio looks different in reality from the form in which it was handed down by the Davidian school. But in the last analysis he had not let himself be so badly deceived. Had not the ideal of the Renaissance, melodious and harmoniously balanced, which now surrounded and took possession of him, always been his natural artistic habitat? In Florence as in Rome he found only confirmation and justification of what had been—at least in the essence of his artistic nature—his being and his striving ever since childhood. It was only natural that his instinct for Raphaelism should become further intensified here on Classic soil. His many—perhaps too many—years of residence in Italy pushed the Gothic, northern, romantic side of his art farther and farther into the background, and he turned away from the extreme archaizing of the Barbus and from the influence of Flaxman which had culminated in the "Wounded Venus."

Ingres himself, always highly sensitive to criticism, had been embittered by the appellation "Gothic" with which for a considerable period both critics and public contemptuously dismissed his work. "It is not possible," he wrote at the beginning of 1807, "that one day I suddenly became Gothic; it is only the comparison with the sloppy and cowardly sort of painting which makes even connoisseurs misjudge my paintings, so that they call Gothic *ce qui est sévère et noble.*" What critics characterized as "barbaric," or as a "return to the childhood of nature," was in Ingres' eyes a "strong and noble" stylization. One could imagine an artist who, starting with the outlook of the Primitifs, would develop the chords which he struck in the "Wounded Venus" into greater harmony and strength. But Ingres did not go any farther in this direction. On the contrary, under Italian influence the Classic and Renaissance component of his style, the static balance which appears in Raphaelesque designs, emerges into greater prominence, especially—and often most disadvantageously—in larger compositions. Still, Ingres retained enough of his abstracting, Gothic quality to prevent his pictures from becoming copies or pastiches of the beloved masters of the Renaissance. Ingres himself objected violently to being counted simply as a slavish imitator even of his idolized Raphael. He once said that he had taken in the art of the great masters like mother's milk, that he had tried to make their sublime qualities his own, and from them had first learned to draw properly; nevertheless, every work of his had his own personal stamp: *J'y ai mis ma griffe.* But it so happens that one feels the impress of this "lion's-claw" most strongly and significantly when the primitive, stylizing element appears below the Classical surface. And it is the works of this sort that—subject matter aside—at first really attracted the romantic writers who had been reproached with their desire to cast their poems in the language of Ronsard, in much the same way as Ingres was reproached for returning to Gothic in his paintings. On the other hand, it is understandable that when the Classic element in Ingres' style gained the upper hand and made his work at once cold and sweet, that Ingres should then have encountered an uncompromising, even if unjustified, opposition from the romantics of his time.

As Gautier said, Ingres lived in Rome *seul, fier, et triste,* and admired Raphael. After his five-year Prix de Rome stipend had run out he earned his living chiefly through small, delicate portrait drawings ordered from him mainly by English travelers; drawings which he himself despised and which today are especially admired. . . .

Apart from certain copies (among others, that of Raphael's "Fornarina"—whose traits are clearly borne by some of his female nudes—and, also, copies of Titian), the Roman years produced a

40. Ingres, *Portrait of Granet* (Musée Granet, Aix-en-Provence, Bulloz-Art Reference Bureau)

large number of original works. Ingres worked slowly, continually reworking certain themes, and carried some of them through more than a decade. He made an endless number of preparatory drawings, often needing nearly a hundred different studies of movement for the placing of an arm. But he was so thoroughly trained by his ceaseless practice in drawing that he could complete extremely fine portrait drawings such as those mentioned above in about four hours and did not need much longer for a painted portrait. It was in this vein that he produced really splendid works. Among these, early in the Roman period, is the portrait of the painter Granet [Fig. 40], built up in a pyramid similar to Ingres' youthful self-portrait and with a wonderful view of Rome in the background. The city landscape here is painted as beautifully and in as simple and cubic a fashion as an early Corot; this is all the more remarkable since Ingres, like David, very rarely painted pure landscapes. In reply to the question of a German landscapist as to how one could best learn to paint a landscape, he answered: *étudiez Phidias, Raphael, et Beethoven, et vous serez le premier paysagiste du monde.* . . .

In these portrait oils and drawings Ingres was free of his historical and Classical constraint, and of any exaggerated pretensions. Thus, for all their realism, they continued the linear abstraction and primitiveness of his early works longer and more intensively than most of his other productions. It is not surprising that for us today Ingres' portraits put everything else he did in the shade (with the possible exception of some of his loveliest drawings of nudes). Naturally he himself held a different opinion. He felt himself to be first and foremost a creator of epic compositions, not a painter of accidental faces. *Je suis peintre d'histoire, je ne suis pas portraitiste,* he was accustomed to say, when, during those financially difficult years in Rome, a customer asked for *M. Ingres le portraitiste.*

But those large compositions containing many figures, which for Ingres represented the essence of his art, today demand considerable effort to understand. Least comprehensible are the subjects drawn from French history. In David's atelier there was a whole group of aristocrats and returned emigrants, the so-called *muscadins,* who favored such historical-patriotic themes. Before this time such subjects had been treated only occasionally (for instance, Vincent's "Murder of the President Molé"). Now, however, they became a fashion which the ruling powers—including Napoleon—understandably encouraged. It was a reaction, and since like everything retrospective it was romantic, Ingres' compositions in this genre drew the romantics' approval. Ingres, who had been in David's studio with the *muscadins,* had also been infected with this plague, which created such havoc in the romantic camp. With his excessive conscientiousness, Ingres worried over every detail of *couleur locale,* that is, the exactitude of his antiquarian properties; with dogged zeal he drew halberds, period costumes, and so forth, producing pictures such as "Pedro of Toledo Kissing the Sword of Henry IV," or "Henry IV Playing with his Children Receives the Spanish Ambassadors," which we can enjoy today only as we would enjoy a masquerade.

The religious pictures, such as "St. Peter Delivering the Keys" (1820, for Trinità de' Monti), are not much better. The "Vow of Louis XIII" (1824, for the cathedral of Montauban), the large picture which helped him to fame and changed his whole position in the social and artistic worlds, is a cross between the historical and the religious genres. In it Ingres' Raphaelism borders upon imitation (even though it was precisely concerning this picture that Ingres protested such a criticism). The Madonna to whom the kneeling king hands his crown and scepter is taken directly, with certain changes, from the "Madonna of Foligno," and the angels with their tablets are essentially Raphaelesque. It is true that the larger winged angels above are somewhat livelier, but on the whole they are academic, and the kneeling king with his purple robe and ruff is in the traditional French style of Vouet and Lebrun. After all this there is little left that is Ingres' own, and one does not quite understand why just this particular picture should have had such a tremendous success. Perhaps it was because in this same Salon of 1824 Delacroix exhibited his "Massacre of Chios" and, needing an upholder of tradition to oppose this revolutionary innovator, the public was happy to find an artist who brought to the conservative point of view such great technical skill and such an irreproachably worthy style. . . .

Through the triumph, in the Salon of 1824, of the "Vow of Louis XIII," Ingres was for the first time on solid ground. His art was no longer written off with offensive epithets such as "Gothic," or even (as had happened) "Chinese"; he no longer, as in his youth, counted as a revolutionary, an opponent of the school of David—a role in which he had fancied himself. Now he became the recognized leader of the conservative tendency, in his own phrase, a *conservateur des bonnes doctrines.* It is not too much to say that in this capacity he felt himself to be the God-given defender of the pure ideal, a kind of pope of Classical Raphaelism. This is the explanation of his obstinate, narrow-minded hate of all dissenters—quite in contrast to David. He even forbade his pupils to look at the Rubens in the Louvre, and if any one of them dared to make some slight concession to colorism, he was counted a deserter and an apostate. For Ingres there was no one more terrible than he who seduced others into the way of such sin; the real Lucifer, the embodiment of all evil, was Delacroix. And because he had to admit Delacroix's great talent as an artist, he was that much more fearful that that baneful influence would spoil or destroy the seed he had sown. Nothing pained Ingres more than that at the World Exposition of 1855, where he had a retrospective showing of his work, he had finally to share top honors with Delacroix, who was given similar space; or that in 1856 Delacroix was at last elected to the Academy, of which Ingres had been a member since 1825. At the base of all this hate lay the insecurity of a by no means outstanding intelligence, a fear of everything that was modern and hence revolutionary. As Baudelaire pointed out, the new romantic school felt itself to be the progressive school, yet Delacroix, who was regarded as its leader, was not nearly so fanatically opposed to Ingres as the latter was to him. Even Baudelaire, the defender of the romantics, accompanied his sharp, just criticisms of Ingres with a dispassionate recognition of Ingres' real merits and talent, and other late romantic critics such as Théophile Gautier were occasionally more enthusiastic about Ingres than were his own followers. This was perhaps because even in his later works Ingres' Classicism remained in many ways essentially romantic: religious themes ("St. Symphorien," "Madonna of the Host"); themes of historical sentiment ("Francis I at the Deathbed of Leonardo da Vinci"); exotic themes ("Odalisques," "The Turkish Bath"); on occasion even Neo-Gothic themes ("Saints" for the Chapel of Sablonville); all these were attractive to the romantic temperament by their subject matter alone. Ingres' fear was not occasioned so much by romanticism itself, or by the attacks on him of the so-called romantics, as by the new colorism and the freer manner of execution which went with it. This fear, and the consciousness that in the last resort he could do nothing against the rising new school, led him to emphatic, nearly hysterical exaggerations of his Classical doctrine. At the same time he continually tried to multiply the external props of his artistic power, not so much because he wished to enhance his personal position as because he wanted to further the true doctrine of the "School." He became Professor at the Ecole des Beaux Arts; in 1834 he had himself named Horace Vernet's successor as director of the French Academy in Rome, whence he returned six years later to Paris with his reputation further enhanced; he became a member of the Institute, Senator, Grand Officer of the Legion of Honor, and maintained a famous school (of which Amaury-Duval has left an amusing account). In short, Ingres had a position such as even David had hardly occupied, and of which the enjoyment was marred only by Delacroix's increasing fame.

When one examines the many works large and small produced during these long years, it becomes apparent that the only really worthwhile ones (with certain exceptions from his last years) are those which still show traces of his youthful style. Most often they simply continue the early themes which occupied him recurrently throughout his life. In all such cases that archaistic and abstracting element, which in his youth Ingres had adopted and made his own, has not altogether disappeared. Naturally Ingres no longer wished to have anything to do with his youthful ideals or with his anti-Davidian revolt. When the charming little work of his Etruscan-Flaxman period, the "Wounded Venus," was later shown him in Paris, he laughed in confusion and said, *O cela . . . c'est un péché de jeunesse.* And more and more he detested the Gothic-primitive. When he had first arrived in Italy he had made sketches from the Campo Santo frescoes in Pisa and from Giotto and was extremely enthusiastic about this early period of art: *c'est à genoux qu'il faudrait copier ces hommes-là.* But when, thirty years or more later, in Rome, he heard that two of his favorite pupils were copying Fra Angelico and the like in Florence and working in a primitive-Christian manner, he was greatly angered: *Ces messieurs sont à Florence; moi je suis à Rome . . . Vous entendez, je suis à Rome. Ils étudient le gothique . . . je le connais aussi . . . je le déteste . . . Il n'y a que les Grecs.* The Greeks now no longer meant "Etruscan" vases, but an ideal seen in the light of the Roman High Renaissance, and in the manner of Raphael. The result was that in many of his more important pictures Ingres became what has been called "a self-conscious Classicist." This category includes his most famous composition, the "Apotheosis of Homer" (Salon of 1827), originally designed as a ceiling decoration for a room in the Louvre, but painted as an immense easel picture without regard to its destined position—an altogether Classicistic approach. Worse than this, however, was the fact that in this picture Ingres set his sights much too high. His aim was to show a kind of "school of Athens" containing all the famous men of ancient and modern times. But a period such as the Restoration in France could not set itself problems similar to those of the High Renaissance, with whose humanistic ideal it no longer had anything in common; nor was Ingres a creator like Raphael who could find the solution of such a problem. In spite of one or two fine single figures (such as the Muses at the base of the throne), and in spite of the clear, brilliant color scheme, the large canvas is stilted and unconvincing. In comparison with Raphael, or even David, Ingres lacked the imagination necessary for such a project; as Baudelaire said, *l'imagination, cette reine des facultés, a disparu. . . .*

In his later years Ingres did continue to produce many excellent portraits. Examples are the famous "M. Bertin," of the newspaper magnate (1832, Louvre); "The Duke of Orleans" (1842); "Mme. d'Haussonville" (Frick), which still has much of the tenderness and grace of the early portraits; the elegant likeness of Mme. Moitessier; his self-portraits, among them the clear and simple one of the Uffizi; the fine portrait of his second wife whom he married in 1856 at the age of seventy-six; and many others. They are still more masterful and accomplished than the earlier portraits, and they do not,

41. Ingres, *The Golden Age, c.* 1860, Oil on Paper Affixed to Panel, $18\frac{1}{4}''$ by $24\frac{1}{4}''$ (Fogg Art Museum, Cambridge, Mass., Grenville L. Winthrop Bequest)

42. Ingres, *The Turkish Bath,* 1859–63, Oil on Canvas, $42\frac{1}{2}''$ Diameter (Louvre, Paris)

as do many of his other paintings, become cheap and trivial. Yet, most of them lack that characteristic charm and that abstraction which makes the pictures of the early period so extraordinarily lovely. There are portrait drawings of the very last period which demonstrate, as surprisingly as those of his youth, Ingres' virtuosity in the handling of a delicate and yet not petty line; an example is that showing his godchild holding a candle in church (1856, Bayonne).

Ingres did, in his late years, produce some pictures which were frighteningly bad (such as the Apotheosis of Napoleon, 1853, for the Hôtel de Ville in Paris). Yet, we must insist that Ingres in his old age did not decay as completely as the old David had in Brussels. There are at least two works which transcend the late decay; works which, even though their conception dated back decades, and though they were based on youthful memories, received their final form only during Ingres' later years. The first is a mural decoration: "The Golden Age" in the Chateau of Dampierre. Begun in fresco in 1841, it was abandoned unfinished in 1850; the composition was fully executed only in an oil painting of 1860 [Fig. 41]. A commission for such a mural scheme, in fresco, must have been very welcome to an artist of Ingres' disposition, because of the opportunity it offered to translate his strong and Classic style into an appropriate medium. From Ingres, or rather from his atelier (Mottez, Flandrin, Amaury, etc.) there had already stemmed a kind of renaissance of fresco painting. Most of it employed an archaizing note which derived from the youthful, "Gothic" Ingres, and dealt with Christian themes; in contrast to this, Ingres himself in this one fresco wished to produce something altogether heathen, something "Greek."

The theme of the Golden Age (which, according to the project, was to have been placed opposite a fresco of the Bronze Age) had long given artists of Ingres' tendencies the opportunity to represent a great group of nudes in the open, resting or moving about in gentle play, in an atmosphere of a serene, law-abiding *dolce far niente.* Poussin, in that lovely work of his old age, "Apollo and Echo," simply strove to represent an *âge d'or.* In fact, the landscape of the background and some figure groups in Ingres' fresco derive directly from Poussin's picture, and the atmosphere and sentiment are more dependent still. Poussin once defined the final aim of any art as "delectation." In such a picture Ingres could give wide play to his delight in the human form and could create groups nobly posed and arranged which, in their intertwining and overlapping, remind one of some works of the antique. No monumental painting by his successors—not Flandrin nor Puvis de Chavannes—surpassed this. Perhaps Chassériau in France and in Germany Hans von Marées (whom the right, unfinished side of the fresco brings to mind) could measure up to this standard. It may be fortunate that the fresco was never completed: for once Ingres could not indulge that zeal for finish and perfection which so often drove him to pettiness in detail.

"The Turkish Bath" [Fig. 42] was even more original. It was first painted, in 1859, as a rectangle, then revised to its present circular form in 1863—the small, out-of-scale figure in the pool was added at that time. In this painting the theme of the early "Bather" (1808, Louvre) is taken up again. Here, with some changes in the pose of her legs and with the addition of a guitar, she is used as a *repoussoir* figure, but she still retains the essence of her original simplicity and chaste naïveté. But around this figure, and far beyond her into the background, there lie, sit, or wallow the forms of naked women, almost a tangle of them. The sensuality of the "Odalisque and Slave" (Fogg Museum) here recurs, much intensified by the sense of compression among the female forms. The immediate source for the theme of this picture was certainly the amusing description by Lady Mary Wortley Montagu, in her Turkish letters of the previous century, of a woman's bath in Adrianople. But, in a more general sense, what we see here is a reflection, even in the "Greek" and Raphaelesque Ingres, of the romantic taste for the exotic and the oriental—a taste already remarked in Gros, expressed most vividly in Delacroix, and present in Ingres' own earlier "Odalisques." Actually, Ingres had always shown in his art his fascination by this particular type of sensuous, sleepy, animal-like woman. In the fullness of her young but phlegmatic flesh and the naturalness of her expression, the "Belle Zélie" of Ingres' youth has much in common with Renoir's women. In contrast to Delacroix, Ingres looked upon his odalisque not as an object full of colorful charm, nor simply as an exoticism, but rather as a type of female. The harem woman lying back upon her cushions, her thick, supple limbs apathetically stretched out to any gaze is the perfect expression of this type. Here too was the beginning of a kind of abstraction, a reduction to an essential core which, even though its form was different, was still related to the archaism of Ingres' youth.

It is amazing that a man eighty years old should have been able to create a work that had both the living warmth and the artistic distance of the "Bain Turc." With all his calculated and stubbornly held limitations Ingres still possessed a tremendous vitality. To appreciate how living Ingres was and still is, one must compare him with his contemporary Cornelius, who played a similar role within the same period in Germany. Both possessed only mediocre intelligence, neither realized the limitations of his talent and so picked out high-flown, literary subjects which he could not master; both harnessed themselves to a rigid system from which escape was difficult, and through their Olympian poses both produced their artistic worst: the *genre ennuyeux*. But while, with some youthful exceptions, Cornelius' every stroke remained wooden, stiff, and lifeless, whenever Ingres stepped down from his self-imagined throne to work more or less for himself he showed an artistic power, an expression of a new creative vision, which has enriched his own world and posterity. This new style had in it both the "Classical" and its contrast, the Gothic-Archaic; it united the "Classicistic" and the "romantic." We have described at length and in detail the elements that throughout Ingres' long life went into the formation of this style, where and why it failed, and where it led to pure works of art. Ingres' historical role lay in his purifying the art of his time by ridding it of the worn-out formulas and gestures of an old, stale Classicism. Out of all Ingres produced during a long and arduous life, posterity could get artistic nourishment only from the drawings and a few pictures: those few works that were impregnated by the "Gothic" and the "Archaic," which thus took on that clear and abstract character which is also found in the Japanese drawings which the great draftsmen-painters of the nineteenth century loved so much. "A Chinese or a Japanese artist who has strayed into Greece" was the description given of Ingres by one of his contemporaries. And in this sense it was not the weak and pious frescoists nor the stilted Neoclassicists, more or less directly connected with his school, who were really Ingres' followers, but Manet, Seurat, and above all Degas.

14. RODIN

Albert Elsen

INTRODUCTION

Rodin is a difficult figure to assess. He has been viewed by some as a rebel, by others as a romantic conservative; and while it is likely that these categories, taken singly, will prove quite unreliable, it is equally likely that each label designates a measure of the truth about Rodin. These two selections from Albert Elsen's writings on the great French sculptor emphasize this problem by affirming both the important position he occupies historically, and at the same time the stubborn dichotomy of this historical position. Rodin emerges as a Janus-image who by his literary tendencies, his passion for the great traditions of the Gothic and the Renaissance, and by his commitment to external anatomy faces the past, but who also looks to the future by stressing a reverence for the integrity of the subjective self.

His bronzes are generally expressive of the restless psychological life of man and this energy is communicated through their mass, surface, and total gesture. When one considers the bronzes—the aggressive thrust of the Balzac monument, the ruggedness of the *Burghers of Calais,* and the awkward stretch of *St. John the Baptist Preaching*—it is apparent that they are conceived according to a different principle from that governing those works designed for finishing in marble. The latter are soft, sensuous, the antithesis of the bronzes. This cannot be explained merely by the differences in media; the basic principle is different.

Like Michelangelo's slaves, or his *St. Matthew* in the Academy at Florence, Rodin's marbles oppose the smoothly finished surfaces of the flesh to the roughly-chiselled matrix of the stone. But unlike the sculptures of the Florentine, Rodin's figures do not struggle to free themselves from their marble prison. Instead they seem to be melting back into the shelter of the stone.

In addition to the two works from which these selections were taken, *Rodin* (1963) and *Rodin's Gates of Hell* (1960), Albert Elsen has published such articles as "The Genesis of Rodin's Gates of Hell," *Magazine of Art,* XLV (1952), which initiated his dominant role in the field of Rodin studies, and "The Humanism of Rodin and Lipchitz," *College Art Journal,* XLVII (1958). He has also edited an important anthology, *Auguste Rodin: Readings on His Life and Work* (1965) which reprints the essays by T. H. Bartlett originally published in 1889, the essay by Henri Dujardin-Beaumetz originally published in 1913, and the well-known essay by Rilke. For Rodin's own views, there is his *Art,* translated by Romilly Fedden (1912) and reprinted under the title *On Art and Artists* (1957). Other selected readings are Judith Cladel, *Rodin, The Man and His Art, With Leaves from His Notebook,* translated by S. K. Star (1917) from the original in French of 1908; the Phaidon editions, Sommerville Story, *Rodin* (1939, 1961); Rainer Maria Rilke, *Auguste Rodin,* originally published in 1903, translated by J. Lemont and H. Trausil (1946), and more recently by G. Craig Houston in Rilke's *Selected Works, I, Prose* (1960). Among articles on Rodin, there are Parker Tyler, "Rodin and Freud: Masters of Ambivalence," *Art News,* LIV (1955) and Albert Alhadeff, "Rodin: A Self-Portrait in the *Gates of Hell,*" *The Art Bulletin,* XLIX (1967) and "Michelangelo and the Early Rodin," *ibid.,* XLV (1963). Also of interest is the review of Elsen's *Rodin* by Ruth Mirolli, *The Art Bulletin,* XLVI (1964) and the review of Elsen's anthology by John Schnorrenberg, *ibid.,* XLVIII (1966). Robert Descharnes and J.-F. Chabrun, *Auguste Rodin* (1967), is a beautifully illustrated volume.

RODIN'S CONSERVATISM

The image of Rodin generally presented nowadays is that of the rebel. In their zeal to legitimize him as the ancestor of modern sculpture, his admirers single out certain aspects of his art for praise while conveniently overlooking others. Thus they give credence to the notion that throughout his life Rodin rebelled against the pontiffs of academic art, most of whom have since been consigned to oblivion. (Who remembers the names of Guillaume, Schoenewerk, Dalou, J.-P. Laurens and Chapuis?) This concept of Rodin as a revolutionary far in advance of his time gains acceptance by default. Today it is difficult to find even photographs to conjure up the look of the nineteenth-century Salons in which Rodin exhibited throughout his career.[1]

But if his disagreement with "the School," as he referred to the Ecole des Beaux-Arts, bears restating, so also do those large areas of agreement. Like Delacroix and Manet before him, Rodin was willing to accept official recognition and honors when they came. He was even elected to the French Academy, although ironically the official vote was cast a few days after his death. Rodin's sculpture, like the painting of Manet and the Impressionists, would have been unthinkable without academic art as a point of departure. Visualizing his sculpture in its original context, it becomes clear that in many ways his modernity is grounded in the conservatism of his time; it cannot be said to have sprung full-blown from an imagination oblivious to the style and subject matter approved by the Ecole des Beaux-Arts. Unlike Cézanne, whose art developed totally independent of official recognition, Rodin produced some of his greatest works thanks to state and municipal commissions.

His theories that art should ennoble, instruct and edify the general public, expressed in innumerable statements after 1900, allied him with his most reactionary colleagues. In his conversations on art published in 1911,[2] Rodin championed sculptors and painters who by embodying in their work the great French national virtues—

heroism, wit, courage, self-denial, and respect for lofty sentiment—made the beholder feel that he himself was capable of noble deeds. "Without doubt, very fine works of art are appreciated only by a limited number; and even in galleries and public squares they are looked at only by a few. But, nevertheless, the thoughts they embody end by filtering through to the crowd."[3] Much of Rodin's own artistic education came from visiting galleries and museums and studying public monuments. His most vivid exposure to the myths of antiquity came not from books, but from works of art in the Louvre and the Salons. Looking upon the artist as a synthesizer and popularizer of culture, Rodin proclaimed that his profession should "bring within the reach of the multitude the truths discovered by the powerful intellects of the day."[4]

By the time he published these statements, Rodin himself had become the supreme pontiff of the art world. Proudly he traced the lineage of his art and dogma back not only to the Renaissance and the Gothic, but beyond these periods to ancient Greece and Rome. If this "grandfather" of modern sculpture could witness the work of his descendants and measure their ideas against his own, he would probably reconsider his belief that his mission was to provide a firm guide for the future by linking his time with the past. There is, in fact, no evidence that Rodin was ever aware of, or in sympathy with, the revolution in sculpture undertaken early in this century by Picasso, Matisse, Brancusi, Boccioni, Duchamp-Villon, Archipenko and others. The artists he admired and praised were his own satellites—Bourdelle, Despiau, Claudel and the Schnegg brothers. What he approved in the early talent of Brancusi, Maillol and Lipchitz was the evidence of their affinity with his own art or ideas concerning the imitation of nature.

A comparison of Rodin's staggering production with that of his contemporaries in the late nineteenth- and early twentieth-century Salons makes it difficult to consider him a precursor of modern art in respect to his subject matter. As was common practice at the time, a considerable portion of his *œuvre* consisted of portraits. A cursory inventory of the themes, titles and characters of his other figures reveals the extent to which his ideas and choice of subjects were common to those of other artists of the time. Characteristic themes were sin, melancholy, sorrow and despair; all stages of love, from desire and the embrace to abduction and rape; sleep, fatigue, awakening; revery, thought, and meditation. Perennial subjects were the inspiration of the artist or writer by his muse; maternity, and exchanges of affection between brothers and sisters; play and peril; self-sacrifice, death for country or for a noble cause; primeval man awakening to nature or to his own soul. Like other artists of his time, Rodin followed the old tradition of personification and used the human figure to embody time, the seasons, the elements and various flora. (In his writings and conversations, he frequently compared natural phenomena, trees, water and clouds with the human body.) His work abounded in angels, spirits and genii, nymphs, satyrs, bacchantes, sirens, centaurs, and endless bevies of dancers and bathers. Biblical figures included Satan, Adam and Eve (both before and after the Fall), Christ, St. John the Baptist and Mary Magdalen. They were rivaled by the pagan legions of Pan, Bacchus, Psyche, Orpheus, Ariadne, and Danaïd, Perseus and the Medusa, Aphrodite, Apollo and Mercury. Some of the most popular heroes and heroines derived from literature were Pygmalion and Galatea, Ugolino, Paolo and Francesca, and Romeo and Juliet. The titles in Rodin's work that refer to Classical antiquity do not decrease after 1900. Rodin's titles brought him notoriety—partly because they offended public notions of how they should be portrayed in art, and partly because he could derive them from a corps of famous literary friends. His frequent practice of giving several titles to the same sculpture, or the same title to different works, makes identification difficult in many cases. Perhaps it was against such labels that the insurgent younger generation of the early twentieth century rebelled, believing that sculpture must be freed from literary influence and from its long subservience to illustration and mute theater.

For Rodin, to give a pair of nude figures a title from Ovid was a natural result of his education. From the time of his apprenticeship, which lasted until he was almost forty, all his decorative work in furniture, jewelry, ceramics, mantelpiece or table ornament, and architectural sculpture was identifiable with antique or Renaissance motives. On the beds, he carved appropriately tender amors: his vases were braced by bacchic idyls; balconies were supported by caryatids; fountains were flanked by huge masks of sea gods; pediments were crowned with allegorical figures representing Fame or the continents. These were the subjects that the public expected in decoration.

Rodin had a startling facility for adapting his mode to his subject, scale and medium. The gigantic and brilliant masks intended for the Trocadéro would stand out as fine Mannerist sculpture and hold their own in the Bomarzo Gardens. His caryatids would seem at home if placed next to those Puget carved for the Toulon Town Hall, while his busts of garlanded adolescents belong in Rococo boudoirs. He was trained both to think and work "in the manner of"—*what* or *whom* depended upon the whim of the client. In the oldest and fullest sense, Rodin trained himself long and well as a professional sculptor. Throughout his life, his talents were available for varied projects in many modes, to those who could pay for them.

Unlike today, in Rodin's youth it was unquestioned that the young artist should work from the human figure. Unless he specialized like Barye in animal sculpture, or in floral decoration, the artist had no alternative. The study of anatomy, and drawing and modeling from the studio model, were a matter of course as part of his training. No French sculptor contested the academic dicta that the human form was the noblest means by which to express the human spirit and great ideas, and that ancient Greece and Rome provided paradigms for the figure's proportion, symmetry and movement. Rodin's chief dissent from the Academy lay in its failure to acknowledge or recognize the beauty of Gothic art, which he considered equaled that of antiquity. Modern appreciation of the Gothic owes a great deal to Rodin—not for his archeological information but for his meaningful reading of its form, and his ability to see it as a view of life expressed in beautiful art that rivals the best of any period.

The nineteenth-century editions of Charles Blanc's *Grammar of the Arts of Drawing, Architecture, Sculpture, Painting* and the reviews of the Salons in the *Gazette des Beaux-Arts* enable us to reconstitute the official views of what sculpture should look like and the services it should perform. To manifest "universal life" in the grand figure style that alone could produce strong personalities represented the triumph of civilization over barbarism, for what the French thought of as their "race." These heroes were expected to show pride, majesty and grace by bodies constructed according to prescribed systems of measurement. A repertory of gestures and facial expressions existed with which to convey exalted thoughts and noble feelings. Rhetorical gestures had to seem natural in accordance with standards derived from Greek and Roman prototypes. In the characterization, eloquence and firm articulation were necessary to bring the message most directly to the beholder. Sculptors were enjoined to choose simple, uncomplicated and stable postures, leaving movement to be extended or amplified by the viewer's trained imagination. Deformity or exaggerated, strenuous movement ranked as heresy. Ugliness was not permissible in sculpture, since it would usurp that immortality of which only true beauty was worthy and would have a negative moral influence upon the susceptible. Though more widely interpreted in practice, beauty was narrowly defined by the School as selective: it was not imitative of a single model but was of a generic type, brooking no idiosyncrasies or flaws in proportion or movement. Given this fixed ideal, the sculptor's task was to find the right model. The sculptor, like his subjects, was expected to "cover his inner fire" and seem always master of himself. Correct work in marble allowed no improvisation, for this grave, formal medium was deemed the least suitable to express transient or vigorous movement. Only in sketches might the sculptor's passion be revealed, and the rough or unfinished be tolerated.

Rodin was in some respects an academician *manqué*. It was not his fault but rather his fortune that he failed three times to gain admission to the Ecole des Beaux-Arts where, in spite of his recognized technical precocity, his youthful eighteenth-century style ill suited the taste of his classically oriented examiners. Rodin admired and emulated much that the School stood for—its discipline, its master-pupil relationships, its study of the past and its provision of public monuments. Throughout his life he sought not to overthrow the School, but rather to reform and liberalize it.

His dissents from its principles and practice were nevertheless critical. One of his many statements summarizing his position on the subject was made in 1899:

> The actual fault of the School is to fear everything outside of five or six agreed-upon formulas. It has made the public likewise timid and fearful of change. Nature offers thousands and still thousands of ideas and movements, all equally beautiful. But a small number of axioms which in truth are deformities have been imposed upon us. When we see an individual or group of human beings wed to the attitudes of such academic work, we understand immediately that we are confronted with something false.[5]

Rodin would have established nature as the stern master and measure of art, with students dedicating their lives to its thoughtful

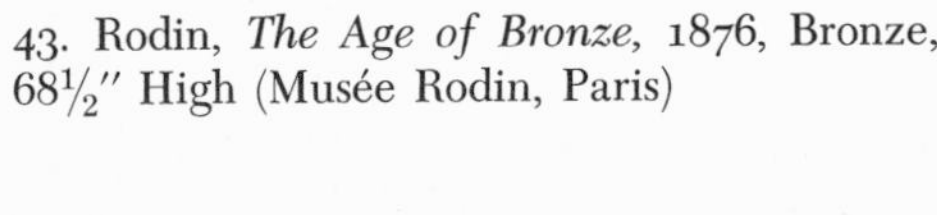

43. Rodin, *The Age of Bronze,* 1876, Bronze, 68½″ High (Musée Rodin, Paris)

imitation. On one occasion, he commented that the School was so committed to convention that it could never look truth in the face. He believed that it was not theories and plaster casts but the experiences of the senses coordinated with the mind which brought the sculptor into contact with life, and thus with truth.

The case for Rodin's importance as an artist who rose above his own conservatism and that of his day must rest on his recognition that official art suffered from too great an aesthetic and emotional distance from life, and that its content was also remote from, and irrelevant to, the deepest human needs of the time. His efforts to close these gaps gave his sculpture its distinction and produced its disquieting impact when it was first exhibited. Rodin attempted to remedy the ills of conservative sculpture and reform public art but contributed to their demise by attracting to his ideas the best youthful talent and by opening the way to more viable alternatives than he himself could ever have foreseen.

By 1876, the date of his first major signed work, *The Age of Bronze* [Fig. 43], Rodin was fully aware of sculpture's dilemma. He recognized that it had degenerated into a demonstration of studio rules, whose mastery produced only formal clichés and empty rhetoric. Having arrogated to itself from ancient art certain norms (often misinterpreted), the School in the name of preserving the eternal verities had shut off all possibilities for growth and flexibility. Rodin saw no opportunity under this closed system for revelation or work inspired by fresh discoveries made either from nature or from great art of the past. Temperamentally unable, in making a major, personal work, to maintain the dispassionate controlled attitude expected of the artist, he reacted against what he termed "polish versus thought" and the frigid rationalization that was supposed to dominate aesthetic decisions. The most enduring of Rodin's precepts was that the artist be tenaciously truthful in translating what he *felt.* An important aspect of his modernity was that he assigned primacy to feeling as the source of art. Just as he cherished unfettered individual intuition rather than blind acceptance of rules, so he rejected the corseting of studio models in arbitrary proportions and predetermined stances that divested them of their human attributes.

Rodin's attitude toward the body was humane. None of his contemporaries had such compassionate understanding, acuity of observation, or sensitive rendering of the nude. He could find humanity in a hand or a foot. As Lipchitz has mentioned, it was the skin rather than the word that for Rodin bore the precious trace of what it meant to live at any time. His desire to make the public and artists seriously aware of sculpture, and of the possibilities for new and meaningful emotional encounters with it, was closely related to his conviction of the need for a sincere awareness of the human body itself. In the body, Rodin saw both man's fatality and his own destiny.

Much of Rodin's modernity rests upon his belief that the artist must devote his life to empirical discovery for and of himself. His empiricism, which denied the possibility of conforming to impersonal norms, was the single trait that above all others prevented Rodin from being an academician and a consistent conservative. The modern ethic that the artist should work from personal experience in ways that he has individually acquired is strongly rooted in Rodin's life and art. This partially explains the natural and violent reactions against him at the turn of the century on the part of younger avant-garde artists, who consciously or not were following his ethic to its logical conclusions.

Rodin himself felt, however, that his empiricism linked him with the great artists of the past, rather than with those of the future. One of his many secretaries has nicely put the sculptor's estimate of his position: "He never claimed that he had introduced anything fresh, but that he had rediscovered what had been long lost by the academicians. The Greeks had possessed it, and so also had the Gothics. But in the official art of the day it was entirely lacking. His contribution . . . was therefore an act of restoration."[6] And to quote Rodin's own words: "It is not thinking with the primitive ingenuity of childhood that is most difficult, but to think with tradition, with its acquired force and with all the accumulated wealth of its thought."[7]

CONCLUSIONS

(FROM *Rodin's Gates of Hell*)

In 1880 Auguste Rodin was commissioned by the French government to create a decorative portal [Fig. 44] based upon *The Divine Comedy*. His preliminary figure drawings, influenced by Dante's poem, suggest that he was preoccupied exclusively with "The Inferno," and especially with themes of passion, violence, and despair. He did not undertake a literal, sequential illustration of "The Inferno," but interpreted the poem's qualities of movement, conflict, and melancholy introspection.

During the formative years for the portal—the late 1870's and early 1880's—the influence of Baudelaire mingled with that of Dante. The fact that Rodin shared Baudelaire's interest in sin, in the vain but inevitable pursuit of carnal pleasure, and in the apparently uncaused moods of depression that make the body a prison of passion, comes to light in his drawing for the *Fleurs du Mal*. Although there is no documentary proof, Rodin's interest in man's perversity and rebelliousness—the consequence of man's indifference to religion and moral values—may have been his reaction to the complex and tense religious atmosphere of the time that saw the undermining of the Roman Catholic Church's authority.

The style and much of the spirit of the Gates come from the major and militant sculptures of the late 1870's—"The Age of Bronze," "John the Baptist," and "Adam." The sculptor's personal and artistic maturity appears in the themes of suffering and striving. But by contrast, he was inexperienced in designing architectural elements, such as a large portal. His admiration for the Renaissance explains the early sketches for the doorway, which are derived from the eastern door of Ghiberti's baptistery. When he began to work in clay and plaster, his thinking became more sculptural and suscepti-

44. Rodin, The Gates of Hell, 1880–1917, 18′ High (Musée Rodin, Paris)

ble to Gothic and Baroque influences. The last model done before the full-scale erection of the Gates was shaped by a personal vision of Hell and the recognition of the timelessness and universality of his theme. He rejected almost all literal references to Dante and Baudelaire, and relied upon movement, light and shadow, and the expressiveness of his anonymous figures to carry his ideas.

From the standpoint of utility, the doors are deficient, although with a few minor changes it would be possible for them to open and close. After 1885, the Gates were no longer intended as an entrance to a building and practical requirements were eliminated. Rodin then indulged his fantasy and the doors assumed a poetic character. The architecture is certainly eclectic, but in good taste and thoughtfully designed as a foil for the agitated sculpture.

Rodin's way of working upon his project included drawing upon older art and literature, upon his own sculpture, and upon observation from life. He became engrossed in the creation of an autonomous sphere of life with its unique space and scale relationships that, in Baroque fashion, narrow the gap between the world of the viewer and the world of art.

The ever-increasing scope of his ideas for the portal, physical fatigue, a more optimistic view of life that emerged during the 1890's, and perhaps a desire for atonement—all these made a definitive realization impossible. Yet though their present state is reconstructed and incomplete, the Gates give a moving presence to Rodin's ideas about society. The subject of the door is the loneliness that results from the absence of spiritual values. Life is an Icarian flight from reality toward the unattainable that ends only in disillusion and destruction. Society provides no checks to restrain nor goals to satisfy the individual. Modern man's problem is the eternal internal hell created by his insatiable passions. And the torment of life continues after death in the form of restless and purposeless movement.

Rodin was one of many modern artists who found in the life of the artist an ideal existence. He insisted upon the artist's freedom of experience; his life and art were based upon empirically derived values that were often at variance with those of his society. In romantic fashion, there is a close connection between Rodin's personal life and the evolution of his art. By 1880, when he began work on the Gates, he could no longer celebrate the rational theories of the Academy or the theology of the Church. "The Gates of Hell" show his desire to interpret the world in terms of his own interior reactions. The core of his most successful art was formed of themes about which he felt most strongly: death, the emotions, the ugly, and the beautiful. The romantic cult of energy had no more distinguished an exponent than Rodin. Through tremendous effort he created a poetical equivalent of the society he lived in. Rather than allowing him to escape from life, his art led him to explore its problems and truths, and ultimately provided an otherwise unattainable form of understanding of himself and his environment.

From an aesthetic standpoint, the Gates are weak in design. They lack a powerful and cohesive facture, perhaps the result both of Rodin's limitations as a composer and of the nature of the problem he had set for himself. The work is richest in its humanitarian sentiments and sculptural details. In the small groups and individual figures can be seen the wellsprings of his art and in some respects his legacy to sculpture.

In many works Rodin raised aesthetic value above ethical or intellectual content. He had explored the expressive properties of structure, volume, light, and rhythm. Recognizing this, Lipchitz speaks of Rodin as "the great composer of light."[8] Though it is possible that some of Degas' daring undated sculptures may have preceded Rodin's work of the late seventies and eighties, it was Rodin's imaginative modeling that reestablished sculpture as exaggeration rather than description or literal imitation.[9] It was the extent and the manner of Rodin's departure from the actual model that strongly influenced Lehmbruck, Matisse, Picasso, Brancusi, and Epstein at the beginning of this century. His use of portions of the body, a technique that served to reduce the literary demands with which sculpture had been burdened, increased his influence on later sculptors. His making the body a study of processes and mobility captured the imagination of Boccioni. Outside of his contemporary followers, Rodin's thoughtful explorations of gesture and his instinct for the significant posture did not manifest an important influence until the work of Lipchitz in the 1930's.[10] The nineteenth-century academic taste for a finished surface and its compartmentalized attitude toward the beautiful and the ugly was ignored by Rodin; his ideas and work helped to expand the aesthetic of modern sculpture. The violence and strenuousness with which artists such as Maillol and Brancusi reacted against Rodin must be counted as an important, though negative, influence. The shadow cast by Rodin, from which so many gifted young sculptors sought to escape, was a partial incentive to the fresh thinking and the daring that led to the revolution in sculpture before the First World War.[11]

To many present-day critics and artists, Rodin's work seems dated. This is owing partly to Rodin's literary affinities, his sentimentality, his Baroque schemes, and his imaging of man exclusively in terms of the external anatomy. Rodin is the culmination of a tradition beginning with the late Middle Ages and reaching down into the nineteenth century in which the artist relies upon the outward appearance of the body to interpret the inner life. Like that of Renaissance and Baroque sculptors before him, Rodin's artistic world was man-centered, and all that was noble or pathetic in human history could be personified in it. During an age of great technical advancement, Rodin's sensibility was unswervingly directed to the private emotional and psychological life. He was convinced that the flesh could mirror the stirrings of the soul. In this century, as a result of Cubism and fantasist art of the twenties and thirties, there has been a widening and enriching of the images of the body, as seen in new and imaginative physiologies, so that advanced sculptors of today such as Lipton, Roszak, and Smith can feel that they have passed the point of no return to realistic external human anatomy. The tragic moral and spiritual problems with which Rodin was concerned in his art have since his time been largely ignored or replaced by the themes of man submitting to a nameless catastrophe, no longer in conflict with his God, but in tension with life itself or confronted by nothingness. Many sculptors recognize, however, that Rodin helped to retrieve sculpture from an intellectual and aesthetic limbo by his rediscovery and energetic demonstration of the power and seriousness of which sculpture is capable. In Simmel's words, "Rodin did not give a new content to the plastic arts, but he gave them for the first time a style by which they express the attitude of the modern soul before life."[12] Man lives by manifestations, and though Rodin may not today supply us with a complete alter image or fulfillment of our needs, he has made an important addition to the richness and variety of modern art that is essential to a speculum of humanity. "The Gates of Hell," like Baudelaire's poetry, expresses ideas and feelings that have meaning at more than one moment in history.

Rodin's Gates are historically valuable as an expression of the *Weltangst* of the late nineteenth century that is also found in the art of Munch, Ensor, and Van Gogh, and that led to the art of the German Expressionists. Meyer Schapiro puts this relationship into focus: "The theme of humanity as a whole is impressive, like the manner of treatment. It points to the twentieth century and particularly to German Expressionism where the image of man is a generalized picture of impulse and suffering. It is also ahistorical, for it represents neither the Last Judgment nor particular events in time; it is a panorama of the soul and the body in abstraction from the culture-forming historical human being who creates the community, art, technology and science."[13]

Rodin's Gates are one of the last works of modern art that attempt to deal with the whole community. They also look forward to the advanced art of this century with its concern for the self rather than the group and with the anonymous hero or victim. Even in bringing together the community he showed simultaneously the traces of its atomization, so keenly felt by artists who have followed. Like the German Expressionists, Rodin presents us with the nonsocial human in his private existence rather than with the social being. The individual has been thrown back upon himself and unremittingly desires fulfillment outside himself. Life is a succession of obstacles that induce both inertia and action. The Expressionists' feelings about man's hopelessness, estrangement, and sense of loss in the vast universe are already present in the Gates.

With his consciousness of man's diversity and unity, his aspirations and dignity tempered by finite capacities, Rodin transforms weakness into spirituality. The range of his art from animality to spirituality is also present in Munch, Van Gogh, Heckel, Nolde, and Lehmbruck. This transformation and this range are symptomatic of the shift in modern times from a religious spiritual art in which the feelings of reverence, faith, and hope formerly addressed to Christ and the saints are transferred to man. The holiness of the living is seen in their suffering, rather than in the passion of the martyrs of the Church.

Like Heckel, Nolde, and Munch, Rodin did not hesitate to draw upon literature—Dante and Baudelaire instead of Dostoievsky—to express his sentiments.[14] For all these artists, literature, art, and life were one. For them, furthermore, art was not creating for pleasure, but the difficult communication of difficult times.

Rodin's lifelong concern was the imaginative rendering of the moral problems of his society.[15] His insights in the Gates preceded by several years the writings of Emile Durkheim. What Durkheim says about societies afflicted by *anomie,* or the absence of moral codes, in his *Suicide,* published in 1897, reads in part like an analysis of "The Gates of Hell."

Irrespective of any regulatory force our capacity for feeling is in itself an insatiable and bottomless abyss. But if nothing external can restrain this capacity, it can only be a source of torment to itself. Unlimited desires are insatiable by definition and insatiability is rightly considered a sign of morbidity. Being unlimited, they constantly and infinitely surpass the means at their command; they cannot be quenched. Inextinguishable thirst is constantly renewed torture. It has been claimed indeed, that human activity naturally aspires to go beyond assignable limits and sets itself unattainable goals. . . . To pursue a goal which by definition is unattainable is to condemn oneself to a perpetual state of unhappiness.[16]

Rodin is the Janus-headed figure of modern sculpture. In one sense his art is addressed to the past and its heritage. He did not consider himself a revolutionary, but often spoke of himself as a worker, insisting that he had not invented anything new, but was simply rediscovering the great tradition of older art. "The Gates of Hell" were for Rodin the descendants of the cathedral portals, Ghiberti's great door, Michelangelo's frescoes—monuments by which the artists had intervened in public life. "The Gates of Hell" also look forward to modern art, for they mark the beginning in sculpture of attitudes toward man that were articulated by the philosopher William Barrett in 1958:[17]

> The modern artist sees man not as the rational animal, in the sense handed down to the West by the Greeks, but as something else. . . . Our time, said Max Scheler, is the first in which man has become thoroughly and completely problematic to himself. Hence the themes that obsess both modern art and existential philosophy are the alienation and strangeness of man in his world; the contradictoriness, feebleness, and contingency of human existence; the central and overwhelming reality of time for man who has lost his anchorage in the eternal. . . . There is a painful irony in the new image of man that is emerging, however fragmentarily, from the art of our time. . . . The disparity between the enormous power which our age has concentrated in its external life, and the inner poverty which our art seeks to expose to view.

The story of its formation and the meaning of the sculpture join "The Gates of Hell" to the great tradition of art which has been involved in the everlasting struggle of mankind for its own mastery.

NOTES

[1] The best sources of such photographs are the albums devoted to French sculptors in the library of the Musée des Arts Décoratifs, and the Archives Photographiques of the Caisse Nationale des Monuments Historiques in the Palais Royal, Paris. Contemporary issues of the *Gazette des Beaux-Arts* contain abundant illustrations of Salon sculpture.

[2] *L'Art: Entretiens réunis par Paul Gsell* (Paris: Grasset, 1911).

[3] *On Art and Artists,* New York, Philosophical Library, 1957, p. 244. This is a translation, with introduction by Alfred Werner, of *L'Art.*

[4] *Loc. cit.*

[5] A. Alexandre, "Croquis d'après Rodin," *Figaro* (Paris), July 21, 1899.

[6] A. Ludovici, *Personal Reminiscences of Auguste Rodin* (Philadelphia: Lippincott, 1926), p. 190.

[7] *Les Cathédrales de France* (Paris: Colin, 1946), p. 180.

[8] *The Heritage of Auguste Rodin,* catalogue of a Bucholz Gallery exhibition, December, 1950.

[9] In his *Pittura, Scultura D'Avanguardia, 1890–1950,* Raffaele Carrieri tries to show that Rodin was indebted to Medardo Rosso for this mode of his style. He says that Rosso was the first to combine in sculpture movement, atmosphere, and instantaneous effect, and to join form to light and the body to air. He also says that Rosso's visit to Paris and an exchange of sculptures with Rodin influenced Rodin's statue of Balzac. Carrieri overlooks the entire development of the Gates many years before, Rodin's earlier discoveries of the use of light in such works as "John the Baptist," as well as the influence of Donatello and the history of older sculpture in the formation of his style.

[10] This comparison is developed in my article, "The Humanism of Rodin and Lipchitz," *College Art Journal,* Spring, 1958.

[11] The best assessment of Rodin's place in modern sculpture that I have encountered has been made by Leo Steinberg in a brilliant review of Andrew Ritchie's *Sculpture of the Twentieth Century.* In stating the grounds upon which Rodin may be claimed for our own century, Steinberg writes, "Rodin does belong to us; not by virtue of his light-trapping modeling, but because in him, for the first time, we see firm flesh resolve itself into a symbol of perpetual flux. Rodin's anatomy is not the fixed law of each human body but the fugitive configuration of a moment. Form is a viscous flow that melts and reconstitutes itself before our eyes. In the 'Défense,' the human form just shaped hangs on the brink of dissolution. The male torso seethes like a blistering sheet of lava. It has none of the resilience of solid forms. A prying finger, one feels, would push through the mass instead of rebounding, as it would from a Greek surface. And the strength of the Rodinesque forms does not lie in the suggestion of bone, muscle and sinew. It resides in the more irresistible energy of liquefaction, in the hot, molten pour of matter as every shape relinquishes its antique claim to permanence. Rodin's form thus becomes symbolic of an energy more intensely material, more destructible and more universal than muscle power. It is here, I believe, that Rodin links up with contemporary vision. The sculptor studying

not states of being, but forms of transition—this is the common factor that unites Rodin's 'Défense,' Picasso's Cubist head, Gabo's spiral theme and Roszak's Spectre of Kitty Hawk." (*Art Digest,* August, 1953.)

[12] Simmel, *op. cit.,* p. 128.

[13] Letter from Meyer Schapiro, January 24, 1954.

[14] While Rodin's use of literary themes was criticized at the beginning of this century by young avant-garde sculptors, today, as seen in the art of Lipchitz and Roszak and many others, there is a willingness to turn again to this source for subject matter and inspiration.

[15] There are some who contend that art should not show human weakness but present man with positive ideals after which his life should be patterned. Simmel has written the most impressive alternative to this view. "If one feels that the end of art is to deliver us from the troubles and disturbances of life, to furnish peace outside of the movements and contradictions of life, one must not forget that the artistic liberation from the anxiety or insufferable character of life can be obtained, not only by taking refuge in that which is the contrary to this agitation, but also, and above all, by the most perfect stylization and the most intense purity of the contents of this reality. [Art such as Rodin's] makes us relive our life in the most profound way, in the sphere of art, and it delivers us precisely from that which we are living in the sphere of reality," (*Op. cit.,* p. 138.)

[16] Emile Durkheim, *Suicide, A Study in Sociology,* pp. 246 ff. This work was called to my attention by Professor Arthur Danto.

[17] *Irrational Man, A Study in Existential Philosophy,* pp. 56–57.

While I am sympathetic with much of Hilton Kramer's characterization of Rodin's art, his assignment of Rodin's views about life entirely to a "proto-Renaissance" conception is obviously at variance with mine. Concerning Rodin, Kramer wrote in his column, "Month in Review," *Arts,* September 1957: "By comparison [with Degas] Rodin looks like the last master of the Renaissance. His vision still adheres to a heroism which often embarrasses the modern eye and makes it ironic. Rodin was still able to draw his themes from the heroic mythologies and draw them straight without mockery or parody or the sense of loss which characterizes so many modern confrontations of heroic myth. He was what everyone said he was—a kind of prophet, prodigious in vision, energy and achievement, and thus even his modern subjects are endowed with a grandeur which, without falsity, has its roots nonetheless in a proto-Renaissance conception of life. His portrait heads tell us what modern life would be like if viewed under the aspect of Classical heroism. Rodin thus stands as the 'father of modern sculpture' in a Freudian as well as in a historical sense. He is both the end and a beginning."

In his *The Nude,* Kenneth Clark has written, "In spite of the vitality with which he maintained this tradition, we feel that with Rodin an epoch and an episode have come to an end. The idea of pathos expressed through the body has reached its final stage and is in decay" (p. 271). In some respects this is true, but Clark might have commented on the art of Lehmbruck, certain phases of Lipchitz, and Marini.

15. THE REACTION AGAINST IMPRESSIONISM

Fritz Novotny

INTRODUCTION

The 1880's were crucial years for French art. There were clear signals out that the artists identified with Impressionism were restive and already probing for new directions. In 1886, they held their final exhibition as a group and went their individual ways. By the end of the decade a new generation of artists had already wrought considerable change, and Cézanne, who belonged to the older generation, was developing his own deliberate discipline which was to have such profound implications for the future of Western art.

Recognizing both the character of this change and the centuries-old burden of transcribing the visible world that still resided in the illusionistic aspects of Impressionism, it is tempting to view the new directions of the 1880's simply as reactive. But to insist upon such an antithetic relationship between Impressionism and Post-Impressionism is to warp the true character and significance of what was happening. The new art was as much the logical extension of Impressionism as its rebel offshoot.

By means of optical mixtures of color and free-patterned brushstrokes—the "microstructure" of Impressionist painting—the effect of a fluctuant, light-filled atmosphere was created. In short, this microstructure served initially an illusionistic function. But the dispersal of optical mixtures throughout and their accompanying texture of brushwork wove together a colored fabric striking enough to draw attention to the surface of the canvas as a distinct entity. It could now be viewed quite apart from its old role as the invisible plane sealing off the illusive dimensions of pictorial space. The picture plane had assumed a new tangibility, and this separation of plane and illusion was surely both a denouement and a beginning.

The selection by Fritz Novotny is one of a series of papers addressed to this problem of the 1880's, and published in *Studies in Western Art, Acts of the Twentieth International Congress of the History of Art,* IV (1963). Of the extensive literature which could be considered relevant to this problem the following selected titles are among the most useful: John Rewald, *History of Impressionism,* rev. ed. (1961); Jean Leymarie, *Impressionism,* 2 Vols. (1955); William C. Seitz, *Monet* (1960) and *Monet: Seasons and Moments* (1960); Clement Greenberg, "The Late Monet" in his *Art and Culture* (1961); Lionello Venturi, "The Aesthetic Idea of Impressionism," *Journal of Aesthetics and Art Criticism,* I (1941); J. C. Webster, "The Technique of Impressionism: A Reappraisal," *College Art Journal,* IV (1944); Richard F. Brown, "Impressionist Technique: Pissarro's Optical Mixture," *Magazine of Art,* XLIII (1950); John Rewald, *Post-Impressionism from Van Gogh to Gauguin,* 2nd ed. (1962); W. I. Homer, *Seurat and the Science of Painting* (1964); Meyer Schapiro, "New Light on Seurat," *Art News,* LVII (1958); Camille Pissarro, *Letters to His Son Lucien,* ed. John Rewald and Lucien Pissarro (1943); H. R. Rookmaaker, *Synthetist Art Theories: Genesis and Nature of the Ideas on Art of Gauguin and His Circle* (1959); and two works of special significance to the Impressionists themselves: Michel-Eugène Chevreul, *The Principles of Harmony and Contrast of Colours,* translated by Charles Martel (1872), and Ogden N. Rood, *Modern Chromatics* (1879), also under the title *Students' Text-Book of Color* (1881). See also the bibliographical section in the headnotes to the selection by Clement Greenberg on Cézanne.

THE REACTION AGAINST IMPRESSIONISM FROM THE ARTISTIC POINT OF VIEW*

My task is to consider the reaction against Impressionism in the purely artistic sphere. This term "artistic" is hardly precise enough, and it is perhaps helpful to add that "artistic" in this instance means the sphere of form, of formal structure. The problem, therefore, is to discern the change that occurred in the domain of form during this period of transformation in the 1880's. If one takes the concept of reaction literally, one has in mind not so much a general change as a conscious trend of opposition against the artistic form of Impressionist painting.

Before considering the specific features of a new form, one must first note that, in that period of transition in the fine arts, form as such acquires a new weight: it stands out, so to speak, quantitatively stronger, and appears more open, more deliberate. Looked at in this way, one must say that for the painters of the new direction, Impressionism had too little form, or that its form was too hidden. And so, in fact, it was: hidden by the naturalism that was felt to be too strong and "unartistic." The intense naturalism hindered a direct effect of form; and conversely, a clear pronounced form, above all in drawing and color, meant a lessening of naturalism. This is an extremely simple and obvious contrast, a mere commonplace. It contains some truth, of course, but it is also inexact. In reality the whole situation was more complex, especially where the relation between naturalistic rendering and form is concerned.

Yet, in the history of painting we know many cases of an extreme naturalism that was no obstacle whatsoever to a very decided formal structure of the painting. Netherlandish art of the early fifteenth century, the paintings of Hans Holbein the Younger, of Vermeer and several other Hollanders of the seventeenth century, and many

*I should like to express my gratitude to Meyer Schapiro for having been so kind as to translate my paper, which was written originally in German.

works by David and Ingres, are classical examples of this fact. In painting of this kind, the effects of form—the composition of lines and masses, arbitrary color, rhythmical play of light and dark—were never constrained by naturalism, precisely because the latter was sufficiently realized in the details, in the rendering of substances, and also in a definite lighting. The relations between these components of naturalism and those elements of form could be quite close and varied; indeed, they had to be, if the unity of the work of art was not to be endangered. And yet the two elements—the naturalistic rendering of the object and the formal artistic order—are not hard to separate in analysis. They belong, in fact, to two different domains. Yet we are still astonished—I remark only in passing—that a naturalism carried to such detail, as in the examples I have cited, should be so compatible with the action of form. But we also know that in the later nineteenth century the relationships were frequently not quite so harmonious.

In Impressionist painting, however, the relation between the naturalistic and the formal content is of an entirely different order from that in the examples cited. In Impressionism, naturalistic detail is not restrained by the form or tied to it in a unified effect; for here, at least in principle, there is no naturalism of detail, whether in the representation of substance, surface, or lighting. In Impressionism each of the two components—form and fidelity to the object—has an altogether different value, a completely different character, from those in the older examples, and their relation to each other has, therefore, become basically different.

The specific naturalism of the Impressionist mode of representation has long been characterized by the catchword "illusionism." The peculiarity of naturalism in Impressionist painting is a specific illusionism, something so obvious that we can use the word without having to define the term more exactly. We must consider more closely here only one aspect of Impressionist illusionism, its relation to form.

It has always been said of Impressionism—and its opponents have clearly meant it as a criticism—that it ignored drawing and composition, or even renounced them in principle. One wonders how true this really is; but it is, at any rate, unquestionable that drawing as the supporting element in composition was in fact negated, and that the conscious, traditional canons of composition were replaced by new kinds of pictorial construction, above all, by the seemingly unintentional or, to speak paradoxically, the emphasized accidental, composition (which by this time had, of course, a certain tradition behind it). One can still argue whether such a composition in general deserves the name. I believe that enough composition in the old sense still remained in Impressionist painting, but was concealed, and precisely because—and this is an important point—a new element of form had become the real bearer of the pictorial effect. This was the microstructure of Impressionist painting. The Impressionist paint-structure of tiny parts, the execution in flecks and strokes, as the constructive basis of the picture, took over the role of composition with large units.

Since we know that this phenomenon did not occur first in Impressionist painting in the narrower sense, in the Impressionism of the later nineteenth century, but had appeared before in several periods of the history of art, in Late Classic illusionism, and in Baroque painting since its beginnings in the sixteenth century, we must indicate, at least briefly, what is peculiar to the Impressionist painting of the second half of the nineteenth century.

Here we must at once note a difference of degree. Never before had the microstructure dispossessed the large elements of form so drastically, and finally almost completely, as happened in the developed Impressionism after the late 1860's. There are exceptions in Baroque painting, particularly in certain late works of Titian, in the art of the seventeenth century (Velázquez and Hals are the best-known extreme cases), and in the eighteenth century (Francesco Guardi). But there the illusionistic effect, the illustrative precision of the whole, and whatever brings out the object, the substance, and the rendering of light, is hardly ever as strong as in nineteenth-century Impressionism. And that itself is a second important point of difference. Here, too, one might speak of a difference of degree, but if we consider both peculiarities together—the heightened significance of the microstructure and the heightened illusionism—and if we observe how much they cooperate and interact, it becomes insufficient to speak merely of a difference of degree; here, rather, something new in principle emerges. Its characteristic formula would be this: an extremely developed painterly form serves an equally extreme illusionistic effect. And further: the peculiar painterly form is carried so far in the conviction that only through the latter could the strong naturalistic effect be achieved. I refer, of course, to the theory of division of color. It was regarded as the means of attaining a maximum luminosity. Yet, it is a question whether this scientific knowledge was only pseudo-scientific; the drive to form, to as free a coloring as possible, was perhaps the more decisive and essential cause. But we shall leave this question aside and for the moment stress the fact that Impressionist painting is at bottom full of form, and precisely so if one considers the already mentioned peculiarity of the great, dominating role of the microstructure. But within this basic constituting role, we may even note various kinds and gradations of strong formal effect. I have already emphasized one of the most important—very important also for the future development of painting—namely, the continually increasing power of strong, pure colors, as unbroken as possible. Another kind is the progressively freer patterning of the brushstroke. And a third is the new significance of the picture plane.

This last is very closely connected with the two other phenomena, the free color and the free "open" brushstroke. But here, in the picture plane, the double aspect of Impressionist form becomes particularly clear. In Impressionist painting the picture plane is still—as strongly as it ever was in a naturalistic mode of representation—a projective screen for the illusionistic effect; as such, it must remain unnoticed. But if one deliberately ignores the illusionistic effect, the picture plane begins to disclose a special kind of life of its own, the self-evident and inevitable consequence of that stepped-up formal independence of the color and brushstroke. To repeat in summary: it is the Impressionist mode of painting full of form. We can phrase it more exactly. In all its aspects it drives the form to greater independence, to sovereignty in color, brushwork, and effect of the picture plane. What limited and constrained it was the commitment to illusion. If this is so, then clearly, in such a situation, at this moment of historical development, the emancipation of form, its strengthening and freedom, could rely in essential features on what already existed. (I need not stress that by this catchword, "emancipation," no value judgment is intended; it refers here mainly to the loosening of the ties with illusion.) It may be said now once and for all that the sharpest reaction against Impressionism was, in fact, this renunciation of illusionistic effect, and we may consider, in turn, how the emancipation, intensifying, or new overtness of form, already latent in Impressionism, were realized in the various fields of the painter's language of expression. This process is an especially exciting drama in the history of modern painting.

What is new in the domain of pictorial structure is quite apparent in so far as we are concerned with the problem of the building up of a picture out of small or large units. There were in that respect two entirely opposed reactions against Impressionism: on one hand, a carrying further and intensifying of the method of construction with small units, i.e., Pointillism; on the other, the exact opposite: forming the picture of large pieces of surface, with summary yet precise silhouettes. This second mode was the more explicitly announced reaction, in fact, a real opposition to the Impressionist method. But Pointillism, too, very clearly stressed something new by the systematization of the microstructure, by relating the small parts to the larger units of the composition, as Signac has expounded it in his programmatic book, *D'Eugène Delacroix au Néo-Impressionnisme.* This is all so clear, it would be superfluous to describe it more closely.

It is not so superfluous, however, to point to the following striking fact: that some of the spokesmen of the new—painters like Gauguin and Van Gogh—who applied the method of construction with large silhouettes (*cloisonnisme*) so broadly and demonstratively, at the same time returned constantly to the Pointillist system. They demonstrated thereby not only their roots in the microstructure established by Impressionism, but also that so decidedly formal an art as the construction out of large silhouettes was compatible with that microstructure. The latter, considered as a form rather than as a method of representation, is indeed not at all antagonistic to the large form and may even be conceived in the same spirit.

Even more clearly than in the brushstroke pattern, the novelty of Post-Impressionist painting is prepared in the domain of Impressionist color. With the turn from Impressionism and its "double aspect," every conceivable way was opened for new significances and functions of color. Even the free unnaturalistic color was already latent in Impressionism. For this, only a short step was necessary, but it led to vast horizons, and it was this step, more than any other formal means, that stamped the total picture of painting after Impressionism. The unconstrained sovereignty of color became one of the chief characteristics of modern painting.

Among all the new functions of color, one stood out above all the others: the conceptual, psychological, and, in extreme cases, symbolically interpreted color. It signifies a radical departure from Impressionism, which had strictly forsworn, at least in its program, the intrusion of any idea whatever in the mere depicting of the

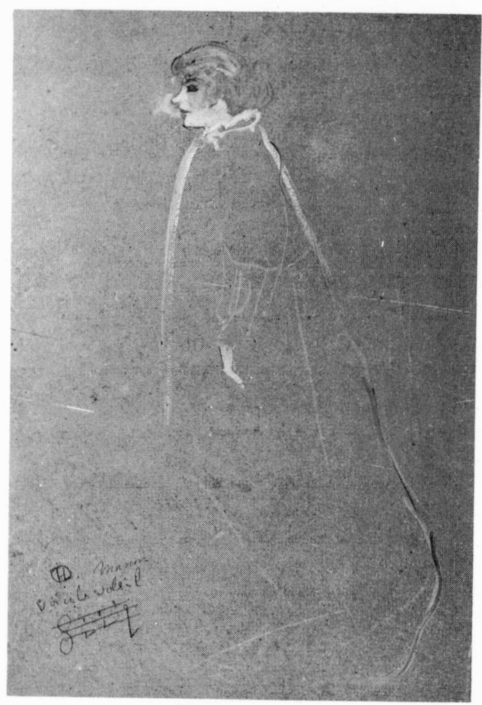

45. Toulouse-Lautrec, *Manon voici le soleil* . . . (Musée Calvet, Avignon)

visible. Here we can only emphasize the fact; it would be hopeless to try to say something about the many possibilities of a new meaning of color; besides, it would take us beyond the problems of form.

But this holds in a very special degree for the third element of form: the particular effect of the picture plane. It is here that a new and un-Impressionist form originates; even more, a new significance in a way more mysterious and less evident than with the paint structure and color. Nowhere is this clearer than in Cézanne's painting, for to no painter of his epoch was the value of the picture plane, its meaning for the pictorial whole, as central a problem as it was for him. This, too, is connected with the limiting of illusionism. In Impressionist painting the picture plane is the projective screen for the rendering of three-dimensional shapes of space and bodies in so decided and extreme a manner that even where it remains visible as a painting ground—as occurs often in the sketchy procedure of this art (Fig. 45)—it suggests space and bodies that are not really represented. In Cézanne's painting it is different, especially in his watercolors (Fig. 46). In these and even in his drawings, the many voids are something other than those in the suggestive method of the Impressionists. The empty areas in Cézanne's pictures, the frequent interruption, submergence, extinction, and re-emergence of contours and forms, have long surprised the contemplators of his art and have stimulated reflection. Since the beginning of our century, this peculiarity has been adopted by painters as something enigmatic and fascinating, comparable to a scientific discovery or invention.

I have, it is true, said that the fleck structure of Impressionist painting also emphasizes the value of the picture plane. Compared with Cézanne's method, however, it is merely an ideal, a logical value, an automatic result, and not the object of a serious artistic preoccupation. One can describe more precisely, though not briefly, how, through the peculiar effect of the picture plane in Cézanne's painting, the entire work becomes a formal structure in a new way. That is understandable if we consider the simple fact that the picture plane is the carrier of all formal means, color, drawing, etc. In endowing the picture plane with a special effectiveness, Cézanne changed the whole appearance of the picture in a fundamental and radical way.

46. Cézanne, *Provençal House*, 1890–94, Pencil and Watercolor, 16½″ by 20″ (Mr. and Mrs. Henry Pearlman)

On this revolutionary occurrence one can quote a sentence from Kandinsky's *Über das Geistige in der Kunst:* "Not a man, nor an apple, nor a tree is represented, but all these are used by Cézanne to form a mental painterly"—or, to put it literally in an un-English form—"a subjective painterly thing that is called a picture." (Let me give this quotation in the original language: "Nicht ein Mensch, nicht ein Apfel, nicht ein Baum werden dargestellt, sondern das alles wird von Cézanne gebraucht zur Bildung einer innerlich malerisch klingenden Sache, die Bild heisst.") In this remark Kandinsky, in the most unpretentious way conceivable, has hit the salient point in the change to the new character of the picture in the painting of our century.

My task here is to speak only of form, and that naturally means a certain arbitrariness, especially since we are dealing with the art of a period of transition from naturalism to the dominance of new forms, to an art that is increasingly form-conscious. Naturalistic painting was not abruptly terminated by a radically opposed autonomous art of form remote from nature. It would therefore be tempting to consider how the penetration of form, whether more or less slow or intense, affected the content of representation or the mode of rendering objects. Such observation would be particularly instructive in the art of the painter of whom I was speaking: Cézanne. In his painting the turn to the new is realized in so hidden a manner that he was incorrectly, yet understandably, counted among the Impressionists, as is still done even today. What is fundamentally new, works secretly, but is extremely effective precisely because, by and large, the external image of nature is preserved in spite of the intensity of form, color, and picture plane. In Cézanne's art, it must be stressed, the image of nature is in principle preserved throughout as a theme from Impressionism. The new kind of form and its new power are compatible with the representation of things. The situation here is, in essence, the same as in Impressionism; but the relation between the values of form and of representation is no longer that of illusionistic effect, and, within the theme of nature common to Cézanne and the Impressionists, there has been a decisive change. Instead of the self-evident and eternally momentary, the enduring and regular stand out; instead of the dominance of light upon which, for the Impressionists, all objectivity rested, there is for Cézanne an equally dominant element for which we cannot easily find a proper designation. But the comparison with Impressionism may help us here. The fleck structure of the Impressionist method and the peculiarity of the picture plane that goes with it, namely the homogeneity of the dense web of strokes, is the formal expression of that basic dominant element of light. Beside it, the picture plane in Cézanne's painting seems more spiritualized. If in this special form of the picture plane, analogous to Impressionism, a particular element is expressed, then this, too, is more spiritualized, somewhat like the visible or felt relationship of things in the picture. The peculiar relation that we have already mentioned, of void and suggested object in Cézanne's pictures, mainly in the watercolors and drawings, and particularly the very characteristic way of forming the contours, show that what binds things is more pronounced than what separates them. While for the Impressionists the binding factor is a bodiless element, namely light and the atmosphere that pervades it, yet still a physical reality, Cézanne's form leads to an immaterial unity to which all individual shapes are subordinate. We are, to be sure, already beyond the sphere of pure form when we note in the specific form of both the Impressionists and Cézanne the expression of an objective content. But if we wish to penetrate more deeply this form of Cézanne in its opposition and reaction to Impressionism, we must consider the single categories of the representation of reality; we must observe what happens, within the framework of so peculiar and novel a handling of the picture plane, to the representation of space, to perspective, to the rendering of substances, etc. We could then define the deviations and deformations that are discretely realized in a characteristic way. In spite of these, we never lose the feeling that a fundamental change has taken place—a reversal, a transvaluation in favor of form.

We have now reached the point where we can compare and summarize the types of reaction against Impressionism in the field of pictorial form. They were, as I have already said, essentially of two kinds.

One is that turn from the Impressionist way of seeing, which does not proceed from form, but from the very beginning opposes Impressionism in its basic attitude to reality. It repudiates more or less radically the representation of the merely visible, and takes as its theme inner processes, thoughts, and feelings. Its formal correlate is the anti-naturalistic decorative form, in short, all that characterizes Symbolism and Expressionism. The reaction against Impressionism here is a radical one, yet in many respects it is also a return to older forms; at least it resumes and rehabilitates already familiar concepts of art, for example, the deliberate painting of ideas or of a romantic attitude. A mode of conception that still existed beside Naturalism has merely assumed a new shape in these cases, and even its form of expression is often hardly new.

The other type of reaction is outwardly less radical. It holds, if only outwardly, to the path of the realistic depiction of reality; it does not abandon Impressionism for an opposite direction, but goes further in the Impressionist sense. Of this type and its form I have already spoken somewhat more fully, and deliberately so, since from a broad point of view it is essentially new. This path in the Impressionist direction, carrying further the Impressionist mode of seeing and its form, led to new domains of form and, as a result, to new conceptions of the picture in general. The Pointillism of Seurat's rigorous form and Cézanne's constructive method are the most significant outcome of this innovation. It is clear that several of the leading Impressionist painters had moved in just this way beyond Impressionism; the best-known and most striking example is Pissarro with his approach first to Cézanne and later to Pointillism.

47. Claude Monet, *Fishermen on the Seine near Poissy*, 1882, Oil on Canvas, 24″ by 32″ (Kunsthistorisches Museum, Vienna)

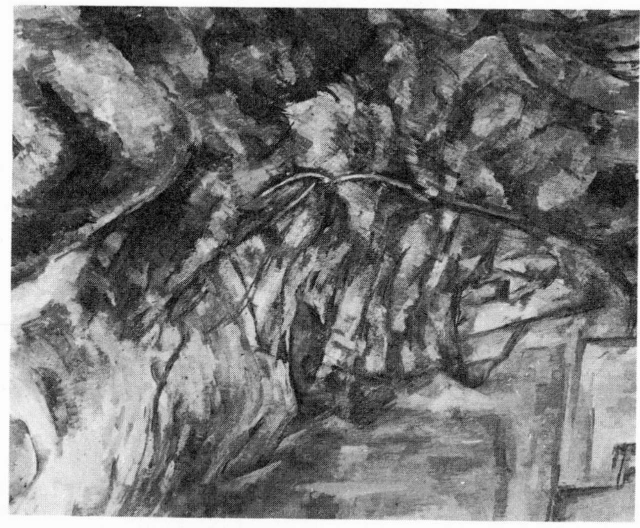

48. Cézanne, *Rochers à Bibémus,* 20″ by 24″ (Musée du Petit Palais, Paris, Photo: Bulloz)

49. Georges Braque, *Maisons à l'Estaque,* 1908, Oil, $28\frac{3}{4}$″ by $23\frac{3}{8}$″ (Hermann and Margrit Rupf Collection, Kunstmuseum, Bern). Permission A.D.A.G.P. 1969 by French Reproduction Rights, Inc.

I should like to show here once again, through several examples, how the reaction against Impressionism and the way to a new art may be recognized in what is outwardly not emphasized, yet is in essence a remarkably pervasive and radical method: a landscape by Monet, *Fishermen on the Seine near Poissy,* dated 1882, in the Kunsthistorisches Museum, Vienna (Fig. 47), a work of Cézanne's later style, *Trees and Rocks in the Quarry of Bibémus* in the Petit Palais, Paris (Fig. 48), and Braque's *Landscape near L'Estaque,* of 1908, in the Rupf Collection in Bern (Fig. 49). Common to all three pictures is the basic attitude to space in the typical, so-called accidental, segment of a landscape without a visible horizon. But precisely in this common feature one can recognize the basic differences with special clarity; the three pictures may be regarded as examples of stages of development on a consistent path which leads to new forms. . . .

This comparison of two basically different reactions against Impressionism requires still further comment, for there is also a connection between them. I have already remarked that the creators of a new form of broad-contoured, large scale composition and a non-naturalistic coloring with symbolic content, Gauguin and Van Gogh above all, built, like the Impressionists, with small units. This shows that not only could both these forms be combined, but also that the life of the small form and its expressive possibilities, as developed in the Impressionist way of painting, or at least latent there, were regarded by the pioneers of Expressionism as an indispensable form. The vibrant restlessness in Van Gogh's animistic pictorial world is quite clearly connected with the color flicker of Impressionist painting, and how much his symbolically charged color, like Gauguin's, is indebted to the free coloring of the Impressionists, is obvious enough.

If so many connections with Impressionism remain in this art which, in dissatisfaction with the Impressionist program, had turned to an entirely different content, how much closer are they in that other type of painting that remained close to Impressionist themes, namely, Cézanne's direction. Here, too, there occurred very soon a turn to a new pictorial world, to an un-naturalistic form, most sharply in Cubism. Superficially considered, this, too, would appear as a strong reaction, a counterswing. But there is still another aspect, the very one that I have tried to present here. So pronounced a pictorial method of representation as that of Impressionism appears to us today as a seedbed for a breakthrough of pure forms. Naturally, I am not thinking of a "blind" law of development, and I shall avoid saying that it had to come. For being a matter of the history of spirit, it could surely have been different. But since it took place as it did, we must note that a highly consistent process is visible here. What is peculiar is the role of form within and beside an extreme naturalism. Was the satiation by this naturalism, by the magic of illusionism, therefore a negative cause, participating more strongly in the reactive turn to the new, or was the positive factor of a compelling seduction by form the stronger? And what part was played by the individual artist? That, of course, is a general question and there are, naturally, several such questions in this context. But I should like to close at this point, for I believe that the theme proposed for my paper was the description of phenomena and not their causes.

16. CÉZANNE

Clement Greenberg

INTRODUCTION

Virginia Woolf, in her biography of Roger Fry, the English critic who was largely responsible for introducing Cézanne to English-speaking viewers, reports how Fry was disappointed, on finally visiting the artist's locale at Aix-en-Provence, to discover so little memory of him there, as if Cézanne had come and gone, leaving scarcely any trace of his presence in that "little bourgeois world." How different it had been in the world of art.

When Clement Greenberg says in this selection that Cézanne's art "endures in its newness" he identifies the essential quality of all great art: its capacity to remain relevant after it has passed into history. The special relevance of Cézanne's work is not to be measured solely in terms of its historical impact, or even by its aesthetic significance, but must also comprehend the patient dedication of the artist to the frustrating labor of realizing his artistic mission. There is surely a supreme poignancy in this, for as Greenberg points out, how unsure Cézanne was of where he was going. For all artists who follow, this knowledge is as awesome as it is reassuring.

The first work in English devoted to the art of Paul Cézanne was Roger Fry's brief monograph, *Cézanne: A Study of His Development*, published in London in 1927, and reprinted several times since. The literature has grown tremendously since then. The following titles, therefore, represent a stringently pared selection: Gerstle Mack, *Paul Cézanne* (1935); Paul Cézanne, *Letters*, ed. John Rewald (1941); Meyer Schapiro, *Paul Cézanne* (1952), a monograph of special importance; Erle Loran, *Cézanne's Composition*, 3rd rev. ed. (1963), an analysis by a painter; John Rewald, *Paul Cézanne*, translated by M. H. Liebman (1950), reprinted in 1959 and 1965; and Kurt Badt, *The Art of Cézanne*, translated by S. A. Ogilvie (1965). See also the review by Alfred Neumeyer, of the last-mentioned work, in *The Art Bulletin*, XLIX (1967). For Cézanne's relationship to the art of the past and analyses of his imagery there are a series of articles by Theodore Reff: "Cézanne and Poussin," *Journal of the Warburg and Courtauld Institutes,* XXIII (1960); "Cézanne's Bather With Outstretched Arms," *Gazette des Beaux-Arts,* 6th series, LIX (1962); "Cézanne, Flaubert, St. Anthony, and the Queen of Sheba," *The Art Bulletin,* XLIV (1962); "Cézanne's *Dream of Hannibal,*" *ibid.,* XLV (1963); "Cézanne and Hercules," *ibid.,* XLVIII (1966); and Sara Lichtenstein, "Cézanne and Delacroix," *The Art Bulletin,* XLVI (1964).

Cézanne's art may no longer be the overflowing source of modernity it was thirty years back,[1] but it endures in its newness and in what can even be called its stylishness. There remains something indescribably racy and sudden for all its familiarity by now, in the way his crisp blue line can separate the contour of an object from its mass. Yet how distrustful Cézanne himself was of bravura, speed—all the apparent concomitants of stylishness. And how unsure at bottom of where he was going.

He was on the verge of middle age when he had the crucial revelation of his artist's mission. Yet what he *thought* was revealed was largely inconsistent with the means he had already developed to meet and fulfill his revelation, and the problematic quality of his art—the source perhaps of its unfading modernity—came from the ultimate necessity of revising his intentions under the pressure of a method that evolved as if in opposition to them. He was making the first pondered and conscious attempt to save the key principle of Western painting—its concern for an ample and literal rendition of stereometric space—from the effects of Impressionist color. He had noted the Impressionists' inadvertent silting up of pictorial depth; and it was because he tried so hard to reexcavate that space without abandoning Impressionist color, and because this effort, while vain, was so profoundly conceived, that his art became the discovery and turning point it did. Like Manet, and with almost as little real appetite for the role of a revolutionary, he changed the direction of painting in the very effort to return it by new paths to its old ways.

Cézanne accepted his notion of pictorial unity, of the realized, final effect of a picture, from the Old Masters. When he said that he wanted to redo Poussin after nature and "make Impressionism something solid and durable like the Old Masters," he meant apparently that he wanted to impose a composition and design like that of the High Renaissance on the "raw" chromatic material provided by the Impressionist registration of visual experience. The parts, the atomic

[1] [Written in 1951.]

units, were still to be supplied by the Impressionist method, which was held to be truer to nature; but these were to be organized into a whole on more traditional principles.

The Impressionists, as consistent in their naturalism as they knew how to be, had let nature dictate the over-all design and unity of the picture along with its component parts, refusing in theory to interfere consciously with their optical impressions. For all that, their pictures did not lack structure; insofar as any single Impressionist picture was successful, it achieved an appropriate and satisfying unity, as must any successful work of art. (The overestimation by Roger Fry and others of Cézanne's success in doing exactly what he said he wanted to do is responsible for the cant about the Impressionist lack of structure. What is missed is geometrical, diagrammatic and sculptural structure; in its stead, the Impressionists achieved structure by the accentuation and modulation of points and areas of color and value, a kind of "composition" which is not inherently inferior to or less "structural" than the other kind.) Committed though he was to the motif in nature in all its givenness, Cézanne still felt that it could not of its own accord provide a sufficient basis for pictorial unity; what he wanted had to be more emphatic, more tangible in its articulation and therefore, supposedly, more "permanent." And it had to be *read* into nature.

The Old Masters had assumed that the members and joints of pictorial design should be as clear as those of architecture. The eye was to be led through a rhythmically organized system of convexities and concavities in which manifold gradations of dark and light, indicating recession and salience, were marshaled around points of interest. To accommodate the weightless, flattened shapes produced by the flat touches of Impressionist color to such a system was obviously impossible. Seurat demonstrated this in his *Sunday Afternoon on Grand Jatte Island,* as well as in most of his other completed group compositions, where the stepped-back planes upon which he set his figures serve—as Sir Kenneth Clark has noted—to give them the quality of cardboard silhouettes. Seurat's Pointillist, hyper-Impressionist method of filling color in could manage a plausible illusion of deep space, but not of mass or volume within it. Cézanne reversed the terms of this problem and sought—more like the Florentines than like the Venetians he cherished—to achieve mass and volume first, and deep space as their by-product, which he thought he could do by converting the Impressionist method of registering variations of light into a way of indicating the variations in planar direction of solid surfaces. For traditional modeling in dark and light, he substituted modeling with the supposedly more natural—and Impressionist—differences of warm and cool.

Recording with a separate pat of paint each larger shift of direction by which the surface of an object defined the shape of the volume it enclosed, he began in his late thirties to cover his canvases with a mosaic of brushstrokes that called just as much attention to the physical picture plane as the rougher dabs or "commas" of Monet, Pissarro and Sisley did. The flatness of that plane was only further emphasized by the distortions of Cézanne's drawing, which started out by being temperamental (Cézanne was never able to master a sculptural *line*) but turned into a method, new in extent rather than in kind, of anchoring fictive volumes and spaces to the surface pattern. The result was a kind of pictorial tension the like of which had not been seen in the West since Late Roman mosaic art. The overlapping little rectangles of pigment, laid on with no attempt to fuse their edges, brought depicted form toward the surface; at the same time, the modeling and shaping performed by these same rectangles drew it back into illusionist depth. A vibration, infinite in its terms, was set up between the literal paint surface of the picture and the "content" established behind it, a vibration in which lay the essence of the Cézannian "revolution."

The Old Masters always took into account the tension between surface and illusion, between the physical facts of the medium and its figurative content—but in their need to conceal art with art, the last thing they had wanted was to make an explicit point of this tension. Cézanne, in spite of himself, had been forced to make the tension explicit in his desire to rescue tradition from—and at the same time with—Impressionist means. Impressionist color, no matter how handled, gave the picture surface its due as a physical entity to a much greater extent than had traditional practice.

Cézanne was one of the most intelligent painters about painting whose observations have been recorded. (That he could be rather intelligent about many other things has been obscured by his eccentricity and the profound and self-protective irony with which he tried, in the latter part of his life, to seem the conformist in matters apart from art.) But intelligence does not guarantee the artist a precise awareness of what he is doing or really wants to do. Cézanne overestimated the degree to which a conception could precipitate itself in, and control, works of art. Consciously, he was after the most exact communication of his optical sensations of nature, but these were to be ordered according to certain precepts for the sake of art as an end in itself—an end to which naturalistic truth was but a means.

To communicate his optical sensations exactly meant transcribing, however he could, the distance from his eye of every part of the motif, down to the smallest facet-plane into which he could analyze it. It also meant suppressing the texture, the smoothness or roughness, the hardness or softness, the tactile associations of surfaces; it meant seeing prismatic color as the exclusive determinant of spatial position—and of spatial position above and beyond local color or transient effects of light. The end in view was a *sculptural* Impressionism.

Cézanne's habits of seeing—his way, for instance, of telescoping middleground and foreground, and of tilting forward everything in the subject that lay above eye level—were as inappropriate to the cavernous architectural schemes of the Old Masters as were Monet's habits of seeing. The Old Masters elided and glided as they traveled through space, which they treated as the loosely articulated continuum that common sense finds it to be. Their aim in the end was to create space as a theater; Cézanne's was to give space itself a theater.

His focus was more intense and at the same time more uniform than the Old Masters'. Once "human interest" had been excluded, every visual sensation produced by the subject became equally important. Both the picture as picture, and space as space, became tighter and tauter—distended, in a manner of speaking. One effect of this distention was to push the weight of the entire picture forward, squeezing its convexities and concavities together and threatening to fuse the heterogeneous content of the surface into a single image or form whose shape coincided with that of the canvas itself. Thus Cézanne's effort to turn Impressionism toward the sculptural was shifted, in its fulfillment, from the structure of the pictorial illusion to the configuration of the picture itself as an object, as a flat surface. Cézanne got "solidity," all right; but it is as much a two-dimensional, literal solidity as a representational one.

The real problem would seem to have been, not how to do Poussin over according to nature, but how to relate—more carefully and explicitly than Poussin had—every part of the illusion in depth to a surface pattern endowed with even superior pictorial rights. The firmer binding of the three-dimensional illusion to a decorative surface effect, the integration of plasticity and decoration—this was Cézanne's true object, whether he said so or not. And here critics like Roger Fry read him correctly. But here, too, his expressed theory contradicted his practice most. As far as I know, not once in his recorded remarks does Cézanne show any concern with the decorative factor except—and the words are the more revelatory because they seem offhand—to refer to two of his favorite Old Masters, Rubens and Veronese, as "the decorative masters."

No wonder he complained till his last day of his inability to "realize." The effect toward which his means urged was not the one he had conceived in his desire for the organized maximum of an illusion of solidity and depth. Every brushstroke that followed a fictive plane into fictive depth harked back—by reason of its abiding, unequivocal character as a mark made by a brush—to the physical fact of the medium; and the shape and placing of that mark recalled the shape and position of the flat rectangle which was being covered with pigment that came from tubes. (Cézanne wanted an "elevated" art, if anyone ever did, but he made no bones about the tangibility of the medium. "One has to be a painter through the very qualities of painting," he said. "One has to use coarse materials.")

For a long while he overpacked his canvases as he groped along, afraid to betray his sensations by omission, afraid to be inexact because incomplete. Many of his reputed masterpieces of the later 1870's and the 1880's (I leave to one side the proto-Expressionist feats of his youth, some of which are both magnificent and prophetic) are redundant, too cramped, lacking in unity because lacking in modulation. The parts are felt, the execution is often exact, but often there is too little of the kind of feeling that precipitates itself in an instantaneous whole. (No wonder so many of his unfinished paintings are among his best.) Only in the last ten or fifteen years of Cézanne's life do pictures whose power is complete as well as striking and original come from his easel with real frequency. Then the means at last fulfills itself. The illusion of depth is constructed with the surface plane more vividly, more obsessively in mind; the facet-planes may jump back and forth between the surface and the images they create, yet they are one with both surface and image.

Distinct yet summarily applied, the square pats of paint vibrate and dilate in a rhythm that embraces the illusion as well as the flat pattern. The artist seems to relax his demand for exactness of hue in passing from contour to background, and neither his brushstrokes nor his facet-planes remain as closely bunched as before. More air and light circulate through the imagined space. Monumentality is no longer secured at the price of a dry airlessness. As Cézanne digs deeper behind his broken contours with ultramarine, the whole picture seems to unsheathe and then re-envelop itself. Repeating its rectangular enclosing shape in every part of itself, it seems also to strain to burst the dimensions of that shape.

Had Cézanne died in 1890, he would still be enormous, but more so in innovation than in realization. The full, triumphant unity that crowns the painter's vision, the unity offered like a single sound made by many voices and instruments—a single sound of instantaneous yet infinite variety—this kind of unity comes for Cézanne far more often in the last years of his life. Then, certainly, his art does something quite different from what he said he wanted it to do. Though he may think as much as before about its problems, he thinks much less into its execution. Having attracted young admirers, he expands a little, has his remarks taken down and writes letters about his "method." But if he did not then confuse Emile Bernard, Joachim Gasquet and others among his listeners, he confuses us today, who can only read what he had to say. I prefer, however, to think with Erle Loran (to whose *Cézanne's Composition* I am indebted for more than a few insights into the essential importance of Cézanne's drawing) that the master himself was more than a little confused in his theorizing about his art. But did he not complain that Bernard, with his appetite for theories, forced him to theorize unduly? (Bernard, in his turn, criticized Cézanne for painting *too much* by theory.)

To the end, he continued to harp on the necessity of modeling, and of completeness and exactness in reporting one's "sensations." He stated his ideal, with more than ordinary self-awareness, as a marriage between *trompe-l'oeil* and the laws of the medium, and lamented his failure to achieve it. In the same month in which he died, he still complained of his inability to "realize." Actually, one is more surprised, in view of the gathering abstractness of his last great paintings, to hear Cézanne say that he had made a "little progress." He condemned Gauguin and Van Gogh for painting "flat" pictures: "I have never wanted and will never accept the lack of modeling or gradation: it's an absurdity. Gauguin was not a painter; he only made Chinese pictures." Bernard reports him as indifferent to the art of the primitives of the Renaissance; they, too, apparently, were too flat. Yet the path of which Cézanne said he was the primitive, and by following which he hoped to rescue Western tradition's pledge to the three-dimensional from both Impressionist haze and Gauguinesque decoration, led straight, within five or six years after his death, to a kind of painting as flat as any the West had seen since the Middle Ages.

The Cubism of Picasso, Braque and Léger completed what Cézanne had begun. Its success divested his means of whatever might have remained problematical about them. Because he had exhausted so few of his insights, Cézanne could offer the Cubists all the resources of a new discovery; they needed to expend little effort of their own in either discovery or rediscovery. This was the Cubists' luck, which helps explain why Picasso, Léger and Braque, between 1909 and 1914, were able to turn out a well-nigh uninterrupted succession of "realizations," Classical in the sufficiency of their strength, in the adjustment of their means to their ends.

Cézanne's honesty and steadfastness are exemplary. Great painting, he says in effect, ought to be produced the way it was by Rubens, Velasquez, Veronese and Delacroix; but my own sensations and capacities don't correspond to theirs, and I can feel and paint only the way I must. And so he went at it for forty years, day in and out, with his clean, careful *métier*, dipping his brush in turpentine between strokes to wash it, and then depositing each little load of paint in its determined place. It was a more heroic artist's life than Gauguin's or Van Gogh's, for all its material ease. Think of the effort of abstraction and of eyesight necessary to analyze every part of every motif into its smallest negotiable plane.

Then there were the crises of confidence that overtook Cézanne almost every other day (he was also a forerunner in his paranoia). Yet he did not go altogether crazy: he stuck it out at his own sedentary pace, and his absorption in work rewarded him for premature old age, diabetes, obscurity and the crabbed emptiness of his life away from art. He considered himself a weakling, a "bohemian," frightened by the routine difficulties of life. But he had a temperament, and he sought out the most redoubtable challenges the art of painting could offer him in his time.

17. CUBISM

John Golding

INTRODUCTION

The first part of this selection recounts, in journalistic fashion, the series of events between 1910 and 1912 that engaged a number of artists and writers and formed the generating context for the Cubist movement. The web of interests and actions outlined here evokes some sense of the vitality and excitement of that brief but crucial period.

The second portion of the selection is a summation of the movement as a whole and its place in the history of modern art.

The most important single document of this movement is the collaborative effort of the Cubist artists and theorists, Albert Gleizes and Jean Metzinger: *Du Cubisme,* published in 1912, and translated into English in 1913. It is available, with some revisions in the 1913 translation, in *Modern Artists on Art,* edited by Robert L. Herbert (1964). Of nearly equal importance is the more familiar work by Guillaume Apollinaire, *Les Peintres Cubistes* (1913) and available in English as *The Cubist Painters* (1949). Among other works in English are the following selected titles: A. J. Eddy, *Cubists and Post-Impressionism,* a pioneer work first published in Chicago in 1914, followed by a London edition in 1915; Alfred Barr, *Cubism and Abstract Art* (1936) and *Picasso, Fifty Years of His Art* (1946); Christopher Gray, *Cubist Aesthetic Theories* (1953); John Golding, *Cubism: A History and an Analysis 1907–1914* (1959) from which this selection was taken; Robert Rosenblum, *Cubism and Twentieth Century Art* (1961) and Edward F. Fry, *Cubism* (1966), a fine anthology of documentary texts. Two articles of interest are Winthrop Judkins, "Toward A Reinterpretation of Cubism," *The Art Bulletin,* XXX (1948); and Edward F. Fry, "Cubism 1907–1908: An Early Eyewitness Account," *ibid.*, XLVIII (1966). Because of the artist's connection with Cubist theory, mention should also be made of the fine catalogue compiled by Daniel Robbins, *Albert Gleizes 1881–1953; A Retrospective Exhibition* (1964).

The following selection is reprinted from John Golding, *Cubism: A History and an Analysis 1907–1914* (1959), by permission of the publishers, Faber and Faber, Ltd., London.

ON THE HISTORY AND CHRONOLOGY OF CUBISM

1910 is the year in which the Cubist painters, other than Picasso and Braque, came together as a conscious group, although many of them had known each other earlier. Metzinger and Delaunay had exhibited portraits of each other at the *Salon d'Automne* of 1906, when both were working in a Neo-Impressionist idiom, and by 1907 Delaunay had met Léger and Le Fauconnier as well.[1] Gleizes and Le Fauconnier became friendly in 1909 after a meeting at the home of a young socialist writer named Alexandre Mercereau,[2] where Gleizes also met Metzinger and Delaunay for the first time in the following year, although these meetings did not lead to immediate friendship, and Gleizes knew little about their work.[3] Léger appears to have joined the circle at Mercereau's later in the same year, probably introduced by Delaunay with whom he was becoming very friendly at this period. The painters also met at the Tuesday evenings held by the review *Vers et Prose* at the *Closerie des Lilas*. This café was the stronghold of the older generation of literary Symbolists, writers like Paul Fort, Stuart Merrill and Verhaeren, but many of the younger literary figures such as Apollinaire, Allard, Salmon and Mercereau (the last two on the staff of *Vers et Prose*) were to be seen there too. Allard had arrived in Paris from Lille in the spring of 1910 and his first contacts were with the future Cubists; because of this, his criticism is doubly interesting as representing their ideas unclouded by outside opinion. Older, more established painters like Signac and Sérusier also frequented these gatherings at the *Closerie* so that the atmosphere, though stimulating, was not particularly radical. Gustave Kahn, art critic of the *Mercure de France*, entertained privately the same group of painters and authors.[4]

The works of Metzinger, Gleizes and Le Fauconnier had been hung together by chance at the *Salon d'Automne* of 1910, but the common characteristics which the critics saw in their styles, and the excitement expressed by the poets and authors at Mercereau's and at the *Closerie des Lilas* over the possibilities of a new school of painting, seem to have made the painters aware of each other. Apollinaire and Salmon in particular, although both were in many ways insensitive to painting, realized that Picasso's latest style contained the elements of a new art, and felt that the work of several other painters was evolving in a similar direction. Gleizes writes, "it was at this moment, October 1910, that we discovered each other seriously, including Robert Delaunay . . . and that we realized what we had in common. The necessity of forming a group, of frequenting each other, of exchanging ideas, seemed imperative." [5] Besides the meetings at Mercereau's and the *Closerie,* the painters began meeting regularly at Le Fauconnier's studio in the rue Visconti as well, where during the closing months of the year they watched with interest the development through successive stages of his *Abondance,* a painting that all appear to have regarded as an important, revolutionary work. Early in the following year Gleizes instituted weekly *soirées* at his studio in Courbevoie. Neither Picasso nor Braque, the true creators of the movement, were present at any of these gatherings.

The first Cubist manifestation took place at the *Salon des Indépendants* of 1911. Largely at the instigation of Apollinaire, Salmon and Allard, the painters had decided to show together as a group. "Metzinger, Le Fauconnier, Delaunay, Léger and I," writes Gleizes, "had decided to show at the next *Salon des Indépendants* . . . but . . . should show as a group, everyone was agreed." They feared that if their paintings were not all shown together most of the impact would be lost; but to ensure that they were hung together, the rules of the *Salon* had to be modified. Usually the committee of the *Salon* appointed a hanging committee which was automatically and unanimously approved by the general assembly at its annual meeting held a few weeks before the opening of the exhibition. With the aid of their literary friends, the painters drew up a pamphlet to distribute to the general assembly, protesting against the chaotic hanging in previous exhibitions, and urging that the hanging committee proposed by the committee of the *Salon* be overthrown. They proposed instead a new list of candidates which included themselves "and certain other painters whom we knew to a greater or lesser extent . . . who seemed to us capable of representing if not a particular tendency at least a certain standard." These included Lhote, Segonzac, La Fresnaye and Marchand.

The maneuver proved successful and Metzinger in particular

received a very large number of votes. Le Fauconnier, Léger, Delaunay, Metzinger and Gleizes chose for themselves *Salle 41* and accepted a few other painters to be shown with them, among them, at the request of Apollinaire, Marie Laurencin. A neighboring gallery contained the entries of Lhote, La Fresnaye, Segonzac, Luc Albert Moreau and André Mare. The dramatic "coup" at the general meeting, coupled with the publicity made by the writers of the circle, sufficed to provoke an exceptional amount of interest in the contents of these rooms even before the *Vernissage.* On the opening day it was almost impossible to get into *Salle 41* owing to the crowds. Next day a violent storm of criticism and derision was let loose in the press,[6] while the long review by Apollinaire in *L'Intransigeant* served to establish him as the champion of the group.[7] The painters themselves, despite the highly organized aspect of the demonstration, appear to have been surprised at the sensation caused by their works and at the sudden notoriety which they acquired overnight. Even without the works of Picasso and Braque the public saw in this manifestation a new departure in art; yet in many ways the *succès de scandale* of the *Indépendants* was due as much to the poets as to the painters.

Shortly after the *Salon des Indépendants,* the *Société des Artistes Indépendants* of Brussels invited the French painters to join them in their yearly show, which was to open in June. The catalogue lists Archipenko, Delaunay, Segonzac, Gleizes, Le Fauconnier, Léger, Marchand, Moreau and Jean Plumet; Metzinger for some reason abstained. In his preface to the catalogue, Apollinaire wrote: "The new painters who made manifest this year, at the *Salon des Artistes Indépendants* of Paris, their artistic ideals, accept the name of Cubists which has been given to them. Nevertheless Cubism is not a system, and the differences which characterize not only the talent but the styles of these artists are an obvious proof of it."[8]

The term "Cubism" had become common usage in the press after the opening of the *Salon des Indépendants,* although Apollinaire himself had referred to Metzinger, who had shown a painting directly influenced by Picasso, as "the only adept of Cubism strictly speaking."[9] Applied to the artists showing at Brussels, the term could have no very definite meaning, and Apollinaire found it hard to identify many specific characteristics shared by the painters, or even to distinguish Cubism from Fauvism: "One feature unites them, for if the principal merit of the painters who have been called the Fauves was the return to fundamental principles as far as color and composition are concerned, the Cubists, in order to extend yet further the province of an art thus renewed have sought to return to basic principles of drawing and inspiration. If I add that the majority of Cubists were formerly considered to be Fauves, I can demonstrate how far these young artists have come in a short time and the logic of their vision.

"Out of these two movements which follow upon each other and fuse so successfully, is born an art that is simple and noble, expressive and precise, passionate in its search for beauty, and ready to tackle those vast subjects which yesterday's painters feared to undertake, leaving them to antiquated, boring and pretentious daubers of the official *Salons*."

Apollinaire concludes: "I believe that in these few words I have conveyed the true meaning of Cubism: a new and lofty artistic movement, but not a rigid school inhibiting talent."

The exhibits in the Brussels exhibition seem to have had in common only a concentration on clearly defined simple forms and a corresponding limitation of color, and very few of them had anything at all in common with the work of Picasso and Braque. Certain critics like Hourcade and Allard, who did not realize the importance of what Picasso and Braque were doing, continued to take a broad view of Cubism as simply a return to a more sober, Classical form of art, and thus to include within the movement a large number of artists who were not strictly speaking Cubist but had been slightly influenced by Cubism. In October 1912 Hourcade wrote: "The term 'Cubism' . . . means nothing if it is used to designate a school: there is no school of Cubist painting. And it is absurd to think that the painters of the *Section d'Or*[10] and others, scattered through the *Salon d'Automne*, share any concern other than that of reacting against the sloppiness of Impressionism. The true definition of Cubism seems to me: *the return to a sense of style through a more subjective vision of nature* (conveyed at times by a stronger emphasis on masses). The main interest of Cubism is the total difference of the painters from each other."[11] However, Vauxcelles's original references to the "cubes" in Braque's work and to his "bizarreries cubiques" had been intended disparagingly, and the term "Cubism" continued to be applied by hostile critics to the work of the more advanced painters whom they could not understand or appreciate, and by perceptive critics to these same

50. Picasso, *Portrait of Daniel Henry Kahnweiler*, Oil on Canvas, 39″ by 28″, 1910 (Courtesy of The Art Institute of Chicago)

artists whom they considered to be pioneers in a new movement. But as the pictorial innovations of Picasso and Braque—the construction of a painting in terms of a linear grid or framework, the fusion of objects with their surroundings, the combination of several views of an object in a single image, and of abstract and representational elements in the same picture [see Fig. 50]—began to influence a widening circle of artists, the style became distinguishable by virtue of these features.

Although until late in 1912 Picasso and Braque lived in Montmartre and had relatively little contact with the other Cubists who lived mostly on the Left Bank or in the suburbs, they did not live in isolation. Picasso had never shown publicly at the big *Salons*, but Braque's Cubist works exhibited at the *Salon des Indépendants* of 1909 were widely discussed and were undoubtedly an influence on some painters, while they must have helped others to interpret

Cézanne in a more intellectual, objective way. The work of both painters could be seen at Kahnweiler's gallery in the rue Vignon and at the small private gallery run by Uhde.[12] Delaunay used to meet Picasso at the gatherings at the Douanier Rousseau's,[13] while Metzinger was a frequent visitor to Picasso's studio in the *Bateau Lavoir*[14] during the early years of Cubism, and was an important agent in transmitting the first discoveries of Picasso and Braque. It was Metzinger who, in his *Note sur la Peinture* of 1910, was the first to write of the fact that Picasso and Braque had dismissed traditional perspective and felt free to move around their subjects, studying them from various points of view. Discussing the painting of Picasso and Braque, he added to some general remarks about the return to a more formal and intellectual art his view that a painting by Picasso was "the tangible equivalent of an idea, the image in its totality. . . . Cézanne shows us living forms revealed by light, Picasso adds a material inventory of their intellectual existence, he establishes a free, variable system of perspective. . . . To purely optical sensations he adds tactile sensations." And of Braque he wrote: "Whether he paints a face, a fruit, the entire image pulses incessantly; the painting is no longer an inert grouping of concurrent masses." Léger was shown the works of Picasso and Braque in 1910 by Kahnweiler and met them later the same year.[15] Le Fauconnier and Gleizes did not meet Picasso until late in 1911, and Gleizes does not record having met Braque at all.

The poets and writers who had been instrumental in organizing the younger painters at the *Indépendants* also played a large part in uniting the different aspects of Cubism. Apollinaire and Raynal in particular moved freely in all artistic circles. Apollinaire, however, remained personally most intimate with Picasso, and it is certain that the literary circle which surrounded Picasso, and which included Max Jacob and Pierre Reverdy, was more advanced than that around Gleizes and Metzinger, whose closest friends, men like Mercereau and Nayral, belonged to the circle of Paul Fort and the older generation of Symbolists.

During 1911 and 1912 the group formed by Gleizes, Metzinger, Léger, Le Fauconnier and Delaunay was expanded to include several new figures. Archipenko and La Fresnaye, who had been unknown to Gleizes before the *Salon des Indépendants* of 1911, began to frequent the Mondays at Courbevoie.[16] Picabia was drawn into the circle, probably by Apollinaire with whom he had recently become friendly. Apollinaire himself was usually accompanied by Marie Laurencin. But most important was the contact established with the Duchamp brothers who exhibited under the names of Jacques Villon, Marcel Duchamp and Duchamp-Villon. Duchamp-Villon, although at that time not personally in touch with the group, was on the committee of the *Salon d'Automne* of 1911 and together with La Fresnaye, Desvallières and one or two others, was largely responsible for persuading the hostile jury to include the paintings submitted by the Cubists. Duchamp-Villon and La Fresnaye were also members of the hanging committee, so that the Cubist painters were able to exhibit for the second time that year as a group. Marcel Duchamp and Jacques Villon had been influenced by the demonstration at the *Indépendants,* and were included in the Cubist room at the *Salon d'Automne.* After this their studio at Puteaux became another meeting place. Franz Kupka, a Czech painter who had come to Paris in 1894 or 1895, and who lived in an adjacent studio, was also drawn into contact with the Cubists. Le Fauconnier and Mercereau continued to entertain weekly, so that the painters and writers were meeting constantly. Metzinger, Gleizes, and Le Fauconnier even planned to publish a review dedicated to the plastic arts, with the collaboration of Jacques Nayral and Mercereau.[17] The participation of many of these painters in the formation of *Les Artistes de Passy* in October 1912, an attempt to transform that district of Paris into yet another art center, is a further sign of the continual emphasis on communal activity.[18] Lhote, who had already established a certain independent reputation, mixed cautiously in Cubist circles, but from 1911 onwards was generally referred to as a Cubist, although his somewhat academic style often gained his exemption from the unfavorable criticism directed at the other painters.

The most significant new figure to join the group, however, was undoubtedly Juan Gris. A Spaniard like Picasso, Gris had arrived in Paris in 1906 and had moved into a studio adjacent to Picasso's in the *Bateau Lavoir.* Although he did not begin painting seriously until 1911, Gris had thus been in a position to watch at first hand the birth and development of Picasso's Cubism. Within an amazingly short time he developed into a highly accomplished and individual painter. As he was a very intellectual artist, he was the ideal figure to take over from Metzinger the task of transmitting the principles of Cubism to the other painters; and since he joined the group at a moment when the movement was striving for greater definition, his influence and importance cannot be overestimated. Marcoussis and Herbin, whose work began to be noticed during 1912 and 1913, had also approached Cubism directly through Picasso and Braque.

The influence of Cubism seems to have been immediate and extensive. One reviewer of the *Salon des Indépendants* of 1912 writes: "Now that the Cubists have grown into a school their works occupy several rooms and are to be seen in several exhibitions,"[19] and another: "the Cubists are to be found in force."[20] Reviewing this same exhibition, both Allard and Apollinaire noticed that for the first time in several years the influence of Matisse and Fauvism was slight.[21] Gustave Kahn wrote: "The exhibition favors the Cubists."[22] To add to the general impact of their work, many of the Cubists had, at the suggestion of Apollinaire, submitted very large canvases—Delaunay's *Ville de Paris* was the largest painting in the exhibition.

That same year (1912) the Cubists also exhibited in Rouen at the *Salon de Juin,* and the movement was rapidly becoming known outside France as well. As early as 1910, Mercereau had sent to Russia an exhibition of works by Gleizes, Metzinger and Le Fauconnier, and a few artists whose aims he felt to be similar.[23] Apollinaire was able to write that the *Salon d'Automne* of 1912 had been persuaded to show the Cubists because of their influence and prestige abroad;[24] the most important and sensational feature in the *Salon* was certainly the *maison cubiste,* for which André Mare and Duchamp-Villon were responsible. Indeed, a painter-critic named Lecomte had resigned from membership of the *Salon* because he felt the Cubists were too numerous and their work too well hung.[25] Finally the storm and controversy raised by the Cubists reached its climax on the third of December 1912 when they became the subject of an *interpellation* in the *Chambre des Députés.* Following the lead of a municipal councillor and amateur photographer named Lampué, who had written an open letter to Monsieur Bérard, Under-Secretary in the Ministry of Fine Arts, in the *Mercure de France,*[26] a Socialist deputy, Monsieur Jean Louis Breton, demanded that measures be taken to prevent the Cubists from exhibiting at the *Salon d'Automne:* "It is absolutely inadmissible that our national palaces should be used for manifestations of such an obviously anti-artistic and antinational kind." The attack was answered by Marcel

Sembat, another Socialist, and a leading member of the party, who was himself keenly interested in modern painting. "When a painting seems bad to one," he declared, "one has an incontestable right, that of not looking at it and going to see others. But one doesn't call in the police."[27] So the matter rested there; but it is a sign of the intense feeling aroused by the new school.

The most important single Cubist exhibition was that of the *Section d'Or* at the *Galerie de la Boétie* in October 1912. In the previous year the Cubists and a large number of their friends had exhibited at the *Galerie de l'Art Contemporain* in the rue Tronchet, under the auspices of the *Société Normande de Peinture Moderne.*[28] This exhibition had received little attention in the press, though *l'Autorité* and *Paris Journal* had referred to it as an "exhibition of Fauves and Cubists,"[29] no doubt through a confusion of terms, but also partly because this seemed the only way of describing the manifold tendencies represented, which were as divergent as at Brussels.[30] The *Section d'Or,* on the other hand, was generally accepted as being Cubist in character. Over 200 works were shown, and the fact that all the artists showed paintings representative of their development during the previous three years gave the exhibition an added air of being a Cubist demonstration.[31] Since Picasso and Braque had not exhibited for some time, and since they had not taken part in the manifestations at the *Salon des Indépendants* and the *Salon d'Automne,* the public were not in a position to realize that their abstention deprived the *Section d'Or* of much of its meaning. The idea of the *Section d'Or* seems to have originated in the course of conversations between Gleizes, Metzinger and Jacques Villon at Puteaux and Courbevoie. Jacques Villon, who was older than the others and seems on that account to have enjoyed a certain authority, is generally credited with having suggested the title.[32] On the second of September 1912 *Gil Blas* announced that Marcel Duchamp was planning to send to the forthcoming *Salon d'Automne* a painting which was also to be called *La Section d'Or.*[33] All the Duchamp brothers were at this time passionately interested in mathematics; Jacques Villon was engaged in reading Leonardo's *Trattato della Pittura,*[34] while Marcel Duchamp was a close friend of an amateur mathematician named Maurice Princet, so that it is not surprising that they should have been responsible for introducing a more scientific note into Cubist discussions. The choice of *La Section d'Or* as a title for the exhibition of the group of painters who appeared at the *Galerie de la Boétie* seems to indicate some dissatisfaction with the term Cubism as applied to their work, and was probably intended to imply that the paintings shown had a more profound and rational basis. Perhaps it was felt also to have a wider, more general meaning. The three organizers, however, and many of the painters most directly concerned, were at this period working in a Cubist idiom.[35]

If the Cubists had been surprised by the violent reactions which they had aroused previously, they seem to have been anxious to attract as much attention as possible with this exhibition. The *Vernissage* was held from nine until midnight, for which the only precedent was the initial opening of the *Salon d'Automne* in 1903.[36] Invitations were issued to vast numbers of people, and many of the guests had to be turned away. Lectures by Apollinaire, Hourcade and Raynal were advertised, and a review, *La Section d'Or,* was published to coincide with the opening; it was edited by Pierre Dumont and numbered Apollinaire, Reverdy, Max Jacob, Maurice Raynal, Salmon, Warnod and Hourcade among its contributors.

As in previous exhibitions, artists like Alcide le Beau, Segonzac and Luc Albert Moreau, whose paintings were related to Cubism only in a most general way, were invited to show, and the title may have been chosen partly to allow for this. But as opposed to the exhibition of the *Société Normande de Peinture Moderne* of the previous year, the majority of the artists showing at the *Section d'Or* were Cubists or painters directly influenced by the movement, and the effect made must have been concentrated. Furthermore, the fact that the exhibition was organized to show the successive stages through which Cubism had passed indicates that the painters were attempting to make their work as comprehensible as possible to the public, and their purpose must have been further served by the demonstration of the affinities between Cubism and the more readily understandable paintings of other artists who shared only a few of their pictorial concerns. The exhibition was undoubtedly a great success, and it put Cubism on the map more than any other exhibition that preceded it.

This same desire to render Cubism more intelligible to the general public, and to define and clarify the movement generally, led Gleizes and Metzinger in the autumn of 1911 to collaborate in writing the book *Du Cubisme,* which appeared in August 1912. Salmon's *La Jeune Peinture Contemporaine,* which contained an

Histoire anécdotique du Cubisme, was published in the following month. Earlier in 1912 Apollinaire had written a series of articles for *Les Soirées de Paris* and these were gathered together with some additional material to form the bulk of his *Les Peintres Cubistes* which was issued in March of the following year. In February and June 1912 Hourcade published articles entitled respectively *La Tendance de la Peinture Contemporaine* and *Le Mouvement Pictural vers une école française de peinture,*[37] in which he attempted to reassess the achievements of the preceding year. Raynal's first significant essay *Qu'est-ce que le Cubisme?* did not appear until late in 1913.[38] All these writings had certain points in common. All emphasized that Cubism was an art of realism, although natural appearances were playing an ever-diminishing part. Painting was to become intellectual, and the painters would depict the world not as they saw it, but as they knew it to be. Apollinaire and Hourcade added that this conceptual or intellectual approach led naturally to a selection of simple geometric forms. The right of the painter to move around an object and combine various views of it into a single image, first stated in writing by Metzinger in 1910[39] and elaborated a few months later by Allard,[40] was quickly adopted by most critics as a central feature of the style, and became related to the conceptual or intellectual aspect. Thus Hourcade felt that an artist could convey more clearly the real nature of an object by showing as many aspects of it as possible, and guided by intelligence rather than by his eye, would resort to geometric forms. Knowing that the opening of a cup is round, it is false to depict it simply as an ellipse; ideally the object is shown as a combination of plan, section and elevation. Emphasizing the intellectual approach, Hourcade was the first of the many writers to relate Cubist painting to Kantian aesthetics, and in one of his articles includes a quotation from Schopenhauer: "Kant's greatest service was to distinguish between the appearance of a thing and the thing in itself, and he showed that our intelligence stands between the thing and us."[41] Hourcade also saw as a second feature of Cubist painting the organization of the whole surface in terms of interpenetrating or interacting planes: "The fascination of the paintings lies not only in the presentation of the main objects represented, but in the dynamism which emerges from the composition, a strange, disturbing dynamism, but one that is perfectly controlled." In *Du Cubisme,* this feature was discussed as deriving from Cézanne:

51. Metzinger, *Danseuse,* 1912, Oil on Canvas, $57\frac{1}{2}''$ by $45''$ (Albright-Knox Art Gallery, Buffalo, N.Y.)

"He teaches us to understand a dynamism that is universal. He shows us the modifications which objects thought to be inanimate impose on each other. . . . He prophesies that a study of primordial volumes will open up unheard of horizons. His work, a homogeneous mass, moves in front of our eyes, contracts, expands, seems motionless or flickers, and proves that painting is not—or is no longer—the art of imitating an object by means of lines and colors, but that of giving a pictorial expression to our intuitions."[42]

On the subject of the abstract tendencies inherent in Cubist painting, however, the writers differed sharply. Apollinaire appeared to see complete abstraction as the goal. In the second section of *Les Peintres Cubistes*[43] he stated: "The subject no longer matters, or hardly matters.[44] . . . The secret ambition of the young painters of advanced tendencies is to create a form of pure painting. This is a completely new kind of expression. It is still in its infancy and not as abstract as it aspires to be."[45] Gleizes and Metzinger, themselves painters, and fascinated by purely formal pictorial problems, also began by seeing abstraction as the logical end, although they rapidly retreated and admitted the need, for the moment at least, of a certain coefficient of realism: "... the painting imitates nothing and ... must justify its existence in itself. ... Yet we must admit that reminiscences of natural forms cannot be absolutely banished, at least not yet. Art cannot be raised to a pure effusion at a single onset."[46] Allard and Hourcade rigorously opposed any suggestion of abstraction in Cubist painting. Hourcade condemned it as un-French: "our tradition calls for a subject and the originality of Cubism lies precisely in its rejection of the anecdote in order to rediscover the subject";[47] and he repudiated the idea that all the painters of the *Section d'Or* had renounced natural appearances: "... it is absolutely false to say that all these painters are turning their backs on nature and want only to produce pure painting."[48] None of the writers realized that the Cubism of this date relied on a balance between abstraction and representation to achieve its effects, and that it was this balance that gave each work a significance on more levels than one. It was only natural that the two artist-writers, Gleizes and Metzinger, should have been the ones who were forced into a position of compromise between the two poles of abstraction and representation [Fig. 51].

But while the *Section d'Or* represented the high point of the Cubist movement as it was presented to the public, and while the influence of Cubism daily became more powerful and widespread, many painters who had been Cubist, or had moved in Cubist circles, were already abandoning the style or using certain aspects of it as points of departure for developing completely new art forms.

CONCLUSION

"One can already foresee the approaching day when the term 'Cubism' will have no more than a nominative value to designate in the history of painting certain researches carried out by painters between 1907–14." So Blaise Cendrars wrote in 1919 in an article entitled *Le Cube s'effrite.*[49] To the majority of people this obituary of Cubism must have seemed rather premature. For Cubism, it was obvious, had survived the war. Léonce Rosenberg, the dealer who had temporarily taken over Kahnweiler's role as the chief patron and supporter of the movement, had by 1919 presented at his *Galerie de L'Effort Moderne* large one-man exhibitions by five well-known Cubists, and was busily encouraging newcomers to the school.[50] Exhibitions by Picasso and by Severini, who had by this time abandoned Futurism in favor of a purely Cubist idiom, were scheduled for the following year. Then, in January 1920, a second exhibition of the *Section d'Or* was held at the *Galerie de la Boétie* with the intention of demonstrating the continued vitality and coherence of the movement.[51] Almost all the Cubists, with the important exception of Picasso, showed at the *Salon des Indépendants* of this same year. After the opening Gris was able to write Kahnweiler: "the *Salon des Indépendants* opened with something of a success for the Cubists, who were taken seriously by the whole—or almost—of the press. Even Monsieur Vauxcelles admits that he has wronged us."[52]

But if at the end of the war Cubist activity was resumed on a large scale, the character of the movement was deeply changed. The great revolutionary days were past. In art, as in politics, things which had seemed outrageous in 1914 were accepted almost without a murmur in 1919. As far as Cubism goes, this is proved by the fact that Vauxcelles, who before the war had been its bitterest opponent, was now able, as Gris noted, to look at it in a more detached and objective way. And in fact, as Kahnweiler has pointed out in his book on Gris, the united front presented by the Cubists in 1920 was not based on any very solid foundations. Gleizes, who was one of the organizers of the 1920 *Section d'Or* and had seen the exhibition as a conscious attempt to revive the spirit and principles of prewar Cubism, was forced to admit that it served only to show how "the idea (of Cubism) as it developed has burst the tiny envelope of the *word* Cubism."[53]

As a movement, then, Cubism had lost the quality of unity and concentration which had made it seem so vital and revolutionary in the years before the war. During the war most of the painters were physically separated from each other, and many of them were temporarily forced to abandon their work.[54] When they were able to resume their normal lives they found that they had lost a sense of continuity in their art. Some, like Braque, hesitated for a while before recovering their sense of direction. Others, like Gleizes and Villon, were immediately drawn towards a more abstract form of expression. For a few painters, such as Léger for example, the war itself provided an intense and positive experience that had an immediate and lasting effect on their artistic development. Then those artists who, like Picasso and Gris, had been in a position to keep Cubism alive during the war, had been forced to work in comparative isolation, and this had served to accentuate the differences between them. New figures, most notably the two sculptors Laurens and Lipchitz, were giving the style a new interpretation.

Nevertheless, although after 1918 Cubism was more diffuse than it had been four years earlier, it is dangerous to overestimate the part played by the war in the disintegration of the school. During 1913 and 1914 Picasso and Braque had already been moving apart stylistically. Gris was asserting himself more and more as an individual artist who was giving the style a different emphasis. In his *Contrastes de Formes,* Léger's researches into the pictorial properties and possibilities of form had reached a point of individuality that placed them outside any category. The Orphism of Delaunay was growing steadily further away from its parent movement. La Fresnaye, who had in any case never been a central figure in the movement, had fallen under the influence of Delaunay and was moving out of the Cubist orbit. The Duchamp brothers, and most especially Duchamp-Villon, had adapted Cubism to the principles and aesthetic of Futurism. By 1914 both Marcel Duchamp and Picabia, whose allegiance to Cubism had in any case always been rather doubtful, were completely Dada in spirit. Lhote and a large number of painters like him, who were referred to as "Cubist," had really only seized on the most superficial aspects of the style and were using them to create an up-to-date academicism; indeed, applied to their work, Vauxcelles' definition of Cubism as "an offensive return to the academy" was apt enough.

It is true that as the original nucleus of the movement was breaking up, the style was constantly attracting new figures. By 1914 a host of minor painters, many of whom have long since been forgotten, had become Cubist or had been touched in a positive fashion by the movement. These were the painters who were, perhaps, most affected by the war. For like Gleizes and Metzinger and the other hangers-on of Cubism, it was they who felt the conscious need to be part of an organized, revolutionary movement. When the major Cubists were physically separated by the war and Paris was temporarily abandoned as the home of the artistic *avant-garde,* Cubism lost the impetus that was necessary to sustain the efforts of the lesser artists. After the painters were able to reassemble again, new forces were making themselves felt; many artists experienced a sense of disillusion and disorientation that prevented them from taking up where they had left off. Although much prewar Cubism had a strong intellectual flavor, its origin had been notably unscientific; it offered no hard and fast rules, no signposts to artistic security and success. Many of the lesser painters began to search for some definite pictorial certainty in the realms of abstraction or in coldly didactic movements such as Purism. Others turned to forms of expression more suited to an emotional and disturbed state of mind. The fact that Picasso, who was still generally regarded as the central figure of the Cubist movement, was working in a naturalistic as well as in a Cubist idiom must have made many people doubtful about the future of the style. In short, Cubism no longer held out the possibilities of a universal pictorial idiom.

And although even before 1914 Cubism had spread with unprecedented rapidity to almost every part of the Western world, it was never to become an international style. For, just as many of the painters who had been originally attached to the school used Cubism as a point of departure for the realization of totally different ends, so artists in Holland, Russia and Germany reinterpreted, indeed occasionally even misinterpreted Cubism to found a whole succession of schools and pictorial idioms that were completely divorced from its ideals. This, it has been seen, was exactly what had been done first of all by the Futurists when they had seen in the pictorial techniques evolved by the Cubists the means of expressing their own violent ideologies. By 1914 abstraction was already a force in European art, and during the war more and more painters became attracted to it. An increasing number of artists, painters like Mondrian, Malevitch, Rodchenko, and even at one point, it appeared, Klee, had come to see in Cubism only the first step towards a completely abstract form of painting.

It is easy to understand how such an interpretation could be placed on Cubism. With Cubism, painting had become further removed from ordinary visual appearances than ever before; the Cubist painters were acutely aware of the formal or abstract side of their art. And we have already seen how from an interest in reducing objects and figures to their simplest basic forms, Léger had passed on to an interest in those forms for their own sake, endowing them with a life and independent existence of their own. Delaunay, by introducing what was really a traditional use of color (as opposed to a Cubist use of it) into Cubist painting, had become fascinated by the spatial and formal interaction between planes of pure color, and had soon come to feel that there was no need for a subject, since these formal problems were really the theme of his art. Mondrian, without entering deeply into the spirit and significance of Cubism, had seized at once on the methods of composition evolved by the Cubists, and fascinated by the superficial patterns in the work of Picasso and Léger (whom, as he himself admitted, he most admired) he embarked on a series of formalized experiments that resulted eventually in the aesthetic of *De Stijl.*

The fact that Cubism gave birth to so much abstract art may be one of the reasons why it has been so consistently misunderstood by the public, and even occasionally by serious critics and historians. Cubism, it must be stressed again, was an art of realism, and it was even further removed from abstraction than from, for instance, Futurism. All the true Cubists had at one time or another come near to complete abstraction, but each of them had almost immediately retracted and reasserted the representational element of their art. After the Cadaquès paintings Picasso produced the comparatively legible portrait of Kahnweiler, and devised a system of pictorial "keys" that would render his paintings more accessible to the spectator. When in the winter of 1911–12 Braque's fascination with the tactile qualities of pictorial space had resulted in a complicated, highly hermetic group of paintings, he hastily reverted to a more comprehensible idiom. In 1915 Gris' dissatisfaction with the descriptive quality of much of his earlier work led him to produce the most abstract of all his works, a still life (now in a private collection in Paris) in which it is impossible to reconstruct with any certainty the nature of most of the objects that compose it; this painting, however, did not solve the problems he was facing and remained an isolated phenomenon in his work. It was in his *Contrastes de Formes* that Léger first detached himself from Cubist aesthetic, although he paralleled these paintings with other, more figurative work, and soon abandoned abstraction altogether. Indeed, it is perhaps not altogether fortuitous that the naturalistic portraits executed by Picasso in the second half of 1915 were more or less contemporary with some of his most hermetic Cubist canvases since those done at Cadaquès five years earlier.

But whatever the future of the movement might have been if

it had not been for the war, it is certainly true that by 1914 the fundamental principles of Cubism had been established and all the most important discoveries and innovations had been made. To the system of perspective which had governed European painting since the Renaissance the Cubists had opposed the right of the painter to move freely around his subject and to incorporate into his depiction of it information gathered from previous experience or knowledge. For the first time in the history of art, space had been represented as being as real and as tangible, one might almost say as "pictorial," as the objects which it surrounded (here one must distinguish between an Impressionistic depiction of atmosphere and the painting of empty, clear space, such as is found before Cubism only in the late work of Cézanne). While the Cubists had not denied the interrelation of color and volume, they had formulated a means of allowing them to exist independently of each other in a single painting; that is to say they were using various pictorial elements in their simplest, purest form, allowing each to retain its separate identity while contributing at the same time to the total effect. Partly in order to solve the pictorial problems that had confronted them in their creation of a completely new pictorial idiom, and partly as a natural result of their concept of the painting as an independent organism, a constructed object with a life of its own rather than as a traditional "work of art," the Cubists had evolved two revolutionary pictorial techniques: *papier collé* and *collage.*

Finally, in their desire to take stock afresh of the world that surrounded them, the Cubists had effectively stripped bare many of the problems that had underlain painting and sculpture since the beginning of time. Artists, except those intent only on duplicating their subject in an illusionistic way, had always been aware of the need to reconcile their representation of it with the abstract demands of the aesthetic medium in which they were working; forms must be balanced to achieve a satisfactory composition, in painting volumes in depth must be arranged to produce also a harmonious surface pattern, and so on. The outlook of the Cubists, it has been seen, was intensely realistic, and a true appreciation of their painting depends ultimately on the spectators' ability to reconstruct or identify its subject-matter. But because they were less directly conditioned by visual appearances than any other school of painting since the Renaissance, they were able to evolve more abstract pictorial and sculptural techniques to solve the problems of recreat-

52. Braque, *Still Life* (*With Word "Vin"*), 1913, Papier Collé, $23\frac{1}{8}''$ by $17\frac{1}{4}''$ (Louise and Walter Arensberg Collection, Philadelphia Museum of Art)

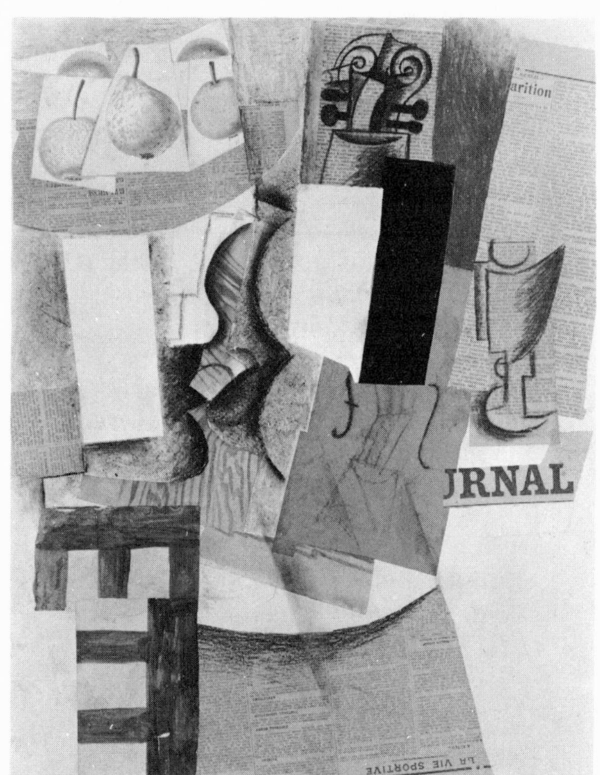

53. Picasso, *Violin and Fruit,* 1913 (A. E. Gallatin Collection, Philadelphia Museum of Art)

ing or reinterpreting the material world through an artistic medium. Never before had the duality between representation and abstraction been so clearly stated as it was in the Cubist paintings of Picasso, Braque, and Gris, in the years immediately preceding the war. In these paintings one is aware at once of the presence of an easily identifiable subject, but the eye is simultaneously stimulated by the presence of an equally obvious underlying abstract pictorial structure with which the representational elements are fused and related. Had any of the problems facing the Cubists remained unsolved before the painters were physically separated by the war, they might have found it necessary to come together again in the same spirit of cooperation that had given the movement such intensity and concentration in the prewar years. But because the nature of the style had been so firmly established during these years preceding 1914, the history of Cubism after the war is largely the history of the artistic development of a series of individual artists who used its principles as the foundation for the creation of their own particular idioms.

In so far as Cubism was a new concept of form and space, involving new pictorial techniques, it is still alive today. Picasso has never relinquished the right to synthesize into his subjects any amount of information or detail, gained by using a variable viewpoint, that he felt necessary to convey more forcefully his vision or ideas of them. *Guernica* is not a Cubist painting, but equally obviously it could not have come into being without Cubism behind it. In Braque's late *Ateliers* there is much the same feeling of spatial materiality and continuity as there is in the works of his classical Cubist period. At the end of his career, when Gris' work could no longer be classified as strictly Cubist, he was still using a "synthetic" Cubist procedure, working from abstraction to representation, marrying a subject to an abstract pictorial substructure. This same process has been used at different times and in modified ways by Braque, Léger and even Picasso. *Papier collé* and *collage* have long since been accepted as recognized methods of work. There is even a reflection of the concept of the *tableau objet* in the aesthetic beliefs of the most radical American painters of the 1950's.

Indeed, the continued life of Cubism, the fact that its influence can be seen around us everywhere today, in painting, sculpture, and even, though less directly and obviously, in architecture and the applied or commercial arts, makes it difficult, perhaps even impossible to assess with complete detachment and objectivity its ultimate role in the history of art. But there can be no doubt that to the historian of the future it will appear as one of the major turning points in the evolution of Western art, a revolution comparable in its effects to any of those which have altered the course of European art, and one which has produced a series of works capable of holding their place amongst the great masterpieces of the past.

NOTES

[1] Unpublished biographical data on Delaunay, compiled by Sonia Terk Delaunay, definitive version 1950.

[2] Mercereau, a journalist and writer of short stories dealing with supernatural happenings, had founded, some years earlier, the *Abbaye de Creteil,* a communal artistic settlement. Gleizes had also participated in this scheme. The *Abbaye* closed down after a few years, and Mercereau busied himself in trying to bring together young Parisian painters and writers.

[3] Gleizes, *Souvenirs,* unpublished, written in the years before 1953.

[4] *Ibid.*

[5] *Ibid.,* on which the following account is based.

[6] *Gil Blas,* 20–21 April 1911, and in *Comoedia, Excelsior, Action, L'Oeuvre* and *Cri de Paris* (quoted in Gleizes).

[7] *L'Intransigeant,* 20 April 1911.

[8] *Les Indépendants, Cercle d'Art,* VIIIème Salon, 10 June–3 July 1911.

[9] *L'Intransigeant,* 21 April 1911.

[10] For the *Section d'Or* see [pp. 290–91 in this text].

[11] *Paris Journal,* 23 Oct. 1912.

[12] There was also a Picasso exhibition at Vollard's in the winter months of 1910–11. Vollard continued to buy Picasso's work until the summer of 1910, although his purchases became fewer, and this exhibition may not have included Cubist work. There appears to have been no catalogue; M. Kahnweiler cannot remember the exhibition at all.

[13] *Picasso et ses Amis,* p. 77.

[14] The *Bateau Lavoir* was the studio building in the rue Ravignan (today known as the place Emile-Goudeau), where Picasso lived from 1904 until 1909; the name seems to have arisen from its resemblance to the washing-boats on the Seine. The building was originally a piano factory, and was known to Picasso and his friends also as *la maison du trappeur.*

[15] Douglas Cooper, *Fernand Léger et le nouvel Espace* (Geneva, 1949), p. 36.

[16] *Souvenirs.*

[17] The plans for this review are discussed in *Paris Journal,* 17 Oct.–30 Oct. 1911.

[18] The formation of this group is discussed in an article entitled *Passy, Nouveau Centre d'Art,* in *Poème et Drame,* Paris, January 1913. The painters involved were Gleizes, Metzinger, Laurencin, Jacques Villon, Duchamp-Villon, Picabia, La Fresnaye and Tobeen. Auguste and Claude Perret were also present at the

meetings in the *Maison de Balzac.* At one of these meetings La Fresnaye read a paper on Cézanne.

[19] J. Laran, in *Bulletin de la Société de l'Histoire de l'Art Français,* 1er fascicule, 1912.

[20] Mourey, in *Journal,* 22 March 1912.

[21] *L'Intransigeant,* 19–22 March 1912; *Côte,* 19 March 1912.

[22] *Mercure de France,* 1 April 1912.

[23] Gleizes, *Souvenirs.*

[24] *L'Intransigeant,* 30 Sept. 1912.

[25] *Le Temps,* 12 Oct. 1912.

[26] 16 Oct. 1912.

[27] *Journal Officiel de la Chambre des Députés,* 1ère Séance du 3 déc. 1912.

[28] This is presumably the same body as originated the exhibition at Rouen the following summer (1912), see p. 290 [Golding] above, although Apollinaire calls it *Société des Artistes Normands* (*Les Peintres Cubistes,* p. 13).

[29] *Paris Journal,* 13 Nov.; *l'Autorité,* 27 Nov. 1911.

[30] The following painters exhibited at the *Galerie d'Art contemporain:* Metzinger, Le Fauconnier, Gleizes, Léger, Dufy, Marcel Duchamp, La Fresnaye, Lhote, Laurencin, Picabia, Friesz, Segonzac, Jacques Villon, Mare, Le Beau, Zak, Verdilhan, Dumont, Lotiron, Marchand, Luc Albert Moreau, Vera, Tobeen, Braque, Girieud, Ribbemont-Dessaignes, Texier, Saint-Deles; and the following sculptors: Archipenko, Duchamp-Villon, Jermant, Nadelman and Halau.

[31] *Paris Journal,* 15 Sept. 1912.

[32] This was confirmed verbally to the writer by M. Marcel Duchamp.

[33] *Gil Blas,* 2 Sept. 1912.

[34] Jacques Lassaigne, *Jacques Villon* (Paris, 1950), p. 4. The *Trattato della Pittura* appeared in a French translation by Péladan in 1910.

[35] The exhibitors were: Metzinger, Gleizes, Villon, Duchamp, Duchamp-Villon, Picabia, Gris, Lhote, La Fresnaye, Marcoussis, Archipenko, Agero, Marchand, Segonzac, Luc Albert Moreau, Vera, Léger, Pierre Dumont, Tobeen, Glanis, Le Beau, Laurencin, Hassenberg, Lewitzka, Tivnet, Ribbemont-Dessaignes, Gav, Dexter, Girieud and Valensi.

[36] *Paris Journal,* 9 Oct. 1912.

[37] In *La Revue de France et des Pays Français No.* 1, Feb. 1912. *Revue Française,* June 1912.

[38] In *Comoedia Illustré,* Dec. 1912.

[39] *Note sur la Peinture.*

[40] In *Sur Quelques Peintres, Les Marches du Sud-Ouest,* June 1911.

[41] *La Tendance de la Peinture Contemporaine.*

[42] *Du Cubisme,* pp. 8, 9.

[43] This section appeared originally in the Feb. 1912 edition of *Les Soirées de Paris* as *Du Sujet dans la Peinture Moderne.*

[44] *Les Peintres Cubistes,* p. 11.

[45] *Ibid.,* pp. 13–14.

[46] *Du Cubisme,* p. 17.

[47] *La Tendance de la Peinture Contemporaine.*

[48] *Paris Journal,* 23 Oct. 1912.

[49] In *La Rose Rouge,* no. 3, 15 May 1919.

[50] By 1919 there had been exhibitions of Braque, Léger, Metzinger, Herbin and Gris, Rosenberg had also shown Laurens and was planning a Hayden exhibition, two new recruits to Cubism.

[51] Yet a third exhibition called *La Section d'Or* was held at the Galerie Vavin Raspail in 1925.

[52] *The Letters of Juan Gris,* p. 75. Letter of 31 Jan. 1920. Kahnweiler was in Switzerland.

[53] "L'Epopée" in *Le Rouge et le Noir,* June–July 1929.

[54] Léger, Braque, Gleizes (very briefly), Marcoussis, Metzinger, Jacques Villon and Duchamp-Villon were in the army as were La Fresnaye, Lhote and the majority of the peripheral figures who had been attached to the movement.

18. THE AESTHETIC THEORIES OF KANDINSKY AND THEIR RELATIONSHIP TO THE ORIGIN OF NON-OBJECTIVE PAINTING

Peter Selz

INTRODUCTION

The first decade of the twentieth century saw European art moving along a number of fronts in the general direction of an art without representational imagery—towards an art purely of colors, lines, and shapes that bore no direct relationship to the appearance of the outside world. If convenience impels us to fix on these years for the genesis of the non-objective art that finally emerged between 1910 and 1914, historical sense urges us to recognize that the process had been gathering force in art and thought for many decades and that the representational habit, with the authority of centuries of tradition behind it, was not easily sloughed. From the superior comfort of our retrospective vision we have probably determined most of the elements that went into this process. We recognize the contributions of the Jugendstil aesthetics of the 1890's, the impact of the Symbolists and Post-Impressionists, of Les Fauves, and Orphism. The "chemistry" of the process may still be imperfectly understood, but it is reasonably certain that Wassily Kandinsky was its final catalyst.

To cite but one symptom of the conditions within which the process was maturing, it is rewarding to read in conjunction with Kandinsky's *Concerning the Spiritual in Art,* that remarkable little book, George Santayana's *The Sense of Beauty* (1896), and particularly Santayana's remarks on the sensuous level of perception. He saw pure sensations of color as being antecedent to the constructive effects of form, and these sensations of color at a fundamental level as having affinities with the qualities of other sensations, especially sound. A general development of the capacity to grasp the connections and to sense these qualities—"sensibility" was Santayana's word for this capacity—"would make possible a new abstract art, an art that should deal with colors as music does with sound." By the end of the century a spokesman for the Jugendstil would speak of "the music of color" and Kandinsky himself, in his *Concerning the Spiritual in Art,* wrote of color as the keyboard on which the artist plays "to cause vibrations of the soul."

For bibliographical details of Kandinsky's *Concerning the Spiritual in Art,* see footnote 5 in this selection by Peter Selz. Kandinsky's short autobiography, *Rückblicke,* can be found in English translation by Hilla Rebay; also "Retrospects" in *Kandinsky,* edited by Hilla Rebay (1945), and translated by Mrs. R. L. Herbert, as "Reminiscences" in *Modern Artists on Art,* edited by Robert L. Herbert (1964). Kandinsky's treatise of 1926, *Punkt und Linie zur Fläche,* was translated as *Point and Line to Plane* by H. Dearstyne and Hilla Rebay (1947). Other selected works of relevance are: James Johnson Sweeney, *Plastic Redirections in 20th Century Painting* (1934); Piet Mondrian, *Plastic Art and Pure Plastic Art, 1937, and Other Essays, 1941–1943* (1945); L. Moholy-Nagy, *The New Vision,* 4th rev. ed. (1949); Georges Duthuit, *The Fauvist Painters* (1950); Peter Selz, *German Expressionist Painting* (1957); and Werner Haftmann, *Painting in the Twentieth Century,* 2 Vols., rev. ed. (1965).

The following selection is a reprint, with permission of the author, Peter Selz, of "Aesthetic Theories of Wassily Kandinsky and Their Relationship to the Origin of Non-Objective Painting," *The Art Bulletin,* XXXIX (1957).

At a time when so much painting is in the non-objective vein, it seems relevant to investigate the aesthetic theories of the artist who was the first champion of non-objective art, or "concrete art,"[1] as he preferred to call it.

It is possible that non-objective paintings may have been painted prior to Kandinsky's first non-objective watercolor of 1910* and his more ambitious *Impressions, Improvisations,* and *Compositions* of 1911. There are abstractions by Arthur Dove, for example, which are dated 1910. Picabia and Kupka began working in a non-objective idiom not much later,[2] and Delaunay painted his non-objective *Color Disks* in 1912.[3] In Germany Adolf Hoelzel ventured into non-objective painting as early as 1910, but whereas for Hoelzel it was merely experiment in additional possibilities, Kandinsky made non-objectivity the very foundation of his pictorial imagery.[4]

Kandinsky formulated his ideas of non-objective painting over an extended period of time. Notes for his essay, *Concerning the Spiritual in Art,*[5] date back to 1901 while the book was completed in 1910. His thoughts were continued in his essay "Über die Formfrage" for the famous almanac *Der blaue Reiter.*[6] Both essays were first published in 1912.[7] These essays are to a considerable extent based on previous aesthetic theory and were very much in keeping with the avant-garde thinking of the prewar years. They also constitute almost a programmatic manifesto for the expressionist generation.[8]

Kandinsky's particular didactic style makes his writings difficult to read and analyze. Kenneth Lindsay in his study of Kandinsky's theories described Kandinsky's peculiar literary style as follows: "Characteristic of Kandinsky's writing is the technique of breaking up the given topic into opposites or alternatives. These opposites or alternatives usually follow directly after the posing of the problem and are numbered. Often they suggest further sets of opposites and alternatives. The sequence of thought is flexible, sometimes abrupt and cross-tracking, and frequently associative. The dominating

*[Later research has indicated that this work must be dated later than 1910, probably 1912 or 1913. Letter from Peter Selz to editor, November 14, 1967.]

54. Kandinsky, *Improvisation 28*, 1912, Oil on Canvas, 44″ by 63¾″ (The Soloman R. Guggenheim Museum, N.Y.)

relativity of the thought process contrasts strongly with the conclusions, which are often positively stated."[9]

THE REJECTION OF MATERIAL REALITY

Kandinsky was always strongly predisposed toward sense impressions. In his autobiography he indicates that he experienced objects, events, even music primarily in terms of color, and he did not conceive of color in its physical and material aspects but rather in its emotional effect. During his scientific studies he lost faith in the rational scientific method and felt that reality could be fully comprehended only by means of creative intuition.

Kandinsky was not alone in his rejection of positivism and pragmatism at the turn of the century. Generally it might be said that "the twentieth century has in its first third taken up a position of reaction against classic rationalism and intellectualism."[10]

Even in the pure sciences the value of the intuitive as against the purely experimental was stressed during the early part of the twentieth century, so that by 1925 Werner Heisenberg was able to formulate the "Principle of Uncertainty," stating that there is a limit to the precision with which we can observe nature scientifically. This did not mean a return to metaphysics, but it indicated the inherent limitations of quantitative observation.

Kandinsky's doubt of the ultimate possibilities of quantitative analysis was shared by many philosophers also. His philosophy finds perhaps its closest parallel in the thinking of Henri Bergson, who taught that true reality can be grasped only through artistic intuition, which he contrasted to intellectual conception. The intellect, according to Bergson, is man's tool for rational action, but "art, whether it be painting or sculpture, poetry or music, has no other object than to brush aside the utilitarian symbols, the conventional and socially accepted generalities, in short, everything that veils reality from us, in order to bring us face to face with reality itself."[11]

Similarly Kandinsky turns away from the representation of visible objects in his attempt to penetrate beneath the epidermis of appearances to the ultimate or "inner" reality.[12] As early as his first encounter in Moscow with the paintings by Monet, Kandinsky felt that the material object was not a necessary element in his painting: "I had the impression that here painting itself comes into the foreground; I wondered if it would not be possible to go further in this direction. From then on I looked at the art of icons with different eyes; it meant that I had 'got eyes' for the abstract in art."[13] Later he wrote: "The impossibility and, in art, the purposelessness of copying an object, the desire to make the object express itself, are the beginnings of leading the artist away from 'literary' color to artistic, i.e. pictorial aims."[14]

Agreeing with earlier writers such as the symbolists, Van de Velde, and Endell, Kandinsky felt that art must express the spirit but that in order to accomplish this task it must be dematerialized. Of necessity, this meant creating a new art form.

It was not only for philosophic reasons that Kandinsky wished to forsake objective reality. Psychological reasons, it seems, also played their part. Speaking about his period of study at the Munich Art Academy, he wrote: "The naked body, its lines and movement, sometimes interested me, but often merely repelled me. Some poses in particular were repugnant to me, and I had to force myself to copy them. I could breathe freely only when I was out of the studio door and in the street once again."[15]

It is significant that the human body, which is found as an almost universal motif in the art forms of most cultures, is here eschewed as subject matter.[16] It is true that the art of the west emphasized the nonhuman aspects during the nineteenth century, when painters turned their attention to still life and landscape. The conscious rejection of the human form, however, is certainly psychologically significant. Indeed a psychological interpretation of the reasons for this response might give us a more profound understanding of the non-objective artist and his work.

From the point of view of the history of aesthetics it is also interesting that Kandinsky's rejection of the forms of nature occurred at approximately the same time as Worringer's publication, *Abstraction and Empathy.* Here Worringer submits the theory that the cause for abstraction is man's wish to withdraw from the world or his antagonism toward it. The lifeless form of a pyramid or the suppression of space in Byzantine mosaics clearly shows that what motivated the creation of these works of art was a need for refuge from the vast confusion of the object world—the desire for "a resting-place in the flight of phenomena."[17] Worringer's thesis of abstraction as one of the bases of artistic creation preceded Kandinsky's first non-objective painting by about two years, and it is important to keep in mind that the two men knew each other in Munich during this critical period.

Kandinsky himself maintained that the immediate cause of his first essay at non-objective painting was the shock of suddenly entering his studio to see one of his paintings lying on its side on the easel and being struck with its unusual beauty. This incident, he believed, made it clear to him that the representation of nature was superfluous in his art.[18] The emphasis on the element of distance in the aesthetic experience found a parallel in the theories of the contemporary English psychologist, Edward Bullough: "The sudden view of things from their reverse, usually unnoticed, side, comes upon us as a revelation, and such revelations are precisely those of art."[19]

Kandinsky felt, however, that he could not immediately turn to "absolute painting." In a letter to Hilla Rebay,[20] he pointed out that at that time he was still alone in the realization that painting ultimately must discard the object. A long struggle for increasing abstraction from nature was still necessary. In 1910 he was still writing: "Purely abstract forms are in the reach of few artists at present; they are too indefinite for the artist. It seems to him that to limit himself to the indefinite would be to lose possibilities, to exclude the human and therefore to weaken expression."[21]

But he was already pointing out at that time that the abstract idea was constantly gaining ground, that the choice of subjects must originate from the inner necessity of the artist; material, or objective, form may be more or less superfluous. He insists that the artist must be given complete freedom to express himself in any way that is necessary according to the "principle of inner necessity." He looked hopefully to the future where the eventual predominance of the abstract would be inevitable in the "epoch of great spirituality."[22]

In 1910 Kandinsky painted his first abstract painting, a watercolor. [See editor's note at beginning of article.] The first large non-objective oil dates from 1911, and throughout 1912 he did both "objective" and "concrete" paintings. After 1912 there were very few "objective" works. His art had become completely free from nature and like music its meaning was now meant to be inherent in the work itself and independent of external objects.

Kandinsky distinguished what he called "objective" art from "concrete" art by distinguishing between the means chosen by the artist. In "objective" art both artistic and natural elements are used, resulting in "mixed art," while in "concrete" art exclusively artistic means are used, resulting in "pure art."[23] In a short article, published in 1935, he gave a lucid example of this distinction: "There is an essential difference between a line and a fish. And that is that the fish can swim, can eat and be eaten. It has the capacities of which the line is deprived. These capacities of the fish are necessary extras for the fish itself and for the kitchen, but not for the painting. And so, not being necessary they are superfluous. That is why I like the line better than the fish—at least in my painting."[24]

The element of representation is thus rejected by Kandinsky for his art. He insists that a picture's quality lies in what is usually called form: its lines, shapes, colors, planes, etc., without reference to anything outside of the canvas. But here occurs an apparent contradiction in Kandinsky's theory, because he—like expressionists in general—did not believe that a picture must be evaluated from its formal aspects. Kandinsky and the expressionists did not agree with "formalists" like Roger Fry, who believe that the aesthetic emotion is essentially an emotion about form. Seeing Kandinsky's first abstractions, Fry concerned himself only with their form: ". . . one finds that . . . the improvisations become more definite, more logical and more closely knit in structure, more surprisingly beautiful in their color oppositions, more exact in their equilibrium."[25]

Kandinsky himself takes strong issue with this theory. In his aesthetics the formal aspect of a work of art is as unimportant as its representational quality.

THE INSIGNIFICANCE OF FORM

Form, to Kandinsky, is nothing but the outward expression of the artist's inner needs. Form is matter, and the artist is involved in a constant struggle against materialism. Kandinsky's words are reminiscent of medieval thought when he says: "It is the spirit that rules over matter, and not the other way around."[26]

The artist should not seek salvation in form, Kandinsky warns in his essay, "Über die Formfrage," because form is only an expression of content and is entirely dependent on the innermost spirit. It is this spirit which chooses form from the storehouse of matter, and it always chooses the form most expressive of itself. Content always creates its own appropriate form. And form may be chosen from anywhere between the two extreme poles: the great abstraction and the great realism. Kandinsky then proceeds to prove that these opposites, the abstract and the realistic, are actually identical, and that form is therefore an insignificant concern to the artist. This he does as follows:

In the "great realism" (as exemplified in the art of Henri Rousseau) the external-artificial element of painting is discarded, and the content, the inner feeling of the object, is brought forth primitively and "purely" through the representation of the simple, rough object. Artistic purpose is expressed directly since the painting is not burdened with formal problems. The content is now strongest because it is divested of external and academic concepts of beauty. Kandinsky preferred this "great realism," also found in children's drawings, to the use of distortion, which he felt always aroused literary associations.

Since the "great abstraction" excludes "real" objects, the content is embodied in non-objective form. Thus the "inner sound" of the picture is most clearly manifest. The scaffolding of the object has been removed, as in realism the scaffolding of beauty has been discarded. In both cases we arrive at the spiritual content itself. "The greatest external differentiation becomes the greatest internal identity:

Realism = Abstraction
Abstraction = Realism"[27]

The hypothesis that the minimum of abstraction can have the most abstract effect, and vice versa, is based by Kandinsky on the postulation that a quantitative decrease can be equal to a qualitative increase: 2 plus 1 can be less than 2 minus 1 in aesthetics. A dot of color, for example, may lose in its *effect* of intensity if its *actual* intensity is increased.[28] The pragmatic function of a form and its sentient meaning are dissimilar, yet abstraction and realism are identical.

Kandinsky cites several examples to prove this thesis. A hyphen, for instance, is of practical value and significance in its context. If this hyphen is taken out of its practical-purposeful context and put on canvas, and if it is not used there to fulfill any practical purpose at all—such as the delineation of an object—it then becomes nothing but a line; it is completely liberated from signification and abstracted from all its meaning as a syntactical sign; it is the abstract line itself. At the same time, however, it has also become most real, because now it is no longer a sign but the real line, the object itself.

It may be argued that Kandinsky uses a very narrow definition of both the abstract and the realistic, and that the line may be a great deal more realistic and more meaningful as a sign, such as a hyphen, in its context, than it is as a line only. It is a valid objection to say that this identity of the abstract and the real holds true only in this verbal analogy, and that Kandinsky has not presented logical proof. Kandinsky, however, was not concerned with the correctness of intellectual thought, or with the proof of his spiritual values. He admits: "I have always turned to reason and intellect least of all."[29]

He concludes his analysis of form by saying: "In principle there is no problem of form."[30] The artist who expresses his "soul vibrations" can use any form he wants. Formal rules in aesthetics are not only impossible but a great stumbling block to the free expression of spiritual value. It is the duty of the artist to fight against them to clear the way for free expression. Often in the history of art, artists were bogged down by matter and could not see beyond the formal. The nineteenth century was such a period, in which men failed to see the spirit in art as they failed to see it in religion. But to seek art and yet be satisfied with form is equivalent to the contentment with the idol in the quest for God. Form is dead unless it is expressive of content. There cannot be a symbol without expressive value.

In his introduction to the second edition of *Der blaue Reiter* Kandinsky states the aim of the book as "to show by means of examples, practical arrangement and theoretical proof, that the problem of form is secondary in art, that art is above all a matter of content."[31]

Kandinsky understood his own time as being the beginning of a new spiritual age when the abstract spirit was taking possession of the human spirit.[32] Now artists would increasingly recognize the insignificance of form per se, and realize its relativity, its true meaning as nothing but "the outward expression of inner meaning."

ART THE AFFIRMATION OF THE SPIRIT

We have seen that in Kandinsky's aesthetics form as well as object, the formal and representational aspects of art, have no importance by themselves and are meaningful only insofar as they express the artist's innermost feelings. Only through the expression of the artist's inner emotion can he transmit understanding of true spiritual reality itself. The only "infallible guide" which can carry the artist to "great heights" is the *principle of internal necessity* (italics his).[33] This concept of internal necessity is the core and the basis of Kandinsky's aesthetic theory and becomes a highly significant element in expressionist criticism in general.

The period of spiritual revolution which Kandinsky believed to be approaching, he called the "spiritual turning point." He perceived indications of this period of transition in many cultural manifestations. In the field of religion, for instance, Theosophy was attempting to counteract the materialist evil. In the Theosophical Society, "one of the most important spiritual movements,"[34] man seeks to approach the problem of the spirit by the way of inner enlightenment. In the realm of literature he cites Maeterlinck as,

". . . perhaps one of the first prophets, one of the first reporters and clairvoyants of the *decadence*. . . . Maeterlinck creates his atmosphere principally by artistic means. His material machinery . . . really plays a symbolic role and helps to give the inner note. . . . The apt use of a word (in its poetical sense), its repetition, twice, three times, or even more frequently, according to the need of the poem, will not only tend to intensify the internal structure but also bring out unsuspected spiritual properties in the word itself."[35]

By using pure sound for the most immediate effect upon the reader or listener, the writer depends on prelanguage signs, i.e., sounds which—like music—do not depend on language for their meaning. This level of signification is also the basis of Kandinsky's non-objective painting. In music Kandinsky points to Schönberg's panchromatic scheme, which advocates the full renunciation of functional harmonious progression and traditional form and accepts only those means which lead the composer to the most uncompromising self-expression: "His music leads us to where musical experience is a matter not of the ear, but of the soul—and from this point begins the music of the future."[36] Kandinsky conceived of music as an emancipated art, which furthermore had the quality of time-extension and was most effective in inspiring spiritual emotion in the listener. Painting, while still largely dependent on natural form was showing similar signs of emancipation. Picasso's breakdown of volumes and Matisse's free use of color for its own sake were manifestations of the turning point toward a spiritual art.[37]

How would the artist achieve full spiritual harmony in his composition? Kandinsky pointed out that the painter had two basic means at his disposal—form and color—and that there was always an unavoidable mutual relationship between them.

In his prewar writings he still did not come forth with a thorough analysis of forms as he did later with his systematic *Point and Line to Plane,* yet he was already stating: "Form alone, even though abstract and geometrical, has its internal resonance, a spiritual entity whose properties are identical with the form. A triangle . . . is such an entity, with its particular spiritual perfume."[38]

But color is the most powerful medium in the hand of the painter. It has a psychic as well as a physical effect upon the observer. It can influence his tactile, olfactory, and especially aural senses, as well as his visual sense, and in chromotherapy it has been shown that "red light stimulates and excites the heart, while blue light can cause temporary paralysis."[39] Color is the artist's means by which he can influence the human soul. Its meaning is expressed metaphorically by Kandinsky: "Color is the keyboard, the eyes are the hammers, the soul is the piano with many strings. The artist is the hand that plays, touching one key or another purposively, to cause vibrations of the soul."[40]

Kandinsky then proceeds to develop an elaborate explanation of the psychic effect of color. This contrasts to the more scientific color theories of Helmholtz, Rood, Chevreul and Signac and closely approaches the psychological color theory of Goethe and metaphysics of color of Philipp Otto Runge. Like his romanticist predecessor, Kandinsky believed that color could directly influence the human soul.[41]

Blue in Kandinsky's system is the heavenly color; it retreats from the spectator, moving toward its own center. It beckons to the infinite, arousing a longing for purity and the supersensuous. Light blue is like the sound of the flute, while dark blue has the sound of the cello.

Yellow is the color of the earth. It has no profound meaning; it seems to spread out from its own center and advance to the spectator from the canvas. It has the shrill sound of a canary or of a brass horn, and is often associated with the sour taste of lemon.

Green is the mixture of blue and yellow. There the concentricity of blue nullifies the eccentricity of yellow. It is passive and static, and can be compared to the so-called "bourgeoisie," self-satisfied, fat and healthy. In music it is best represented by the placid, long-drawn middle tones of the violin.

White, which was not considered a color by the Impressionists, has the spiritual meaning of a color. It is the symbol of a world void of all material quality and substance. It is the color of beginning. It is the "sound" of the earth during the white period of the Ice Age.

Black is like eternal silence. It is without hope. It signifies termination and is therefore the color of mourning.

By the symbolic use of colors combined "according to their spiritual significance," the artist can finally achieve a great composition: "Color itself offers contrapuntal possibilities and, when combined with design, may lead to the great pictorial counterpoint, where also painting achieves composition, and where pure art is in the service of the divine."[42]

Kandinsky's color symbolism is in no way based upon physical laws of color or the psychology of color vision. He himself pointed out when writing about color that "all these statements are the results of empirical feeling, and are not based on exact science."[43] This may even explain his own inconsistencies such as his statement in *Concerning the Spiritual in Art* that "red light stimulates and excites the heart"[44] contradicted by his assertion that "red . . . has brought about a state of partial paralysis."[45]

It is also true that specific colors call forth different associations in people as well as cultures. Specific reactions to specific colors have never been proved experimentally. Max Raphael in his book, *Von Monet bis Picasso,* points out that colors have had altogether different meanings for those individuals most occupied with them. Yellow, for example, signified the earth for Leonardo, had gay, happy characteristics for Goethe, meant friendliness to Kant and heavenly splendor to Van Gogh, suggested the night to Gauguin and aggressiveness to Kandinsky.[46] We might add that it symbolizes jealousy in German usage, an emotion which is associated with green in English idiom.

Such examples could be increased *ad infinitum* and it is very doubtful that Kandinsky attempted to set down scientific rules for color associations. He was articulating his own personal associations; he stated: "It is clear that all I have said of these simple colors is very provisional and general, and so are the feelings (joy, grief, etc.) which have been quoted as parallels to the colors. For these feelings are only material expressions of the soul. Shades of color, like those of sound, are of a much finer texture and awaken in the soul emotions too fine to be expressed in prose."[47]

In his second significant book, *Point and Line to Plane,* subtitled "A Contribution to the Analysis of the Pictorial Elements," Kandinsky presented his grammar of line, forms, and space in a manner similar to his color theory in *Concerning the Spiritual in Art.*

It is the task of the painter, according to Kandinsky, to achieve the maximum effect by bringing his media, color and form, into orderly and expressive composition. Each art has its own language, and each artist, be he painter, sculptor, architect, writer or composer, must work in his specific medium and bring it to the expression of greatest inner significance. But once painting, for example, is divested of the scaffolding of natural form and becomes completely abstract, the pure law of pictorial construction can be discovered. And then it will be found that pure painting is *internally* closely related to pure music or pure poetry.

SYNTHESIS OF THE ARTS

Kandinsky points out that human beings, because of individual differences, differ in the type of art expression to which they are most receptive. For some it is musical form, for others painting or literature, which causes the greatest aesthetic enjoyment. He also realized that the artist could achieve aesthetic effects in sensory fields not limited to his own medium. He was much interested, for instance, in Scriabin's experiments with sound-color combinations. The re-enforcement of one art form with another by means of synaesthesia will greatly increase the final aesthetic effect upon the receptor. The greatest effect can be obtained by the synthesis of all the arts in one "monumental art," which is the ultimate end of Kandinsky's aesthetics.

Kandinsky here continues the nineteenth century tradition—from Herder to Wagner—with its desire for a union of all arts. Kandinsky believes that a synthesis of the arts is possible because in the final analysis all artistic means are identical in their inner meaning: ultimately the external differences will become insignificant and the internal identity of all artistic expression will be disclosed. Each art form causes a certain "complex of soul vibrations." The aim of the synthesis of art forms is the refinement of the soul through the sum-total of these complexes.

In his essay "Über Bühnenkomposition"[48] and in his "Schematic Plan of Studies and Work of the Institute of Art Culture,"[49] Kandinsky outlines the possible steps to be taken for the achievement of "monumental art." Present-day drama, opera, ballet are criticized as much as the plastic arts. By discarding external factors in "stage composition,"[50] particularly the factors of plot, external relationship, and external unity, a greater internal unity can be achieved. Kandinsky then experiments with such a composition, "Der gelbe Klang."[51] There he attempts to combine music, the movement of dancers and of objects, the sound of the human voice (without being tied down to word or language meanings), and the effect of color-tone, as experimented with by Scriabin.

Kandinsky admits that his "stage composition" is weak but believes the principle to be valid. It is necessary to remember, he maintains, that we are still at the very beginning of the great abstract period in art. Materialism still has its grasp on modern activity and is not as yet completely vanquished. But the new, "the spiritual in art," already manifests itself in most fields of creativity.

Kandinsky made his first attempt at the realization of a synthesis of the arts when he proposed and founded the Institute of Art Culture in Moscow in 1920, a comprehensive institute for the study and development of the arts and sciences. Kandinsky was active in this organization as vice-president for about a year; then political pressure forced his resignation and he found a similar field of activity in the Bauhaus in Weimar, which he joined in 1922.

CONCLUSION

Expressionism, which began by shifting emphasis from the object to be painted to the artist's own subjective interpretation—reached in Kandinsky the total negation of the object. In this respect he was of great inspiration to succeeding artists. The final phase of Expressionism also became the beginning of an altogether new artistic concept, non-objective painting, and Kandinsky was heralded as its innovator by the following generation, even by painters such as Diego Rivera working in an altogether different style: "I know of nothing more real than the painting of Kandinsky—nor anything more true and nothing more beautiful. A painting by Kandinsky gives no image of earthly life—it is life itself. If one painter deserves the name 'creator,' it is he. He organizes matter as matter was organized, otherwise the Universe would not exist. He opened a window to look inside the All. Someday Kandinsky will be the best known and best loved by men."[52]

In his rejection of the representational aspect of art, Kandinsky cleared the way for new values in art. By experimenting with the possibility of an expressive—rather than a formalistic—art in the non-objective idiom, he threw out a challenge which performed a most valuable function in the history of modern art. Through his activity as an aesthetician as well as a painter he was able to write a series of books which fully articulate his ideas and have become as influential in the history of modern painting as his paintings themselves.

Kandinsky's aesthetic theory continues, among other things, the precept that the elements of painting—lines and colors and their combinations—evoke emotional associations in the observer. This precept is basic to Expressionism, although not original with the Expressionist movement. Much of it is implied in romanticist aesthetics and clearly stated in the theory of empathy. It is set forth differently in Paul Signac's theory of Neo-Impressionism and occurs again in Bergson's *Essai sur les données immédiates de la conscience.*[53] It is significant for an understanding of symbolism and its corollary *Jugendstil,* and was reiterated by such men as Gauguin, Denis, Sérusier, Walter Crane, and August Endell.

Kandinsky's essays, however, are exceedingly important because they were written by the man who himself was the innovator of non-objective painting. Now in the total absence of representational objects the plastic elements were to become sole carriers of the artist's message. This probably is why he felt called upon to express verbally what he had done in his painting through the intuition of "inner necessity."

In the analysis of his color theory it was pointed out that no direct parallels can be established between the artist's statement and the observer's response. Both projections rest on highly personal and subjective factors. This, however, does not greatly differ from music. It has, for example, been shown that the major and minor modes are by no means endowed with characteristics which would call forth identical reactions in different listeners.[54] A great deal depends on previous experience and training.

As Kandinsky himself has indicated, prose cannot express the shades of emotion awakened by sound and color. Each person may verbalize differently about the experience of a work of art and his verbalization may be at great variance with that of the artist. Yet direct communication can take place on a primary visual (preverbal) level, before either spectator or artist articulates. It is toward this level of communication that the art of Kandinsky and other Expressionists was directed.

NOTES

This article is based on a chapter of the author's book, *German Expressionist Painting*, University of California Press. It was originally a part of a doctoral dissertation, "German Expressionist Painting from Its Inception to the First World War," University of Chicago, 1954. The author wishes to acknowledge his debt particularly to Drs. Ulrich Middeldorf and Joshua Taylor, under whose supervision this dissertation was prepared. The translations are by the author unless otherwise indicated in the footnotes.

[1] Wassily Kandinsky, "Abstrakt oder Konkret," *Tentoonstelling abstrakte Kunst* (Amsterdam: Stedelijk Museum, 1938).

[2] Kupka's *Red and Blue Disks* in the Museum of Modern Art, New York, is dated 1911–1912, but it is just possible that this date was added later.

[3] Germain Bazin in his biographical notes to René Huyge's *Les Contemporains* (Paris: Editions Pierre Tisné, 1949), cites 1914 as the year in which Delaunay did the first non-objective painting in France. This author is able to predate this by two years, since he has seen Delaunay's *Color Disks* (Delaunay Studio, Paris), a completely non-objective painting, dated 1912. It remains possible, however, that Picabia did nonobjective paintings in Paris before then. Recently it has been maintained that the self-taught Lithuanian artist, M. K. Čiurlionis, painted non-objective pictures between 1905 and 1910 (Aleksis Rannit, "M. K. Čiurlionis," *Das Kunstwerk*, I, 1946–47, pp. 46–48, and *idem*, "Un pittore astratto prima di Kandinsky," *La Biennale*, VIII, 1952, no. 8). Čiurlionis' work is now in the Čiurlionis Gallery in Kaunas. The reproductions included in Mr. Rannit's articles on Čiurlionis, however, are highly symbolic abstractions, verging on the fantastic art of Kubin, Redon, or some Surrealists.

[4] Hans Hildebrandt, *Adolph Hoelzel* (Stuttgart: W. Kohlhammer, 1952), p. 14.

[5] Kandinsky, *Concerning the Spiritual in Art* (New York, Wittenborn, Schultz, 1947). This book was first published by Piper in Munich as *Über das Geistige in der Kunst* in 1912. The first English translation was undertaken by Michael Sadleir under the title *The Art of Spiritual Harmony* (London, 1914). The first American edition, called *On the Spiritual in Art*, appeared in 1946 (New York, Solomon R. Guggenheim Foundation). The 1947 edition, authorized by Mme. Kandinsky and translated by Francis Golffing, Michael Harrison and Ferdinand Ostertag, will be used here because it is much closer to the original text.

[6] Kandinsky and Franz Marc (eds.), *Der blaue Reiter* (Munich: R. Piper and Co., 1912).

[7] In 1926 Kandinsky published his most systematic treatise, *Punkt und Linie zur Fläche* (Bauhaus Book, IX, Munich, Albert Langen Verlag, 1926). This book, translated as *Point and Line to Plane* by Howard Dearstyne and Hilla Rebay (New York, Solomon R. Guggenheim Foundation, 1947), was written at the Bauhaus and elucidates most clearly Kandinsky's thinking during this later period. It falls, however, beyond the realm of discussion in this study.

[8] "If *Der blaue Reiter*, published by R. Piper, is taken together with Kandinsky's *Das Geistige in der Kunst*, as a unity, then this double volume is just as

much *the* book of the prewar years as Hildebrandt's *Problem der Form* was *the* book of the turn of the century. The separation of the two generations is already made clear in the title, which emphasizes form in the one and spirit in the other." Hans Hildebrandt, *Die Kunst des 19. und 20. Jahrhunderts* (Handbuch der Kunstwissenschaft) (Potsdam-Wildpark, 1924), p. 382.

[9] Kenneth Lindsay, "An Examination of the Fundamental Theories of Wassily Kandinsky," unpublished doctoral dissertation, University of Wisconsin, 1951. Dr. Lindsay establishes incisive relationships between Kandinsky's theories and his paintings. While doing research in Kandinsky's studio in Neuilly-sur-Seine during the spring of 1950, I had adequate opportunity to compare my interpretations with those of Lindsay, which has led to a fruitful exchange of ideas. In a good many instances our interpretations differ, especially as to the placing of emphasis.

I am also indebted to Dr. Klaus Brisch for many provocative ideas on Kandinsky. I unfortunately have not been able to see Brisch's doctoral dissertation, "Wassily Kandinsky: Untersuchung zur Entstehung der gegenstandslosen Malerei," University of Bonn, 1955.

[10] Thomas Mann, *The Living Thoughts of Schopenhauer* (New York: Longmans Green and Co., 1929), p. 29.

[11] Henri Bergson, *Laughter* (New York: Macmillan, 1911), p. 157.

[12] Very much the same idea is expressed by Franz Marc: "I am beginning more and more to see behind or, to put it better, through things, to see behind them something which they conceal, for the most part cunningly, with their outward appearance by hoodwinking man with a façade which is quite different from what it actually covers. Of course, from the point of view of physics this is an old story. . . . The scientific interpretation has powerfully transformed the human mind; it has caused the greatest type-change we have so far lived to see. Art is indisputably pursuing the same course, in its own way, certainly; and the problem, our problem, is to discover the way." (Franz Marc, diary entry, Christmas 1914, in Peter Thoene [pseud.], *Modern German Art*, Harmondsworth, Pelican Books, 1938.)

[13] Kandinsky, "Notebooks," quoted in Nina Kandinsky, "Some Notes on the Development of Kandinsky's Painting," in Kandinsky, *Concerning the Spiritual in Art*, p. 10.

[14] Kandinsky, *Concerning the Spiritual in Art*, p. 48.

[15] Kandinsky, "Text Artista," *Wassily Kandinsky Memorial* (New York: Solomon R. Guggenheim Foundation, 1945), p. 65 (hereafter cited as "Text Artista"). This is Kandinsky's autobiography, written in 1913 and first published under the title *Rückblicke* by Der Sturm in Berlin in the same year.

[16] Franz Marc, turning toward non-objective painting shortly before his death, gave a very similar reason: "Very early in life I found man ugly; the animal seemed to me more beautiful and cleaner, but even in it I discovered so much that was repelling and ugly that my art instinctively and by inner force became more schematic and abstract." (Marc, letter, April 12, 1915, in *Briefe, Aufzeichnungen und Aphorismen*, Berlin, 1920, II, p. 50.)

In this respect Kandinsky and Marc differed decidedly from their associate in the Blaue Reiter, Paul Klee, who was always concerned with creating symbols to interpret man and the forces of nature: "The naked body is an altogether suitable object. In art classes I have gradually learned something of it from every angle. But now I will no longer project some plan of it, but will proceed so that all its essentials, even those hidden by optical perspective, will appear upon the paper. And thus a little uncontested personal property has already been discovered, a style has been created." (Paul Klee, June, 1902, "Extracts from the Journal of the Artist," in Margaret Miller [ed.], *Paul Klee* [New York: Museum of Modern Art, 1945], pp. 8–9.)

[17] Wilhelm Worringer, *Abstraktion und Einfühlung* (Munich: R. Piper and Co., 1948), p. 29. First published Munich, 1908. English edition: *Abstraction and Empathy* (London: Routledge and Kegan Paul, 1953).

[18] Kandinsky, "Text Artista," p. 61.

[19] Edward Bullough, "Psychical Distance as a Factor in Art and an Aesthetic Principle," *British Journal of Psychology,* v, 1912, pp. 87–118.

[20] Kandinsky, letter to Hilla Rebay, January 1937, *Wassily Kandinsky Memorial,* p. 98.

[21] Kandinsky, *Concerning the Spiritual in Art,* p. 48.

[22] *Ibid.,* p. 77.

[23] Kandinsky, "Abstrakte Kunst," *Cicerone,* XVII, 1925, pp. 639–647.

[24] Kandinsky, "Line and Fish," *Axis,* II, 1935, p. 6.

[25] Roger Fry in *The Nation,* August 2, 1913, quoted in Arthur J. Eddy, *Cubists and Post-Impressionism* (Chicago: A. C. McClurg and Co., 1914), p. 117.

[26] Kandinsky, "Text Artista," p. 64.

[27] Kandinsky, "Über die Formfrage," *Der blaue Reiter,* p. 85.

[28] *Ibid.,* p. 84.

[29] Kandinsky, "Text Artista," p. 71.

[30] Kandinsky, "Über die Formfrage," in Kandinsky and Marc, *op. cit.,* p. 88.

[31] *Der blaue Reiter* (2d ed.) (Munich, 1914). p. v.

[32] This idea is very similar to Herder's theory of Inspiration: J. G. Herder, *Ideen zur Philosophie der Geschichte der Menschheit* (Leipzig, 1821).

[33] Kandinsky, *Concerning the Spiritual in Art,* pp. 51–52.

[34] *Ibid.,* p. 32. Kandinsky himself—as Lindsay has pointed out ("An Examination of the Fundamental Theories of Wassily Kandinsky," pp. 208–213)—was not a member of the Theosophical Society. He admired, however, the cosmology of Mme. Blavatzky which attempted to create a significant synthesis of Indian wisdom and Western civilization. The antimaterialistic concepts of the Theosophical movement attracted a good many artists and writers yearning for a new religious spirit during the early part of the century. Besides Kandinsky: Piet Mondrian, Hans Arp, Hugo Ball, William Butler Yeats.

[35] Kandinsky, *Concerning the Spiritual in Art,* pp. 33–34.

[36] *Ibid.,* p. 36.

[37] *Ibid.,* p. 39.

[38] *Ibid.,* p. 47.

[39] *Ibid.,* p. 45.

[40] *Ibid.*

[41] The following remarks about color are taken from "The Language of Form and Color," *Concerning the Spiritual in Art,* Chap. VI, pp. 45–67.

[42] *Ibid.,* pp. 51–52.

[43] *Ibid.,* p. 57n.

[44] *Ibid.*, p. 45.

[45] Kandinsky, "Text Artista," p. 75.

[46] Max Raphael, *Von Monet bis Picasso* (Munich, 1919), p. 102.

[47] Kandinsky, *Concerning the Spiritual in Art*, p. 63.

[48] In Kandinsky and Marc, *Der blaue Reiter*, pp. 103–113.

[49] Kandinsky, "Text Artista," pp. 75–87.

[50] By "stage composition"—*Bühnenkomposition*—Kandinsky is referring to the totality of movement on the stage.

[51] Kandinsky, "Der gelbe Klang," in Kandinsky and Marc, *Der blaue Reiter*, pp. 119–131. The possibilities of such a synthesis in the film were not yet explored in 1912.

[52] Diego Rivera, quoted in "Notes on the Life, Development and Last Years of Kandinsky," in *Wassily Kandinsky Memorial*, p. 100.

[53] Bergson, *Essai sur les données immédiates de la conscience* (Paris, 1904).

[54] Christian P. Heinlein, "The Affective Characteristics of the Major and Minor Modes in Music," dissertation, Johns Hopkins University, Baltimore, 1928; quoted in Lindsay, "An Examination of the Fundamental Theories of Wassily Kandinsky," p. 104.

19. FRANK LLOYD WRIGHT AND TWENTIETH-CENTURY STYLE

Vincent Scully, Jr.

INTRODUCTION

This selection is the keynote paper in a series of five on the subject of Frank Lloyd Wright and his contemporaries delivered at the Twentieth International Congress of the History of Art in 1961. In this paper Professor Scully plots Wright's work in the context of international developments in architecture during the first half of the twentieth century and in relation to a likely thrust of fresh architecture in the second half. Of particular interest are the remarks concerning Wright's relationship to past traditions; the full reciprocal circle of Wright's early impact on European architecture through De Stijl channels to the International Style, and from the latter back to Wright in the form of a "regenerating influence"; and the comparisons between Wright's architecture from 1902 to 1906 and that of Louis I. Kahn from the mid-1950's to the early 1960's.

Apart from Wright's own publications, much of the basic literature is cited in Professor Scully's bibliographical note at the end of this selection. Additions to this should include Norris K. Smith, *Frank Lloyd Wright: A Study in Architectural Content* (1966); H. A. Brooks, "Frank Lloyd Wright and the Wasmuth Drawings," *The Art Bulletin,* XLVIII (1966); Mark L. Peisch, *The Chicago School of Architecture: Early Followers of Sullivan and Wright* (1965); James Birrell, *Walter Burley Griffin* (1964); and the series of papers mentioned above, published in *Studies in Western Art, Acts of the Twentieth International Congress of the History of Art,* IV (1963).

Of the architect's own writings mention should be made of *An Autobiography* (1932); *The Future of Architecture* (1953); *Frank Lloyd Wright on Architecture,* ed. by Frederick Gutheim, 2nd ed. (1960); *Frank Lloyd Wright: Writings and Buildings,* ed. by E. Kaufmann and Ben Raeburn (1960). In a special category is the important publication edited by Arthur Drexler, *The Drawings of Frank Lloyd Wright* (1962); and for contextual material there are Henry-Russell Hitchcock, *Architecture: Nineteenth and Twentieth Centuries* (1963) and Henry-Russell Hitchcock and Philip Johnson, *The International Style: Architecture Since 1922* (1932).

Some years ago a student asked Frank Lloyd Wright how he could make his own work wholly original. Wright replied, in effect, "You can't. I invented a new architecture . . . about 1900, and all you can do is learn its principles and work with them." At the time, this answer seemed to me to be one of unparalleled, if delightful, arrogance. Now I am not so sure that it was far from being the simple truth. And the period of Wright's work upon which the scholar must concentrate, in order to seek out the truth, is the period cited by Wright himself, that which spanned the two centuries and came to a close at about the fateful date of 1914.

In this distinguished company I make no pretence of being prepared to produce fresh data about Wright. Nor can all the many qualities of his work be discussed or illustrated here. Instead, despite the risk of repeating what I, or others, have written elsewhere, I should like to present a thesis for argument, developed as follows: first, that Wright not only created a style of architecture but also, through his long life span, carried that style through all its possible phases; second, that Wright's early work, of the period noted above, was more solely his own than the work of the later periods normally was, and more fully embodied a balance between his two major principles of design than the later work usually did; third, that out of one of those principles the International Style of the following decades took form, and out of another the new architecture of the second half of the century—the architecture which may succeed that of Wright—would now seem to be making its beginning.

This thesis as a whole implies that Wright's work indeed had two major separable aspects and sought two distinct objectives which he himself was able to merge only when at his most complete. Both these objectives were built into Wright's life by the circumstances of his birth. One was the creation of building form through a totally integrated structural system; the other was the creation of spaces which were, in his own term, "continuous." The first objective derived from the Gothic Revival theory of the middle of the nineteenth century, and into the Gothic Revival Wright was, literally, born. As we all know, his mother determined before his birth in 1869 that he should be an architect and, to that end, hung nineteenth-century engravings of English cathedrals in the room she had prepared for him. Her impulse may be taken to have been picturesque, transcendental, possibly partly Ruskinian in tone. Some of these attitudes were to cling to Wright all his life, and he read Ruskin later. But, as he himself tells us, the book that most affected him and which, in his own words, "was the only really sensible book on architecture in the world," was Viollet-le-Duc's *Dictionnaire raisonné.* Here the attitude was a tough and mechanistic one, expressive of nineteenth-century positivism and scientism and insisting that the forms of Gothic architecture derived purely from the logical demands of its skeletal structural system. In this way the later nineteenth century was able to see Gothic architecture according to its own pragmatic and materialistic image of reality and to embody such, as Banham has otherwise shown, in its own architectural theory.[1]

But Wright was also born into another engrossing nineteenth-century attitude, one which achieved its greatest symbolic force in America. This was the sense of continuous expansion, of the endless opening up of the environment. The print of 1868 by Palmer and Ives, comprehensively entitled *Across the Continent: "Westward the Course of Empire Makes Its Way,"* makes this point. All was to flow on endlessly, boundlessly, in the unity that comes with flow. Physical space, biological evolution, and the democratic future were alike regarded in terms of such unified progress forward.

Here, then, were two concepts, structural and spatial, and both directly expressive of the major goals and symbols of their time. Wright was to set himself the task of integrating the two through the chemistry of his art, and of weaving them into single organisms at once unified and serene. Before his birth and in his childhood the way was already being prepared for him. During the mid-century the American Stick Style, carried by the Pattern Books which began with those of Andrew Jackson Downing, had attempted to apply Gothic Revival principles of structural expression to American domestic programs and wood frame techniques. And Wright tells us that when, as a beginning architect, he first settled in Oak Park in 1887, it was not the new houses but Mr. Austin's "old barn vertically boarded and battened," that he loved. But by this time, when he himself was about to build, the other image, that of spatial continuity, had become dominant in American work. It had begun in England during the sixties, with Richard Norman Shaw's tile-hung "old English" houses planned around living halls, and later in the United States to be associated with American colonial work and called Queen Anne. This mode was introduced into America by Henry Hobson Richardson in his shingled Watts Sherman House of 1874, where the horizontal continuity of the surface, expressive of the new continuities of interior space, was made even more decisive. By the mid-eighties such spatial continuity reached a point in America never approached by the English houses. Wilson Eyre's Ashurst House of 1885, with its horizontally extended and open interior, its projecting porches, and its bands of windows, is an excellent example. By 1886, another architect of this Shingle Style, Bruce Price, had organized the new open interior space into that cross-axial type which had been popular in North America since Jefferson's time; and Wright's own house in Oak Park, of 1889, was closely derived from the houses of Price, although the cross-axial plan was not yet employed in it. Around 1900, however, when Wright came into his first maturity, as in the Ward Willitts House, he used Price's cross axis to create a set of horizontal continuities which recall those of Eyre but are infinitely more decisive and are extended with low ceilinged compulsiveness. Indeed, the house as a whole seems to have passed beyond the underlying picturesque eclecticism of the Shingle Style into a new style that is entirely its own. It is true, as many critics have pointed out, that other sources of inspiration can be seen here, such as the Japanese Ho-O-Den at the World's Fair of 1893. The stripping, the cross-axis, and the projecting roofs are common to both, but Wright has so woven together the structural and cladding elements, reminiscent of those of the Stick Style, that the building fabric as a whole is now completely in accord with the continuously expanding spaces it defines.

With these wooden houses of the beginning of the century, therefore, Wright's integration of continuous space with frame structure was already complete. Instantly, in 1902, he turned to the same problem in masonry, where his image of continuity could be given permanent, monumental form. Here I must apologize for recalling a sequence of development that is familiar to us all, but the need to do so will, I hope, be apparent at the end of this talk. In the Heurtley House the direct influence of Richardson's eminently permanent masonry can be felt, as from the Glessner House in

Chicago, which Wright knew at first hand, or from the Quincy Library, which was well published. But Wright divides Richardson's engrossing shell, with its volumetric gable roof, into separate planes, across which the wooden spanning elements stretch with the running continuity of bridges. Spatial movement and sculptural mass were in this sense combined. Immediately, having developed his masonry as plane, Wright turned to masonry as pier. Perceiving the vertical demands of such, he also sensed the volumetric bay which the pier somehow wants to bound. So, in the Hillside Home School, also of 1902, the four piers support a symmetrically placed hip roof, defining a volume of space which is fundamentally static but which is brought into the cross axes of spatial expansion through projected window bays and cantilevered ceiling planes.

In 1904 a further step was taken in the Martin House, where the piers were exploited to the full as space definers, marching outward in companies to form the major spaces and, where the axes cross, grouping in fours to create smaller service spaces for heating and lighting equipment. Thus the unification of spatial desires with structural and mechanical demands is so complete that the house approaches the integration of a working machine. The only exception to this is the widely overhanging roof, where the desire for horizontal spatial extension causes steel beams to be concealed in the wooden structure and so introduces an element lacking the inner structural rationale of the other forms. But in the Larkin Building—also of 1904 and now tragically demolished—the spatial continuity was contained by the building fabric, and the integration of space with structure was complete. Concrete beams supported brick parapets, threaded horizontally through the vertically continuous piers, and capped them above. The whole was a tensile unity in which major and minor volumes were structurally formed through the bay system into an industrial cathedral that should have delighted Viollet-le-Duc. The mechanics never faltered. The thickness of the piers received the filing cabinets; vertical circulation was clearly separated into corner towers, and all these major, minor, and service spaces worked together to create the building's exterior form. The only captious elements, the globes and putti, seem related to European developments of the period, as perhaps to Olbrich's Sezession Building, in Vienna, of 1898–99, whose romantic-classic, geometric severity Wright's building also shared.

Yet it is clear that this industrial form could not have been built as it was without the example of Louis Sullivan, and its vertical piers and interwoven horizontal spandrels recall those of Sullivan's first great skyscraper, the Wainwright Building of 1890–91. Wright has recorded his emotion when Sullivan laid the first sketches for the Wainwright Building on his drawing board. But Wright himself was attempting something fundamentally different from the master's work. Sullivan's building was integrated façade design, at most a schematic description of the character of the spaces it contained, but Wright's was an integral embodiment of those spaces. Sullivan's building was conceived as a standing body, with a base, a middle, and an end, and can therefore be described, as Sullivan described it, in terms of the classic column. But Wright's solids, though supremely strong, expressed the volume of space they defined. Thus the exterior of his building was that of a container of spaces and is to be read not as a column but as a galleried cavern.

This difference, which I have discussed elsewhere, is important because of the fundamental polarity in attitude it reveals. When Sullivan looked at Richardson's work, as for example at the Marshall Field Warehouse, of 1885, he saw it not in terms of spatial definition, but in anthropomorphic and humanistic terms with which Wright had nothing to do. So, in his *Kindergarten Chats,* Sullivan wrote of this building, "Here is a man for you to look at. A man that walks on two legs instead of four, has active muscles . . . lives and breathes . . . in a world of barren pettiness, a male."[2] Therefore, in his own Guaranty Building of 1895, designed after Wright had left the office, Sullivan developed Richardson's forms further in terms of skeletal skyscraper construction and caused the building truly to stand upon its legs, stretch, and stir. In these ways it became primarily the expression of a physical presence rather than of a spatial environment. Indeed, the Guaranty Building, with its doubled piers and its calculated drama of compression and tension, purposely overrode its description of its space and structure in favor of the sculptural unity of its body. Such intentions have ultimately Hellenic rather than medieval backgrounds; they seem related to the Greek rather than the medieval revival of the early nineteenth century and, in part, to the general Classicizing reaction of its close. They have become central to some mid-twentieth century architecture other than Wright's. So the late skyscrapers of Mies van der Rohe stand upon exposed columns and multiply their vertical mullions in order to achieve bodily unity in terms which, though now rather frozen, are still Sullivan's figural rather than spatial ones. More forcefully, the late buildings of Le Corbusier culminate this modern expression of the human presence and its act. They stand as muscular forces, and mask, where necessary, both their interior spaces and their actual structure in order to appear to be the sculptural embodiments of powers with which men can identify their own.

But Wright's way was the opposite. Perhaps no less sculptural, it yet sought a sculpture that was constructivist and environmental, rather than figurally active, in effect. Unity Temple, of 1906, culminated its integration. Here, as Wright most lucidly describes in his *Autobiography*, square hollow piers, flat planes, crossed beams and projecting slabs in poured concrete all worked together to create the kinds of space desired, and the building's plastic solids wholly revealed both the shapes of those spaces and the structural process whereby they were formed.

If Unity Temple may be regarded as a culmination of Wright's integration, the Robie House documents his movement beyond it toward a more arbitrary state. Now the desire for continuous space most movingly dominates the fabric. The heavy masses of brick are lifted by that compulsion, and the steel-concealing, low-hipped roofs take wing. In that sense the solids burst apart, like—as so many critics have pointed out—those of contemporary Cubist painting. At the same time, the Robie House, designed as if in exaltation, sums up several hundred years of American imagery. The containing, protective box of Colonial architecture, which had exerted considerable influence upon the architects of the Shingle Style and thus upon Wright himself, now splits around the central fireplace mass and embodies to the full the nineteenth-century feeling for spatial expansion and flight.

With this house Wright summed up his earlier intentions and burst their boundaries. Its completion in 1909 coincided with a decisive break in his own personal life. Thereafter he had no fixed place in the American nineteenth-century suburban culture—and especially middle western suburban culture—that had nourished him. Indeed that culture itself, as a creative milieu, began to break up by the time of World War I. The reasons for this are still in dispute and cannot be developed here, but the fact remains that the middle western suburb had been prepared to support the idealistic radicalism of its architects: it then became, and has generally remained, carefully conservative. It is as if Wright, having lost his functional place—and never again to have around him so mature and productive a group of followers, associates, and sympathetic but free and equal critics as the other architects of the Prairie School had been—was now forced to seek out only the most grandly personal and mythic of objectives. So, at the Midway Gardens of 1914 he forced his earlier forms into vast spatial continuities, like those of some nineteenth-century American landscapes, where the solid shapes, however symmetrically framed, are eaten through by space and slide forward and out continuously under the empty sky.

After 1914, now personally involved in the tragic flux of American culture and totally uprooted from his past, Wright seems to have felt a need to begin again upon cultural foundations more wholly permanent. His overt dependence upon precedent, here upon Mayan forms, became much more marked than it had been in any of the work done between 1900 and 1914. A wish for overwhelmingly stable mass dominates, spatially appropriate perhaps in the A. D. German Warehouse of 1915, less so in the Barnsdall House of 1920. There, too, the desire for structural integrity was entirely given up in order to achieve the Mayan mansarded roof profile in lath and plaster. And even when, in his splendid block houses of the twenties and his inspired 1929 project for St. Mark's Tower, Wright achieved once again a complete integration of structure and space, and Mayoid inspiration was still seen as much to the fore.

Yet, through these decades so difficult for him, the influence of Wright's work had acted more strongly than any other single force to give form to the new architecture of modern Europe, and the special way it had acted is of critical importance. Wright's work had become generally known through the great Wasmuth publications in 1910 and 1911. From such publications Berlage, whose Amsterdam Bourse of 1903 had also been a brick structure with an enclosed court, saw the Larkin Building as an eminently machine architecture, as Banham has shown. We may assume that Berlage understood, in other words, its complete integration of function and structure. The formal influence of Wright upon other Dutch architects and upon Gropius in the teens need not be discussed here. But the Dutch De Stijl group of the late teens and early twenties, whose members also admired Wright, must be considered. This group appears to have seen Wright's work not in terms of integration but through its own predilections for line and plane, Classicizing severity, and the abstract manipulation of space. This is important because it was clearly through De Stijl that the International Style of the twenties found its characteristic shapes. The process, whatever it also owed to both Cubism and Futurism, can be traced almost step by step from the illustrations in Wasmuth. If we take a photograph of the side of the Ward Willitts House from the 1911 volume and concentrate upon the running, asymmetrical pattern of dark stripping, we can derive from it a painting by Van Doesburg of 1918. Ignoring the lines and focussing upon the advanced and recessed masses, we arrive at a construction, a constructivist sculpture, by Van Tongerloo, of 1919. Hollowing out the masses and seeing the surfaces as thin, sharp-edged planes defining volumes of space, we approach a house project by Van Doesburg, of 1922. Finally, stretching the whole out once more into an asymmetrical organization of interlocked, thin-surfaced boxes, we come to Gropius' Bauhaus of 1925–26, and to the full International Style. The bounding solids are now merely planes which exist to define volumes. There is no structural mass and no question of structural and spatial integration; in fact the space definers and the supporting members are normally kept separate, one from the other. The relation to the machine, which was of persistent importance in European theory, and of which Banham has brilliantly made so much, is now not, as in the Larkin Building, primarily in how the building functions as a working machine, but how, industrially glazed and brightly stuccoed, it looks.

The fullest understanding of Wright's continuity of space was shown during the twenties by Mies van der Rohe, as a comparison between a plan of 1906 by Wright and one of 1923 by Mies clearly shows. And Mies' Barcelona Pavilion of 1929, itself a piece of constructivist sculpture, is a synthesis between Wright's fluid, American planning, as reinterpreted by De Stijl, and the Classicizing containment that was also desired by European sensibility. At the same time the planes are everywhere detached from the structural columns and therefore act purely as arbitrary space definers. Such separation is to be contrasted with the integration of space and structure in a somewhat similar project by Wright, the Yahara Boat Club, of 1902, published by Wasmuth in 1910. If, however, we step forward instead of back in Wright's work, we find that the influence of Mies and, very secondarily, of other European architects of the International Style, has, by the thirties, come to exert a direct and indeed regenerating influence upon Wright's own design. The "parti" of the entrance side of the Goetsch-Winkler House of 1939, for example, shows the relationship very clearly. Wright's earlier influence upon Europe now bore fruit for him, but, as indicated, a certain metamorphosis had taken place in the process. Now, for example, Wright creates his space almost entirely by flat planes rather than by an interwoven skeletal fabric. In wood in the Usonian Houses (though steel flitches were often inserted between their joists) and in reinforced concrete in such a great masterpiece as the Kaufmann House, Wright found various ways to make those planes structural, but the dominance of International Style intentions seems clear. So the Kaufmann House, though creating a splendidly complex and serene spatial ambient, and being itself a structure of much daring, is also a kind of mature constructivist sculpture, recalling types developed by the Europeans out of Wright's earlier work.

Finally, when he attempted to escape from the International Style through the continuously curvilinear forms of his last decades—which themselves (like those of the Johnson Wax Building) reveal other immediate sources of inspiration that need not concern us here—Wright often manipulated the solids, whether as walls or columns, so that all structural demands and expressions were, visually, denied by them and it was truly, in his own words, "space, not matter," that became the reality. Similarly, it is clear, as the researches of Folds have shown, that Wright was never entirely sure how the continuous spiral of the Guggenheim Museum was to be constructed, so that, in the final version, the vertical piers, which do much of the actual work, are in conflict with the helical conception of the space, and injure it. All this sharply contrasts with the balance between solid and void in the similarly top-lighted and galleried Larkin Building, where the members, fully creating the space and expressive of it, were structurally convincing as well.

Wright may therefore be said to have pushed his style to its ultimate, space-dominant, solid-denying phase—to what may perhaps be referred to as its Late Baroque phase. That is to say, if Brunelleschi stated a clear principle of the relation of solid to void, and of structure to space, and Alberti and others developed the system into a balance between mass and space, in which solid and void were sculpturally interdependent, so the Late Baroque may be said to have dissolved the solids in favor of the space, bending them entirely to the service of the total environment they created. If a similar course can be traced in Wright, it can also be perceived in the International Style as a whole. Because that style had begun, by Wright's last years, to exhibit characteristics that were almost Rococo. The lacy fragmentation of mass in Yamasaki's recent work is one example among many, while Stone's fluttery elegance in his project for a National Cultural Center is even more striking. Many recent Russian works, most of them apparently inspired by Stone, show the same characteristics. So Stone's project of 1961 closely resembles one of the schemes submitted in the new competition for a Palace of the Soviets, of 1959, which in turn seems to have taken as its point of departure Stone's American Pavilion at Brussels, of the year before. The new Rococo is thus strikingly international.

If, therefore, the International Style saw Wright purely in terms of defined space, and if it and he seem to have reached concluding phases together, we are compelled to ask how the fresh architecture of the second half of the century is to take shape. Where is it to begin? That question is significant for this paper because the answer would appear to be that the new architecture is now beginning not where Wright ended but where Wright began, and, as indicated earlier, is apparently developing according to one of his principles, the structural one. Several names might be associated with this movement, but the one which most architects would, I think, now advance as essential is that of Louis I. Kahn, and it is Kahn whose influence upon architectural students, at least in the United States, is presently greater than that of any other architect. This is not the place to describe Kahn's unusual career or to analyze his theory and design in detail. I should only like to point out that, from about 1955 to the present, his development has paralleled that of Wright between 1902 and 1906 in almost every significant detail. I do not say that this relation to Wright was necessarily conscious on Kahn's part; indeed, the fact that it was probably unconscious makes it doubly significant. Clearly enough it has followed a course laid down in Kahn's own theory, which is itself ultimately based upon Viollet-le-Duc and Choisy: functional ("What," as Kahn puts it, "does the building want to be?"); integrational, as he insists, like Wright, the architecture is the "making of spaces" and that those spaces should be defined by structure. At the same time, considerable influence from some of Le Corbusier's later buildings in brick and concrete, such as the Maisons Jaoul, has obviously played an important part.

Yet the parallel with Wright seems central, since Kahn's fully mature projects can be said to have begun with his archaic Trenton Bath House of 1955. Here hollow piers support hipped roofs to create structurally conceived bays of space which closely recall Wright's Hillside Home School, of 1902. To go further, the plan of the Bath House is cross-axial, defined by the piers. In this it of course strikingly recalls Wright's work, like the plan of the Gale House of 1902. But here a difference is apparent. Wright's squares interlock, and the axes penetrate each other, creating the kind of continuously fluid space that was so expansively extended in the Ward Willitts plan. Kahn's spaces are not continuous, but separate. The squares do not interlock; each volume has its own roof cap with oculus, and in the central unroofed square the opposite geometric shape, a circle, is inscribed. The Kahn plan is thus intended to be static and fixed; Vitruvian and Renaissance conceptions, and indeed the cubes and spheres of Brunelleschi, are recalled. Where, however, Brunelleschi could define his spatial areas with slender, solid columns, Kahn's piers are hollow, containing those services which are essential to most modern buildings and which, therefore, Kahn now integrates into the structural and spatial concept as a whole. We have, of course, seen this before and in exactly this sequence. Wright's Martin plan, of 1904, with its grouped columns containing heating and lighting elements, comes to mind, as do the hollow piers of Unity Temple. So, too, in sequence, comes Kahn's project for the Trenton Community Center as a whole, now recalling the columnar groupings of the Martin House and making both major and service spaces with them. But again Kahn caps each bay with its own precast, hipped roof, even where the demands of the spaces below require that the column system be interrupted. In this way Kahn again rejects the nineteenth-century image of expansive continuity in favor of the separateness of parts, but, as with Wright, it is the structure that makes the space and the two together which produce a convincingly fresh and powerful form.

The same holds true in Kahn's Medical Research Laboratories for the University of Pennsylvania, completed in 1960, when the next step in the sequence, that to the Larkin Building, is taken. Again, vertical service towers, clad in brick, house stairways and, here, ventilating ducts, while the floor levels are defined by horizontal spandrels plaited, as by Wright, through vertical piers. At the same time, Kahn's cantilevering of the floor levels off exposed columns recalls the system used in the Philadelphia Savings Fund Society Building of 1930–32, designed by George Howe, later one of Kahn's closest associates and mentors, and William Lescaze, while the stepped diminution of the cantilevered precast trusses was prefigured in the similar beam treatment of one of the buildings in Richard Neutra's Rush City Reformed Project of the twenties. Now, however, Kahn makes the space through an interweaving of the toughly scaled armature of the reinforced concrete skeleton, as Wright had done, but the space itself differs once more. The functions are surely less integrated with the structure—here in Kahn a cross-axial structure—than Wright's admittedly simpler program permitted, but there is a difference of intention as well. Wright's spaces pull the observer in, enclose, release, soothe him, drawing all finally together into an expansive harmony; but Kahn's spaces are exposed, pushed out by the structural members, not sequential but fundamentally separate, while the scheme of the complex as a whole avoids Wright's embracing envelope to insist upon the separateness of each structurally conceived, eight-columned tower.

The larger differences between Wright and Kahn can now be determined. Wright develops fluid spatial sequences, Kahn units of space. Wright will, if choice be necessary, override the structure in favor of the space; Kahn, if necessary, the space in favor of the structure. Wright emphasizes the continuous plastic unity of parts, Kahn their jointed separateness. Wright insists upon the expansiveness and serenity of the environment, Kahn upon its pressures, difficulties, and demands. Both earnestly attempt to balance human desires against the intrinsic physical requirements of the thing made. Wright will normally, and with lyric fervor, opt for the former; Kahn, with a kind of tragic intensity, for the latter. The first set of attitudes adds up to a late nineteenth-century view of human possibility, the second to a mid-twentieth-century perception of human fate. So each of these buildings belongs to the best thought of its own generation, but that they also belong to the same family is clear. And it seems most important for the future of American architecture that the relationship should be a familial one, because Kahn, for the first time among those Americans whose work has consistently recalled Wright's, seems not a follower, but a descendant.

Their mutual sequence is by no means concluded. Kahn's project of 1960–61 for the First Unitarian Church in Rochester recalls Wright's Unity Temple of 1906. Their exteriors are strongly fortified masses, lighted primarily from above and expressive of the deeply enclosed volumes they contain. Kahn, however, avoids Wright's projected roof slabs, expressive of spatial interlocking and horizontal continuities. So, too, a plan for church and school resembling Wright's was considered but rejected by Kahn on spatial and functional grounds. And again, though in the final plan the units are brought into a closer grouping by Kahn, they still retain their spatial, structural, and formal separateness and discontinuity, and are not woven into interlocking echoes of each other as Wright, with his concern for rhythmic unity, has them. At the same time, a system of precast bent slabs, supported on crossed beams, forms Kahn's top-lighted roof, and recalls in this way Wright's system in the Temple.

The church at Rochester is now under construction, and many other projects by Kahn are developing the creative sequence further. Some, like that for the Salk Center in California, seem to show evidence of influences from sources that were also important to Wright in his later years. What this may foretell cannot be determined at present. (It is discussed in detail in my recent book on Kahn.)

It is now apparent, however, that a family of principle, of complicated ancestry but brought to form by Wright, produced, comparatively late in his own life, a new champion, who may, perhaps most significantly, be creating another indigenously American school. The forms of that family rise across the general picturesque eclecticism of much of the century and indeed across the International Style of the intervening years. The two generations differ in the fundamental spatial symbol to which each adheres, but they are alike in the governing desire for spatial and structural integration that binds them. Each, though considerably more concerned with the mechanics of function than the International Style usually was, still belongs to the tenacious Western tradition of solid, monumental building in common materials, as the International Style had not always seemed to do. Their specific ancestry lies in that large segment of Western experience which has been primarily concerned with the construction of interior spaces. Their opposite, equally important today, is eventually Hellenic in ancestry, and seeks, with subjective idealism, to embody the human act in architectural form. They, however, seek to image not the human body but the objectively realistic force of the settings constructed for it.

There is clearly room and need for both symbols in the modern world, and indeed both have been sought by it in one way or another since its beginnings. Wright's and Kahn's principle, whatever its backgrounds, has been especially sympathetic to Americans, since, under the prod of anarchic change, it passionately insists upon the need to produce a permanent environment that shall be abstractly moral, insofar as it embodies fixed principle and law. Ironically enough, the fluid instability of modern times destroyed Wright's building. But it now comes to life once more through the revival of an intention that was most succinctly stated by its builder many years ago, when he wrote, "Above all, integrity." [3]

NOTES

[1] Reyner Banham, *Theory and Design in the First Machine Age* (New York, 1960).

[2] Louis Henry Sullivan, *Kindergarten Chats* (Lawrence, Kansas, 1934).

[3] Since this talk was intended to reappraise and realign material already well known, it is presented here as given, without footnotes. For the same reason its numerous illustrations have all been omitted since most of them can be easily found elsewhere, as in my books: *The Shingle Style* (New Haven, 1955); *Frank Lloyd Wright* (New York, 1960); *Modern Architecture* (New York, 1961); and *Louis I. Kahn* (New York, 1962). For further photographs of Wright's work the reader is referred to Henry-Russell Hitchcock, *In the Nature of Materials; 1887–1941; The Buildings of Frank Lloyd Wright* (New York, 1942), and for the early period to Grant C. Manson, *Frank Lloyd Wright to 1910: The First Golden Age* (New York, 1958).

20. ART AT MID-CENTURY

Harold Rosenberg

INTRODUCTION

These selections by one of the foremost critics of contemporary art stand in a special relationship to the art they deal with. When they were written this art was being produced, or was still a reasonably fresh phenomenon. Such commentary therefore accepts the risks of the moment along with the artists themselves. For in the flux of the moment there is little of the security to be found in the relatively stable medium of history that surrounds the older arts of the museums and art-history texts. History has a slow, settling process of evaluation, the accretion of countless opinions and dialogues, that functions quietly and inexorably as both preserver and destroyer. For the critic of the contemporary scene this process has barely begun.

For futher study of recent and contemporary art forms there are a number of periodicals which illustrate and review the current art scene, such as *Art News, Art in America,* and *Art International,* to name but a few. Exhibition catalogues are another excellent source. Of these, the following titles should prove very useful: *The Art of Assemblage,* ed. Wm. C. Seitz, Museum of Modern Art, New York (1961); *The New York School, The First Generation: Paintings of the 1940's and 1950's,* ed. Maurice Tuchman, Los Angeles County Museum of Art (1965); *The Responsive Eye,* ed. Wm. C. Seitz, Museum of Modern Art (1965); *Directions in Kinetic Sculpture,* ed. Peter Selz and George Rickey, University of California, Berkeley (1966); *Primary Structures,* ed. Kynaston McShine, The Jewish Museum, New York (1966); and *American Sculpture of the Sixties,* ed. Maurice Tuchman, Los Angeles County Museum of Art (1967). Of special interest is the article "Sensibility of the Sixties" edited by Barbara Rose and Irving Sandler, *Art in America,* LV (1967), which consists of statements by contemporary artists.

PAST AND POSSIBILITY

Consciousness of art history rules the art of our time and is the key to what takes place in the galleries of New York, Los Angeles, Paris, Warsaw, Tokyo. It affects not only the objective status of new works, the conditions under which they are valued and acquired, but the impulses that enter into their creation, their aesthetic meaning, in fact, their very existence as works of art.

In all periods, the sense of tradition governed the responses of artists and their audiences. History-consciousness is something different. Tradition is aware of the past as a single complex of forms extending through the present into the future. In contrast, the modern sense of history recognizes that the past is made up of diverse cultures which by action in our time are being resolved into a future unity, the "one world" of democracy, of science or of The International Style. As tradition was an inescapable ingredient of the art of earlier centuries, proposing both what to paint and how to paint it, the consciousness of history is in a modern painting or sculpture as palpable as its form or motif—often, as in "overall" abstraction, the art-historical reference is the *only* content. Much of the difficulty in grasping contemporary art comes from ignoring this element. To appreciate a new picture it is not enough for the observer to know what trees or women bathing look like. He must have some inkling of the reflections cast upon the painting by other paintings (this is the case even when there are trees or bathing girls in the picture). The old pleasure of seeing "life" inside the frame must be augmented, if not replaced, by the stimulation of recognizing an inspired side glance to, say, "Les Demoiselles d'Avignon." Art history decides what art is. In turn, art decides what shall move us as beauty.

The density of meaning in a modern painting is always to some degree an effect of the artist's engagement with the history of art, including ideas about it. A work with a thin background of visual and intellectual experience of the art of other times will not outlast a prevailing fashion. A historically ignorant painting has no better claim to attention than the ideas of an economist who never heard of the Stock Market Crash.

This judgment too is, however, subject to being overruled by future events. The public survival, for no matter what reason, of a work or style affects its actual aesthetic worth for an indeterminable period. Objects are visually changed by the years, usually for the better, thus coming to justify the opinion, perhaps originally erroneous, that caused them to survive. The glamor of temporal distance, itself an aesthetic quality, or the mental equivalent of one, spreads an aura upon styles, whether in a wall decoration, furniture or hairdos, that have won a place in the common memory. By their mere presence in the history of art, even in a state of being overgrown by later forms, works act upon taste to inflect it in their own direction. Art becomes valuable through creating the values by which it is valued. By means of longevity alone a painting may acquire a power of moving us unknown to its creator or its erstwhile admirers. A style once accepted continues to occupy a level of the educated imagination from which it may be summoned to the surface by psychological or cultural circumstances. Thus all preserved works are candidates for revival. Periods of reaction against yesterday's enthusiasms seem to be growing constantly shorter, if we may take as indications the recent fuss about Monet or Art Nouveau.

A new art mode to replace Abstract Expressionism was felt to be long overdue, if for no other reason than that some of the leaders had been with us for as many as twenty years. By all the presumed laws of vanguardism, no innovating style can survive for that length of time without losing its radical verve and turning into an Academy. This is especially the case with a revolution that has succeeded—the high prices and international publicity of Gorky, Pollock, de Kooning, Kline, Hofmann, Rothko, Gottlieb, Guston, David Smith, Lassaw, Motherwell and half a dozen related figures provided additional proof that whatever adventure they may have had in common belonged to the past. Thus for several years upon the closing of the galleries in the spring, Abstract Expressionism was, like Adonis,

> Whose annual wound in Lebanon allur'd
> The Syrian damsels to lament his fate,

55. Hans Hofmann, *Liebestraum,* 1954 (Hans Hofmann Estate)

prepared for burial. In this instance the loudest among the attendant damsels were the art critics of *The Herald-Tribune* and *The New York Times;* they were assisted by the anonymous commentators and caption writers of *Time* and *Life,* a handful of literary "humanists" urging subject matter versus abstract art, plus dealers and spokesmen for younger or "out" artist groups. As the outcries of farewell to the old new art reached their shrillest pitch, numerous candidates for the succession were watched with the fascination of a tight-rope act. "Beyond" Action Painting appeared Neo-Dada incorporations of random objects, from fenders of wrecked automobiles to stuffed beasts; high-relief paintings built up with mortar or plastics; motorized sculpture; one-color canvases; paintings produced by rolling nude ladies in pigment; adaptations of the art of children, lunatics, policemen and embroiderers of pillow slips; "happenings" combining visual effects with melodramatic life-situations. Alongside these all-out shock probes came various "back to sanity" manifestations aimed at the restoration of significant social or moral motifs or familiar aesthetic concepts: West Coast Neo-Impressionist landscape painting; Samuel Beckett-doom-type-Existentialist "images of man," featuring the Chicago School of mutilated torsos; extensions of "pure" painting in hard-edged divisions of the canvas, with flat, clean surfaces and analytically related colors in the Mondrian-Albers-Glarner tradition; soft-edge "imagism" of one or two simple shapes on a bland ground.

Finally, . . . the election settled on Pop Art, with its emphasis on mimic mass media (comic-strip blowups and mock advertising displays) but reaching into the entire kitsch environment of present-day public life.

Apparently, however, dissatisfaction of the art audience with the rate of innovation is not enough to force the pace of art history. Certainly, Pop Art earned the right to be called a movement through the number of its adherents, its imaginative pressure, the quantity of talk it generated. Yet if Abstract Expressionism had too much staying power, Pop was likely to have too little. Its congenital superficiality, while having the advantage of permitting the artist an almost limitless range of familiar subjects to exploit (anything from doilies to dining-club cards), resulted in a qualitative monotony that could cause interest in still another gag of this kind to vanish overnight. Also, and perhaps because of the same superficiality, Pop's roster of individual practitioners was not impressive, even taking youth into account. . . . Speaking of the current situation in American art, all that can be said definitely is that Abstract Expressionism is no longer the latest mode, though it may well still be the newest in terms of potential originality and depth. . . .

The frustrated search for the new turn, both extremist and conservative, was duplicated throughout the Free World and in some of the Soviet satellites. At international exhibitions as in the United States works aimed at scandalizing taste educed no shock and those directed at elevating it evoked no meaningful trend. One thing had been learned from the notorious mistakes of the past one hundred years, and the lesson was thoroughly confusing. It was that no new work, no matter how apparently senseless, repulsive or visually vacant, could be rejected without running the risk that it would turn up as a masterpiece of the era. The story of the Ridicule Of The Radicals—of the Impressionists, Van Gogh, Matisse, Modigliani, Duchamp—had become part of the folklore of painting. Today, no one is more conscious of it than the professionals. Some try to make up for the old errors by coming out uncritically for each new move. Others shift attention from the bad record by levelling their complaints not against it but against the fact that it has brought about an epidemic of aesthetic permissiveness that is even worse than being wrong, and which is presumably curable by returning to the old attitudes that caused it. Cheerleading and stern "values" are, however, equally sham when people refuse either to resist what they dislike or to value their values.

New art is an unlimited risk for the intelligence. It calls upon intuitions that reach past the guide lines of concepts—indeed, this is one of its chief attractions. Nor is the risk any the less with art whose novelty consists in reverting, like the paintings of Balthus or the drawings of Giacometti, to earlier aims of painting, to museum surfaces or to semblances of places, things or people. Denouncing such work for not being "abstract" can be as silly as denouncing Newman for being "empty." History is not safe even for the anti-square. This final judge stands on the side of all artists as a continuing threat to all pronouncers of judgment. It stands also on the side of all charlatans and salesmen as a continuing insult to informed opinion. Modern consciousness of art history throws all standards on the roulette of success, not in money but in survival.

The dependent and shifting nature of art values, not only on the market but intrinsically, is uppermost in the mind of today's art collector, whether he buys for himself or as the representative of an institution. Acquiring a work is acquiring a piece of art history, or it is acquiring nothing (beyond, that is, an object of personal enjoyment in the same class as a cat or a souvenir). In signing his check the collector asserts his belief in the future presence of the work as a significant point attained by art as a whole. History, however, is open to anything and the merit of the chosen painting or sculpture has—at best—only the authentication of a present-day consensus. This consensus is all but certain to be supplanted, as others have been in the past. In the last analysis, committing himself to a painting is the collector's own act. Through it he courageously (recklessly?) affirms not only his aesthetic judgment, from whatever source it be derived, but the conviction that he can predict where art is going. Pride in this foresight, rather than the charm of a given painting, is often the motive of the new collector, as indicated by the practice of buying works at a glance or even over the telephone.

A collector who has acted early within a trend that continues to hold has earned the same respect as an investor who bought IBM at 30. But he has gained much more. By his act he has identified himself with the work in its adventure through time, and together with it he will enter into the history of art. In America, the growing popularity of the study of contemporary art history since the War has produced the novel spectacle of the collector as hero. One who landed early on the shores of Abstract Expressionism is invited to lecture on his deed like a Marine colonel in the first wave at Iwo Jima.

While there are still old-style collectors who simply buy paintings they admire, collecting art has become, through the pervasive sensitivity to time and survival, a career with metaphysical overtones, a means to immortality or at least to indefinitely protracted mention in the public record. With this stake in the reputations of "their" artists, collectors are often more passionately positive about art values than artists or critics. To preserve their heroic moment from dilution, some pronounce the ultimate evaluation: that after the works collected by them art entered a lasting decline. "Today," Peggy Guggenheim concluded her revised autobiography, "is the age of collecting, not of creation." Miss Guggenheim's position is, of course, self-defeating, since if there were nothing for new Balboas of the studios to discover the age of collecting would be finished too. To maintain the present impetus of art acquisition, there must be a continual flow of new creations, on each of which one or more discoverers may triumphantly ride the stream of time.

Prophets are notorious manipulators. To anticipate events is to attempt to control them. The attempt to *make* art history is implicit in the work of every contemporary school of art and in all serious criticism, including that which takes the form of buying art works, exhibiting them, awarding foundation grants. In our time those who are content merely to paint pictures or to contemplate them are out of touch, either through choice or through ignorance, with the dynamics of creation in the arts; their norm is to be found in the canvases and picture gazers at the outdoor shows in Washington Square. Art, including its appreciation, has become an area of conflicting powers.

Can the "art world" be rigged? Since the first appearance of the experimental modes in painting the charge of manufactured support has been advanced innumerable times. After a century of reiteration, it is still repeated with undiminished passion. Someone must be *behind* this art which, obviously, has no appeal to the eye or message for the intellect. To insist on the aesthetic value of a head with vertical lips, or a canvas splattered with thrown paint or with nothing on it but a few ribbons of color, one must either be a principal of the conspiracy or one of its dupes. In the nineteenth century proof of the hoax was presented by the Impressionist sunset which a mule painted with its tail; last week the proof was Action Paintings made by chimpanzees. (I am not sure I can explain the switch from the mule to the chimpanzee, unless it signifies that the plot of modern art against humanity has become more ominous, in that what was behind the mule was only its tail while behind the chimp is the menacing figure of the trainer as Big Brother.) The idea of the hidden aesthetic string-pullers inspired the Nazi doctrine of the corruption of German folk expression by "degenerate art." In the United States, the continued creation and exhibition of Abstract Expressionist works has been laid to stimulation by a clique of critics, dealers, art editors, museum officials and college art departments. Not long ago the chief art critic of *The New York Times* attributed to Alfred Barr of the Museum of Modern Art the power to turn movements in art on and off at will. Mr. Barr hastily repudiated this apotheosis as the Goddess of Art History.

Since everyone who has to do with art in any capacity is engaged in propelling it somewhere, the question of undue influence is less a problem of morality than of power. It is in regard to the power to define art in accordance with the relativity of values introduced by the historical consciousness that modern painting impinges directly on politics. Totalitarian societies destroy the provisional nature of contemporary art and regulate by edict what art is and shall be. In a democracy influence exists, but there can be no exclusive influence; even the force of a great idea is limited by the democratic right to opinionatedness and ignorance. Art comes to be the result of a balance among the things it is asserted to be by the self-elected individuals who create it and devote themselves to it.

The constant shuffle of powers gives new importance to the art critic and art functionary, particularly those who undertake to predict. It has been claimed that having abandoned nature the creation of art now takes off from critical concepts. It is undeniable that an unprecedented interplay now exists between art and ideas. Yet the importance of the conceptual element can easily be exaggerated. Occasionally, a critic overexcited by the spotlight will lend his weight to some "law" that must prevail in the art to come.

Detecting the hint of a torso or a table in an "abstract" painting, one critic happily applauds the inevitable self-reassertion of Nature in painting and warns the stubborn against holding out. Another logician of inevitability, having noted a tendency toward increasing economy of means in painting, declares that from now on good painting will be identifiable by its simple shapes, thin pigments and untouched areas of canvas. In the bewildering outpouring of styles and assumptions, any theory offers a footing, and in the carry-over from the past both critics will be right: the visible world will reappear and so will paintings reduced to finger exercises with the medium. By the same token, however, only artists lacking in vision and intellectual vitality will submit to being directed by the formulas of critics, so that in picking the "right" works the danger of being misguided is as great as ever.

For the artist, the replacement of tradition by historical consciousness compels a continual choosing among possibilities. The decision to follow one aesthetic hypothesis rather than another is a matter of professional life or death. The release of art from the one-way push of the past is inseparable from a permanent uneasiness, related to the anguish of possibility from which all free men suffer. This uneasiness both artists and their audiences will have to learn to endure.

ACTION PAINTING: CRISIS AND DISTORTION

"In Greece philosophizing was a mode of action"—KIERKEGAARD

Action Painting solved no problems. On the contrary, it remained at its best faithful to the conviction in which it had originated: that the worst thing about the continuing crisis of art and society were the proposals for solving it. In the thirties American art had become active, having gratefully accepted from politics an assignment in changing the world. Its role was to participate in "the education of the masses." Painting and sculpture were to overcome at last their bohemian isolation and gain an audience of ordinary folk in the Classical manner. An enticing outlook—except that practice was to disclose that to educate the masses the educator must himself take on the essential characteristic of the masses, their anonymity. For the contemporary mind no prospect holds a deeper dread. In practice the art of the social message found itself shuffling feebly between the action-inspiring poster and the aesthetic ideal of personal style.

The war and the collapse of the Left dissolved for the artist the drama of The Final Conflict (the only kind of conflict which, in the realm of the spirit, love or politics, might justify putting aside the conflicts of creation). The social crisis was to have no closing date and had to be accepted as the condition of the era. If it ever did end, nothing would be left as it was now. Thus art consisted only of the will to paint and the memory of paintings, and society so far as art was concerned consisted of the man who stood in front of the canvas.

The achievement of Action Painting lay in stating this issue with creative force. Art had acquired the habit of *doing* (as late as a decade ago it was still normal for leaders of the new art to stage public demonstrations). Only the blank canvas, however, offered the opportunity for a doing that would not be seized upon in mid-motion by the depersonalizing machine of capitalist society, or by the depersonalizing machine of the world-wide opposition to that society. The American painter discovered a new function for art as the action that belonged to himself.

The artist's struggle for identity took hold of the crisis directly, without ideological mediation. In thus engaging art in the life of the times *as the life of the artist,* American Action Painting responded positively to a universal predicament. Where else but in this crisis would any living individual ever live? Throughout the world, works from New York reached to individuals as possibilities for each. Paintings produced painters—a development greeted with jeers by shallow minds. Painting became the means of confronting in daily practice the problematic nature of modern individuality. In this way Action Painting restored metaphysical point to art.

There was not in Action Painting as in earlier art movements a stated vanguard concept, yet it carried implicitly the traditional assumptions of a vanguard. Devoid of radical subject matter—except for occasional echoes in the titles of paintings and sculptures of prisons, the Spanish Civil War, Pennsylvania coal towns—Action Painting never doubted the radicalism of its intentions or its substance. Certain ruptures were taken for granted. Foremost among these was the rupture between the artist and the middle class. Commercialism, careerism, were spoken of disdainfully as a matter of course. If the antagonism to conventional values had been shifted inward, from, say, the group manifesto to dialogues between husbands and wives, the self-segregation of the artist from the "community" was still the rule. Indeed, the first gesture of the new painting had been to disengage itself from the crumbling Liberal-Left which had supplied the intellectual environment of the preceding generation of artists.

The rejection of society remained unexpressed. This may have deprived Action Painting of a certain moral coherence and reduced its capacity to resist dilution. Its silence on social matters is not, however, decisive either as to its meaning or its public status. Anti-social motifs in art are of doubtful consequence—society calmly takes them in its stride and in time extends its rewards to the rebels who painted them. This has been the case with nineteenth-century Realism, as with Dada, Expressionism, Surrealism, even Social Realism. To explain the success of Action Painting as the pay-off for an opportunistic turning away from the issues of the day requires a blend of malice and ignorance. A rich Action Painter stoically enduring the crisis of society in his imported sports car makes a good butt for comedy but the loudest guffaws come from cynics for whom sales prices are the ultimate measure.

Another vanguard assumption taken up by Action Painting with fullest intensity was that which demanded the demolition of existing values in art. The revolutionary phrase "doing away with" was heard with the frequency and authority of a slogan. The total elimination of identifiable subject matter was the first in a series of moves—then came doing away with drawing, with composition, with color, with texture; later, with the flat surface, with art materials. (Somewhere along the line Action Painting itself was eliminated.) In a fervor of subtraction art was taken apart element by element and the parts thrown away. As with diamond cutters, knowing where to make the split was the primary insight.

Each step in the dismantling widened the area in which the artist could set in motion his critical-creative processes, the irreducible human asset in a situation where all superstructures are shaky. It had become appropriate to speak of the canvas as an arena (at length the canvas was put aside to produce "happenings").

On the "white expanse" a succession of champions performed feats of negation for the liberation of all. "Jackson broke the ice for us," de Kooning has generously said of Pollock. It is possible,

56. Jackson Pollock, *Cut-out*, 1949, Oil on Canvas, 24″ by 31″ (Ohara Art Gallery, Kurashiki City, Japan)

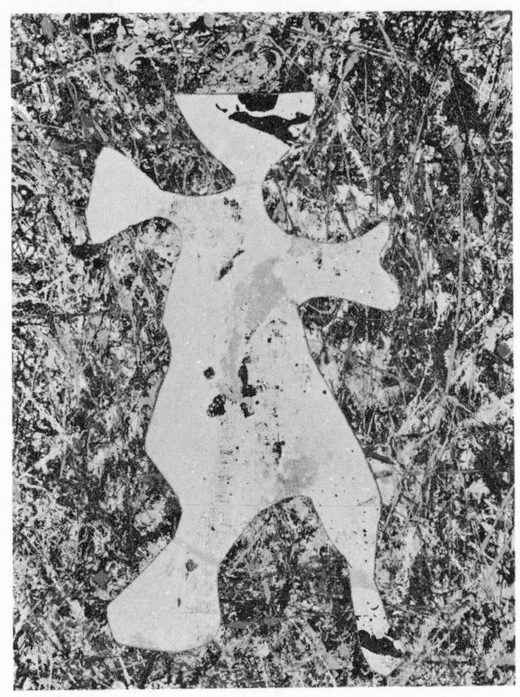

to paraphrase Lady Macbeth, to stand not on this order of the breaking. Be that as it may, behind Pollock came a veritable flotilla of icebreakers. As art dwindled the freedom of the artist increased, and with it the insignificance of gestures of merely formal revolt. The content of paintings became more important than ever before.

Action Painting also pressed to the limit the break with national and regional traditions which, by an historical irony, the political internationalism of the thirties had strengthened. As noted above, the crisis-nature of Action Painting made it a major language of social disaffection wherever experimental art was not barred by force.

To forget the crisis—individual, social, aesthetic—that brought Action Painting into being, or to bury it out of sight (it cannot really be forgotten), is to distort fantastically the reality of postwar American art. This distortion is being practiced daily by all who have an interest in "normalizing" vanguard art, so that they may enjoy its fruits in comfort: these include dealers, collectors, educators, directors of government cultural programs, art historians, museum officials, critics, artists—in sum, the "art world."

The root theory of the distortion is the academic concept of art as art: whatever the situation or state of the artist, the only thing that "counts" is the painting and the painting itself counts only as line, color, form. How *responsible* it seems to the young academician, or to the old salesman, to think of painting "as painting" rather than as politics, sociology, psychology, metaphysics. No doubt bad sociology and bad psychology are bad and have nothing to do with art, as they have nothing to do with society or with real individuals. And about any painting it is true, as Franz Kline once said, that it was painted with paint. But the net effect of deleting from the interpretation of the work the signs pointing to the artist's situation and his emotional conclusions about it is to substitute for an appreciation of the crisis-dynamics of contemporary painting an arid professionalism that is a caricature of the aestheticism of half a century ago. The radical experience of confrontation, of impasse, of purging, is soaked up in expertise about technical variations on earlier styles and masters. The chasm between the artist and society is bridged by official contacts with artists and by adult-education and public-relations programs. Artificial analogies are drawn between features of Action Painting and prestigious cultural enterprises, such as experiments in atomic laboratories, space exploration, skyscraper architecture, new design, existential theology, psychotherapy. An art that had radically detached itself from social objectives is recaptured as a social resource. In turn, society is deprived of the self-awareness made possible by this major focus of imaginative discontent.

As silencing the uneasy consciousness of contemporary painting falsifies the existing relation between art and society, it also inverts the relation between the artist and art. The exclusion of ready-made subjects and the reduction to the vanishing point of traditional aesthetic elements are conceived not as effects of the loss by art of its social functions, on the one hand, and of the artist's sentiment of distance from accepted standards of value, on the other, but as a victorious climb up a ladder of vocational progress. The tension of the painter's lonely and perilous balance on the rim of absurdity is absorbed into the popular melodrama of technical breakthrough, comparable to the invention of the transistor. Sophistries of stylistic comparison establish shallow amalgams which incorporate contemporary art into the sum total of the art of the centuries. By transferring attention from the meaning of the artist's statement to the inherited vocabulary, modern works are legitimized as art to the degree that they are robbed of sense. The longing which Eisenhower recently expressed for art that did not remind him of contemporary life is shared by the functionaries of the art world, who, however, are professionally equipped to prevent *any* art from bringing up this disturbing reference.

The will to remove contemporary painting and sculpture into the domain of art-as-art favors the "expert" who purveys to the bewildered. "I fail to see anything essential in it [Action Painting]," writes Clement Greenberg, a tipster on masterpieces, current and future, "that cannot be shown to have evolved [presumably through the germ cells in the paint] out of either Cubism or Impressionism, just as I fail to see anything essential in Cubism or Impressionism whose development could not be traced back to Giotto and Masaccio and Giorgione and Titian." In this burlesque of art history, artists vanish, and paintings spring from one another with the help of no other generating principle than whatever "law of development" the critic happens to have on hand. Nothing real is "anything essential"—including, for example, the influence on Impressionism of the invention of the camera, the importation of Japanese prints, the science of optics, above all, the artist's changed attitude toward form and tradition. In regard to historical differences the critic's sole qualification is his repeated "I fail to see," while name-dropping of the masters supplies a guarantee of value beyond discussion. Yet grotesque as this is, to a collector being urged to invest in a canvas he can neither respond to nor comprehend, it must be reassuring to be told that it has a pedigree only a couple of jumps from Giotto.

Anything can "be traced back" to anything, especially by one who has elected himself First Cause. The creator, however, has not before him a thing, "traceable" or otherwise; to bring a work into being he must cope with the possibilities and necessities of his time as they exist within him. The content of Action Painting is the artist's drama of creation within the blind alley of an epoch that has identified its issues but allowed them to grow unmanageable. In this situation it has been the rule for creative performance to be a phase in a rhythm of confusion, misery, letting go, even self-destruction—as the formula of Thomas Mann had it, of the alliance of creation with sickness, at once moral and physical. The lives of many, perhaps a majority, of the leading Action Painters have followed this disastrous rhythm from which creation is too often inseparable. Who would suspect this inception of their work from the immaculately conceived picture-book biographies and the gasping-with-admiration catalogue notes, in which personalities have been "objectified" to satisfy the prudery of next of kin and the prejudices of mass education?

The suppression of the crisis-content of Action Painting in the interests of promoting it as art has given rise to a counter public-relations which denounces this art as historically inconsequential and as gratuitously subversive of aesthetic and human values. The ideological assault against Action Painting reaches the same pitch on the Right and on the Left. The former refuses to acknowledge that its standards are empty abstractions, the latter that its techniques for making history have proven fruitless. The happy fiction that the art of our time is a fulfillment of the art of the ages thus finds itself at war with the fiction that our time could find a fulfillment if it were not for the perversity of contemporary artists—a conflict of echoes in a vacuum. Art criticism is probably the only remaining intellectual activity, not excluding theology, in which pre-Darwinian minds continue to affirm value systems dissociated from any observable phenomena.

The crisis that brought Action Painting into being has in no wise abated, though the political surface of the crisis has grown a bit calmer with the lessening of the threat of nuclear war. In regard to the trends of mass culture, the situation of the artist and the position of art itself, all indications are that the crisis has been deepening. The major change of the past ten years is that with more buying and selling of art the consciousness of the crisis has been further dulled—perhaps the spirit of abandonment has been furthered by the increasing difficulty of dealing with it. With desperation driven underground, the will to act has weakened and the inability to do so become less disturbing. I am describing the inner reality of the much-advertised success of vanguard art.

The future of Action Painting, relieved of its original stress, is not difficult to predict. Indeed, it was already visible a decade ago, before its acquisition of a name propelled it in the direction of a Style. "The tremors produced by a few expanses of tone or by the juxtaposition of colors and shapes purposely brought to the verge of bad taste in the manner of Park Avenue shop windows are sufficient cataclysms in many of these happy overthrows of Art. . . . Since there is nothing to be 'communicated,' a unique signature comes to seem the equivalent of a new plastic language . . . etc." With the crisis-sentiment displaced by the joys of professionalism, it remained only to make labels of Anguish and Spontaneity. I do not wish to imply, of course, that artists have any greater obligation to be troubled or in doubt than other people.

The idea of this "trans-formal" art was never a simple one, nor would it be wise to attempt, as is often proposed, a very close description of it. An action that eventuates on a canvas, rather than in the physical world or in society, is inherently ambiguous. As Thomas Hess has argued, art history lies in wait for the Action Painting at its beginning, its middle and its end (what lies in wait for art history?). To come into being such a painting draws on the methods and vocabulary of existing art; in its process of production it invokes, positively and negatively, choices and references of painting; upon completion it is prized within the category of painting values and "hangs on the wall." In sum its being a work of art contradicts its being an action.

To literal minds the presence of a contradiction invalidates either the description or the object described. Yet it is precisely its contradictions, shared with other forms of action (since all action takes place in a context by which its purpose may be reversed), that make Action Painting appropriate to the epoch of crisis. It retains its vigor only as long as it continues to sustain its dilemmas: if it slips over into action ("life") there is no painting; if it is satisfied with itself as painting it turns into "apocalyptic wallpaper."

I have said that Action Painting transferred into the artist's self the crisis of society and of art. It was its subjectivity that related it to the art of the past, most immediately to that of another desperate decade, the Germany of the twenties, from which it drew the misnomer "Expressionism."

There is also a non-subjective way of reacting to a crisis—perhaps this way belongs to a later phase in which hope and will have been put aside. I refer to the impassive reflection of the absurdities which become the accepted realities of daily life, as well as the emblems of its disorder. The projection of these absurdities according to their own logic produces an art of impenetrable farce, farce being the final form, as Marx noted in one of his Hegelian moments, of action in a situation that has become untenable. It is as the farce of rigid anxiety that I interpret the current revival of illusionism in art through techniques of physical incorporation of street debris and the wooden-faced mimicry of senseless items of mass communication. Here again, however, the crisis-content of the work is already being camouflaged in critical how-to-do-it interpretations which amalgamate the new slapstick art with an earlier aesthetic of found materials and popular images.

In that it dared to be subjective, to affirm the artist as an active self, Action Painting was the last "moment" in art on the plane of dramatic and intellectual seriousness. The painters in this current have kept to the tradition of the human being as the ultimate subject of painting. All art movements are movements toward mediocrity for those who are content to be carried by them. The premises of Action Painting, however, are still valid for individual beginnings.

THE GAME OF ILLUSION: POP AND GAG

In earlier times the hero was "represented" by a statue of marble or granite. In Moscow today the tomb of Lenin contains the actual body of the leader as a statue. The tomb is the world's greatest collage; it incorporates a non-art object, the body, into a traditional aesthetic structure. The effect is to convert the corpse into something which affects the imagination in the manner of a work of art but with the weight of actual fact.

The transformation of things by displacing them into art and of art by embedding it in a setting of actuality is the specifically twentieth-century form of illusionism. "The noises of waves, revolvers, typewriters, sirens, or airplanes," explained Erik Satie, a contemporary of the Cubists, in commenting on his ballet *Parade,* significantly subtitled *Ballet Réaliste,* "are in music of the same character as the bits of newspapers, painted wood grain, and other everyday objects that the Cubists frequently employ to localize objects and masses in Nature." In short, the man-made is introduced into the order of trees and waves. Another artist of the First World War era, Jean Arp, contended that his sculptures ought to be come upon as one comes upon a stone polished by a stream; that is to say, that his creations were on a par with those of geology.

No doubt this mixing of art and nature derives to a large extent from urbanization. The city dweller's "nature" is a human fabrication—he is surrounded by fields of concrete, forests of posts and wires, etc.; while nature itself, in the form of parks, a snowfall, cats and dogs, is a detail in the stone and steel of his habitat. Given the enormous dissemination of simulated nature through window displays, motion-picture and television screens, public and private photography, magazine advertisements, art reproductions, car and bus posters, five-and-ten art, it is plain that in no other period has the visible world been to such an extent both duplicated and anticipated by artifice. Surrounded by artistic copies of presidents, scenes, famous events, we become in the end largely insensitive to the distinction between the natural and the made up. The ghostliness of an environment loaded with doubles thus augments the fascination which the game of substituting the image of the thing for the thing itself and vice versa has held for painting since artists, somewhere around the middle of the nineteenth century, lost their patience with mere picturing. The most pervasive term in modern art is "New Realities." It has been used as the title of vanguard art magazines, of art movements (both abstract and ultra-representational), and of group exhibitions. Painters and sculptors in every mode, from Albers to Shahn, have applied to themselves the name "Realist" (being "New" usually goes without saying). Since it signifies something different for everyone who uses it, the label is meaningless. Its popularity does testify, however, to the belief, all but universal among twentieth-century artists, that a work of art ought to be a thing added to the world of things rather than a reflection of things that already exist. In short, while the work of art today is not illusory in the sense of being a representation, it is of a nature to give rise to new forms of mystification through drawing the spectator into an invented realm not unlike that of his everyday life.

Imagine that a cut of pie manufactured by Ma So-and-So, Inc., which looks and tastes like plaster, is reproduced in plaster and set in a display case, and that next to it is a poster on which the pie is painted with such luscious realism of color and tone that you can taste the blueberries. To extend this game of the real pie that is ersatz and a painted pie that is full of the flavors of memory, an artist creates out of plastic or fabric a segment of pie that looks like fabric, not pie, that is utterly non-suggestive of flavor, and that is six feet long. It is neither a real pie that lacks pie qualities nor a fake pie that seems real. This "sculpture" is an illusory object like the poster, but since it creates no illusion, it is logically, just what it is, that is, a reality. Yet a piece of plastic or fabric pie is not real, either. It is the bastard child of illusion, and its only excuse for existence is to enter into the processes of the aesthetic imagination as they have developed during the past century, so one would not be inconsistent in considering this inedible nonlikeness of pie pure art. The only hindrance is that the pie does not look like art; it is purposely not like art any more than it is like pie. But its looks are beside the point. It exists as a demonstration model in an unspoken lecture on the history of illusionism as it occurs in both painting and the streets of big cities. Since the purpose of the pie is to dispel illusion, it might more properly be called a criticism object than an art object. To emphasize his point, in case anyone missed it, the artist (critic) suspends from the ceiling of his gallery a pair of denim pants about size 64 (presumably one who eats six-foot pies will need the largest pants he can get).

This is art comically talking about contemporary art in terms of things—a kind of farce ballet, with credits due to *Ballet Mécanique* and *The Gold Rush.* The performance should be appreciated by anyone who has reflected on the Pygmalion fable or experienced the shock of running into Mr. Schweppes, parted whiskers and all, not in an advertisement but face to face on Fifth Avenue. In a civilization in which public events and personages exist for us primarily through the communications media, in which events often are made to occur exclusively for those media, discourse on illusionism is entirely relevant.

The pie and the pants I have described are, with perhaps some difference of detail, the creations of Claes Oldenburg, who at the outset was the most skillful gamester of illusion of the New Realism, as this type of art is named by the Europeans, with paranoiac persistence, or Pop Art, as it is called in the United States and in England. Yesterday's generation of illusionists was headed by Robert Rauschenberg and Jasper Johns.

On Halloween in 1962, Sidney Janis, whose gallery represented de Kooning, Rothko, Guston, and other top Abstract Expressionists, opened a two-locations exhibition of "factual" (i.e., illusionistic) painting and sculpture. Under these auspices, and after fifteen years of the austerity of abstract art, the new New Realism hit the New York art world with the force of an earthquake. Within a week, tremors had spread to art centers throughout the country.

A good part of the impact was attributable to the fact that illusionistic art is easy to talk about, in contrast to abstraction, whose rhetoric had been reused until it was all but exhausted. This was a powerful advantage for the new work, since much of contemporary painting and sculpture is art only through having sidled, leaped, or been smuggled into the universe of art words.

Coupled with the sudden availability of language was the sense that art history was being made, in that it was from the leading emporium of American abstract art that these appetite-wrecking collations and misplaced home furnishings, advertisements, and comic strips were peeking. Exhibitions with much the same content had been given one or two years earlier by the galleries of individual Pops and the style had been covered by the Museum of Modern Art in its massive "Assemblage" exhibition. The visual puns of Rauschenberg and Johns, Larry Rivers' adaptations of playing cards and cigarette packages, and, long before these, the refined associationism of Joseph Cornell's "boxes" had connected American illusionist vanguardism with the "ready-mades" of Duchamp, Schwitters, Man Ray, and other artists of the First World War period. But with the Janis Gallery converted to the Pops, art politics sensed the buildup of a crisis. Was this the long-heralded dethronement of Abstract Expressionism? Conversation turned to speculation about treachery, secret motives, counterstrategies. What was generally disregarded was that this gallery had prospered by following the decisions of art history without handicapping itself by preferences of taste or ideology. With the New Realism, the Sidney Janis Gallery ventured for the first time to create a bit of belated art history on its own account—an undertaking not unusual in the present art situation.

The New Realists exhibition proves on analysis to be itself an "assemblage" uniting half a dozen tendencies of the art of the past fifty years. Most of the European exhibits, amounting to more than half the total, and a few of the American had no connection with the theme set for the show by the new United States anti-appeal art packages. Some, like Enrico Baj's "Style Furniture," Mario Schifano's "Propaganda," and Tano Festa's "New Shutter" (these artists are all Italian), merely employed everyday images and surfaces to create works of art in the conventions of Cubism, Expressionism and Neo-Plasticism. Yves Klein's sponge sculpture and reliefs, Peter Agostini's plaster clothesline and Robert Moskowitz's "Untitled," a handsome gray-on-gray using as its upper half a glued-down window shade with wrinkles, were in the same category of work in accepted art forms created out of odd stuff. In contrast to these things-as-art, other works in the exhibition did not belong because they were simple *things*, without overtones of dream or the power of self-comment. These included accumulations of swords and faucets by Arman and Jean Tinguely's skeletal radio receiver, both from France. One of Tinguely's two "Works in Progress," a refrigerator that razzed the spectator who opened it, did belong; so, too, did the ominous cord-and-wrapping-paper bundles of another Frenchman, Christo.

In the past, the Europeans have had a much more sophisticated visual vocabulary of illusion than the Americans, while we have plunged into the dream-fact and, as they say, made it work—from millions of chock-full-o'-nuts sandwiches to a lighted waterfall on top of a Broadway building.

Among the Americans in the show, the most imaginative and critically conscious were Oldenburg, Jim Dine, and George Segal. All three use paint and modelling materials to cause the idea of art to abut upon commonplace objects without lending glamour to them. Oldenburg's plastic-steeped ladies' underwear brought to Fifty-seventh Street shoppers an atmosphere not very different from that induced by windows on Fourteenth Street. The essential distinction between the gallery objects and the store objects considered as objects was the art reference of the Oldenburgs, provided by the identification of their maker as an artist and the place of exhibition as an art gallery. This amounted to getting rid of art qualities on a scale that goes far beyond the famous "White on White."

Dine incorporated a lawnmower into art by leaning it against a canvas marked with some Impressionist strokes of green paint, which had also splashed down on the mower. Similarly, carpenters' tools, soap dishes, and a lead pipe become art by hanging or jutting from painted surfaces. The implication was: art is paint and canvas and anything connected (literally) with it—a formula that satirizes the abstract painting of the past ten years.

Segal's plaster family sat around a wooden dining-room table, one member holding in his plaster hand a beat-up aluminum coffeepot. The imprecisely realistic creatures seemed to suffer physically from the fatiguing weight of actual wood and metal, and in this group and in his strangely anguished "Bus Driver," flanked by a genuine coin receptacle, the game of illusion reached a pitch of pathos that belongs equally to sculpture and the theater. Segal was the only

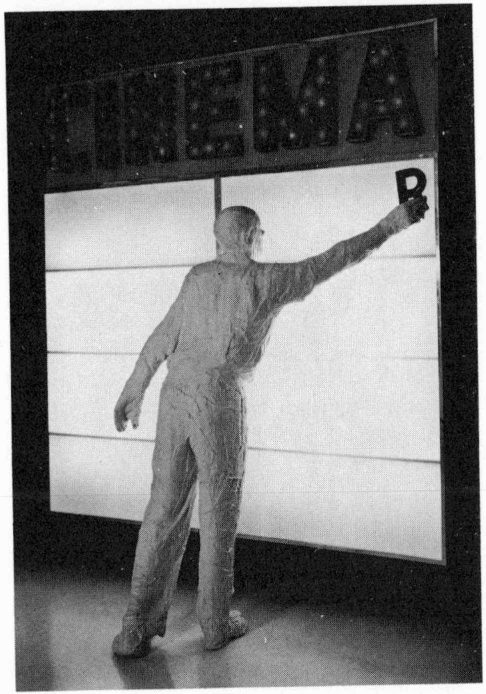

57. George Segal, *Cinema*, 1963, Plaster Statue, Illuminated Plexiglass, Metal Sign, 118″ by 96″ (Albright-Knox Art Gallery, Buffalo, N.Y. Gift of Seymour H. Knox)

exhibitor who used the new illusory combinations to create a new feeling rather than as a commentary on art.

In the two years following the Janis show, Oldenburg and Dine had run out of ideas and Segal had ceased to be touching. The art of these men depends on surprise, and no effect is more difficult to obtain in a situation swamped by promoters.

Other Pop artists varied from tiresome decorator's apprentices matching gags to genuine artists in search of a new way. Old-fashioned street and shop signs and the patterns stenciled on packing cases aroused in Robert Indiana a nostalgia for Americana. Tom Wesselmann reiterated the common point about art and fake by inserting a reproduction of a "fine-art" portrait behind a cutout of the smiling lady who offers standard brands, hamburgers and hot dogs. Like James Rosenquist's paintings composed like collages, this was advertising art advertising itself as art that hates advertising. Wayne Thiebaud, a serious painter, depicted rows of sandwiches, salads and ice-cream sundaes in perspective instead of the more customary rows of trees and shrubs. Art lovers who discussed Thiebaud in terms of "painterly" qualities seem to me to have missed his point, which was to be painterly but with "no artificial color added." Something similar but with motives that aroused

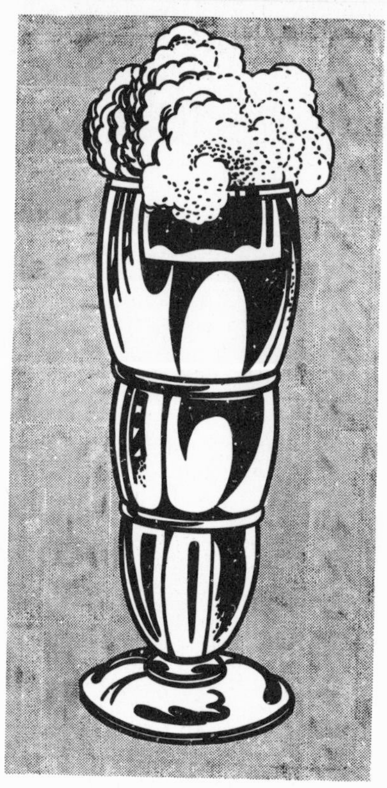

58. Roy Lichtenstein, *Ice Cream Soda,* 1962, Oil on Canvas, 64″ by 32″ (Collection: Myron Orlovsky)

suspicion was true of Roy Lichtenstein, an Abstract Expressionist suddenly retooled to blow up comic strips. Andy Warhol offered columns of Campbell's Soup labels in narcotic reiteration, like a joke without humor told over and over again, until it carried a hint of menace (later, he reiterated electric chairs).

The new American illusionist contrivances have a deeper identification with commercial art than the plagiarism or adaptation of its images. They share the impersonality of advertising-agency art-department productions. They are entirely cerebral and mechanical; the hand of the artist has no part in the evolution of the work but is the mere executor of the idea-man's command, though in this case the artist himself is usually the idea-man (sometimes the idea for a work comes from friends or sponsors). Nor is the self of the artist engaged by the process of creation. As a phase in the history of modern illusionism, the American contributions to this exhibition, with the exception of Segal's, represented a hyper-objectivism that kept the game of fictions in the air without a landing spot in reality.

If, as some have maintained, there is terror in this art, it comes from its irremediable deadpan—a grin in porcelain.

The attempt to purge Abstract Expressionism by polemics against it in the art pages of the press produced nothing more than ideological nagging. The purging of art by works of art based on a different premise is, however, always vitalizing. Those artists, dealers, and curators who functioned on the assumption that the look of Action Painting was sufficient to authenticate a canvas were put on notice by the new illusionist objects that any image, including Coca-Cola lettering or the numbers on a pinball machine, could be equally viable. In sum, there is no greater aesthetic virtue in copying a de Kooning than in copying the design on a beer can. If you do either, you are talking to the audience about itself, not engaging in creation. In dramatizing this principle, Pop Art has been a contribution to art criticism.

THE ART OBJECT AND THE AESTHETICS OF IMPERMANENCE

In defining a poem in terms of its psychological effect on the reader Poe introduced time into criticism. "All excitements," he argued in "The Poetic Principle," "are, through a psychal necessity, transient" and half an hour "at the very utmost" is the limit of "that degree of excitement which would entitle a poem to be so called at all." There are, of course, poems that take longer to read. But though it is physically present on the page, for Poe "a long poem does not exist."

A comparable time limit on paintings was proposed recently by Marcel Duchamp, except that instead of considering the audience's capacity for "excitement" Duchamp reflected on how long the stimulating power of the work itself can last. Discussing "the short life of a work of art," he declared that a painting possesses an aesthetic "smell or emanation" which persists for twenty to thirty years, after which it dissolves and the work dies. As illustration, Duchamp mentioned his own celebrated "Nude Descending a Staircase"; despite all the fuss about it, he said, the "Nude" is dead, "completely dead."

As against the common-sense notion of the poem or painting as an object to which the beholder reacts, Poe and Duchamp pose the idea of the work as a temporary center of energy which gives rise to psychic events. To attribute independent power to things is a species of fetishism; but the fetishes of these artists are of a modern variety because their potency is measured by the clock. In the introspection of Poe and the history consciousness of Duchamp, an interval of portentous time replaces the transcendental "thing" of the older aesthetics and the older magic. The work of art is like an irradiated substance; when its charge dies down it begins to *last.*

The concept of painting as involved in time is of fairly recent origin. The French Catholic philosopher, Étienne Gilson, analyzing the nature of painting in his *Painting and Reality,* refers to "the *received* [i.e., accepted] distinction between arts of time (poetry, music) and arts of space (sculpture, painting and, generally speaking, the 'arts of design')." Gilson endeavors to uphold this distinction by arguing that though the aesthetic experience of a painting continues for so many minutes then ceases, the painting itself has a physical existence in space and that it is this spatial existence that determines the nature of painting as an art. The spatial concept has, however, Gilson admits, been meeting resistance among modern aestheticians and artists, probably from artists most of all. Gilson finds himself in direct conflict with Paul Klee's assertion in his "Creative Credo" that Lessing's famous separation in the *Laokoön,* between arts of space and arts of time is out of date in twentieth-century space-time thinking. It takes time, Klee explained, for a dot to turn into a line, for a line to form a surface, and so forth; in sum, for the picture as a whole to come into being out of its parts. It takes time also for the spectator to appreciate it—"leisure-time," said Klee, plus, he added (quoting the nineteenth-century phenomenologist, Feuerbach), a chair to keep the fatigue of the legs from distracting the mind. All this phenomenology of action and response is applicable, Gilson concedes, but only to "the genesis of the work of art and of its apprehension by a beholder." A painting is of time when it is considered as an encounter between the artist and his audience. It belongs to space when it is conceived as a thing, that is to say, as Gilson puts it, "from the point of view of the work of art itself."

The notion of the art object as worthy of being considered from its own point of view apart from the artist's act of creation and the excitement of the spectator is of capital importance in regard to twentieth-century art. A painting is set aside as a thing independent of the human circumstances surrounding it not merely for the sake of philosophical completeness but for ideological purposes. This is made amply clear by Gilson in *Painting and Reality.* Art which is, in his words, "in keeping with the physical mode of existence that belongs to painting," that is, with the mode of spatiality, will conform to and uphold values of stability and permanence; which means that it will oppose the evanescent-energy concepts of Poe, Duchamp, Klee and other contemporaries. From the essential "thingness" of painting Gilson derives an aesthetics of quiescence, contemplation, pattern, as against the "action" tradition of such paintings as Gericault's "Epsom Derby" or Jacques-Louis David's "Bonaparte Crossing the St. Bernard." Paintings like the David and the Poussin "Rape of the Sabine Women" are to be restudied in such a way as to transform their "motion in time" into "visual pattern in space." Gilson carries his concept to the literal conclusion that the still life is the supreme subject of painting since "in a still life nothing acts, nothing gesticulates, nothing does anything else than to be"—a formula of negatives curiously homologous with the anti-Expressionist pronouncements of Ad Reinhardt. In sum, the concept of the art object becomes the basis for imposing on paintings a mental "set" or gridiron of values—in this instance, the values of a religious quietism over and apart from the actual experience of both painters and spectators.

Gilson's metaphysics of the art object provides (in reverse) a clue as to why so many modern paintings and sculptures are deliberately produced out of materials that change or fall apart. The short-lived work of art, as dramatized, for example, by the self-annihilating "sculpture" exhibited by Tinguely a few years ago in the garden of the Museum of Modern Art, displays art as an *event.* To underscore the phenomenon of creation and its effects on the beholder as the exclusive content of a painting, some twentieth-century artists have been willing to condemn the work itself to extinction. Duchamp, though he doubts that aesthetic shock is any longer possible, seems himself shocked by the degree to which contemporary artists connive at the self-destruction of their products. "It's the most revolutionary attitude possible," he has asserted, "because they know they're killing themselves. It is a form of suicide, as artists go; they kill themselves by using perishable materials." Apparently, Duchamp can endure the thought that his "Nude" is dead but is awed that a work shall vanish and take its creator with it.

The painting with a "short life" is an antidote to the painting as an object that obstructs the psychic transaction between the artist and the spectator. One who today reacts with excitement to Duchamp's "Nude" is, in the opinion of her creator, stimulated by "the thing he has learned" rather than by the painting itself. From the artist's point of view, better a dead work than one enveloped forever in abstractions. In the end, Duchamp acknowledges that his notion of the fading aroma or "soul" of a painting may be a fantasy. But it has vital, practical function: "it helps me make a distinction between aesthetics and art history."

The aesthetics of impermanence stresses the work of art as an interval in the life of both artist and spectator. Compositions into which found objects are glued or affixed or from which they protrude or are suspended make art subject to time on equal terms with nature and commodities for daily use. A German critic's description of a work by Kurt Schwitters shows the direct connection between the embodying of time in a contemporary work and bringing the spectator into contact with the artist: "The MERZbau is a three-dimensional assemblage to which new elements were *merzed on* for sixteen consecutive years until, eventually, it grew upwards through two stories and downward into a cellar in Schwitters' house in the Waldhausenstrasse in Hanover. The important thing is for the spectator to stand *'in'* a piece of sculpture." (His italics) The yellowing and crumbling newspapers in a collage of Picasso or Schwitters incorporate a rhythm of aging equivalent to the metamorphosis of characters in Proust's *Remembrance of Things Past,* composed in the same period. Art that deteriorates more or less visibly is the reply of the twentieth-century mind to the fixated aestheticism of Dorian Gray.

Action painting, which has usually refrained from attacking the physical integrity of the canvas (though there are notable examples of perishable Action Paintings by Pollock, de Kooning, Kline and others), has focussed on the inception of the work in opposition to, as Klee put it, the "end product." Its vocabulary tends to describe its creations in terms of their coming into being: expressions that conceive of a painting as beginning to "happen" or as "working itself out" are typical. Some Action Painters apparently concluded that the picture ought to be begun and finished in Poe's "half an hour" as a guarantee of authentic excitement. In Action Painting the artist is the first spectator and the audience is invited to repeat with him the experience of seeing the work take shape. Mathieu, for example, actually made painting a picture into a public performance; and analogies have often been drawn between Action Painting and the paintings executed as a spectacle by Zen monks. From Action Paintings to "happenings," which carry painting and sculpture over into theater, took only a single logical step—a final step, by the way, which in art one should always hesitate to take. In the "happening" the art object, Gilson's "physical existence," is abandoned altogether and composition turns literally into an event.

As an art form the "happening" is superfluous, as are such other coarser manifestations of transience as audience-participation collage and decollage (reassembling torn fragments of posters), art controlled by timers or by photoelectric cells, "making art by eating" (done both in New York and Paris; art-eating has the advantage of combining the art exhibition and the artists' party, the two chief tourist attractions of the art world). Today all works of art have become happenings. A Giotto and a Kaprow are events of differing duration in the psyche of individuals and in the history of art. Ontologically, a painting may be an immobile object to be contemplated; in this respect, however, there is nothing to differentiate it from any other object, and, as we have seen, it can be made to move and act by "ontologists" of a different persuasion. More relevant to the philosophical definition of art than its inherent spatiality is its function in a given human environment. In terms of what it does, the chief attribute of a work of art in our century is not stillness but circulation. Whether through being moved before multitudes in exhibitions and reproductions or through being made available to multitudes in *their* movements, as in the great museums, it is circulation that determines the nature and significance of paintings in the contemporary world.

Circulating as an event in art history, the painting sheds its materiality, it assumes a spectral other self that is omnipresent in art books, illustrated articles, exhibition catalogues, TV and films and the discourses of art critics and historians. Composed in the first instance of the painter's motions in time, the picture also exists temporally in the frequency-rate of its public appearance. To introduce it into and identify it as part of the cultural system, it must carry an art-historical tag that relates it to paintings of other times. Thus the painting becomes inseparable from language (one of Gilson's temporal media); in actual substance it is a centaurlike being—part words, part art supplies.

It is inspiring to imagine with Professor Gilson a painting engaged in "the simplest and most primitive of all acts, namely, to be." To witness an enactment of isolated being, however, one would have to seek out a painting hidden from curators and reviewers. Perhaps a little more than other contemporary museums, the Guggenheim has dedicated itself to hooking up its exhibits historically. Its "Six Painters and the Object" show linked comic strip and billboard art to Seurat and Léger. Its "Cézanne and Structure in Modern Painting" exhibition rounded up such widely separated contemporaries as Jenkins and Marca-Relli, Ferren and Albers, as "heirs of Cézanne" with whom "structure is the guiding principle." Van Gogh has been similarly "explored" in relation to twentieth-century Expressionism, i.e., has been stuffed under a stylistic label with artists far removed from him in motive, intellectual character and conception of the object. It is probably futile to object that these tags interfere with the apprehension of the works shown; and no doubt there are theoretical grounds for connecting Cézanne with "structure" and even the rationale of structure. Yet one would like to see Cézanne associated for a change (and to help free the physical presence of a Cézanne from its ideological casing) with Expressionism and even (via de Kooning and Hans Hofmann) with Action Painting, and to see Van Gogh brought forward among painters of "structure," by way, for example, of his color theories. After all, historical continuity depends on the facets chosen for emphasis, and nothing could be more misleading than the bifurcation of the history of modern art into Formalist and Expressionist limbs. It ought no longer be necessary to point out that every valid artist is both—that Kline is a Formalist, Newman an Expressionist, as well as the vice versa. Mr. Daniel Robbins, who prepared the catalogue for "Cézanne and Structure," strove heroically to enunciate this synthetic character of modern creation: of Albers' "Homage to the Square" series he wrote that the "primary effect is emotional and closely tied to nature," and, noting qualities in Alber's painting that he found "baffling," "moving," "equivocal," he concluded that "in terms of the conventional sense of structural aesthetic, it produces a sense of frustration." Then why include

Albers in the theme of "Cézanne and Structure," unless a "conventional" and "frustrating" label is better than no label at all?

Once set in motion, a work survives apart from its physical body. Indeed, the art object tends more and more to dissolve into its reproductions and to fixed opinions regarding its meaning. Exhibited for limited periods, frequently to illustrate a concept, the original painting retires leaving the image in the catalogue or historical or biographical monogram by which it is "placed" and comprehended. Duchamp is probably mistaken: perishable materials will not prevent artists from achieving immortality in the future chronicles of art. Today, painters are renowned in places where not a single painting of theirs has ever been displayed; why should they not be equally famous in areas of time never reached by their actual products?

Impermanence of the art object arose as the artist's weapon against art as an intellectual prop for changeless ideas. Today, however, impermanence has become a stylistic device, eagerly appreciated in terms of aesthetic precedents. Refuse, old newspapers, rugs—ephemera symbolizing the moment of vision when anything that lies at hand is sufficient for aesthetic excitement—are embalmed in bronze or plastics to insure the works composed of them against the ravages of time. Art cannot transform the conditions of its own existence. The struggle to preserve the direct encounter between the artist and the spectator will, however, no doubt continue by one means or another. To *épater le bourgeois* may prove far easier than to exorcise the art historian. Perhaps one should look forward to masterpieces on such themes as "The Abduction from the Studio" and "The Rape of de Kooning's Women."

21. THE MECHANIZATION OF ART

Edgar Wind

INTRODUCTION

We are all familiar with the juxtaposition of art and mechanization as representing two mutually exclusive processes. Whether we believe this to be an obsolete romanticism or a salvable idea, it continues to plague us. This selection by Edgar Wind ranges through a variety of situations in which the art and mechanization theme and attendant value judgments are evoked: the illuminated manuscript and the invention of printing; photography, the film, and television; reproductions of works of art that present huge monuments and small coins on the same scale of the printed page; the scientific cleaning and restoring of pictures; the engineering of recorded music; mechanical enlargements and reductions of sculptural models; and many other instances that pose fascinating questions about the nature of the relationship between art and mechanization. The value of such a selection as this lies in its evocative power. It suggests questions that lie well beyond its specific content. And whenever the question involves such alternatives as automatisms or personal choice, one suspects that the chafing issue behind it all is not whether individual acts resulting in the creation of unique objects are superior to the repetitive and predictable actions of machines producing repetitive and predictable objects, but rather who—or what—is at the controls.

For further reading consult Herbert Read, *Art and Industry*, rev. ed. (1954), first published in 1934; Lewis Mumford, *Technics and Civilization* (c. 1934), also available in 1963 paperback with critical preface; Siegfried Giedion, *Mechanization Takes Command* (1948); *Bauhaus 1919–1928*, ed. H. Bayer, W. Gropius, and Ise Gropius (1952); Lewis Mumford, *Art and*

Technics (1952), especially the essay "Standardization, Reproduction, and Choice"; Herbert Read, *To Hell With Culture* (1963), particularly Chapter 14, "The Great Debate"; Lewis Mumford, *The Myth of the Machine* (1967); and J. Reichardt, "Computer Art," *Studio*, CLXXIII (1967). For a nineteenth-century view, see William Morris, "The Aims of Art," originally published in 1887, and available in *Realism and Tradition in Art, 1848–1900*, ed. Linda Nochlin (1966).

It might be thought that art and mechanization are mutually exclusive. An artistic performance is a creative act, unique and unrepeatable, whereas it is of the very essence of a mechanical event that it can be repeated, and often is. To say that a creative artist would not incline to repeat himself exactly is an understatement: he is incapable of it. If two paintings ascribed to a great master look identical, it is more than likely that at least one of them is a copy by another hand. The rule is the same as in the study of handwriting. A man's signature varies because he writes spontaneously. When two signatures are exactly the same, a suspicion of forgery arises.[1]

There are anecdotes about Mozart which illustrate the point in music, although they may well be legendary. It is said that, when asked to repeat an improvised piece, he would unfailingly improvise a variation of it. As a child of seven, while accompanying a singer extempore, he changed the accompaniment with every repetition. According to Grimm, who reported this incident in his *Correspondance littéraire* (1 December 1763), "he would have done it twenty times over if he had not been stopped."

It was in a similar spirit of creative exuberance that Renoir denied in a conversation with Vollard that the chemistry of pigments ever forced him to regularize and repeat his procedures: "In painting, you know, there is not a single process that can be made into a formula. For instance, I once attempted to fix the quantity of oil that I add to the paint on my palette. I couldn't do it. Each time I have to add my oil at a guess."[2] The statement is the more remarkable as it comes from a meticulously trained technician who started as a painter of porcelain.

Even if we suppose that Renoir was exaggerating a little, or that Vollard embellished the statement while recording it, the bias of Renoir's remark is clear enough: he held fast to the old belief that art is degraded by mechanization. I call it an old belief because it antedates our age by at least 500 years. The invention of printing, for example, and the use of woodcuts for the illustration of books, filled the Duke of Urbino, the famous Federigo da Montefeltro, with such dismay that he would not allow a printed book to enter his library. For him the act of reading a classical text was desecrated by the contemplation of the printed page. Words that were beautifully written by a scribe seemed to address his eye and mind in a personal way which was obliterated by mechanical type; and a manuscript illuminated by hand-painted miniatures gave him a pleasure that no woodcut could equal.[3]

It would be easy to dismiss this attitude as sheer snobbery, the kind of preciousness that is sometimes found among modern collectors who have turned Veblen's principle of conspicuous waste into a policy of sound investment. That an ingredient of vanity and calculation may have entered into the Duke of Urbino's disdain of printing I would not deny: [4] but there is more to it than that. The first printed books were made to look like manuscripts, some were even doctored with handpainted initials, or colored washes imposed on the woodcuts, or by being printed specially on vellum, to satisfy the kind of fastidious taste which the Duke of Urbino had cultivated. Thus he cannot be entirely blamed for having regarded this new manufacture as an impertinent and vulgar cheat.

At its first appearance a newly mechanized art always looks like a fake, because it models itself on an unmechanized or less mechanized kind of art. Before the film had found its own powerful idiom, it looked like degraded theater, just as television now often looks like degraded film. Thus, when Ruskin spoke of what he called "vile manufacture," he did not mean to distinguish between vile and honorable manufacture. All manufacture seemed to him vile because it was the opposite of honorable craftsmanship in which the artisan controlled his work by his own hand, whereas in manufacture the production was surrendered to a machine, an automaton that mimicked and falsified living craftsmanship and thus was nothing but its cheap, deceptive double.

Although it is obvious that Ruskin overstated his case, there is no denying that there are aspects of mechanization which justify some of his apprehensions. In the creation of monumental sculpture, for example, it is economical for the artist to confine his work to a small model and delegate the enlargement of it to a mechanical instrument which, point by point, transposes the small shapes to a huge scale. The machine treats forms as if they were indifferent to size, although every perceptive sculptor knows that they are not.

The same problem in reverse arises with medals or coins, where it is expedient to make the model on a larger scale, which is then brought down to the right size by the reducing machine. As a result, the ordinary coin or medal looks as vacant as the ordinary public monument.[5] On the progressive mechanization of carving, duly upbraided by Ruskin in *Aratra Pentelici* for weakening and effacing "the touch of the chisel as expressive of personal feeling or power," it is worth consulting the *Encyclopaedia Britannica.* Fifty years ago (1911) the article on Sculpture noted that "in the opinion of many artists the use of the mechanical pointing-machine is responsible in a great measure for the loss of life and fire in much of modern sculpture." In the most recent edition (1960) we read instead that "with the help of a pointing-machine the present mechanical system of carving is easy to learn and free of responsibility because it is mathematically exact."

If Ruskin said that "a great sculptor uses his tool exactly as a painter his pencil, and you may recognize the decision of his thought, and glow of his temper, no less in the workmanship than the design," the same thought applies with little variation to architectural workmanship as well: its quality declines if a machine is allowed to superimpose its own habits on the artist's style. Prefabricated window-frames, for example, when inserted into otherwise conventional buildings, produce a jarring monotony of fenestration in which architecture is victimized by mechanics. I hasten to add that these dreary cases speak not against mechanization as such, but only against bad and inflexible mechanization, an unimaginative use of machinery which the creative modern architects have triumphantly overcome. Entering as they do into the spirit of a mechanized process, with the same intimacy as the manual craftsman felt for the tool in his hand, they project their imagination into every part of the mechanism, and thus render mechanization itself expressive. In such cases we do not have a "mechanization of art," but on the contrary an artistic use of machinery; and if this ideal relationship of mechanical instrument to art were universal, there would be no argument.

But even these modern achievements, as is well known, are travestied by "vile manufacture." The streamlined constructions required for airplanes and racing cars are transferred to cars not designed for such speeds but intent on suggesting them by borrowed rhetoric. Thus the streamlined taxicab is built so low that we must double ourselves up in order to get in or out of it. The beautiful and comfortable chairs invented by Mies van der Rohe are parodied in the mass-produced, streamlined chair constructed according to a technological idea of being seated and hence allowing no one to sit as he pleases.[6] The streamlined knife, fork, and spoon are likely to interfere with the act of eating by making us needlessly conscious of it. The false rhetoric of mechanization persistently obliges us to look sharp, thus reversing the effect of those antimacassars which obliged even Ruskin to look comfortable.

It would be tempting to dismiss all this as a passing fashion that need not be taken too seriously, were it not that many cities are already disfigured by fake-modern buildings that will stand for a long time. Equipped with the newest facilities of engineering, architectural design requires of its craftsmen exceptional powers of resistance not to let any part of the machinery usurp a function that belongs to the architect himself. The temptation to let the machine have its way increases with the perfection of machinery; every new instrument producing new routines which only a master can rescue from automatic proliferation. Perhaps this explains why modern buildings are either superb or miserable. The tension is too great to allow for decent mediocrity. In that respect the architecture of our age is indeed like an airplane or a racing car. The only alternative to perfection is disaster.

A particularly destructive use of mechanization is its illicit extension to the past, as for example in the refacing of ancient buildings. Since no modern machinery can produce the exact double of an old façade, every stage of major repair would seem to call for fresh architectural invention. Replacements cannot be made by rote. Where complete repetitions have been attempted with machine-cut stones and the old ornaments recarved, they look like replicas or facsimiles of the building that has vanished. Thus the refacing of Wren's Sheldonian Theatre in Oxford may be studied one day as a monumental example of the naive obstinacy and self-delusion that bedevil a mechanical age. In the nineteenth century Viollet-le-Duc thought, because he was a skillful and vigorous engineer and had the support of an inspector of monuments as energetic as Prosper Mérimée, that he could restore French cathedrals to their original splendor. Today his name has become a byword for nineteenth-century Gothic; yet few of those who smile at Viollet-le-Duc seem to recognize his fallacy in their own confident pursuit of exact restoration. "The Church of Vézelay," wrote Mérimée, "is now restored in the most complete manner, and if one of its abbots of the thirteenth century were to return from the dead, no doubt he would find it just as he had left it.[7] It is worth recalling here a remark made by Auguste Prost in 1885: "To remake (*refaire à neuf*) an ancient monument . . . is to place oneself before this dilemma: either to falsify it by failing, or to produce a pastiche by succeeding." Prost admitted the necessity of restoring corroded parts: "but to set oneself the task of replacing a decayed work in its entirety is . . . to cause the certain loss of the object that one is dismounting." In describing what had happened before his own eyes to the cathedral of Metz, he recorded a typical sequence of events: "On voulait réparer d'abord; on a été conduit ensuite à vouloir restaurer, et aujourd'hui on démolit ce qui restait du vieil édifice, pour le reconstruire entièrement." [8]

The same problems and delusions occur in the so-called "scientific" cleaning of pictures. Conscientious restorers are always guided by an awareness that they cannot touch a painting without interpreting it. The danger arises when the attempt is made to reduce the burden of exegesis by delegating a major part of it to a chemical solvent which, it is hoped, will safely remove superimposed layers of paint or varnish, and so lay bare the artist's original work without having altered it by the contact.[9] The belief that a painting of, say, the fifteenth century can be returned with scientific certainty to its pristine state, as if five hundred years of existence had left no trace on it, is of course a chemical as well as a historical absurdity. Even if the material history of such an object were reversible, which it is not, the restorer's own vision cannot be wound back to a fifteenth-century optic except by an effort of historical imagination that is subject to all the hazards of learned inference. "Does not the eye altering alter all?" [10] In an age of art-historical inquiry, which increasingly converges with studies in the history of science, it is surprising that some museum curators still fail to realize that after a short passage of time the "scientific" treatment of a picture will be datable to the year. Style will be recognized in cleaning as easily as it used to be in overpainting: for no one can jump over his own historical shadow.

That these adventures of restoration are often pursued today in a reckless spirit, and on a much larger scale than should be necessary, is due to a scientific as well as an aesthetic fashion. The notion that every old picture must be cleaned is like certain outdated medical fashions that made it obligatory for every respectable person of advanced age to "take the waters." In the preservation of pictures these restorative ablutions are encouraged by a desire for freshness at any cost, even if it entails fragmentation. After a picture has been decomposed, the painting is "honestly" left in a half-raw state—an artificial ruin or, to put it more charitably, a carefully prepared scientific specimen which, like any other product of technical skill, registers some of the peculiarities of the technician. Since the mechanics of stripping down a painting reverses the sequence in which it was built up, it is almost inevitable that processed pictures acquire a surface that looks machine-made, resembling the hard luminous gloss of mechanical reproductions, with brute colors in glaring juxtaposition. The satisfaction aroused by paintings reduced to that state may probably be ascribed to the fact that vision has increasingly been trained on derivative prints, which tend to over-define an image in one direction by fixing it to a mechanical scale.

That our vision of art has been transformed by reproductions is obvious. Our eyes have been sharpened to those aspects of painting and sculpture that are brought out effectively by a camera. What is more decisive, in the artist's own vision we can observe the growth of a pictorial and sculptural imagination that is positively attuned to photography, producing works photogenic to such a degree that they seem to find a vicarious fulfillment in mechanized after-images: as if the ultimate hope of a painter or sculptor today, apart from having his works placed in a museum, would be to see them diffused in comprehensive picture-books, preferably in an illustrated *catalogue raisonné.*[11] What has optimistically been called the "museum without walls" is in fact a museum on paper—a paper-world of art in which the epic oratory of Malraux proclaims, with the voice of a crier in the market place, that all art is composed in a single key, that huge monuments and small coins have the same plastic eloquence if transferred to the scale of the printed page, that a *gouache* can equal a fresco.[12]

On these assumptions it is only logical that the color print threatens to become the medium on which a painting must count for being remembered. That Picasso has consciously adjusted his palette to the crude requirements of the color process I would not say, but his paintings suffer remarkably little in this singularly coarse form of reproduction. They suit it almost as well as Van Gogh. With a growing adjustment to the color print, it is natural that the objects best suited to that medium should be preferred to works that are too intricate for it, machinery thus dictating a selection that sponsors a stylistically regressive taste. The art of the *douanier* Rousseau has thus an advantage over that of Titian because his color effects, being schematic and plain, can be simulated more easily by the printing press.[13]

The same forces are active also in music. Originally the gramophone record produced an echo of the live performance, with all the peculiarities of the performer's attack. It served as a substitute for a concert, removed by one degree from the real event. For that reason musicians and amateurs of music inclined at first to despise the substitute, with much the same vigor as the Duke of Urbino displayed in his resentment of printing. However, recording—like printing—developed its own style: it became an idiom with a particular aesthetics. Marked idiosyncrasies of phrasing, for example, which may be startling and impressive in the concert hall, can grate when they are heard too often. Recording therefore tended to file them off, aiming instead at a technical finish which would allow for constantly repeated hearing. It is a well-known fact that gramophone records are now often put together piece by piece, each piece a polished unit in a musical *collage* which no living performer has played as a whole. The ear thus gets adjusted to dehumanized sounds, and there can be no doubt that, ever since, the style and the quality of performances have changed toward a more even mechanical proficiency, not only for the purposes of recording but retroactively in live concerts as well. In some instances composition itself has begun to aim for the recorded tone, prescribing a style of musical performance that lends itself to *montage* and stereophonic projection,[14] just as the mechanized idiom of the film has decisively shaped certain styles of dramatic writing and acting that subordinate the range of human expression to the capabilities of the screen.[15]

The situation reminds me of a historic occasion in Washington when the newly founded National Gallery of Art was opened by President Roosevelt in 1941. He was expected to address the guests, and many who had often heard him speak so effectively over the radio, were curious to see in what manner he would address an audience face to face. They found that he did not address them at all. The speech was broadcast, and from the first the President's mind was concentrated on the microphone before him. It was a graceful speech addressed to the world outside, while those in his immediate presence were like eavesdroppers, listening in on a performance not intended for them. No doubt, those listening to the broadcast assumed that they were getting only a reflex of his speech, a sort of echo, but they were mistaken: what seemed like an echo was the substance.

In the enjoyment of art this curious reversal seems to me one of the fundamental dangers of mechanization. The medium of diffusion tends to take precedence over the direct experience of the object, and more often than not the object itself is conceived with this purpose in view. We are given the shadow for the thing, and in the end we live among shadows, and not only believe that things are made for the sake of their shadows, but find that this is actually the case. Not that this condition is without promise. Many a brave new world of things was made out of shadows firmly shaped by an artist, but the boldness required for that task has increased with the ease of evading it: for it is both the strength and the weakness of a mechanized medium that it can replace personal choice by automatisms which, however economical in other walks of life, are artistically blank and wasteful. No mannerism is more stultifying than one caused by a machine.

An easy pride in the advances of mechanization is therefore just as unfounded as that proverbial phobia of it which was justly ridiculed by J. B. S. Haldane: "There is no great invention, from fire to flying, which has not been hailed as an insult to some god."[16] To assume, as Ruskin did in his weaker moments, that an art must lose its authenticity whenever it delegates part of its function to an ancillary craft is an aesthetic superstition. Ideally, on that theory, the composer should be a singer, the poet a bard, the architect a builder, mason, and bricklayer. It is true that some of the arts still survive in that uncorrupted state. The painter has not yet delegated his brush, nor the draftsman his pencil, and there are even sculptors who have not delegated their chisels. And yet, some of the creative expansions of art—in architecture, music, and drama—could never have taken place at all if the artist had always remained his own instrument, or the only authentic instrument of his art. A prudent skepticism about mechanization, particularly when it overreaches itself, should not deny the positive part that machinery and substitution have played in artistic growth.

To my mind one of the most enlightening of antimechanical protests lies buried in that quizzical American book, *The Education of Henry Adams*. Always scrupulously attentive to historical ceremony, particularly when he foresaw that it might be fatuous, Adams took a few steps of his own, in the year 1900, to inaugurate the twentieth century. He went to Paris and visited the World Exhibition, where he stood, bemused and bewildered, before the forty-foot dynamos in the Great Hall. He understood little about engineering and, perhaps for that reason, viewed its progress with misgiving. He reflected that, since 1893, "the automobile had become a nightmare . . . almost as destructive as the electric tram which was only ten years older, and threatening to become as terrible as the locomotive steam engine itself." To regain his balance, Adams withdrew to the cathedrals of Chartres and Amiens. Here, worshipping at the shrine of the Virgin, he meditated on the fate of those who were worshipping at the shrine of the dynamo. Adams was the kind of man who feels that on a memorable occasion it is important to make a memorable statement. Although he did not agree with Gibbon's evaluation of the Gothic style, he envied Gibbon for having dismissed all Gothic cathedrals in one single sentence by saying: "I darted a contemptuous look on the stately monuments of superstition."[17] Adams longed to dart just such a look on the stately monuments of engineering, but for that he was too shrewd; he knew that these forces had to be reckoned with, and although he distrusted them intensely, he prided himself on being a good judge of forces. He therefore composed for his autobiography, under the year 1900, a chapter entitled "The Dynamo and the Virgin." In it he contrasted the modern powers of steam and electricity with the force exerted by medieval faith. "All the steam in the world," he writes, "could not, like the Virgin, build Chartres."

This memorable remark is worth analyzing. According to it, the Virgin built Chartres; which is clearly a metaphor, and presumably it means that faith in the Virgin inspired the building of the cathedral. But Chartres was not built by faith alone. Like other French Gothic cathedrals, it was built by carefully calculated engineering. The master-builders who constructed ribbed vaults and flying buttresses would have been much displeased with an admirer of their work who discounted their mathematical and mechanical ingenuity. The antithesis between modern engineering and medieval spirituality is one of those facile and fallacious disjunctions by which we get trapped when we regard art as naturally opposed to mechanization. On the side of art Adams disregarded the mechanical energies that had been harnessed to produce an admirable building, while on the side of mechanics he considered the energies in the raw, unrelated to any purposes they might subserve. Thus we get a fine antithesis between mechanization and spirit, produced by mental omissions on both sides.

A philosophical inquiry into artistic utensils would probably show that the problems associated by us with mechanization lie dormant in the use of the simplest instrument. A mere pencil or piece of chalk in the hand of an artist extends his range beyond his natural self. Is not all art a form of self-extension, as in Carlyle's definition of man as "a tool-using animal"? [18] Any instrument, it is true, brings with it the danger that it might enslave the man that it is meant to serve. Thus the pencil dominated Meissonier, Menzel, and Muirhead Bone, and their perception became as mechanical as their skill. Yet a vision without instrument is an equivocal ghost: there is no "Raphael without hands." [19] As for Mozart, he may have disliked the mechanics of copying, but once he had put pen to paper, the notes could be read, recopied, distributed and played, and with the help of modern mechanization the performances in their turn can be recorded and the records replayed *ad libitum.* Repetition, however unattractive to Mozart, seems as essential to the continued existence of his music as spontaneity was to its creation. What is more, certain chances offered by mechanical repetition were explored with great spirit by Mozart himself. He composed rondos, fugues and *ritornelli* for little clock-work organs and magical music-boxes in the collection of Count Josef Deym, whom he jestingly called "the watch-maker." [20] How spontaneously he enlivened automatic toys is best known from Papageno's *Glockenspiel* in "The Magic Flute." Mozart could thus adapt his genius to mechanization, but only as a marginal exercise. Imagine that all of Mozart's music were readjusted to suit the needs of "the watchmaker"! Yet it might well be argued that, in the last analysis, listening to a gramophone or a tape recorder, or to any of the more advanced machines of electro-acoustical engineering, is like listening to a superior sort of musical clock.

No matter how perfect these robots may become, music would shrink if it were composed primarily for them; just as painting would shrink if it were conceived as a perfected form of print-making.[21]

It remains one of the memorable facts in the history of engraving, a craft comparable with the production of musical disks, that some of the most notable contributions to that medium came from artists who were primarily painters and turned to engraving only intermittently. Strongly mechanized crafts, to remain responsive to art, will always require the kind of irregular refreshment which engraving received from the *peintre-graveur.* Otherwise a composer's skill might eventually be learned by a computer, and in that case, as has been well said, both will have wasted their time.[22]

NOTES

[1] Friedländer, *Der Kunstkenner,* p. 33. Against this view F. Winkler has claimed (I think, mistakenly) that Van Eyck, the Master of Flémalle, Dürer, Holbein, Baldung Grien, Mabuse, and also Ter Borch produced exact duplicates of some of their pictures (*Berliner Museen: Berichte* VII, 1957), pp. 37 ff. He was right, however, in suggesting that the subject deserves a more systematic study than it has so far received. See also B. Nicolson, "Terbrugghen repeating himself," *Miscellanea D. Roggen* (1957), pp. 193–203.

[2] Vollard, *Recollections* (translated by V. M. Macdonald), p. 266; cf. *Souvenirs* xii, 2: "En peinture voyez-vous il n'y a pas un seul procédé qui s'accommode d'être mis en formule. J'ai essayé de doser l'huile que j'ajoute à la couleur sur ma palette. Eh bien, je n'ai pas pu y arriver. Je dois, à chaque fois, mettre mon huile au jugé."

[3] Vespasiano da Bisticci, *Vite di uomini illustri del secolo xv,* ed. A. Mai and A. Bartoli (1859), p. 99: ". . . tutti iscritti a penna, e non v'è ignuno a stampa, che se ne sarebbe vergognato." Pope Alexander VII acquired these manuscripts for the Vatican Library where they now form the famous *Codices Urbinates.*

[4] Had the Duke of Urbino been consistent in his prejudices, he might have extended his disdain of manufacture from printed books to his hand-written library. The scribe who copied one manuscript from another, was he not a degraded mechanic compared with the rhapsodes who had recited the *Iliad* live? At the time of the rhapsodes, no doubt, there must have been critics who fastidiously regretted the better days when the poets themselves recited their songs and had not yet delegated that function to a tribe of menial substitutes, etc.

[5] Ruskin attacked the mechanization of sculpture in *Aratra Pentelici* (1872), §178; *Works,* ed. Cook and Wedderburn, XX (1905), p. 326.

On the pitfalls of mechanical enlargement, the debate on Graham Sutherland's tapestry for Coventry Cathedral revealed some illuminating details: According to the Chairman of the Edinburgh Tapestry Company (letter to *The Sunday Times,* 10 June 1962, p. 12), the artist supplied the weaver with only a small design, which was photographically enlarged by one hundred. The technique and history of the reducing machine are clearly set forth by Sir John Craig, *The Mint* (1953), pp. 299, 321, 341 f., 358 f. The final result is worth noting: "By repetitions of the process at different positions along the bar, reductions are obtained to different scales. . . . All identical patterns, such as portraits, on a series of coins from a crown-piece to a Maundy are thus reproduced from a single original" (p. 359). For the ill effect on the art of the medallist, see C. H. V. Sutherland, "The Art of the Modern Medal," *Journal of the Royal Society of Arts* CIII (1955), pp. 545 ff.; also Sir George Hill, *The Medal: its Place in Art* (British Academy, 1941), p. 6.

[6] Chairs designed by Mies van der Rohe—the MR chairs (1926), the Barcelona chair (1929), the Tugendhat and Brno chairs (1930), and conchoidal chairs for manufacture in plastics (1946)—are illustrated in Philip Johnson's monograph on Mies van der Rohe (1947), pp. 54, 56 f., 172 f. Many of the hackneyed tubular chairs that have become standard office furniture ape the elegant MR chairs.

[7] Article in *Le moniteur universel,* 30 December 1854, reprinted in *Lettres à Viollet-le-Duc* (1927), pp. 215 f.

[8] A. Prost, *La cathédrale de Metz* (1885), pp. 271 ff. On the destruction of Saint-Front in Périgueux by restorers, see Le Corbusier, *Quand les cathédrales étaient blanches* (1937). As for washing the stone, however preferable to refacing, Le Corbusier anticipated the problem in a memorable sentence: *Les cathédrales étaient blanches parce qu'elles étaient neuves.* The pleasure is dubious of seeing a wrinkled old face restored by artifice to the color of youth. The color does not suit the wrinkles. It is a delusion to claim that such buildings look new; they look just what they are—old buildings washed. The blunted edge of the stone, combined with the luminous surface, recalls the paper and print of "washed books" or "washed engravings." Whether the life of these buildings will be shortened by the increased porosity of the stone is another question.

[9] For a concise account of the technical problems set by the stratification of paintings, see A. E. Werner, "Scientific Techniques in Art and Archaeology," *Proceedings of the Royal Institution of Great Britain* XXXVIII (1960), pp. 211–33, with further literature. At a conference held in Rome, September 1961, an important debate took place between Stolow, Keck, Ruhemann and others on the effect of solvents such as acetone on varnish and paint (reported in *Studies in Conservation* VI, 1961, pp. 123 ff.). Stolow remarked: "once sclvent has been allowed to come into contact with a paint film, an irreversible change takes place—that of leaching."

The official inquiry of 1853, by a Select Committee of the House of Commons, into methods of picture-cleaning at the National Gallery produced a Report that is still worth consulting (cf. C. Holmes and C. H. Collins Baker, *The Making of the National Gallery,* 1924, pp. 24 f.). The question was then, as it is now, whether "glazings" and other final touches by the Old Masters were being removed (cf. *Burlington Magazine* CIV 1962, nos. 707, 716). The Gallery's case is painstakingly argued in The Director's Report, The National Gallery (1962), pp. 67–87 ("Renewal of the Controversy over Cleaning"), but the reasoning is not faultless. On p. 77, for example, it is suggested that because the Gallery's restorers do not regard themselves as infallible "they are reluctant to add their own interpretations to what is revealed when the additions made by less scrupulous restorers have been removed"—which seems to imply that the technique of removal is infallible and that judgments on "less scrupulous restorers" can be completely free of interpretation. Yet the very next sentence proposes that "by general consent Titian was one of the most original and adventurous of all painters" and for that reason the bold colors laid bare by recent cleaning are unlikely to deviate from his original vision. Whatever the historical validity of this particular interpretation of Titian's style, the denial that it *is* an interpretation would be absurd. The stubborn claim *hypotheses non fingo* is a basic misapprehension of method. No restoration is well-directed if it does not make stylistic assumptions, which are of course open to debate. The belief that in any phase of his work the restorer can divest himself of this uncertainty is not only illogical: it is dangerous.

[10] Yeats, *Essays and Introductions* (1961), p. 159.

[11] Some of the best catalogues of modern art have perhaps unwittingly helped to shape the working habits of younger artists. Paintings brought forth in rows and classes look irresistibly like illustrations for the artist's future *catalogue raisonné*. Is it possible that, in the place of the patron, it is now the cataloguer who looks over the artist's shoulder? As is well known, the cataloguer's excusable love of order has occasionally obscured the art of the past by forcing its profuse growth into linear sequences. Today, linear sequences seem to dominate growth. The catalogue has become an aesthetic force.

[12] Although it is difficult to conceive, Malraux seriously holds in *Le musée imaginaire* that it is through the levelling effect of reproduction that supra-personal forces are discovered in art: "La reproduction, et elle seule, a fait entrer dans l'art ces sur-artistes imaginaires . . . qui s'appellent des styles" (p. 52)—as if a common style emerged from the obliteration of differences. Merleau-Ponty recalled in *Signes* (p. 57) how a documentary film, by slowing down the motion of Matisse's hand, made the painter's brush stroke appear as a long premeditated action. If such an enlargement were juxtaposed with a real gesture of deliberation, the difference between them would vanish. As Merleau-Ponty rightly says, Malraux's "spirit of painting" works too much "from behind the painter's back," *une Peinture qui travaille derrière le dos du peintre* (p. 81), a failing here explained by Malraux's reckless individualism: "Quand on a enfermé l'art au plus secret de l'individu, la convergence des œuvres ne peut s'expliquer que par quelque destin qui les domine."

[13] Since the ordinary photographic plate is sensitive to a larger range of shades than can be recorded in color, the best black-and-white reproduction of a Titian, Veronese or Renoir is comparable to a conscientious piano transcription of an orchestral score, whereas the color print, with rare exceptions, is like a reduced orchestra with all the instruments out of tune. Color photographs and color prints have indeed fostered a coarseness of vision in art that is likely to be increased by color television. It would be tempting to reply that color distortion is a technical imperfection that is bound to be overcome with the progress of science, but this is an evasion of the actual problem: for it is precisely during the time-lag that vision is mechanically shaped and coarsened.

[14] See *The Times*, 20 July 1961, p. 8: "The composer's demand that [the choruses] be prerecorded on tape and stereophonically reproduced in the theater not only produced beautiful and exciting effects but made it possible for the chorus to get them right piece by piece, and the pieces to be assembled." Scherchen used prerecorded choruses in Schoenberg's *Moses and Aaron*, Bruno Maderna in Nono's *Intolleranza 1960*. In such composite arrangements for the stage, which are becoming increasingly frequent in modern opera, live voices and a live orchestra

are placed against recorded sounds; and since the records are set and hence inflexible, the living sounds must abide by the dead ones.

[15] In the art of the film, mechanization has achieved the peculiar triumph of reducing the aesthetic experience to an instantaneous response. The full effect of a film must be manifest at first sight; otherwise it is not a good film. Hence only a few of the great films increase in depth at a second viewing, but as they were not designed for that purpose, this is hardly a valid criterion for judging their quality as films. It is nevertheless well worth analyzing exactly what kind of pleasure we get from a good film when we see it for the second or third time. It is often not so much a pleasure of spontaneous response as one of reflective recognition, an appreciative awareness of how the instantaneous effect, designed for a single viewing, was originally achieved. As the by-product of an avowedly popular art, the film has thus inadvertently engendered (much like jazz) a particularly finical sort of critical *expertise.*

That films have lasting moments of genuine lyricism and produce great exhibitions of the actor's art, which are worth reexperiencing for their own sakes, is undeniable; but even here the fact remains that the actor in a film adjusts his capability to that of the screen, where sequences are built up out of episodic "shots," and the necessity of thus concentrating his performance on relatively short, discontinuous pieces may gradually disable him for the living stage.

[16] J. B. S. Haldane, *Daedalus* (1924), p. 44.

[17] *The Autobiographies of Edward Gibbon,* ed. John Murray (1896), p. 263; also *Memoirs of my Life and Writings,* ed. G. Birkbeck Hill (1900), p. 309 note.

[18] *Sartor Resartus* I, v.

[19] Lessing, *Emilia Galotti* I, iv (speech of Conti the painter): "Why do we not paint directly with our eyes! So much gets lost on the long way from the eye through the arm to the paint brush! Yet the fact that I know what got lost here, and how it got lost, and why it had to get lost, makes me proud, and prouder than I am of all that I managed to save. . . . Or do you think that Raphael would not have been the greatest pictorial genius if by mischance he had been born without hands?"

[20] Mozart's compositions for mechanical instruments: K. 594, 608, 616; cf. A. Einstein, *Mozart* (1945), pp. 153, 268 f.

[21] The same argument may help to define the artistic merits and limitations of photography. What precludes photography, as Croce put it, from becoming "entirely art," although it may have "something artistic about it" (*Estetica* I, ii, *ed. cit.,* p. 20), is the crucial surrender of the pictorial act to an optical or chemical agency which, however carefully set up and controlled by the photographer, must remain automatic in its operation. If the photographer's skill and taste become obtrusive to the point of obliterating the automatism, the photograph looks contrived: there is not enough genuine photography in it. It follows that an aesthetics of photography would have to stress the importance of an agent outside the photographer's control, a partly unpredictable component which, in a successful photograph, plays in with the photographer's intentions. The term *photogenic* refers to an adventitious felicity which the photographer must catch in an object but not devise. In that respect his skill and tact are inseparable from *reportage* (as in Cartier-Bresson). According to S. Kracauer, *Nature of Film*

(1961), the aesthetics of the cinema rests on the same principle: he rejects High-Art photography as incompatible with genuine filming.

For a detailed criticism of deliberately artistic photographs, see H. and A. Gernsheim, *The History of Photography* (1955), pp. 176 ff.; also H. Gernsheim, *Creative Photography: Aesthetic Trends 1839–1960* (1962), pp. 13, 73 ff. While it is now generally acknowledged that the Victorian aberrations of Rejlander (cf. Beaumont Newhall, *Photography, a Short Critical History*, 1938, pl. 36) are pseudo-photographic as well as pseudo-pictorial, this genre is as illicit in its modern form, even if indulged by Steichen or Man Ray (*ibid.*, pls. 50, 72); cf. Kracauer, *op. cit.*, p. 10.

[22] P. Laird, "Composers or Computers?," *The Listener* LXV (1961), pp. 785 f. The increasing emphasis on pre-compositional thought and construction, to which this article draws attention in contemporary music ("the composer's interest has shifted from the music to the method by which it is written"), was observed in poetry by Valéry. He suggested in 1920, while reflecting on the heritage of Mallarmé, that pure poetry, like pure philosophy, is defined *par son appareil, et non par son objet:* "It seems that constructive thought, which used to enter into verse, . . . has now withdrawn to the phase of its preparation" (*Variété* I, pp. 100 f.). It is easy to see the same shift of emphasis in the theoretical preliminaries of abstract painting. As Lévi-Strauss put it sarcastically: "C'est une école de peinture académique, où chaque artiste s'évertue à représenter la manière dont il exécuterait ses tableaux si d'aventure il en peignait" (*La pensée sauvage*, 1962, p. 43 note). Pure art has this feature in common with mechanization, where it is self-evident that constructive thought is withdrawn from the event as such into its preparation: the event is then released automatically.

Index

INDEX

Index

INDEX

Index

Index

Index

Index

Index

INDEX

Index